D1559417

X——THE PROBLEM OF THE NEGRO
AS A PROBLEM FOR THOUGHT

AMERICAN PHILOSOPHY

Douglas R. Anderson and Jude Jones, series editors

X—THE PROBLEM OF THE NEGRO AS A PROBLEM FOR THOUGHT

NAHUM DIMITRI CHANDLER

FORDHAM UNIVERSITY PRESS   NEW YORK   2014

Copyright © 2014 Fordham University Press

All rights reserved. No part of this publication may be reproduced, stored in a retrieval system, or transmitted in any form or by any means—electronic, mechanical, photocopy, recording, or any other—except for brief quotations in printed reviews, without the prior permission of the publisher.

Fordham University Press has no responsibility for the persistence or accuracy of URLs for external or third-party Internet websites referred to in this publication and does not guarantee that any content on such websites is, or will remain, accurate or appropriate.

Fordham University Press also publishes its books in a variety of electronic formats. Some content that appears in print may not be available in electronic books.

Library of Congress Cataloging-in-Publication Data
is available from the publisher.

Printed in the United States of America

16 15 14   5 4 3 2 1

First edition

THE
AMERICAN
LITERATURES
INITIATIVE

A book in the American Literatures Initiative (ALI), a collaborative publishing project of NYU Press, Fordham University Press, Rutgers University Press, Temple University Press, and the University of Virginia Press. The Initiative is supported by The Andrew W. Mellon Foundation. For more information, please visit www.americanliteratures.org.

Contents

Acknowledgments

For the appearance of this work, I must, above all, thank my editor at Fordham University Press, Helen Tartar. And, I am most deeply thankful. For, since first speaking with me in the autumn of 1993 about the project of which this book is an expression, she has remained steadfast—for what is now a generation of thought, at least—in her affirmation of my efforts to think the work of W. E. B. Du Bois anew and to address certain concerns in modern social thought from my somewhat peculiar path of thinking. A scholar, a writer, simply could not hope for more, in a lifetime. She has, indeed, changed my world. I hope that herein she can find some sense of the measure of my gratitude and appreciation, as well as some retrospective value in seeing this discourse into a new public presentation. And for that event, such as it is, I also thank Tom Lay of Fordham Press, who with the kindest prodding has shepherded this book into its present form, and Tim Roberts, of the American Literatures Initiative.

Then, this text was gifted with two anonymous readers, who were kind enough to make themselves known to me, Fred Moten and David Lloyd. It is hard to imagine any other two readers who might have engaged the study in such a fundamental manner, affirmatively critical to the limit, in such a way as to not only push me to render this discourse at the highest level that I could bring to the table, now, but by way of their own exemplary paths of inquiry and questioning, to recognize my own work as part of a renewed horizon of shared discourse and urgent concern with thinking anew today. When this study grows up, I hope that it will be like David's own beautiful discourse under the heading *Irish Times: Temporalities of Modernity* (Keough-Naughton Institute for Irish Studies at the University of Notre Dame, 2008) from which I drew inspiration in my final revisions to my own study, with which it shares much, in particular on its "lower frequencies," as Ralph Ellison suggested in another context. And then, too, for me, Fred Moten has been from our first discussion the first voice of my generation to which I listen;

to discover in the event that he had given a listen to this locution—anonymously, as it were—heartened me to try to bring to it another order of voice. I hope that he hears herein, and on every page, all that we share.

And then, from somewhere near the mid-point of the journey entailed in the making of this book, Franc Nunoo-Quarcoo and Maria Phillips became essential to its realization—most fundamentally, in matters of the spirit. They have been there, always, at the other end of the line, waiting, patiently, affirmatively, ever-hopeful. A master of the graphic arts, Franc has tendered his remarkable genius for the shaping of the cover design. For their contribution to both layers of its form, both its inside and its outside, this book, then, belongs also to them.

For those who know what it means to write, they will doubtless understand that I write with two hands: one is that of my wife, Ayumi, as she attends to certain practices of our shared life, in particular the close care just now of the still toddler son, Aaron Eisuke, that we share and hold together in family; the other, is mine, as I try to trace in outline the nightlines and dreams that come to me in the darkness of thought, inscribing them, attending thus to other forms of our life, sharing them with her, all the while. This book is hers too. Her dreams, at least some of them, are recorded here, just as well as mine. I hope all who read it remember this.

At the outset of any textual reference, I must thank Danielle Kovacs, curator of collections in the Department of Special Collections and University Archives at the W. E. B. Du Bois Library of the University of Massachusetts Libraries, and the trustees of the David Graham Du Bois Memorial Trust, respectively, for assisting me on numerous matters over many years and for ensuring scholarly access to so much work by and about W. E. B. Du Bois, most especially that contained in the papers of W. E. B. Du Bois housed at Amherst.

"Anacrusis," the opening text for this study, was published in an earlier, slightly shorter version, without certain annotations (which, although mainly prepared in the autumn of 1991, are presented here for the first time), under the title "Between" in *Assemblage: A Critical Journal of Architecture and Design Culture* 20 (April): 26–27. I thank Thomas Keenan and Eduardo Cadava for the suggestion of the idea, and Mark Wigley as guest editor, for the invitation to contribute to the special issue "Violence Space." During the time of the first composition of this text, Sue Hemberger, academic officemate and intelligence *extraordinaire*, the eighth wonder of the world, in my judgment, read every line and affirmed the thought at its inception—which still means the world to me.

Chapter 1, "Of Exorbitance: The Problem of the Negro as a Problem for Thought," was previously published in a form proximate to its presentation here in *Criticism: A Quarterly Journal for Literature and the Arts* 50, no. 3 (2008): 345–410. I thank Wayne State University Press and Jonathan Flatley of *Criticism* for permission to republish it. An early version of some sections of this chapter were presented at the conference "The Academy and Race: Toward a Philosophy of Political Action," sponsored jointly by the Department of Philosophy and the Department of Africana Studies at Villanova University, March 8–10, 1996, and subsequently published in *Callaloo: A Journal of African American and African Arts and Letters* 19, no. 1 (1996): 78–95; thus, I also thank *Callaloo* and its editor Charles Rowell, for kind consent to the republication of those revised sections here. That important conference was organized by Kevin Thomas Miles, who remains for me a principal philosophical interlocutor on these matters. Several diverse configurations of thought, position, and intellectual generation were gathered for the first time at that conference, and the impact of the interlocutions inaugurated there remain widely distributed, even if not always explicitly so, across the disciplines of philosophy, literature (comparative as well as English), and the social sciences, in the United States. It thus remains a signal moment for my own intellectual generation. (See Chapter 1 note 55 below for references on this matter.) I also thank Mae G. Henderson and Julie Elizabeth Byrne for conversations related to the development of the earlier version of this chapter. The second half of the chapter was initially brought to full formulation during my year as a member of the School of Social Science at the Institute for Advanced Study, Princeton, New Jersey. While there, I was supported by fellowships from the National Endowment for the Humanities and from the Ford Foundation that I wish to acknowledge and for which I remain grateful. As well, I received the support of the faculty, staff, and other members of the School of Social Science during the 1998–99 academic year. I thank the faculty of the school, especially Professors Joan Scott and Michael Walzer, and the late esteemed scholars, Clifford Geertz and Albert O. Hirschman (in particular the latter, who by way of a fundamental sense of hospitality, took a notable interest in my concerns with the work of W. E. B. Du Bois), for their intellectual generosity and hospitality during that time. Above all, the interlocution of Professors Charles Sheperdson, Thomas Flynn, Nancy Hirschman, and Kamran Ali, for which I am deeply thankful, often led me to think further on these matters than I had yet thought possible. Just as important, I wish to note in deepest thanks that this essay in the first full version of its present form was prepared during the autumn of 2004 in Zarautz, in the Basque Country, on the northern coast of Spain, where I was able to remain for a time and write, through the kind generosity of Karmele Troyas and Arturo Coello Leyte and through the careful life friendship of Alberto Moreiras and Teresa Vilarós-Soler, while on a sabbatical.

Chapter 2, "The Figure of the X: An Elaboration of the Autobiographical Example in the Thought of W. E. B. Du Bois," revised here, was published in earlier form in Smadar Lavie and Ted Swedenburg, eds., *Displacement, Diaspora and Geographies of Identity* (Durham, NC: Duke University Press, 1996), pp. 235–72. Sections of this chapter were presented at conferences organized by the Centre for Research in Ethnic Relations at the University of Warwick, May 21–23, 1993, and the Department of German Studies at Emory University, March 25–27, 1993; to the Department of English, Duke University, February 3, 1993, and the Department of Anthropology at Princeton, University, January 11, 1993; and at the Workshop on the Politics of Race and the Reproduction of Racial Ideologies, University of Chicago, May 2, 1992. The initial formulations outlined here were first presented at sessions of the American Anthropological Association, on "Displacement, Diaspora, and the Geographies of Identity," in Chicago, November 20–24, 1991, organized by Smadar Lavie and Ted R. Swedenburg, and on "Transnational Subjectivities of Africans in the Diaspora," in San Francisco, December 2–6, 1992, organized by Helan E. Page and Donna D. Daniels. Smadar Lavie and Robert Gooding-Williams read this essay in its entirety and gave me distinct and principled responses; Lavie's response indicated in the introduction to *Displacement, Diaspora an Geographies of Identity* was especially thoughtful, for which I am most appreciative and from which I have benefited beyond that interlocution. I thank David Theo Goldberg for our early and ongoing dialogue; Abebe Zegeye and Julia Maxted for the wonderful invitation to Warwick; Angelika Bammer for her unfailing generosity, of which her sense of critical responsibility and the invitation to Emory were just a small part; Thomas Holt for the freedom and openness of his response to Du Bois, which teaches by example; and Sue Hemberger, gifted scholar, teacher, and friend, whose questions in her own engagements in American and African American literature and social thought have been formative for mine.

Chapter 3, "The Souls of an Ex-White Man: W. E. B. Du Bois and the Biography of John Brown," was published in an earlier, somewhat shorter version in *CR: The New Centennial Review* 3, no. 1 (spring 2003): 179–95. I wish to acknowledge and thank both Scott Michaelsen, coeditor of that journal, and Michigan State University Press, its publisher, for permitting its revised publication here. It was presented in several contexts. At the Collegium for African American Research, Wesphalia Universität, Münster, Germany, it was read in public for the first time and dedicated to Herbert and Fay Aptheker on March 20, 1999, as part of a panel on Du Bois at the millennial turn, where the engagement and papers by fellow panelists Robert Bernasconi, David Farrel Krell, Ronald A. T. Judy, and Kevin Miles, and the careful hearing and questions by Robin Blackburn from the audience, made the experience historic. At Cornell University, it was presented by way of the invitation of Nancy Hirschman under the auspices of the Department of Government through the "Crossing Borders/Crossing Boundaries: A Dialogue Between Political Theory, Political Science, and Related Disciplines" lecture series on April 25, 2000, on the occasion of which I was especially gifted with the presence and questions of Hortense Spillers, Leslie Adelson, Susan Buck-Morss, and Milton Curry. And then, it served as the text for the opening session of the Faculty Seminar Series of the Program for Comparative American Cultures, while I served as chair of that program, at Johns Hopkins University, on November 14, 2000. Through the generous invitation of Kalpana Seshadri of Boston College, a generosity of more than one occasion, for which I remain grateful, it was presented on March 16, 2001 in the Seminar on Post-Colonial Studies, based in the Humanities Center at Harvard University, on the occasion of which Lewis Ricardo Gordon and Paget Henry, both then of Brown University, notably joined the discussion and gave the text their most considered engagement, on the line of an ensemble of questions about intelligence and intellectual practice in "black," which remains with me today. Finally, it was also read with considerable courtesy in absentia by the panel organizer and chair, my then senior colleague Sara Castro-Klaren of Johns Hopkins University (and for her affirmation, I remain grateful today, for she had been kind enough to think of me for the invitation to present the paper, whereas in the event I regretfully could not make the journey to New York) as part of a panel "Teaching and Resisting Genre: Beyond Literary and Cultural Studies," organized under the auspices of the Division on the Teaching of Literature, Modern Languages Association, at the annual meetings, December 28, 2002, in New York.

    Chapter 4, "Originary Displacement: Or, Passages of the Double and the Limit of World," was published in an earlier form, under its main title only and without the section under the subheading "Theoretical Conjunction," in *boundary 2: an international journal of literature and culture* 27, no. 3 (fall 2000): 249–86, a special issue, "Sociology Hesitant: Thinking with W. E. B. Du Bois," edited by Ronald A. T. Judy. The majority of the essay that forms the basis of this chapter was first prepared during the winter months of 1993 and then further developed during the fall of 1994, although certain key elements were developed as noted below in the spring of 1988. The earlier version of this chapter, or sections of it, were presented in several contexts. A section was presented at "The Re-mapping of Scholarship: A Working Conference on African Peoples in the Industrial Age," sponsored by the Center for Afroamerican and African Studies at the University of Michigan, September 30–October 1, 1994; I thank Earl Lewis and Robin D. G. Kelley for their hospitality on that occasion, and Francis Abiola Irele, Sylvia Wynter, and Joe Trotter for their dialogue during this conference. At Duke University, I presented a portion of the essay as part of the W. E. B. Du Bois Lecture Series sponsored by the Program in African and African American Studies, March 25, 1996; I thank George Elliott Clarke, Lee Baker, Jan Radway, Jonathan Goldberg, and Fredric Jameson for their critical engagement on that occasion. In early 1998, the essay was read in several contexts: at the Johns Hopkins University, sponsored by the Program in Comparative American Cultures and the Humanities Center, for which I thank Robert Reid-Pharr, Katrina McDonald, Walter Benn Michaels, Neil Hertz, and Frances Ferguson for their engagement, and Virginia Hall for her editorial assistance; at a conference on the "New World Orders? New Terrains in an Era of Globalization," at the University of California at Irvine, for which I thank Richard Perry and Bill Maurer for the invitation; in a seminar sponsored jointly by the Department of African and African American Studies, the Department of Anthropology, and the Humanities Institute at the University of California at Davis, for which I thank Zoila Mendoza for her indefatigable support on the occasion, Carol Smith, Georges Van Den Abbeele, Patricia Turner, and Aklil Bekele for making it work, and my former teachers Cynthia Brantley, Desmond Jolly, and Carl Jorgensen for their continued generosity and affirmation, and Frederic Jameson, my senior colleague at Duke at the time, for a considered second hearing on the Davis occasion and his further comments, most of which remain at stake for the future life of these thoughts; at the first meeting of the Working Group on Law, Culture, and the Humanities at the Georgetown University Law Center, for which I thank Austin Sarat, Ken Mack, and Brook Thomas for their engagement. Too, I must note that at the inception of the work presented here, in the book as a whole, but especially in this chapter, the American Bar Foundation (ABF) made available to me a fellowship of several years duration under the aegis of its law and social science program. While the problematics of law articulate only within the depths of this study (hardly at all in the form of the concerns of positive law), the support of the ABF allowed me the space to pursue fundamental research on the philosophical and moral premises of legality, as such, and to situate them amidst general questions of social theory, which has in turn informed virtually every page of this study. Thus, I thank especially William L. F. Felstiner, whose idea it was to start the program that brought me to the ABF, which he directly adjudged, Bryant Garth and Robert L. Nelson, subsequent executive directors of the ABF, who continued to enable my work there, but especially Christopher L. Tomlins, for his example in scholarship (even though he did not know it then), and Elizabeth Mertz, who remains a most decisive mentor for me (even though she never claimed such), showing the finest sense of what it might mean to be a scholar, manifesting both the most profound intelligence, yet always as a part of a community of learning, something that she has always held in the highest regard. This inception is all still with me, a generation forward and ongoing.

"Parenthesis" was prepared and presented for the inaugural symposium of the project *Issues in Critical Investigation, The African Diaspora*, convened by Professor Hortense Spillers within the auspices of the Department of English at Vanderbilt University, Nashville, Tennessee—September 30 to October 1, 2011. I thank Professor Spillers for her always inimitable example and intellectual friendship that seems already of a lifetime, in stellar form on the event, as well as my fellow panelists Ronald A. T. Judy, Fred Moten, and Tiffany Ruby Patterson, and other participants in the conference, notably Milton Curry, Ifeoma Nwankwo, and Nicole Waligora-Davis, for their engagement in the event. A version of this chapter is forthcoming among the proceedings from that conference to be published in *Palimpsest: A Journal on Women, Gender, and the Black International*; I thank the editors of that journal, Tiffany Ruby Patterson and T. Denean Sharpley-Whiting, along with SUNY Press for permission to include that text as part of this chapter. The opening passages of this chapter were also presented as part of an introduction of

Cedric Robinson on the occasion of the second of two seminars that he presented under the title of "Staging Black Radicalism" through the auspices of the Critical Theory Institute and the Program in African American Studies at the University of California, Irvine, February 6, 2012. I thank not only Professor Robinson for his profoundly generous example of decades, but also Tiffany Willoughby-Herard for her own previous exemplary introduction of Professor Robinson, along with Jared Sexton and Kyung Hyun Kim, respectively of the programs named above, for the invitation and opportunity to offer my own thoughts on that rich and quite remarkable occasion.

Note on Citations

Where possible or appropriate the citations given herein to texts by W. E. B. Du Bois will be to the thirty-seven volumes of *The Complete Published Writings of W. E. B. Du Bois*, published by the Kraus-Thomson Org. Ltd., edited and introduced by the late Herbert Aptheker, from 1973 to 1986, as well as to the six volumes of Du Bois's texts published by the University of Massachusetts Press, also edited and introduced by Aptheker, three of selected correspondence and three of selections of other texts, including previously unpublished texts and documents, from 1973 to 1985. Specific bibliographical details for the texts cited from among these volumes can be found in the list of references at the end of this study. With three texts, however, further detail is necessary. With *Dusk of Dawn*, originally published in 1940 but cited herein from its 1975 reprint as a volume in *The Complete Published Writings*, where appropriate and as an aid to the reader, I have usually indicated within my text the chapter, or subsection thereof, that is under discussion, for pagination varies somewhat among the most commonly accessible editions of this text (Du Bois 1975c). This edition is cited in the text as *Dusk* followed by page number. *John Brown*, originally published in 1909, was reissued by Du Bois in 1962 on the occasion of the centennial of the Emancipation Proclamation, with a new preface and textual additions, and reprinted in *The Complete Published Writings*. The reader may find it useful to note that whereas I make reference in Chapter 3, both directly and by interpretive implication, to the last two chapters of the biography, none refer to the 1962 additions and thus my references can be usefully indexed from any complete extant edition of the study (Du Bois 1973). This edition is cited in the text as *John Brown* followed by page number. *The Souls of Black Folk: Essays and Sketches*, however, is cited herein from the first edition of its original publication (Du Bois 1903f); the second edition, which has no major changes from the first, is available online in a scholastically reliable electronic form (Du Bois 1903e). It is cited in my text from the first edition as *Souls* followed by page number, chapter, and paragraph number. In addition, three early essays by Du Bois—"The Conservation of Races" of 1897, "Strivings of the Negro People" from later in 1897, and "The Study of the Negro Problems" of early 1898—while occasionally cited according to their original publication (details for which may be found in the bibliography [Du Bois 1897a; Du Bois 1897b; Du Bois 1898b]), they are more generally cited from the reedited, complete (as originally published or as extant but unpublished among the papers of W. E. B. Du Bois), and annotated versions of these texts included in *The Problem of the Color Line at the Turn of the Twentieth Century: The Essential Early Essays*, forthcoming from Fordham University Press (Du Bois Forthcoming[a]). These three essays are cited in my text as follows: "The Conservation of Races" as CR, "Strivings of the Negro People" as SNP, and "The Study of the Negro Problems" as TSNP, respectively, followed by pagination and paragraph number (for example, CR 22, paras. 1–3) from this forthcoming edition of early essays by Du Bois. Finally, as indicated in the endnotes, throughout this study I occasionally take reference to material that may be found only (as original documents or in microfilm form derived therefrom) among the Papers of W. E. B. Du Bois, Special Collections and University Archives, Series 3, Subseries C, MS 312, University of Massachusetts Libraries, housed in the W. E. B. Du Bois Library at the University of Massachusetts, Amherst. Currently maintained by the staff of the Department of Special Collections and University Archives of the University of Massachusetts Libraries, the original papers were compiled and edited by Herbert Aptheker, whereas the microfilm edition was supervised by Robert C. McDonnell.

ANACRUSIS

For Cecil Taylor[1]

W e must desediment the dissimulation of a war.
Yet, no speech can pretend to offer a commensuration with the massive violence of the *disaster* that was in Los Angeles.[2]

How can we speak of the massive violence that preceded what has been called the rebellion or riots in the streets of Los Angeles? How can we speak of the violence of a beating that had occurred before it had occurred? How can we find words, fashion a discourse responsible to the unnameable sense that overtakes one in hearing of the utter verdict in *California v. Powell*? That is, how can we even hope to fathom the insidious pain, the psychic destruction (which is anything but "psychological"), the torture, the physical and sexual convulsion, the horrendous unending repetition of violence upon violence that was, and remains, the violence of the verdict itself?

We cannot pretend to *speak* of these things. We reach a limit; our limit. We cannot know, we cannot (only) name, here, in this domain. We, must be, responsible; only.

In the face of incommensurability—I call this entire "thing," long before the beating itself and yet to come, the *disaster*—in the face of such, we cannot *speak*, as in depart from or arrive at truth. We can only respond, make a choice—a decision—in short *judge*, in other terms, *be responsible. We must act as if we were responsible.* For, we will, always, be responsible. This, it seems to me—strangely enough—without "words" and speeches, communicates with the response of tens of thousands in Los Angeles, and across the country (and this "country" is not homogeneous with the United States of America). The violence of everyday life was re-dressed. It was not exactly concealed, as in fully clothed, before. Yet, its shape, the organization of its folds, its layering was, perhaps, irreversibly re-marked. We must recall one key aspect of the performativity of what is often called, poorly, spontaneous rebellions: we must hold it analytically irreducible that, as they say, ". . . happens" (and we have only this language, "some*thing*" happens). I leave my proof to the debate wherein some will try to deny this unnameable, and, hence, acknowledge its operation. I wish to remark, among this, one theme: we build even on our "failures" (and failure is unavoidable and necessary). "Los Angeles," or the "country," will (never) (only) be the "same."

There must have been an explosion, an irruption somewhere, from the beginning of time, as time, and thus yet beyond time, neither time nor not time, indeed displacing time, before beginning, cavernous and massive, fractual, infinitely so; an earthquake or a volcano; a black hole in the whiteness of being, in the being of "whiteness."[3] And Du Bois can assist us in recalling this ancient volcano, more ancient than that already ancient volcano that we call "Los Angeles," "the Los Angeles riots," or the "rebellion in Los Angeles," in 1992, the *disaster* already and yet to come. Du Bois meditates, reflects, dark as night, or light, black-light, in the structure of this opening.

> Between me and the other world there is ever an unasked question: unasked by some through feelings of delicacy; by others through the difficulty of rightly framing it. All nevertheless, flutter round it. They approach me in a half-hesitant sort of way, eye me curiously or compassionately, and then, instead of saying directly, How does it feel to be a problem? they say, I know an excellent colored man in my town; or I fought at Mechanicsville; or, Do not these Southern outrages make your blood boil? At these I smile, or am interested, or reduce the boiling to a simmer, as the occasion may require. To the real question, How does it feel to be a problem? I answer seldom a word. (*Souls*, 1–2, chap. 1, para. 1)

This is our text: a fragment, an opening, of *The Souls of Black Folk*. We will, in the course of this brief itinerary, try to mark or re-mark our inhabitation *of* it. To do this requires the displacement of a question, indeed, a certain double displacement. Two questions, double, one displacing the other, or the other displacing the one. On the one hand, we will not *ask the question* of being. We *know* that such is impossible. Hence, on the other hand, we will ask only the question *of being.* Du Bois, as we know, can hardly ask: "How does it feel to be a problem?" And, thus, he, or his discourse, at any rate we, come(s) upon the *impossible itself:* How can one ask, "how does it feel *not to be* a problem (for example, white)?" And so it seems, *the question* destroys itself. It seems we are in a black hole. But then again it could be white. And so our preamble must end; or fold.[4]

We shall try, then, to read with Du Bois; writing. In this scenography, nothing comes on the scene punctually. Nothing comes on the scene on its own terms; which is to say, it comes on the scene on other terms. Distinctions move laterally or obversely vibrating through chains and networks of associations. It is in this lateral, or obverse, movement that we can describe the formation of form. Everything in this paragraph moves by indirection. Nothing settles down. Form would be deflection as indirection; for each movement is inflected back into itself, doubled and redoubled by the differences that organize its formation. The prose itself, by its syntax and the con*fusions* of its meanings, remain not only the site of a question, but the very movement or form of a question.

The very first word of this first paragraph of *Souls*, the *word* "between," inaugurates itself as and according to a kind of logic. The *word* "between" could present itself, recalling certain semantic sedimentations, as both defining and defined by an opposition, as producing and produced by an oppositional logic. Such a logic would presuppose or intend the possibility that a distinction could be made radical: either/or, all *or* nothing; without remainder (Aristotle's law of contradiction or noncontradiction). The *word* "between" would, in the case of an oppositional coherence, on the one hand, appear (as explicit theme or proposition and implicit metaphor) as that very thing which separates the one and the other, "me and the other"; appearing to offer them *its* own coherence as their possibility. As presented, "Between me and the other world there is . . . ," this oppositional determination of the *word* "between" is precisely the propositional theme of this sentence. And, I would suggest, this thematized oppositional positioning communicates with a formal aspect. By one entire aspect of its grammar, according to its function as a preposition, this *word* appears as that quite solid structure which gives

the referent for this prepositional phrase, "me *and* the other," its specific
and determining sense. It would, on the other hand, by the (unavoidable)
structure of its enunciation, assume its own predication: "there," "there
is," "is ever." The verb seems to explicitly thematize its capacity to predicate sense (redoubled, if you will, since this is just the *word* "being" folded
into the precomprehension of being): it is the third person singular of the
present indicative of the verb "to be."[5] This stable solid structure that is
presented as the *word* "between" would authorize the movement of an
oppositional logic and a reading of it as radical.

Yet, the character of Du Bois's demonstration, the style of his discourse,
can be thought to disrupt the stability of the distinction authorizing this
opposition, this oppositional logic. Another sort of logic, could, perhaps,
be elucidated, one that would take over the radicality assumed by the
oppositional logic and make it its own. By its syntax, by another aspect of
its grammar, and by the rhythm of its rhetorical style, Du Bois's sentence
registers, in a certain fashion, the radical possibility of this other logic.

Du Bois's sentence could have *begun* with the assumption of predication. The claim of an oppositional logic would have been accentuated.
For example, the sentence could have been written as *"An* unasked question *is* ever between me and the other world," or as *"There is* ever an
unasked question between me and the other world," thus not only presupposing predication and nominality, but almost aggressively asserting
its hegemony.

Also, Du Bois could have begun his sentence, *"In* between me and
the other . . . ," almost asserting a firm presupposition of spatial locus,
of space already confirmed. In the instance of each of the examples
given, the *word* "between" could have then been considered as a sort of
structural metaphor of a determinate object *between* two determinate or
stable objects.

Du Bois's sentence (and hence his essay and book of *Souls*) does not
begin this way. (Although we shall never make it to the end, nor will
it end in such a manner.) In the placement of a preposition (a grammatical form whose function is that of the articulation of relations)
at the very inception of this sentence, the *word* "between," having the
punctual rhythm of an en medias res inauguration, Du Bois's syntactical
style produces a hyperbolic force in the relation of the preposition (the
word "between") and its object or referent (the *words* "me and the other")
in the prepositional phrase "Between me and the other" such that the

preposition is introduced as condition of its referent, rather than vice versa.[6] According to the *movement* of its rhetorical force, *as a discourse*, Du Bois's style makes tremble, by its accentuation, all sedimented commitments that would submit a reading of the *word* "between" in this sentence to an oppositional logic. On the one hand, the apparent stability or objectivity of the terms of the referent, "me" and "the other" is qualified. Not only can neither term enter on its own basis, as we shall see, but the entire nominative status of the noun phrase is made secondary to a structure from which it derives its sense both syntactically and grammatically. This, most simply, is a signifying structure. However, according to another movement, it is the articulation of the unnameable itself; which is not to say, the inarticulate. On the other hand, having itself thus disrupted the supposed repleteness of the elements of its referent, thus also disrupting the stability of its would be out-side, this concept-metaphor, this syncategorem, "between," could not organize its own coherence, and thus it remains only as a movement of dissimulation.[7]

At this juncture we can already recognize that we are in the midst of another logic, an other logic, logic *of* the other. Even at its nominal best, "between" would be the nonlocatable site of at least double meanings (and thereby never only double), taking sense from the play of forces (always) beyond or otherwise than strictly delimitable site. Literally, so to speak, there would be a double force, of the play produced by (or, rather *as*) the operation of the terms "me and other." Opposition would be just one moment of the movement of such logic, and in its possibility it would remain nonradical.

This trembling that is inaugurated by the preposition resonates with the dissociation at work in the articulation of the elements of the noun phrase that comprises its referent. According to the style of Du Bois's formulation, we recognize, not only a grammatical construction, but a rhetorical force (both syntactic and semantic) set loose by the syntax, the movement, of "between": the referent itself is not simply an element or elements but is itself a movement. In the noun phrase "me and the other" (which, in the context of the opening prepositional phrase is the referent of "between"), the conjunction "and" echoes and resonates with that aspect of the rhetorical force inscribed by the preposition "between."

Yet, if this is so, what of this *word* "between"?

A lateral gesture and step in this first sounding of an enunciation still yet to come—that is to say, even as we are attempting to mark or remark an incipient locution—a certain gathering of a few annotations, may allow some displacement of a hesitation that would arise if one were to maintain a strict commitment to *theoria* as arising from or committed to the pure, thought as pure, as if it were an apparition apart from its necessary and ineluctable articulation as a practice .

(1) As a word, "between" cannot set us adrift in the movement of the opening that I am attempting to trace in these few lines. We can see this when we approach the question of its semantic horizons. (a) As a preposition, according to the *Oxford English Dictionary*, abridged edition, it refers to a space already presumed.

> I. Of a simple position. Of a point. 1. The proper word expressing the local relation of a point to two other points in opposite direction. 2. Used of a similar relation of two immaterial objects figured as lying in space; or of a relation, figured as spatial to two material objects. 3. Of time: In the interval following one event or point of time and preceding another. . . .
>
> II. Of intervening space. As separating or connecting. 6. Expressing the relation of the continuous space, or distance, which extends from one point to another, and separates them, or of a line which passes from one to the other and unites them. 7. Used in reference to any objective relation uniting two (or more) parties and holding them in a certain connexion. . . .

(b) And its sense as an adverb is perhaps even more emphatic, even more resolute or "quasi-substantive": "1. Of place: In an intermediate position or course . . . 2. *To go between*: to act as a medium or mediator. . . . " (emphasis in original); "1. Anything occupying an intermediate position, an interval of time. . . . " Understood primarily as a semantic unit, "between" is nothing other than a relational marker that comes on the scene of presentation after certain given terms or entities enter into relationship.

(2) Yet, when tracked according to the movements of Du Bois's discourse, as given in our strophe, if you will and for example, of *The Souls of Black Folk*, his inscribed enunciation, a scene of writing, what we might call its pragmatics, its syntactic force, "between" would delimit any simple notion of its spatiality or presupposed relationality. It would instead accede to the most general disruption of boundaries. As a movement, a syntactical one, we might say, "between" dissipates any simple notion of inside and outside, of above and below.

(a) Hence, "between" as tracked in the movement of Du Bois's inscription may be understood to name the opening of the sense of space, of spatiality, rather than confirm it. We raise into view then two formulations of the grammatical sense or meaning of this word given by the *Oxford English Dictionary* that offers resource for the path of thinking that I am proposing here that we undertake. It tells us that "between" joins and separates in the same status, demarcating the cusp or the possibility of an "Excursion on a Wobbly Rail" that we have followed in Du Bois's passage—allowing Cecil Taylor's example with regard to the matter of so-called tradition to attune us here.[8] Along this formally given pathway, I have begun to offer the thought that "between" marks the opening of historical distinctions. Here we can further recall from the *Oxford English Dictionary* that "in all senses *between* has been, from its earliest appearance, extended to more than two." Here we come upon something of the utmost implication: the double is never only double, proliferating its marks without end. The motif of the double even runs throughout the semantic history of this word. The modern word combines the Old English *betweonum* and the Middle English *bitwenen*, retaining in this history, in turn, a schema of sedimented heterogeneous origins. And we might underline here that "between" is an English word, as distinct from the Latinate prefix *inter*, which contributed to the French *entre* (which the text of Stéphane Mallarmé solicited Jacques Derrida to read so closely at a turning point in the latter's path, as I note below). According to the *Oxford English Dictionary* it was along this conduit that those words with the *inter* prefix were brought into Middle English. Whereas the *inter* prefix in English, *interval* for example, seems to give itself over to a presupposition of given terms, "between," with its sedimented histories marked by a generative doubling seems to maintain a lability, an encoding of a ruinous yet felicitous devolution, for such a determination. We can understand this figure of the double in the history of the English word "between" itself as nothing other than a sedimentation of that unnameable generative force that gives language to itself.[9]

(b) Further, then, on another level I have suggested that "between" should be understood in the text of Du Bois as a certain naming of a movement that we might just as well describe or illustrate as the unnameable itself. But if my practice, in the wake of Du Bois, names the unnameable and seems thereby to give up the rigor of the question at stake in its discourse, this apparitional failure is far from fatal. Instead, I have

reflexively followed, or been lead by, a "word"—"between"—that by definition cannot be commensurate with the network or chain of concepts,
conceptual ensembles concept-metaphors and problematics in which I
might seek to enmesh it. My cultivation of this "word" is here a paleonymic practice, maintaining it with respect to the limitations, or sediment, that still seems to encrust or encase it. It cultivates or maintains a
theoretically insufficient term. (And just what is the status of *theoria* here;
and what, precisely, could sufficiency or insufficiency, mean here?) Thus,
I have sought to affirm the hyperbolic character of Du Bois's practice
and to elaborate some of its effects of catachresis. It responds, thereby, to
that which is excessive to any simple claim on the *movement* of thought
as *practice*.[10] Only philosophy, or an idea of theory, as the thought of
the pure, as a pure thought, a standing above and apart, could claim, or
pretend, to inhabit a ground or position from which such a situation or
practice could be understood as parochial. But, then, again, it might just
find itself caught up in the movement of "between" as we find ourselves
attempting to follow it in and by way of the discourse and inscriptive
practice of one W. E. B. Du Bois.

Let us now return—still moving in lateral and obverse step—to our
attempt at a path through and with our text, a fraction, of *The Souls of
Black Folk*, proper.

This "and"—"between me and the other"—suggests that for their
respective and most precise sense each term must refer to the other. It
marks a movement in which relation is, or better, gives, historicity. This
resonance thereby suggests that the source of this "between" could not be
from any supposed or presupposed respective self-originating entity or
identity ("me" and "the other") of this noun phrase. Rather we find affirmation for reading the constitutive force of the movement of between
as the opening of difference itself. The conjunction "and" suggests the
mutuality of the constitution of the respective senses of the pronouns
"me" and "the other." This mutuality in difference, as difference, disrupts
the logic of a stable boundary, an oppositional logic, that would authorize the assumption or production of terms self-identical to themselves.
This mutuality is in turn analogous to the rhetorical parallel (which is
nothing in fact), their common structure as relations, of the preposition
"between" and the conjunction "and." Redoubling the syntactical force
of the two prepositions of this opening sentence, "between" and "and,"
coursing or interlacing one with the other, Du Bois's discourse can be

understood to bring the ensemblic problem of predication, of nomina-
tion, of (the presupposition of) sense or commitment to presence to issue
with acute force and precision. The theme and form of Du Bois's entire
discourse are announced in radical fashion with this preoccupation and
making tremble of the logic *of being*.

The trembling that we noticed at the inception of this sentence continues to resonate throughout its entire formal structure. We find that
right at the center of this sentence, so to speak, that its object (the strange
"unasked question") has been radically displaced. Rhetorically, it comes
on the stage only after the ground has been affected by the disruptive and
desedimenting movement of "between." It is "presented" only second-
arily. Moreover, it is presented or re-presented under the sign of absence,
displacement, nonpresence ("an *unasked* question"). The grammatical
object, by the syntax and the semantics (determined by its syntactic
deployment) of its production, is precisely that which cannot come on the
scene on its own terms; indeed, it has no punctual presence at all. Moreover, it redoubles the syntactic structure of between, since it not only
resonates with the syntactic force set loose according to the movement of
"between," but as the object, the objective, of the *theme* it comes on the
scene precisely *as* the displaced and displacing structure of "between."
At best its invisible and unheard movement might be re-marked only
after the fact, if at all, in the dispersed and dissimulated movement of
an endless elaboration of questions; a remarking that would already be
inscribed in this unnameable movement *of* between. No small question
that, thematically, as such, it remains unasked, and perhaps unaskable.

It remains, that by its formal structure alone, "between" is nothing
in itself. It remains that by the style of its enunciation, "between" is the
dissimulated simulation of a scene of dissimulation.

Such is the very stage or frame (of what shall we name us?) as a
problem.

This is also to say that simulation, the general possibility of death,
is—if there is such—always the nonsimple. Which is also to say, here
or there, in the turning, we must speak, always, of art, or a politics, of
a politics of the art of—and yet otherwise than—what has for too long
gone by way of the name of death.

And so, what if burial means, at least, both containment and loss, per-
durance *and* dissipation, even beneath the ocean, bottom, *or above* the
builded city? And, here, as we turn toward another folding, may I remark

it in catechresis—inscriptive but not literal, architectural but not architectonic—by way of the figures of parenthesis, of the so-called cantilever?

What, then, if rhythm is not time, or space?

A decryptic, elliptical rhythm announces itself, refusing, thereby, to
state its theme, remaining, resting, perhaps; only. Within the fold of the
practice that yields such, a shudder or a thrill, a graphic amber, an asonic
sonority, may gather or arise—as, yet otherwise, than the envisaged, the
sounded, and the sonorous.

It may give the "re-resonance" of those "silent tongues," of a history of
the future that is not yet, as that which remains.

This may only be given in the work or practice announcing an impossible possible crossing, beyond both future and past. Let us say here,
recalling, again, the making of a way out of no way, a "jitney," perhaps.
Too, if it may come at all, it is always otherwise than in time. That is, it is
given, if at all, as other than one, as the time of making, *of* time, as it were,
as it will have been made, "after all."[11]

And, if it is to become our own way, what can we say, or give as mark,
or remark, a resounding, or re-resonance, drawn or withdrawn, from the
gift of giving, of poïesis? Abyss? Or Passage? Wave, or Sedimentation?
What of Indentation? Perhaps? And yet, there is more to come.

And, yet still, no proper is given, of name. For, it is no name; it is all
names; it is, whatever we may call us, as name.

It is thus that I propose we undertake, in turn, as a form of our own
responsibility, even as we remain without measure, of success, across this
millennial passage, a gesture or step, at least a turn, toward a desedimentation of dissimulation—of an epoch of war—and toward that which
will have only ever been that which will have remained.

CHAPTER ONE

OF EXORBITANCE

The Problem of the Negro as a Problem for Thought

For Jacques Derrida, am memoriam[1]

In a classical philosophical opposition we are not dealing with the peaceful coexistence of a *vis-à-vis*, but rather with a violent hierarchy. One of the two terms governs the other (axiologically, logically, etc.), or has the upper hand. To deconstruct the opposition, first of all, is to overturn [*renverser*] the hierarchy at a given moment. To overlook this phase of overturning [*phase de renversement*] is to forget the conflictual and subordinating structure of the opposition. Therefore one might proceed too quickly to a *neutralization* that *in practice* would leave the previous field untouched, leaving one no hold on the previous opposition, thereby preventing any means of *intervening* in the field effectively. We know what always have been the *practical* (particularly *political*) effects of *immediately* jumping *beyond* oppositions, and of protests in the simple form of *neither* this *nor* that. When I say that this phase is necessary, the word *phase* is perhaps not the most rigorous one. It is not a question of a chronological phase, a given moment, or a page that one day simply will be turned, in order to go on to other things. The necessity of this phase is structural; it is the necessity of an interminable analysis:

the hierarchy of dual oppositions always reestablishes itself. . . . [O]
n the other hand—to remain in this phase is still to operate on the
terrain of and from within the deconstructed system. By means of
this double, and precisely stratified, dislodged and dislodging, writing, we must also mark the interval between inversion, which brings
low what was high, and the irruptive emergence of a new "concept,"
a concept that can no longer be, and never could be, included in
the previous regime. If this interval, this biface or biphase, can be
inscribed only in a bifurcated writing . . . then it can only be marked
in what I would call a *grouped* textual field: in the last analysis, it is
impossible to *point* it out, for a unilinear text, or a punctual *position*,
an operation signed by a single author, are all by definition incapable
of practicing this interval.[2]

Problematization

When speaking of the question of the situation of the Negro American as a matter of thought, we must begin by recognizing the historical problem, or the historical form of the problematization of existence,
the kind of problematic, that has organized its emergence and rendered
both its necessity and its possibility.[3] That problematization is, in a word,
since the sixteenth century, the double and reciprocal articulation of the
institution of modern slavery and its aftermath, including colonialism,
in continental Africa, in the Americas, and in the Caribbean, on the
one hand, and the emergence of a global practice of distinction among
humans that has come to be placed under the heading of an idea, or concept, of race, on the other.

As much as or more than almost any other social configuration or
grouping of peoples in the modern era, this historical situation has posed
for Africans, especially of the so-called diaspora, an exposed or explicit
question about the forms of historical existence and the grounds of
reflexive identification.

Inheriting or confronting, in any case inhabiting, this situation, African American or diasporic intellectuals of the United States from Phillis
Wheatley, Benjamin Banneker, or Olaudah Equiano of the eighteenth
century, including David Walker, Maria Stewart, Frederick Douglass,
Frances Harper or Alexander Crummell of the nineteenth, to W. E. B.
Du Bois and Anna Julia Cooper of the turn to the twentieth, for example,
elaborated an ensemblic discourse that in each case proposed (albeit in

heterogeneous ways, often in the same discourse) the production of a subjectivity, subject position, or profile in discourse that they or later intellectuals, through readings of their work, have marked as Africanist. This question was raised for them not only in terms of their own practices and their own sense of identity or identification, but in terms of the question of the relationship of existence, essence, and identity in general. In the originary passage of the founding of their mundane inhabitation as a problem to the problematization of their own itinerary of existence, this figuration or configuration, perhaps in terms of social and historical practice in general, but certainly in discourse, enacted or enabled the elaboration of a fundamental questioning of the possible character and order of social and historical being in general. For, indeed, although it is rather typically assumed, too simplistically, that the grounds of historical and social existence and identification were placed in question for "Africans," or "Negroes," or "Blacks," configured in this vortex, what is not so typically remarked is the way in which a fundamental questioning of the roots of identification and forms of historical existence for "Europeans" or "Whites" was also set loose at the core of this historical problematization. Indeed these very terms perhaps can be thought as pertinent only in the devolution of the rhythmic turns of this vortex. The profound character of this interrogation and its full implication remain to be elaborated. For, indeed, even though it has remained an exorbitance for traditional forms of thought in Europe and America, this questioning can certainly be thought of as concerned with the most fundamental questions that have been gathered in the modern era under the heading of ontology, and it can also be understood to pose the questions concerning the possibility of truth that the history of metaphysics in the modern era, whether as philosophy or as theology, has called its own. Indeed, it may yet remain the very historical cusp of the announcements of such so-called general considerations.

For much of the past two decades it has been a rather perennial fashion to register a certain kind of critique of the enunciations that I have described as "Africanist." This critique has been directed especially at the work of African diasporic intellectuals from the United States. Over the course of its devolution, a privileged object of such critique remained the work of Du Bois. Further, such critique was almost always placed as the opening or clearing epistemological and political operation for the staging, or setup, of a self-proclaimed new project in the study of African Americans in the United States, the African diaspora in general, or now a domain placed under the loosely concep-tualized umbrella term "Africana." These critical pronouncements of the past two decades are, finally, always placed under the heading of a de-essentializing critique of (African American or diasporic) concep-tualizations of identity and of practices of identification. As such, these critiques as they have been announced since the mid-1980s remain in one entire sense simply part of a broad and diverse contemporary con-figuration that has made thematic the heterogeneous structure of iden-tification and social practice.[4]

Yet, it remains that however much one affirms the questioning of the idea of a simple essence as the ground of supposed identity, identifica-tion, and historical existence, across the heterogeneity of its enunciation, this perennial critique is in turn questionable in one entire and funda-mental aspect of its elaboration. It naively implies that a nonessential-ist discourse or position can be produced. As such, it presupposes an oppositional theoretical architecture at its core, in the supposed and self-serving distinction between a discourse or position that does not operate on the basis of an essence and those that do. It thus all the more emphati-cally presupposes a simple essence as the ground of its discourse, in both conceptual and practical, that is, political, terms.

Yet, no practice in general, no practice as thought, in a sense that we can still refer in a certain way to a *radical order* of question, can simply mark or absolutely delimit its own inhabitation of the presumption of essence.[5]

It is thus that in the presupposition of such a replete position, this cri-tique seems unable to recognize in the *historical situation* of the African American the most mundane of circumstances: that there is not now nor has there ever been a free zone or quiet place from which the discourse of so-called Africanist figures, intellectuals, writers, thinkers, or schol-ars might issue. And this can be shown to be the case in general. Such discourse always emerges in a context and is both a response and a call. In this specific instance, it emerges in a cacophony of enunciation that marks the inception of discourses of the "African" and the "Negro" in the modern period in the sixteenth century.[6] At center of this cacophony was a question about what we now often call identity and forms of identifica-tion. On the surface, its proclaimed face, it was a discourse about the status of a putative Negro subject: political, legal, moral, philosophical, literary, theological, and so on. On its other, and hidden, face, was a question about the status of a putative European subject (subsequently understood as an omnibus figure of the "White"), the presumptive answer to which served as ground, organizing in a hierarchy the schema of this discourse, and determining the historically supraordinate elaboration of this general question. This hidden surface, as ground and reference of identification, along with the exposed surface that showed forth as a question about "Negro" identity, must be continually desedimented, scrutinized, and re-figured in their relation. It is the status of the identity that takes its stand in the shadows, or the system that it supposedly inaugurates, that is so often assumed in the de-essentializing projects that remain perennially afoot in African American and African diasporic studies. Or, if this "European" or "European American," or later "White," subject (presumptively understood as a simple whole despite its remarkable "internal" heterogeneity), or the system presumed to originate with it, is not simply assumed, the necessity, rigor, patience, and fecundity of antecedent Africanist discourses, as they have negotiated a certain *economy*, one within which such discourses (antecedent and contemporary, diasporic and continental) function, is too easily diminished, if not outright denied, in the perennial de-essentializing critique of the immediately past and present intellectual generations.[7]

The economy at work in Africanist problematics, as they articulate the problem of principle or ground, especially as the interwoven questions of tradition or forms of social existence and practices of distinction according to a mark or concept of race, can be stated quite simply. In the face of a distinction, a judgment of value, a recognition of a difference in any sense whatsoever, even or especially if the mark is understood to indicate or name an absence or a putative "nothing," one cannot bring that distinction or mark into question by the postulation of a simple denial of the integrity or ground of the distinction and difference that has been proclaimed; that is, by counterposing either the fullness of a directly oppositional claim, or a measure of neutrality, to the distinction in question. Not only does the apparent direct denial of a distinction, or an apparent refusal of acknowledgment thereof, do so in the very statement or practice of such a gesture, but the force of that implicit and buried recognition will function all the more powerfully in defining the terrain and organizing the field in which the critical discourse operates, limiting and specifying its critique, because such a denial has in fact not overturned existing hierarchies (conceptual and political) of power and authority. It will, in an essential sense, leave the *status quo* intact.

Such is the paradoxical *aeconomy* that takes shape for any practice as the announcement of form, the mark, the sign, or the *phaenomenon*, regardless of the premise of the ostensible ground of such as the real or the imaginary.

Thus, if one's practice would operate on the order of fundamental thought and be general in its practical theoretical implication, it is necessary in articulating oneself in the historical space in which discourses of the Negro emerge and resound to produce a double and redoubled discourse. The enunciation of Africanist figures in discourses of the Negro emerge in a hierarchically ordered field in which the question of the status of the so-called Negro is quite indissolubly linked to a presupposition of the homogeneity and purity of the so-called European or its derivatives. Their discourse is historically coextensive and interwoven with the inception of what philosopher Kevin Thomas Miles once proposed in a felicitous phrase during an interlocution on the question, one might call the "*project*" of (white) purity in the modern era.[8] This situation, or more precisely problematization, yields for African American thinkers what I call the *problem* of purity, or the problem of pure being. To inhabit such a discursive formation, perhaps in a structurally contestatory fashion, one cannot, under the premise of the ultimate incoherence of such a presupposition or proclamation of purity, of the (im)possibility of the pure, simply declare in turn the status (as prior, for example) of a neutral space or position.[9] One must displace or attempt to displace the distinction in question. This necessity is perhaps all the more astringent when the distinction in question is a claim for a pure origin, a pure identity, an ultimate ground of identification. Such a displacement can be made general or decisive only *through* the movement of the productive elaboration of difference—as articulation—perhaps even according to necessity as the performative announcement of a differential figure. Such a production makes possible a delimitation of the claim of purity and prepares the ground for an elaboration of its lability. In the historical situation of the African or Negro American, as has been said in many ways, in many forms of enunciation, but to take W. E. B. Du Bois's formulation from the "Forethought" of the *Souls of Black Folk: Essays and Sketches*, one has to establish, despite all its paradoxes and risks, in the domains of sociality and political inhabitation, for example, the character of an origin of "world."[10]

Or, as I prefer to put it, one might speak of an originary scene of possibility. This necessity can be understood to establish its claim in an order that is as radical, or more so, as all that has been called transcendental in philosophy since the eighteenth century. And its enigmas demand that one find a traversal that moves otherwise and perhaps beyond the limits of that tradition of questioning. It can thus be said that to fail to undertake this differential elaboration would leave the critical position enclosed in the horizon of the declarations of the same or the simple. Yet, especially in the case of the question of the subject, of subjectivation and the movements of identification (individual and collective), in the practical theoretical horizon of the question of "world," one must elaborate not just a negative difference, identity, or identification, which is always recuperable to an ultimate claim of an absolute, of pure being or concept, by way of something like a movement of speculation such as that proposed in the thought of G. W. F. Hegel, in particular all that he placed under the heading of his neologism *Aufhebung*. A thought of the negative in this sense might still remain a simple stage in the consolidation of an original or destined being as a subject that would proclaim itself as absolute. What is at stake then is situated at a level somewhat more radical than the negative in general. Nor is it a matter of establishing a predicate of some kind. The originarity that one must remark in the situation of an Africanist problematic since the sixteenth century can emerge for thought only within an approach that attends to that within historicity and existence that would distend form in general, distantiate presence or its derivatives, disseminate any presumptive sense of being. As a practical theoretical operation it must be elaborated in, or along the track of, the movements of the opening of the general possibility of difference, possibility thought as the remark of both sides of the limit, of limit as the form of the appearance of possibility, of possibility as the announcement of the limit of limit, and perhaps the passage beyond such. There is no absolute origin here, no absolute beginning, no final difference. The modifier general, here, should suggest a formulation in which difference is understood as nothing in and of itself. Yet, it is radical that one must begin with the constituted. Difference named under the heading of such "world" or "worldhood," then, must be elaborated simultaneously as a question of the radical possibility of difference, of the general possibility of the otherwise; yet, it should also be understood as remarking the "fact" that there is difference (maintaining thereby a critical inhabitation of a situation, historical, at once temporal and spatial). And of course the pertinence of the sameness of time, of punctual temporality, would thereby be displaced from its traditional privilege in modern thought in Europe and the Americas. Originarity here would be understood in such a way that the movement of difference, passage, in every sense, is the very possibility of marking any inside or outside and before and after.[11] Such movement is the very form of the organization of the inside of the inside and the outside of the outside. Its temporality will always have been only that which will have been. Such difference, or movement of difference, not only proposes the possibility of a desedimentation of the presumption of purity, or pure being, inhabited as a problem and problematic by Africanist thinkers, but it would also remark the most fundamental dimension of the configured possibility of that which could, perhaps, be considered new in the world in general and in any sense. In this passage, the sovereign gesture of becoming would remain always at stake in that which is not yet born, in that which always arrives on the threshold of historicity too late or after the fact: the new would be this interminable process of becoming such. The new would always only arrive by way of a second time or even an apparently secondary time. The implication of such a practical theoretical thought addresses itself to the most general contemporary proclamations of idea, of system, of the whole. As such, it announces itself on an order of the political that would exceed all existing senses of horizon.

Such is the outline of the always "doubled" or enfolded character of the gesture required in a critical or desedimentative "Africanist" inhabitation of this problematic. (1) Such gesture would affirm an always nominal subject *position*, never an empty form, that is to say never simply a form and never a simple transcendental. (2) It would go by way of an elaboration of the latter's always already differential condition of possibility. What I have proposed to call a "redoubling" would be not only (a) this further elaboration of the ways that this "identity" or identification that one has adduced to contest the discourses of purity is itself heterogeneous, elaborating the differential production of the proclaimed identity (or difference), but also (b) the way in which the movement of this problematic in general arises and takes its organization only through an *agonistic* mode of irruption. This interminable passage through the *agon*, this redoubled inhabitation of the middle passage or a certain maintenance of ambivalence (both of which remain radically otherwise than the neutral) is a theoretical passage that is at once a politics and the practice of an art. This agonistic movement would thus attend to the general order of question in this apparently quite parochial problematic.

In the course of the present chapter I propose the opening of Du Bois's discourse to such an elaboration.

Yet, the practice of Du Bois should be understood as only a certain kind of example or even as a counterexample to the aforementioned perennial premise, an exemplarity which if understood in a certain manner might assist us in reopening the impasses of contemporary thought.

Now, this further elaboration would be the work of critical thought as participation in a tradition. Certainly such critical, or desedimentative, practice would require recognition of the necessity inscribed in antecedent practices of thought. This inhabitation of a nominal critical tradition should be given some further specification. It must (1) maintain a recognition of the necessity of this double gesture and (2) elaborate this necessity as both the possibility and condition of its own practice, in that it always emerges on the scene late and by way of its other, in all senses, and that it cannot accede to the fullness of its own voice, its own declared or willful position within knowledge and power. More sympathetically, we might index this redoubled enunciation as displaced in relation to both (a) its recollection of antecedent practices and (b) its possibility of setting loose a thought whose fullness is always yet to come. This "yet to come" is the spacing or timing of the operation of a nominal critical, or desedimentative, practice, of its possibility and its devolution. This is the order of a paleonymic problematic encoded in the task of theoretical labor in our time.

These formulations propose a strategic intervention enunciated here in an idiom of thought that we might call epistemological, conceptual, and theoretical, which is yet, and more fundamentally, also on the horizon of an ontological problematization of existence, in discussions of the question of the Negro or Negro American as a problem for thought, certainly of discourse and knowledge, but also of historical existence in general. They seek to help expose or bring more into relief a path, or better, paths, of interwoven tracks for retracing and reformulating the question through the operation of a kind of desedimentation and paleonymic practice in thought. In the matter of the problem of the Negro in

the Americas, or perhaps in general, as a problem for thought, one movement of tracks or traces would direct us in a certain descension along
the discursive levels of a project of purity. Another movement of traces
would solicit an inhabitation of the impress that remains of the rhythm
or step of certain figural movements within a discursive field, not so
much by removing them from the soil of their embeddedness or ground
and bringing them back to life, but by a kind of labor of desedimentation that would mobilize—that is, disturb—the lability of the shifts and
fault lines that configure the ground that surrounds them. In this latter
practice, while working across and into such a field of heavily eroded
yet impacted terrain, in the duration of a breaking up and resifting of
worked-over and apparently exhausted deposits, it might be that there
arises a kind of sliding and shifting, a certain dynamis, a certain conjunction of movement and weight, yielding a destabilization of ground,
field, or domain, a movement that could expose sediment that had been
deeply locked and fixed in place, or set into relief new lines of possible
concatenation, or turn up old ground into new configurations of its elements. Such a practice, that is, might turn up new soil on old ground. In
the following considerations, I pursue each track or movement of traces
respectively, if not simply in separation.

Conceptual Notes on the Discourses of the Project of Purity

Although we are generally well aware of the extent, shape, and force
of the discourses that sought to propose (that is, to find or establish as
actual and existing and, further, to proclaim the superiority or suprem-
acy of) a social subject understood as "White" or "(White) European"
as they were articulated in the early nineteenth century, and we even
know something of the moorings of such discourses in eighteenth-
century social, political, and economic developments, the *infrastructural
organization* of that discursive formation, its organization according to
certain presuppositions, often and especially as premises, which are fundamental to an entire metaphysics, in which and according to which, the
dominant positions in the discourse of the question of the Negro in the
Americas has unfolded since the sixteenth century, is not so well recognized and is far less often thought. Once we concern ourselves with following the track of the interwoven character of these enunciations—that
is, the irruption of a discourse concerned with the status of a European,

and, later, "White," historical subject, along with that concerned with the African or Negro—the metaphysical infrastructure of the discourse comes into view, and we can begin to think it from within the possibility of its own commitments. At that juncture, as well, contemporary criticism of the strategies of critical response by antecedent Africanist thinkers in discourses of the Negro to projects of "White" superiority becomes questionable.

Although almost no discursive positions were rigorously systematic and fully elaborated in the eighteenth century, certain key themes and questions that marked out the terrain on which the discourses of the Negro later took shape in the Americas in the nineteenth century were already spelled out in Europe and the New World colonies by the time of the American Revolution.[12] With roots in a configuration of discourses in both Europe and the Americas that took a distinctive shape from the middle of the eighteenth century onward concerning the differences of peoples from around the globe in general, and concerning the specific character of Africans and African American slaves (in a hemispheric sense) in particular, there emerged during the last decades of the eighteenth century and the first half of the nineteenth century a distinctive discourse in the United States concerning the Negro.[13] (1) At its infrastructural core the eighteenth-century discourse was organized around one titular question: Are Negroes human, and if so, are they "fully" human? On the basis of what criteria should their status in relation to (other) humans be judged? And, is that relation one of fundamental, or relative, sameness or difference? And, of course, the question, What is the human? (or, "What is Man?") is always and everywhere at issue, even if only implicitly. This question was especially articulated as a discourse concerning the humanity of Negro slaves. A privileged heading or topic through which this discourse was played out—which in the sense of the project of philosophy was not one among others—was the question of Negro ability or capacity, especially moral and intellectual.[14] (2) The practical and operative question, which presumed Negro inferiority in body and mind, was quite specific: Is their inferior status the effect of their (social) condition, or an effect of their (physical) nature? This practical thematic yielded, further, a sheaf of types of reflections upon the general practical question, "What should be done if the Negro slave is emancipated?" (3) Yet, hidden within both of these questions, and essentially the corollary of the question concerning the humanity of the Negro, even as it is in all truth not less fundamental, was a question about the status of a putative European American or "White" identity. Seldom stated explicitly and in those terms, this latter form of the question acquired its legible organization in conjunction with a stricture against the intermixing of the "races." It is with regard to this latter question that the metaphysical appurtenance of this discourse comes into view. For, at its root, the implied question of this discourse, the hidden question about a European American or "White" identity or identification, brings into view the fact that the adjudication of the status of the Negro implies a prior determination of the grounds for deciding any identity or position as one thing or another; for example, by way of a distinction or heading that has come to be called "race." The question is an ontological one (even if it is not radical or rigorously fundamental): On what basis and in what manner can one decide a being, and its character of existence, as one kind or another? What emerges as decisive at the limit and in the conceptual and propositional sense is the problem of grounding, in some fashion that would be absolute, a socially observable hierarchy that one might wish to affirm. At this juncture, I can begin to name the philosophical appurtenance of the distinction in question, for the only manner in which such a claim could be made was to assume, in the ontological sense, that a distinction was absolute, oppositional, or pure, that in an analytical sense it could be understood as categorical.[15] On that basis then, one could insist upon the categorical difference of the "Negro" (or African) and the European (or "White").

In each of its three aspects, this discourse rests on two interlocked premises: on the one hand, it presupposes the possibility of an infrastructural organization of an oppositional distinction of thought, that of producing an ontological distinction, in this case both between humans and an other and among humans, determining any so-called human being as one kind of thing or another. Hence, it also presupposes the social practice of such a distinction (by which I mean the specific character of the deployment and operation of such a distinction in constituting the effective operation in any actual circumstance or event of the basic terms in play. With regard to human groups, these would be terms such as "Negro," "European," "Indian," or "Chinese," and the logically non-symmetrical character of any list of examples is part of the discursive problem at hand). Further, on the other hand, it presupposes the status of a European, Euro-American, or "White" identity, subject, or mode of identification as coherent, as homogeneous, as a pure term. On that basis, this latter term can be figured as the norm or orientation—that is, as *origin* or *telos*—of the devolution of historical subject position or production of social identity, prescribed as such by general operations of power, authority, and law.

According to these premises, even if by a multitudinous and contradictory movement of logic, even if considered human, the Negro is produced as an exorbitance for thought: an instance outside of all forms of being that truly matter. That is to say, something called the Negro is understood as approachable or nameable from within the architectonic of reason as nonetheless privative and withdrawn in the telic unfolding that is recognized as the claim of reason—that is, in the movement of the economy of *ratio*—it announces an exorbitance that cannot be reduced therein, as it is in Immanuel Kant's disregard or necessarily contradictory inhabitation, in the context of the question of the Negro, of his own critical project.[16] Or the Negro is ambivalently positioned as outside of transcendental historicity, circumscribed within a privative nature, as in G. W. F. Hegel's philosophy of history.[17] Or the Negro slave is proposed as outside, or without standing within, the democratic bequest of the commonweal, as in Thomas Jefferson's ruminations on the state of the Virginia Commonwealth following the American Revolution.[18]

This ensemble of questions, especially the commitments and the premises that make them possible as questions, but also the formal concepts that acquire their organization within these terms, despite the later development of a certain coherence in their discursive elaboration and some specification of themes, map out a general organization of an essential part of a discursive formation regarding the Negro in the long American eighteenth century. They comprise an essential discursive organization of the principal questions that make possible a certain horizon of thought for all nineteenth-century discourses of the Negro, even if they are not exhaustive or absolutely determining in every instance and if they remain at times deeply sedimented.[19]

A brief reading of a sheaf of Jefferson's *Notes on the State of Virginia*, where his discourse explicitly addresses the question of the Negro, along the track that I have proposed, might well allow me to specify a little more the general character of the problem of the Negro as a problem for thought.[20]

Although the theme of slavery runs throughout the book *Notes on the State of Virginia*, Negro American slaves are discussed directly in only two sections: Query VI, titled "Productions Mineral, Vegetable and Animal," and Query XIV, titled "Laws," with the principal discussion in the latter section. Situated in a discussion of prospective legislation that would ostensibly be taken up by the Virginia Assembly, and specifically by way of producing a discourse on a proposal to amend state law to the effect that when a general revision of the common law inherited from England was completed, "all slaves born after [its] passing" would be emancipated, Jefferson develops a question concerning the capacities of Negroes and their status in the commonwealth. Jefferson's discourse on the Negro is a discussion of the merits of such a provision, although in fact neither the law nor the amendment were ever formally addressed in the form discussed by him. We can schematize the key questions that took shape in Jefferson's discourse on this provision. They could be said to exhibit the organization of some basic themes that function in general discourses on the Negro. What makes Jefferson's discourse exemplary here is less his propositional declaration of belief in Negro inferiority in relation to "Whites" or Europeans, for in terms of the eighteenth century he was rather unique in his more or less fully elaborated enunciation of such a view. Thus he is not representative in the manner of a typification. Rather, he is exemplary of a problem for thought in that the questions that organize his discourse show the way in which an ontological problematic is situated at the heart of the discourses of European or "White" superiority, as given, for example, in enunciations with regard to the so-called problem of the "Negro."[21]

The first question, concerning the general grounds for deciding the humanity of Negroes, especially Negro slaves, is never directly posed in its bare form as such; for example, under the heading of the suggestion that Negroes are not physiologically, or "biologically," human. However, this border is broached occasionally, yet persistently, in Jefferson's text by the description of the Negro as slave and then specifically as chattel, the juxtaposition (even if "favorable") of the Negro American slave to an animal (such as the "Oran-ootan") or the privilege of physical attribute in posing the question of the character of the being of the Negro. Rather, the burden of Jefferson's discourse *presupposes* a Euro-American norm of what it means to be human. This premise is never interrogated in and of itself here. With this ground enabling a judgment, Jefferson systematically scores Negro American slaves for not measuring up. The most important censure on his part is his judgment that the supposed Negro inferiority (supposedly evident in empirical circumstances) "is not the effect merely of their condition of life," their social conditions, for example the conditions of enslavement, but is due to their "nature." Whereas, on the other hand, for example, in Jefferson's perspective, the supposed poor status of North American Indians was due to their social conditions and was not due to their nature.[22]

In the second instance, Jefferson's text poses the question, "What is to be done if the Negro slave is emancipated?" Would they be capable of being, or should they be, considered part of the Virginia Commonwealth or the new American republic? Writing of an eventual colonization scheme that would have followed in the wake of emancipation according to the original proposal to change the inherited English common law, Jefferson affirms this provision, maintaining that Negroes were not or would not be assimilable to the commonwealth, which is perhaps best understood in this context as both a legal institution, a "state," and as the putative horizon of a "nation." He argued essentially that there were too many differences between Euro-Americans and Negroes to allow a common ground of inhabitation. Describing them as "political" differences, he suggested that there were too many "prejudices" and "memories," bad history, so to speak, on the one hand, and too many "natural distinctions," on the other, to allow peaceful coexistence of these two groups. He then went on to outline what he called "physical and moral" differences that he believed would be an obstacle to the "incorporation" of Negroes. In this discussion, Jefferson lays out his greatest catalog of supposed Negro inferiorities. The physical differences that he emphasizes are color, body form, and body texture (for example, hair), while providing a rambling list of others. The key motif here is that European bodies are the model, the norm, the *telos* of physical type or attribute.[23] The "moral" differences, as Jefferson calls them, might just as well be called intellectual. What is rhetorically striking about this discussion is the unmitigated authority for peremptory judgment that is assumed by Jefferson. Comparing the Negro unfavorably to the North American Indian, he dismisses a range of Negro intellectual activity as beneath the most fundamental level of mental and moral ability or capacity.[24]

Jefferson's extensive dismissal of Negro intellectual capacity essentially maintains that the Negro does not merit membership in the commonwealth and, by extension, in the nation or even the "state" as a whole. The Negro has no standing in the commonwealth.

A third question, "What is the status of a European, European American, or 'White' subject or identity?" (and likewise the question of the grounds for deciding a racial subject or identity as one thing or another) is both hidden and exposed, in Jefferson's writing, by way of its declaration of, and commitment to, a certain stricture: no intermixing of the races. And this question is also situated within both of the prior questions, functioning essentially as the corollary of the question concerning the humanity of the Negro. A concept of the purity of identity as a fixed, natural (physically or "biologically" given), even metaphysical character is operative here. Jefferson seems unable to pose the question of the relative status of "social condition" or "nature" with regard to whites. Again and again, he juxtaposes Greek or Roman slaves with Negro American slaves, suggesting that great intellectual accomplishments were made by the former despite horrible treatment, whereas the latter in his judgment have failed to produce any lasting contribution to civilization despite comparatively better treatment. He concludes such juxtapositions with a persistent refrain. His explanation for the contributions of the Greek and Roman slaves is in the logical form of a syllogism. Yet, the conditional form of the syllogism, often marked by the conjunction "if," is set aside here for a declaration. As such, the conditional premise is claimed as an analytical *precondition*, and hence is presupposed (and not open to the question of its justification), for any meaningful utterance on the topic, rather than as a *condition*, a term in the analysis, which would require some account of its status. Jefferson writes of these ancient slaves, by way of explanation, "But they were of the race of whites. It is not their condition then, but their nature, which has produced the distinction."[25] In terms of an inquiry that would offer itself as analytic—that is, one that would be without presupposition or would give a self-reflexive and justifying account of such form of premise—Jefferson presupposes, and not only presumes (on the order of a naive opinion), a ground in nature, given a certain concept of the natural, in order to establish and maintain the hierarchy he wants to affirm. The ambivalence that some commentators have long accentuated in Jefferson's discourse can be understood as motivated by an uneasiness with the impossibility of grounding this assumption (that is, validating his presupposition, his implicit but nonetheless committed premise) about nature, specifically the nature of white folks, only on empirical evidence.[26] For this evidence could be faulty. Jefferson would have preferred some proof that would be absolute, that one could claim was absolute law, in that, as one might construe it, such evidence would be logical or ontological. Yet nature (and even God) reveals itself (himself) only through signs. Hence, Jefferson could not claim absolute proof. Thus, the hesitation and ambivalence recorded in the following passage:

> To justify a general conclusion requires many observations, even where the subject may be submitted to the Anatomical knife, to Optical glasses, to analysis by fire, or by solvents. How much more then where it is a faculty, not a substance, we are examining; where it eludes the research of all the senses; where the conditions of its existence are various and variously combined; where the effects of those which are present or absent bid defiance to calculation; let me add too as a circumstance of tenderness, where our conclusion would degrade a whole race of men from the rank in the scale of beings which their Creator may perhaps have given them. . . . I advance it therefore as a suspicion only, that the blacks, whether originally a distinct race, or made distinct by time and circumstances, are inferior to whites in the endowments of both body and mind. (Jefferson 1972 [1787], 143; Jefferson 1984a [1787], 269–70)

What should be emphasized here is that his ambivalence is ultimately organized by the status he can or cannot claim for white identity, not (ultimately), as is usually supposed, by what he can or cannot claim for Negro identity. Jefferson's worry about the truth of the socially existing hierarchy, in colonial Virginia for example, in the system of slavery, is also immediately a worry about the moral status of the practices that are the social performance of this hierarchy. The presupposition of moral superiority of the European or Euro-American *vis-à-vis* the Negro or African American that is maintained in almost all European positions in the discourses of the Negro of this time is thus legible. To the extent that the *truth* of this hierarchy is questionable, the premise of the supposed superior moral status of the European, or later the "White," is unstable, as well. This moral insecurity can be tracked by way of these oscillations of Jefferson's enunciations on the Negro—that is to say, the track or trail of a profound insecurity about his own moral status—which is thus resolutely presumed (as unassailable opinion) or declared (in uncritical analytic presupposition) again and again, perhaps as a way of forestalling an open consideration of the question. In Query XVIII, this sedimented motif comes to the fore and affirms the orientation of our reading. Although these two passages come from different overall discussions— the first embedded in a discussion of Negro ability or capacity and the latter in one about the institution of slavery—the theological reference connects these passages and specifies their root premises as concerned with human faculty and hence ontological status. Jefferson writes:

> And can the liberties of a nation be thought secure when we have removed their only firm basis, a conviction in the minds of the people that these liberties are of the gift of God? That they are not to be violated but with his wrath? Indeed I tremble for my country when I reflect that God is just: that his justice cannot sleep forever: that considering numbers, nature and natural means only, a revolution of the wheel of fortune, an exchange of situations, is among possible events: that it may become probable by supernatural interference! (Jefferson 1972 [1787], 163; Jefferson 1984a [1787], 289)

Jefferson's questions, in light of the history of the devolution of monarchial authority afoot in his time and in light of the question of the universality of Christian salvic dispensation so profoundly posed in his time, might be well gathered in the singular question: What is the relation of "our" people to a sovereign authority, be it ecclesiastical (political or scientific) or divine? Thus, the question of the enslavement of Africans and their descendants in the Americas poses the question of the ultimate authority that would support "the nation" or "the people" as one committed to such an institution. This, then, is the question of the relation of sovereignty to enslavement.[27] And that question broaches the question of metaphysics at the heart of the problem of the Negro as a problem for thought. Jefferson's rhetorical and discursive disposition here, however, forecloses a critical inhabitation of this question. His deepest commitment, even in the latter passage quoted, is to the resolution of the status of "our people," those Americans who would be otherwise than African or Negro, particularly those who in part by way of the very historical process of which Jefferson's discourse is a part come to be called "White." Thus, all of the logical aporias that circulate in the concept of origin and the ensemble of concepts surrounding it are not, and cannot, be thought as questions by Jefferson's discourse. And it is ultimately this putative white identity that Jefferson is most concerned to affirm.[28] Hence, it is no wonder that, although it is only obliquely stated, Jefferson's entire discourse is organized by the *telos* of preventing, or justifying the preclusion of, the mixture or intermixture of any kind among the races.[29]

The so-called Negro question announced as exorbitant to the true concerns of Jefferson's discourse in one sense passes through the barriers that would be presumed to quarantine and contain it and, in a manner not unlike that common process known in cuisines throughout the Mediterranean region in which an aromatic liquid that is slowly but integrally absorbed into a grain, is not only itself transformed into something quite other than its original form but also transforms all that surrounds it. Within Jefferson's discourse, it is such a movement that announces another kind of exorbitance, one that remains irreducible within his discourse. It is at this juncture of the reflective and rhetorical displacement of one question of exorbitance by another that the futile intransigence of Jefferson's practice in thought here can be discerned.

In the face of the primordial ambivalence of the appearance of the phenomenon, of the sign in general, the discourse proposed by Jefferson, and any discourse such as his, must always presuppose its ground and not just presume it; not only does it inhabit the precomprehension of ground, it declares it as a telos. The only premise by which such a claim or insistence upon categorical difference could ostensibly or formally be sustained would be to assume, in the metaphysical sense, that in general a distinction could be made absolute, oppositional, or pure.[30] Only on such a basis, then, could one hope to secure the social and historical claim of the categorical difference of the "Negro" or African and the "White" or Euro-American. The stricture upon the intermixing of the races that we have adduced in Jefferson's thought, and this would maintain its pertinence in all later discourses predicated upon such an oppositional distinction among humans in its most sedimented traditional form, even if not insisting upon this stricture explicitly, thus maintains within itself a fundamentally philosophical—that is, essentially metaphysical—question. The discourse advanced in Jefferson's text cannot open itself to a true or fundamental questioning of its own premises. It is a dogmatism in the midst of the Enlightenment.

It is important perhaps to underscore that this dogmatic position is not the *foundation* for an Africanist discourse in the discourses of the Negro. The incipit of this dogmatic discourse in the project of purity is already a solicitation: the problem of the African or Negro slave. It is a solicitation that sets loose a trembling in the inaugural enunciations of this discourse in the scene of North America of the sixteenth through eighteenth centuries. The inaugural enunciations of this position are already a response. As such, this position in discourse certainly *should not be hypostasized, in and of itself, as the founding* discursive movement or formulation of an Africanist discourse or the project of an African American or African diasporic studies. While it is certainly an instituting condition for the emergence of an Africanist discourse, it is a part of the violent play of the whole problem of the Negro, not its foundation.[31]

The Problem of the Negro as a Problem for Thought

In the face of such a dogmatism, one cannot assume the position of contemplation and neutrality as the first or final gesture. At the level of metaphysics and the most fundamental claims about existence, any ostensible interlocutor positioned as the object of such a discourse is always already engaged in an antagonistic encounter and relation of positions. (The conditions of actual dialogue would perhaps not be met by this situation.) As such, to set afoot a claim in this situation or encounter, an enunciation that would address the opening and telic projection of such a dogmatic position is necessary; that is, the very terms of the encounter, in a discursive sense, would have to be subjected to a certain kind of questioning. Such a questioning can unfold only by way of a double gesture: not only must the ground of the dogmatic claim, the assertion of a certain hierarchy (here among certain groups of humans), be brought into question, but the possibility of another kind, or order, of distinction must be posed and the dispersed figurations that become articulable by way of it given their elaboration.

This situational requirement of a double gesture on the part of any discursive figure or figuration that would or must engage the discourses of the project of purity, as exemplified in the texts of Thomas Jefferson, names the deeply conflictual and constitutively conjoined relation of knowledge and power that stands at both the historical and conceptual juncture of any project that would purport to elucidate something like a Negro or African American or African diasporic figure as an object of knowledge and understanding. In the sense of its announcement as position or ensemble of positions within such an antagonistic field of a discourse, something like an African American studies or an African diasporic studies, or, as I prefer to call it, the discourse of the "problem of the Negro" as "a problem of thought," must always have something at stake. Whether it is the case of the trembling of ontological edifices that it makes possible or the encrusted instituted formation that it cannot dislodge, by way of examples, there are always real and effective positions and consequences in play in the movement of its discourse.

The Configuration of the Practice of W. E. B. Du Bois

I believe that I can further specify the character of this problematic by way of some recourse to the example of W. E. B. Du Bois.

At the level of the irruption of discourse and social practice in general, the work of Du Bois might be situated among (even if as an original production) various configurations of the generations of figures in discourses of the Negro.[32] In this regard, Du Bois's discursive itinerary might be understood as exemplary (but not as a telos, in the final instance) of the problematic that attends any such discursive inhabitation.

Yet, at the level of the formalization and epistemologization of discourses of the Negro, the resonance or pertinence of Du Bois's practice for contemporary questions in African American and African diasporic studies remains singular. This singularity has, quite simply, to do with his principled conceptualization of the Negro, the African American for example, as an object of thought the horizon of possibility and becoming of which would be illimitable. The principled elaboration of this conceptualization led Du Bois to formulate a complex and differential program for the study of the Negro. It is distinguished epistemologically by the *combination* of the micrological infrastructure of his conceptualization of the problem of African American and Africanist identities in general, which simultaneously names the Negro or Negro American as a heading for knowledge and disarticulates the premise that such a heading is a simple essence, in conjunction with the macrological, indeed global, breadth and historical scope of his conceptualization of the field of Africanist studies (especially of the diaspora), which formulates the way in which the structural character of modern systems as such only come into formation by way of the historical trajectories in which an Africanist situation is dispersed throughout its interstices. That is to say, both the object and the field, in Du Bois's terms, are essentially differential in terms of conditions of possibility and comparative in terms of an horizon of realized understanding or knowledge.[33]

On both of the levels named, of discursive possibility and of epistemological project, respectively, even if in differing ways, Du Bois remains an exemplary example by which to suggest the interest of the different and differential positioning that I propose for future elaborations of African American or African diasporic studies, or interventions with regard to this heading, in the United States as they seek to engage or transform discourses of the Negro.

My reference to Du Bois here is intended to have a distinct contemporary bearing. To the extent that every generation since the 1960s, including the generation of that pivotal decade, has sought to reinvent or "rebirth" the field of African American and African diasporic studies, I wish to redirect attention in contemporary discussion, in a certain way, to the generosity and resourcefulness of antecedent practices of thought and Africanist figures in discourses of the Negro.[34] I propose to refer our recollection to not only the 1960s or the 1940s or the 1920s or even to Du Bois's thought in general, but in particular to that work acquiring its orientation in the late 1890s, to the initial stages of the itinerary and work of Du Bois.

In the late 1890s, Du Bois undertook his first systematic attempts to think the question of the Negro as a whole. We can trace the movement of this attempt in three essays written and published in 1897. That year was pivotal in Du Bois's itinerary, for in that year he first systematically formulated the essential presuppositions of his own reflexive inhabitation of the "Negro Problem." In one sense, I am simply placing in configuration three essays from that year: "The Conservation of Races," written in the early spring of that year; "Strivings of the Negro People," written later in the spring and subsequently revised and republished as the opening chapter of The Souls of Black Folk; and "The Study of the Negro Problems," written during the early autumn.[35] Across these three essays, Du Bois's practice outlines a double movement. We can trace the movement of this double gesture within the conceptual organization and under the rhetorical umbrella, of the "The Conservation of Races."

I. On the one hand, when Du Bois attempts to think the question of the Negro, especially the ontological question concerning the ground of the being called the Negro, he initially proceeds according to the logic of opposition that dominated the discourses of the Negro during the eighteenth and nineteenth centuries. This was a quite traditional ontology, moreover an exceedingly overdetermined one; that is, the discourse of scientific evolutionism as it pertains to the so-called human and the concept of race operative at the core of this conjunction. In this movement of his thought, as he follows traditional logic, the entire question becomes confounded. The question of the Negro is confounded with the concept of race, as the Negro, an entity that Du Bois describes as historical through and through, is nonetheless placed by him under the analytical heading of a certain thought of the *ideal*, a *telos*, as if realizable on the basis of a given destiny, which gives it the appearance of an absolute and predetermined entity. The question of race, organized around a concept of the pure or the simple, about which Du Bois has already named profound and telling hesitations due to the impossibility of validating its supposed ideal properties by any empirical measure, is construed by Du Bois as always, in practice a question of mixtures, and changeable, malleable, historically specified, properties (CR, [1987a]: 3–5, paras. 8–12).

Yet, as a putative origin of a world or worldhood, as the figurative scene of originary ideals, even if they are yet to come, the Negro past appears in the present as a retrospective justification for itself. The heading for that retrospection, in this essay, is the concept-metaphor "race."

In this movement of his thought, although deeply critical of the concept of race, Du Bois is unable to displace the order of its pertinence and must use it to distinguish the historicity that he wishes to bring into view. Hence, his questioning of the concept of race, although precisely solicitous of the concept of race at the level of its specific statements, is also unable to categorically dispense with its nominal promise, and thus appears indecisive with regard to its place in the architecture of his conceptualization of the Negro question as a whole. And, even this apparition is not so simple. Further, although yielding an account that is more or less accurate at the level of its actual description of the contemporary conditions of the Negro, there is a logical *aporia* that marks the opening of his discourse (indeed, any discourse) and obscures the intense questioning and inquiry (and hesitation concerning the most apparent possible answers) into the grounds of a so-called Negro identity and, hence, identity as such. That conundrum is simply the logical *aporia* that requires that he speak *as if* that which he wishes to bring under one coherent analytical frame already exists as such an epistemological (or reflective) entity. He cannot open any question whatsoever concerning the Negro without speaking as if the Negro as such is a given and presumably a singular identity. In one entire movement of his discourse, Du Bois *seems* to presume what in fact he is seeking to question. Perhaps this is the price of criticism.

II. On the other hand, Du Bois persistently and systematically described, and dramatized, the actual *character* of the lives of Negroes, both in terms of their experience and in terms of their inscription within certain social systems, in such a way that its excessiveness to this given or inherited ontology (or logic) is made thematic.

In part, we might say that this was due to his critical response to the *practice of racial distinction*, and this would be more in the form of a provocation and solicitation than an instituting foundation. For we must recall that although compelled in the "The Conservation of Races" to set the stage for a statement of the Negro problem with traditional concepts, Du Bois in this address continually resists subordinating the historical and social situation of Negro lives to them. Above all, in this essay, and in others of the period and throughout his life, Du Bois privileged the theme of Negro *capacity*, the way in which an infinite horizon of possible forms of becoming opens within their own *existence*; a position construed such that it is radically excessive to any idea of a fixed or given essence in any simple sense. It was, perhaps, this critical response that led him to interrogate the concept of race in the opening stages of this essay even as he felt compelled to use it.

In another sense, we can say that Du Bois's reckoning of the excessiveness of the lives of Negroes to traditional ontology, which would be oriented by a commitment to determine the Negro as one thing purely and simply (Socrates' question "what is . . .?" construed in a dogmatic fashion), was due to the fidelity of his attention to the *historical experience,* the historial character of the sense of being of Negroes (and not just their systemic inscription): that the originary sense of their being is that of the necessity of making a way, of finding a way, an inhabitation that is always, through and through, historial—one that *must* be made, or always, originarily, remade, anew. This would be the threshold by which their sense of world could be announced, if possible, if such will ever have been possible, however differential the terms or heterogeneous the genesis of such. And, this historical form of origin would be the very opening of exorbitance within their sense of being: of an ineluctable and threshold displacement of the origin *and* of the always renewed opening to that which is beyond any given form of being.

This would be a sense that could be approached, if at all, only by way of understanding and interpretation, a mode of inquiry that should be distinguishable from an account that would be primarily description. Instead, it is an approach akin to something that was called understanding, or more properly *Verstehen*, by his immediate predecessors such as Wilhelm Dilthey, Georg Simmel or his contemporaries such as Max Weber and Émile Durkheim.[36] Finding such an approach was, perhaps more than any other preoccupation, Du Bois's principal or most fundamental concern as a scholar, a practitioner of the still nascent human sciences, in the opening stages of his career: to outline the contours of an historical coming into being; that is, to render legible the sedimented layers of an African American inhabitation of the world.

To situate such an historical existence, he proposed many methods, many ways of accomplishing this goal, of developing access to this experience, directly or indirectly. These included historical research, sociological fieldwork, statistical description, physical and anatomical analysis, and photographic and other forms of visual documentation among others. He called for and practiced many modes of literary production, including the short story, the travelogue, poetry, drama, the novel or long fiction, the essay, and autobiography, to name several. The essay, in general, remained perhaps his favored form. One of these practices, autobiography, remains the site of some of Du Bois's most poignant interventions. He turns to the autobiographical at decisive moments in the "The Conservation of Races." It opens and sets the stage for *The Souls of Black Folk: Essays and Sketches.* Indeed, this register of reference or tone dominates the book, which itself was a collection of essays.

Ultimately, all of this was construed epistemologically—that is, gathered and organized in a theoretical sense—under a critical reflection, that Du Bois called a kind of "interpretation" (TSNP, [1898b]: 18–20, paras. 39–42). And such practice would in turn be otherwise than simply a response to a given object of attention, whether understood as material or ideal; it would also entail the possibility and necessity of a certain production or performance that would itself be a form of such an inhabitation, of such a sense of world, that would itself exemplify such a possibility.

Along these lines, a concern with the historial or existential order of Negro life, Du Bois systematically came upon the *sense of being* of the Negro as not just one thing or another, but as richly and fundamentally double. I recall the famous passages.

After the Egyptian and Indian, the Greek and the Roman, the Teu-
ton and the Mongolian, the Negro is a sort of seventh son, born with
a veil and gifted with second-sight in this American world,—a world
which yields him no true self-consciousness, but only lets him see
himself through the revelation of the other world. It is a peculiar
sensation, this double-consciousness, this sense of always looking at
one's self through the eyes of others, of measuring one's soul by the
tape of a world that looks on in amused contempt and pity. One ever
feels his two-ness,—an American, a Negro; two souls, two thoughts,
two unreconciled strivings; two warring ideals in one dark body,
whose dogged strength alone keeps it from being torn asunder.

The history of the American Negro is the history of this strife,—
this longing to attain self-conscious manhood, to merge his double self
into a better and truer self. In this merging he wishes neither of the
older selves to be lost. He would not Africanize America, for America
has too much to teach the world and Africa. He would not bleach his
Negro soul in a flood of white Americanism, for he knows that Negro
blood has a message for the world. He simply wishes to make it possible
for a man to be both a Negro and an American, without being cursed
and spit upon by his fellows, without having the doors of Opportunity
closed roughly in his face. (Du Bois *Souls*, chap. 1, paras. 3–4)

Although critical of the indecisiveness and incoherence that this sense
produced in Negro political and social life, private and public, and
deeply responsive to the *violence* of the *sense* of this double heading of
existence, the actual experience of this sense, Du Bois never ceased to
affirm this heterogeneity as *also* a good, a resource, in general.[37] Indeed,
in the "The Conservation of Races," Du Bois's vision of this double
reference of the Negro, as American and Negro, is cautiously but quite
assertively hopeful (CR, [1987a]: 5–6, paras. 14–18). Moreover, when he
announces this theme in "Strivings of the Negro People" (which became
the first chapter of *The Souls of Black Folk*) in the paragraphs just cited,
Du Bois marks the structure of possibility of subjectivation that arises
with this sense, which he calls "double-consciousness" at the level of
the subject and "second-sight" at the level of the socius in general, with
both a positive and negative sign. It manifests not only as a kind of loss,
a disarticulation of ostensible purpose, but also as a kind of "gift," a
distantiation of ostensible horizon as a limit. Thus, it is finally, and
quite radically, the movements of displacement and the forms of kinetic
coherence that can be mapped along the passageways of the irruption
of a kind of "double-consciousness," that enable, as both a freedom and

a responsibility, a certain powerful *historial* sense, a "second-sight in this American world," and perhaps beyond it to another world, beyond the possible as a given horizon.[38] This sense makes possible the complex point of view and reflection elaborated as the narrative of "Strivings of the Negro People" and later *The Souls of Black Folk: Essays and Sketches* as a whole. This sense, and the reflection that it invites, enabled, perhaps, the desedimentation of the (violent and destructive) conditions of its own possibility, and perhaps their ultimate displacement at the level of finality or effects, by way of a distantiation of the topical pertinence of their ostensible bearing. That is to say, that in Du Bois's discourse the movement of the production of "double-consciousness" also makes possible the opening for a powerful critical reflection upon scene of its own historical production, which can be named precisely under the heading of a kind of "second-sight." The sense of being a Negro at the turn of the century in the United States for Du Bois is anything but some pure or simple habitation in the world.

This thematic, if followed in all its difficulty, nonetheless displaces the pertinence of traditional ontology. A simple yes/no or either/or question will simply not suffice to situate this identity or determine the sense of identification of this being. The undecidable status of such a sense not only contradicts the conservative understanding of the law of identity formulated in the Aristotelian principle of noncontradiction, which is a philosophical statement of the kind of ontological presupposition that remains the deepest ideal, formal, or logical—that is metaphysical— resource of the discourses of the project of purity (of those discourses that have committed themselves to the presupposition of the possibility of pure being, and, thus, indeed, have hence committed themselves to the very *idea* or traditional *concept* of race), but accounting for the alogical logic that organizes the structure of appearance of such a being, perhaps, displaces the ultimate pertinence of that principle. It marks the scene of a certain exorbitance. Having no strictly delimitable scene of origin or presumptively final sense of habitus, the African American subject is quite often "both/and," as well as "neither/nor."[39] Remaining faithful to the problem of understanding the actual lives of Negro people, in particular his own—that is to say, approaching that life in terms of its historiality, its opening toward a future that is otherwise than simply the past in the future—Du Bois was not only led to produce a description of an original sense of being in the world, but to elaborate a sense of being that in itself could not be reduced to some simple essence, of either the past or of a future.

Yet having begun to elucidate that the Negro was not some absolute and pure entity, grounded in some pure or primordial origin or organized in relation to some fixed or simply given telos, yet working in the face of the dominant positions in the discourses concerning the Negro at the turn to the twentieth century, those that projected the evacuation of the Negro in fact or concept, Du Bois could not simply leave the field unmarked. To have taken the declaration that the concept of race is incoherent and that races do not exist, thus that all concern to produce the conceptual, political, and historical figure of the Negro American on the scene is "racialist" in turn, would only have left the existing hierarchies firmly in place.[40]

Thus, it is no accident that in the third essay from this momentous year in Du Bois's itinerary, "The Study of the Negro Problems," Du Bois puts forth a comprehensive plan calling for an exhaustive study of the Negro in the United States. He formulates this project more systematically, comprehensively and, with regard to a concept of truth, more rigorously than had been done up to that time. This is the site of a fundamental innovation in discourses called scientific or academic concerning the Negro—one of Du Bois's central contributions—not yet well or widely understood in terms of its general implication for any projection of the human sciences, then or now. I consider this text the founding programmatic statement projecting an African American Studies in the United States.[41] Du Bois outlines a twofold epistemological frame in which the Negro people would be studied in terms of their historical situation or environment, the "social" environment, an order that I call *historial* (or systemic, historicities in a general sense), and in terms of their internal development, an order that I call *existential* (or experiential, historicities in a specific sense). In this latter concern, Du Bois describes the object of analysis as the *sense of world* for Negroes, what he calls "a distinct social mind," that which his German contemporaries called a *Weltanschauung*.[42] He writes that this aspect of such a project, in terms of such a whole projection,

> should aim to study those finer manifestations of social life which history can but mention and which statistics can not count, such as the expression of Negro life as found in their hundred newspapers, their considerable literature, their music and folklore, and their germ of aesthetic life—in fine, in all the movements and customs among

them that manifest the existence of a distinct social mind. (TSNP [1898b]: 20, para. 42)

This was an original appeal. It was not until the 1960s that Du Bois's call would begin to be answered in a comprehensive manner. When such a view arrived in historiographical scholarship, for example, it produced a major reorientation of both African American and American history.[43] Du Bois had rightly suggested that this shift in epistemological frame could propose something new, not only for how we understand that entity called "America," but also how we conceptualize sociality and historicity in general.

What should be emphasized here is that in each moment of Du Bois's movement or itinerary, his inhabitation of what I remarked earlier under the heading of the problem of purity or annotated as the discursive projection of the premise of the onto-epistemological possibility of pure being (putatively as both an historical existent and a claim in knowledge about such) his understanding of the grounds of the Negro is first and foremost historical. Despite his proclamation of the need for those understood socially to be Negro to bond together for political, legal, and economic empowerment, he never defines the Negro as first or only one thing. Du Bois, thus, even in his use of it, explicitly resituates the status of the concept of race, even as his committed intellectual generosity (toward discourses premised upon a traditional scientific concept of race and, in particular, at this stage in his itinerary) and the limitations of the concept of *istoria* (historicity or culture) do not allow him to make the displacement radical. (As I suggest later in this chapter, these concepts, like all concepts, can be understood to refer to an essence.) Du Bois thus criticizes the grounds of the concept of race, suggesting that it be understood as nonphysical, as historical, and as otherwise than natural in the simple and given sense of the reproduction of a fixed essence or mode of being. That so-called races change is indeed the most embedded reference of the concept in this text:

> Certainly we must recognize that physical differences play a great part . . . yet no mere physical distinctions would really define or explain the deeper differences—the cohesiveness and continuity of these groups. [Du Bois uses alternately the terms "races" and "nations."] The deeper differences are spiritual, psychical, differences—undoubtedly based on the physical, but infinitely transcending them. (CR[1987a]: 3, para. 9)

At no point is Du Bois's understanding of the *essence* of the Negro an idea of a *simple* or *pure* essence. I recall here that in the middle stages of the "The Conservation of Races," as he outlines the different "races," which he defines as historical entities, Du Bois describes the Negro in the United States as "the most indefinite of all" (CR, [1987a]: 3, para. 8).[44]

The Delimitation of the Situation of W. E. B. Du Bois

What we are left to meditate upon then is this conundrum: Du Bois's intervention was not de facto decisive at one opening of a new century, yet, perhaps, it remains that his practice may function de jure as such at another. And this pertinence would, precisely, obtain by way of the paradoxical and only apparitional indecisiveness of the movements of his itinerary.

For his accomplishment could not have been in fact decisive. First, the concept of *istoria* as such is always recuperable to an essentialist commitment. While the attribution of context may in the strict sense remain ultimately illimitable, the concept of *istoria* can organize itself only if an horizon is understood as given or determinable, present in general. Thus, this concept poses for thought a necessary and unavoidable complication. Secondly, with regard to contemporary thought, all of the formalizations of a concept of the phenomenon, sign, or symbol that underpin our current conceptualizations of historicity or identity were hardly in the enunciative stage of their articulation or elaboration at the time of Du Bois's first of writing during the 1890s. And, even so, these developments are too easily and perhaps too often misconstrued if they are understood to have broken free of the paradoxes that attend the concept of essence. If one thinks of the work of Edmund Husserl, Max Weber, Émile Durkheim, Sigmund Freud, Ferdinand de Saussure, and Franz Boas, these elaborations were nowhere construed at, say, 1895, to the extent that they were unfolding just a decade and a half later.[45] Moreover, it remains an open critical question of the extent to which the infrastructural developments of the conceptualizations of the concept of the phenomenon, of the sign, or the social, so essential to each were construed in such a way even after the turn of the century as to enable such a radicalization.[46] In the work of Franz Boas, this rethinking was not decisive until near the end of the first decade of the century. And even then one can trace a certain indecision and hesitation by Boas around the question of the Negro, or the question posed for thought under its heading.[47] And the same can be said of others.

At any rate, Du Bois is certainly an original figure in a configuration of thinkers problematizing and rethinking an inherited conceptualization of essence, or the sign, and all of its dispositions or its dispersal as matters of historicity, sociality, intentionality, or psychic activity.

We can remark this originality in a paradoxical fashion; that is, by suggesting the extent to which Du Bois's situation was both embedded within the situation of post-Enlightenment thought in general and yet conforms to an enigmatic economy, the specificity of which bears no simple translation into another itinerary of thought, particularly within this turn-of-the-century configuration.

Although the decisive questions that concerned figures such as Husserl, Weber, Freud, Durkheim, de Saussure, or Boas had their roots in the devolution of science that followed in the wake of the revolutions for thought produced in the work of Descartes and Kant—that is, in the idea of thought as science or the idea of practical reason—the dissolution of all previous understandings of unity can well be understood as the problem of the maintenance of the other on the horizon of a putative infinite understanding. An elucidation of this problem in the middle of the nineteenth century necessarily entailed the production and clarification of the structure of existence, of being in general, as not reducible to a simple anteriority. In the provenance of the question of the Negro, we should underscore that this would withhold especially any supposed absolutely determining or final ground in physical or natural existence. It was in the space of this problem for thought that a theory of the displacement of the origin in general became decisive. For the nonreducibility of the structure of existence, in all its possible modalities or hierarchies, to the simple, demanded, then, that the ground of the presentation of being be rethought.

It is this general problematic for thought that decisively marks the practice of this configuration of turn-of-the-century thinkers. It is in this context that the commonness of the concern with the phenomenon, with the status of the sign, or the status of the symbolic, in the movement of the socius in the work of Weber, Boas, Durkheim, or de Saussure can be situated. Each turned away from the reference of the symbol or the sign to a simple or given anteriority, proposing thereby and instead the thought of its productivity. Likewise, it is in this context that one can recognize the problematic that Husserl and Freud, as examples, share in common with this configuration and with each other: each moved away from an a priori determination, given by their respective formations, of that within consciousness that opens toward its other, a biologistic referral in Freud's case and a psychologistic one in Husserl's itinerary, to attempt to think the horizon of consciousness as otherwise than simply given. In this sense, one can say that a general displacement of the presumption of historicity or consciousness as a unitary structure was set in motion by the turning that is registered here and that the thought of a certain dynamism of this heterogeneity was projected toward a new, or another, elaboration.

On the surface, Du Bois's problematic appears far more specific than those of his contemporaries, seeming at first glance almost parochial.

I. Hence, to the extent that the transformation that I have just recalled would be understood as general, pertaining to the social, consciousness, or being as such, Du Bois's thought would appear as derivative at best. It would be subsumed on two levels, certainly by way of the formal or logical subordination of the general to the particular, but also by way of the relative parochiality of the Negro or African American example in the face of the universalism of thought as science as such. Such subsumption is both legitimate and welcome to the extent that the Negro or African American example is recognized and situated as part of the problem of thinking historicity in general and as such. Indeed, Du Bois often appealed to his contemporaries for such subsumption as an *inclusion* of the question of the Negro as a problem and primary scene for what he called sociological thought; that is to say, for a science of the social or the human in general.

II. Yet, on another level, and to the extent that the problem of the Negro maintains sedimented within in it a question about the grounds of that entity, its possibility, and its becoming, the answer to which cannot be decided or given simply by thought under the heading of science or knowledge—that is, in the horizon of the demand for truth—to the extent that the question at issue broaches the matter of the very possibility of such an entity (that is, to ask, for example, how something like the Negro or African American is possible, or what after all could be or become the possible destiny of such a being, or to pose the thought that perhaps it is nothing, or could not exist at all), a patient meditation upon the conundrum of its emergence as a problem for thought, here by tracking the movements of the itinerary of Du Bois, exposes another layer, other layers, within the bedrock of thought as knowledge, of philosophy as science. That layer (or layers) is exposed or brought into relief in a certain way—that is, opens in a certain way—*within* this quite specific question. It is the question "What is (the) human?" This question is not asked here with the presumption that there can be a simple or final answer, for it only arises in the domain of the question of the Negro when that domain has been dislodged from its presumed ground. To the extent that neither a natural (putatively simple) nor an historical *essence* can situate this entity, the very concepts of the same and of difference as they are construed to situate the human as such, at an ontological level, seem almost incoherent when formulated to account for it. This incoherence of thought is registered all the more strongly at the epistemological level of generality. If being under the heading of the Negro is not and, perhaps, cannot be fully given—that is, rendered available for thought as science or philosophy—then perhaps the ultimate pertinence of such a project, or at least its founding and final aim, which would be the naming of the truth of being, is secure or at risk in something like the problem of the Negro as a problem for thought. A tracking of the problem of the Negro for thought. A tracking of the problem of the Negro for thought exposes, then, the fault lines within the layers of sedimentations that have gradually gathered as the very historicity of modern thought. These fault lines, and the shiftings that they both register and make possible, direct us toward an instability in the architectonics of any thought, or thought as practice, that would simply declare its position with regard to the question of essence (especially, for example, as the question of the status of the sign or under the heading of another term such as the symbolic), whether it be of origin or end, or of the universal or of the particular.

Thus, Du Bois's situation with regard to this configuration cannot be simply configured as a derivative one. This matter can be outlined according to both its similarity and its difference.

A. It holds a fortiori that all of the questions at stake in the work of his contemporaries in this turn-of-the-century ensemble, for example, are also at stake in the question given to him as his problematic and is open, more or less, within his own discourse. I have given some brief indication of such a motif earlier, especially with regard to the question of understanding, or *Verstehen*.

At this juncture, before following out the disposition maintained in this motif a bit further, several commonalities in this configuration should be remarked, even if only in brief. (1) In each case, including that of Du Bois, the decisive questions took their definitive shape in the work of each thinker from the middle years of the decade of the 1890s through the first decade of the twentieth century. (2) In the work of each thinker, including that of Du Bois, a routine or given form of conceptualization encountered certain difficulties. While these were difficulties of conceptualization or formulation, of methodological practice, and of explanation, the genetic production of these difficulties in the practice of knowledge referred not only to understanding the epistemological as a simple mode of existence. Rather, they entailed also, in no simple fashion, the whole horizon of thought and of existence, of the organization of power as force in transformations of *techne* in a general sense wrought on a planetary scale across a long nineteenth century. Their announcement as thought is only one form or mode of their maintenance or being. These difficulties issued as a crisis in the practice of thinking, of thinking as a practice in the pursuit of knowledge, of thought as science. In each case, then, a given or routine form of problematization, of making something the site of a question, came into crisis. (3) In each case, with the exception of Du Bois, this shift in conceptualization eventuated in an implication that was formative, or became central, to a discipline of knowledge.[48]

Du Bois certainly recognized himself as part of, and as participating within, the open horizon of science in his time. His affirmation, rather than negation, of the transformations of thought afoot in this configuration should be presumptively understood as general.[49] Operating without the benefit of an ultimately definable ground or apparently stable object of inquiry, Du Bois proposed no grand theoretical *summa*. His thought is marked by a certain apparent nominalism, one that yet operates within definitive commitments and nonetheless practices a profound immanent sense of a whole, in a certain way. At this juncture, we will simply name the latter possibility. If there is a certain methodological necessity to his practice, the demand for which is not simply subsumable to a project of science or truth, it remains that such apparent nominalism may yet be understood according to another horizon, of thought in general, in which the general epistemological bearing of his practice should nonetheless be legible or open for an elaboration of a certain kind.[50]

B. While it remains without emphasis under the heading of science in the apparently philosophically naive and derivative question of the Negro as it appears in Du Bois's discourse, all of the questions of the ground of existence and being encountered by this configuration are posed in a fundamentally distinctive manner. This distinctiveness, this profound and paradoxical originality, operates in twofold, on the two mundane levels of intellectual subjectification (given by way of a horizon or contextualization of some kind) and projection (given as the forms and practices of responsibility to a question), which is to remark, respectively, the way in which the problem that is the site and scene of Du Bois's work is given to him for thinking, and the way in which he inhabits this problematization in his practice.

1. The specific theme of Du Bois's problematic concerns the status of African Americans in the United States and hence in the historical frame of what has been called modernity. It is this question that he is given to think. When one begins to unpack this question, one discovers a series of embedded paradoxes that govern and shape the task of Du Bois's thinking. These paradoxes have to do with the very shape of the itinerary of the question of essence in his discourse. In the itineraries of his contemporaries, the question of essence arrives not just as an unacknowledged presumption but appears as a presupposition.

a. That is to say, it was presupposed, in the traditional discourse given to each, that an essence could be found; that, in an essential way, the object of inquiry was marked by the possibility of recognizing it in the fundament of the simple or the pure (for example, as it was in the psychological discourse, specifically neuropathology, of the end of the nineteenth century for Freud).

b. In Du Bois's situation, no such presupposition was possible with regard to the object of his thought, the condition or ground of the Negro. Or, at least, such a presupposition could not be easily maintained. Indeed, in Du Bois's case, his problematic arose precisely because the given or dominant presupposition was that such an essence could not be found. Or, at least so it seemed. For in another register, embedded or buried within the first, concerning the Negro as inessential subject, was another presupposition, operating as a form of prejudgment, in which it was precisely a supposed absolute and primordial bond of essence to nature, to physical being especially, in the case of the Negro, that is found to govern discourse, reflection, and thought. (If the formulation just adduced seems somewhat obscure, that is itself due to the impossibility of addressing the paradoxical structure of this problematic under the heading of a thesis or declaration. This is the conceptual and rhetorical register of the central difficulty negotiated in Du Bois's thought. To the extent that we

seek, in these few lines, to elucidate something of Du Bois's thought, this
difficulty must be reproduced as a problem in our own enunciation.) In
this sense, it can be said that in a general way, the distinctive character of
Du Bois's situation and discourse may be brought into relief when placed
in the context of this configuration: it is marked by an ensemble of specific paradoxes that requires an ensemble of ironic critical gestures and is
generally paradoxical *and* may be construed as ironic with regard to the
situation and forms of discourse and critique common to this turn-of-
the-century configuration.

2. This motif of the paradoxical and its ironic play can be abstractly
elaborated in terms of the order of example (or exemplarity) that we are
following here, that given with reference to some generality, a form of
context—that is, to say, with regard to the terms of enunciation or discursive premises and critical practice more common to the problematic
of these other thinkers and with regard to those terms of problem specific
to the problematic of Du Bois.

a. Traditional forms of problematization, or, certainly, the most usual
form of a problematic in this configuration of thinkers, entail a certain
mode of existence or practice in which the coincidence of an essential
order of being, an essence of some kind, and that which is understood to
represent such, that which would sustain it for knowledge in and as its
representation, is presumed. Then, in the general sense of practice among
those in this configuration, as such a mode of existence or social practice
encountered certain difficulties and became a problem for thought, this
presumption of coincidence entered a devolution and was brought into
question.

Yet, even this traditional movement of problematization is itself paradoxical. This is so for at least two reasons. First, any form of routinization of existence is always founded on the basis of a crisis. This is what
one might call a founding violence or violence of the origin. Secondly, a
given form of problematization of such a routinization reproduces this
disjunction, to use de Saussure's terms, as a disjunction of signifier and
signified, re-marking, thus, the routine as a certain practice of crisis or
as in practice a devolution of essence. The presumption of an essential
ground, then, covered over precisely the noncoincidence of supposed
essence and its sign. Thus, in the forms of discourse and problematization generally common to this configuration of thinkers, and perhaps in
the horizon or historicity of post-Enlightenment thought in general, the

task posed by the problematic is to bring into question a given presumed or supposed relation between an essence and that which ostensibly represents it. This is the movement of thought and critical discourse that I have remarked earlier by recalling the various breaks with an inherited conception—given by certain relatively established disciplines of knowledge—of their respective principal objects of study introduced in the work of various thinkers of this configuration. The linkage that they were each led to question was a supposedly absolute or an ultimately determining one between a sign, or a symbol, or the phenomenon, and its ostensible ground in an essence.[51]

b. Du Bois's problem, the form of problematization that situated his enunciation(s), can be understood in this common or traditional manner in one aspect of his path of inquiry. However, because there is a certain originality or distinctiveness in the character of the specific problematic given to him, he had to also move in another direction, apparently opposite, *in the same movement of his thought,* and here the philosopheme "same" is confounded. This is because, in Du Bois's problematization, a crisis of meaning, or the noncoincidence of essence and telos, is the given presupposition, the presumption of the mode of existence by which his problem of thought is given to him. In this way his problematic differs from the traditional pattern or the one most common to this configuration. It is thus the latter's ironic double, once brought into critical relief as I am seeking to do here; to speak of one is to imply the other.

(1) This paradox, or a kind of *general structure of irony,* with regard to Du Bois's discourse or practice in relation to the practice(s) of others of this configuration, is produced through *a form of irony that is specific* to Du Bois's discourse (even if we cannot say that it holds only for his in the final instance). At its root, Du Bois's problem entails two interwoven forms of routinization, or social practice, whose references to the concept of essence are the double of each other. It is the status and character of these interwoven forms of social practice that Du Bois must rethink. (a) One form of social practice, the practice or experience of being a Negro, whatever might be such, takes it most original root in the disjunction or displacement of such practice from a (supposed) simple ground in essence. (b) The other, a certain practice toward (those understood as being representative of) the Negro, takes its most original ground in the ordering of practice in a supposed absolute or primordial essence. The interwoven character of these forms of social practice mark this problem

as precisely social and historical, rather than only ideal (in this sense, ideal references what Kant spoke of as matters of "pure reason") and especially not only formal (concerning, for example, a conundrum of logic or rhetoric). This situation cannot be resolved through an analysis or an analytics. And this interwoven character, situated rhetorically in the movement of the double genitive (for example, of whose referential structure means both from and about something), specifies this question as one about the production of historical or social subjects. This doubling at the core of Du Bois's discourse means that the traditional form of enunciation, or strategy of critical thought, would be incommensurate with the economy (in a sense that is at once conceptual, theoretical, practical, or political; that is, the laws or necessities that must be confronted in thinking about the object or matter of concern) of Du Bois's problematic. This incommensuration would arise because a simple affirmation or negation of the ground of either practice, being a Negro or being toward a Negro—that is, a declaration of a simple truth with regard to either practice—has the paradoxical effect of reproducing as a presupposition of thought precisely what one is seeking to question. There is no safe or pure position to be taken within this problematic. It is an economy.

As a matter of style, or the rhetoric of the forms of enunciation, irony with its constitutive risks would be the mode of discourse by which one might inhabit this difficulty, at best and at worst, for always both are possible.[52]

(2) We can further formulate this paradoxical economy as it pertains to any critical decision or response, on two levels, and then summarize its implication for thought in this domain. (a) First, we can notice it with regard to the experience of being Negro. (Perhaps in this specific rhetorical space it is useful to recall that, fictional or not, it is a lived sense.) If, on the one hand, Du Bois simply affirms the stated and presumed disjunction between the Negro and some supposed original and primordial ground, his discourse will have the ironic effect of affirming the supposed vacuity of the Negro as social being. It would affirm all those varieties of discourse that would evacuate the Negro in fact or concept. If, on the other hand, Du Bois only questions this proclaimed disjunction of the Negro and some ground as a thetic alternative, a declaration of opposition to a given thesis, he would simply presume the Negro as a primordial being. His discourse would, then, be simply the specular opposite of the thesis of the Negro without an essence or ground, producing no displacement

of either its logic or the status of its postulation with regard to ontological ground. (b) Secondly, we can recognize this economy with regard to certain practice(s) toward the Negro, those practices taking their epistemological reference (however indirectly or passively) from the concept of race, the practices of racial distinction in general. If, on the one hand, Du Bois only questions this practice of identification, proclaiming the nonexistence or nonessential status of the distinction operated in this practice, insisting on its absence of ground or fundament, then he is left with a certain incapacity to disturb the existing practice (which, as a necessarily semiotic process, operating in the domain of the symbol, the sign, or the phenomenon, will function regardless of one's adjudication of its truth as a question of ground), to overturn the hierarchies that are nonetheless maintained in the name of this material fiction. If, on the other hand, Du Bois only affirms the Negro as the unity of a natural, or physical, essence with an essence of idea, spirit, or sense, under the heading of the concept of race, his discourse will reproduce not only this concept, but thereby implicitly affirm the violence of the practices carried out in its name. (c) Thus, third, and finally, we can recognize that the necessity of a certain strategy of thought, moving simultaneously in two apparently contradictory directions, means that Du Bois must acknowledge in a certain way his participation in the game he wishes to overthrow, his complicity with some of the most embedded premises of the systemic structure (in every sense) that he seeks to make the object of a radical critique. Du Bois's discourse is thus doubly inscribed. In the problematization that his discourse traverses, the question of the Negro is positioned within the problem of essence or sameness, of difference or truth, as the paradoxical double of each, and vice versa. This double position (if it can still be called one) is the originary difficulty of Du Bois's early thought. Thus, a certain nominalism in Du Bois's practice cannot be discounted too quickly. Du Bois had to move beyond absolute declarations, even as he had to make them or appear to make them. Du Bois, then, was engaged in an extremely powerful and entrenched economy. It is the labial structure, or dispersed traces, or sedimented remains, of this difficulty that I have sought to begin to track and outline here. This paradoxical structure is the economy of the discourses of the Negro.

Certainly, then, with reference to Du Bois, we can say that not only did the itinerary of the historically current construal of the problem of the phenomenon or concept of the sign have its bearing on his practice, but that more generally and fundamentally the problem of the concept of essence was at stake in his situation in such a way as to issue as an acute and aporetic question of critical strategy. It brought into relief, thereby, in this domain and in a certain way, an aporia that is general to thought or practice as such: the critical operation always returns one to a location within the terrain of the field that has been engaged. (The further question, of course, is whether such return is simply in the order of the same or whether there is a way in which a kind of a reinscription can enfold the possible passage of the *différend*. That is to say, in a certain discourse, the question is whether the return or repetition effects a new relief of the marks that would reinscribe such a field, thereby giving another exposure, a rearticulation, of their impress for thought and practice in the dynamis of their relation now both old and yet new.) This seems obvious in the conceptual sense when one thinks of the "The Conservation of Races," for example. I have also suggested here, thus far, the extent to which it was a difficulty general to Du Bois's early thought and not just to that essay. Perhaps elaboration can remark the possibility for the irruption of a thought otherwise than the simply given in Du Bois's inhabitation of this difficulty.

The historical pertinence of the difficulty here is more than just the persisting implication of a conceptual conundrum in any practice that has now become recognizable by way of a certain critical thought. This problematic also has bearing in another sense of historicity, the worldly sense of a mundane temporality; that is, in strategic institutional political practice. In order to displace the determination, or determinative effects, of a hegemonic institution one can carry out the full displacement of such only by crossing the threshold from open criticism to a declaration of authority. Without assuming power according to, or by way of, some existing institution within the status quo, a project of criticism cannot attain its mark. If it does not attain such a position, its very maintenance is always open to a quite worldly and unkind intervention. Such an intervention, of the unkind sort, for example, intruded upon Du Bois's project in the early stages of his itinerary in a major way—precisely at the peak of his first activity in the academy. Surely Du Bois had certain institutional supports during this period, from 1896 to 1910, to carry out his projects, a faculty position at Atlanta University and prominent publishers for his articles and books, for example. Yet, as he would claim during the later years of his life, especially, he was targeted in this early moment, from

1903 onward, by Booker T. Washington's "Tuskegee Machine," an attack that lead to the withdrawal of funding for his home institution, Atlanta University, and for his academic work, and that eventually forced him to leave the academy in 1910 (and we have a substantial archival basis for confirming this judgment; more or less, it is now recognized that a similar scene was replayed in the 1930s).[53]

For reasons that were both essential and historical, Du Bois's intervention could not *in fact* have been ultimate or final. We can specify the status of this de facto limit just a bit further. Not only was he limited, on the one hand, in the mundane sense by both the concepts, and their possible construal, available to him *and* by the strategic opportunities for overthrowing the dominant institutionalized positions in the interpretation of the Negro question, but more fundamentally, his practice could only be radical by remaining open, unfinished, unresolved in its engagement with the paradoxical announcement of the problem of difference, or sameness, of being as essence, in matters pertaining to the Negro as a problem.

And it must be emphasized that it is for this principal reason, the sense of the open inscribed in his texts, that there remain major passages of Du Bois's discourse wherein there are further interventions whose full force remain to be elaborated.

Perhaps one such desedimentative motif that might well be followed in Du Bois's work, for example, but which in the logic of its organization may be understood as not just one among others, is the question of the grounds of so-called White identity. Tracking it might allow one to see how in this "half-named" question, the so-called Negro question, there is *an entire horizon that is taken for granted in the domain of the problem of the Negro for thought*, that is the taken-for-granted question of the presumption of the possibility of a pure or simple ground for being as such. However, in an affirmative sense, a certain delimitation of Du Bois's discourse, by way of future engagements with it, might expose another thought of freedom, of possibility, of another world, of democracy, an illimitable becoming therein, something beyond, perhaps, the problem of the Negro as a problem for thought.

However, according to another temporality, that of the concept and practice of thought as a posing of the illimitable within existence as a problem, authority that would affirm Du Bois's practice de jure remains yet to come. In this double inscription that I have sought to decipher, if it is thought with regard to the depth structure of the questions legible within its frame, the itinerary of Du Bois's discourse tracks a rift that opens within any philosophical premise on the question of essence. All cannot be thought at one go, in one gesture; one can never be certain, or sure, of a final move. This condition or difficulty of thought, here, in this domain, points toward, or leads one in a descension toward, a general question of the possibility and ground of being: first, of something like a "Negro," but then, also, of something like a "human," and all the borders that seem to appear under that heading (of the "animal," for example, or of sexual difference, or even of "gender"), and perhaps beyond, to the question of a certain exorbitance that is announced on the order of being. Such is the manner according to which an apparently quite parochial question can lead one in the direction of a desedimentation of a generalized and radicalized question of existence or possibility and difference and sameness. Set in motion by way of a form of historical problematization of existence in which an ontological question announces itself at the heart of the problem of the Negro as a problem for thought, a certain sliding and shifting of metaphysical bedrock can be registered. Critical discourse or practice, such as that of Du Bois's or that of antecedent Africanist figures, inhabits this lability, is possible only by way of it, and can maintain itself, if at all, only by moving along these borders or ridges or fault lines. The sedimentation configuring what remains of such passage can be traced and disturbed by a practice that follows these fault lines, these fractures, within existence and historical being. And, this lability is not and cannot be contained within the border, or frame, in which it was announced. Thinking this situation, Du Bois's, of the Negro as a problem for thought, produces a delimitation of his discourse and the question of the Negro in general.

If by way of a certain labor of thought, then, we fold Du Bois's discourse back across the textuality of this configuration of thinkers from the turn to the previous century, it produces a series of shuddering, decryptic effects. It makes it possible to gather each of the principal interventions of those thinkers, accede to the radicality of their thought, to think with them to the limit (a certain infinitization) with regard to science and knowledge, and then ask another question: What, after all, are humans, *if there is such*, as "Negro" or "Negro American"? This small question, by way of its double and reciprocal interrogation, of the "human" (or "Man") or of the "Negro," which Du Bois poses, for example, in the afterword to *The Philadelphia Negro*, reinaugurates thought (that is, thought in general, as exemplified in this configuration of thinkers) in or as this domain of the Negro as a problem for thought. For, the thought of "the dream-work," of "intentional structure," of "signification," of "social fact," of the problem of "motivation," or of webs of "meaning," all confront the paradoxes that arise in this domain wherein origin and telos, habitus and being, are in ceaseless and irremedial withdrawal. All such forms of knowledge, even as a transcendental exploration, when they must address the question of the Negro, are distended by way of an infrastructural movement in which being as existence, and telos as origin, cannot be brought to a punctuality. That something like a Negro or African American, or African diasporic subject, cannot and should not be the final object of a project of science or knowledge, guaranteeing such a project by way of its givenness as an object, its coherence serving as the fundament of a science, is not an unwelcome limit. Rather, it is the very movement of freedom.

This confounding of all attempts to make of the problem of the Negro or African American a determinate field of science or secure object of any science directs us to rethink such efforts. And the necessity of this rethinking would hold a fortiori for any science in general in which something like the Negro as a problem would be at stake; that is to say, a certain exorbitance for thought announces itself. It directs us in two ways. (a) First, it directs us to reconsider the way in which the problems of thought, in particular as science or knowledge, are *historial* in their becoming and, as historicity, the scene of an ontological problematization of existence. Du Bois formulated the study of the Negro as "study of the Negro *problems*" (my emphasis). Such a rethinking might connect with a rethinking of the history of science or knowledge and a displacement of it in the direction of a history of thought, in which the latter would be the ways in which an irruption within the fabric of existence, or rather an agonistic irruption as existence, renders such being at issue. All that Du Bois places under the heading of the problem of the sense of being of the Negro, for example, under the heading of "double-consciousness," or "second-sight," would find renewed pertinence there: now, not so much as the scene of a parochial interiority but as part of a renewed thinking of the historicity of systems of subjectivation. But, not only as a heading for a thematized problem of inquiry, but also as a thematizing concept-metaphor, making possible a question about the very possibility of our own inquiry, the thought of our time, that would seek to understand forms of problematization as such.[54] Likewise the problem of the color-line as it is announced in Du Bois's thought might become not so much the determinate object of a science, such as the sociology of race relations or a history of racialized behaviors, but an historicizing conceptualization of the posing of a fundamental, even if historical, question of forms of existence in which hitherto unknown systems of sameness and difference emerged. It should go without saying that all of our critical projects would also be thematized by this concept-metaphor, the "problem of the color-line." Thinking it might require inquiry to readdress some fundamental concepts by which historicity has been thought thus far, such as authority, power, and economy, and to question anew the conditions of thought; that is, not only the conditions of historical research by way of the critical investigation of disposition or memory or the informative or archive in general, but the conditions of thought in general. The problematic of the "problem of the color-line" might well reveal itself as a paradoxically exemplary root, at once particular and general, determined and determining, of the transcendental illusions that reason sets afoot in the movements of its itinerary. Thinking such might well lead us to rethink the still contemporary horizon bequeathed to us as the advent of critical thought itself—that is, to think the historicity of the thought of the transcendental, to pose not simply the thought of a transcendental historicity but to elaborate a thought of the historicity of the transcendental as discourse and tradition. (b) Secondly, this situation directs us to that within this problematization that poses the ontological question at the root of knowledge of existence, at the root of knowledge of the social or historical. In this latter aspect, it directs us to that within the problem of the Negro which poses a question beyond historicity or sociality as given. As such, it poses the question of the possibility of something like historicity in general and opens toward a thinking on the border, or beyond, of truth as science or knowledge. This question would address, for example, what Du Bois so often placed under the heading of *ideals*, but not as a matter that is simply mundane or one which is a debate among positions, rather as a matter that is more along the lines of his thought about *chance* (in the context of knowledge, of truth or science, especially as logic) or *freedom* (in the context of ethics and morals, of human "will," and this would be the most crucial problem for him).[55] It directs us to that generative sense of exorbitance as possibility. It could turn our attention from within this domain of the Negro as a problem for thought to that which is other than a relation of knowledge, other than concept or category. Thinking this problematic, this situation, in a certain way, helps to resituate science and knowledge, as thought as such, by redirecting them or sending them again toward a reinhabitation of their instituting borders and, perhaps, a thinking beyond them.

I have proposed Du Bois's itinerary as exemplary in a paradoxically epistemically singular fashion of the paradoxes attendant to any thought that would inhabit the problem of essence as an explicit form of problematization, underscoring specifically the originary complications that mark every strategic gesture, that encode every decision of method or style. Thereby I have affirmed Du Bois's acceptance of the *question* of the Negro, in a certain way, and his irreverent inhabitation of it. And, I have suggested that by way of this paradoxical and ironic exemplarity perhaps entire strata within Du Bois's thought that remain to be desedimented, sifted, or traced. While my ultimate concern is certainly not to simply reconstitute the figure of Du Bois as some final or ultimate paternal figure, it is still the case even in our own time that his features as a thinker, or an intellectual, and the rhythm and step of his practice remain so poorly understood. This is in part due to the very discursive formation that he was so concerned to question. Thus, I have had in part to adduce and name in a different way the figure of Du Bois as a titular guide for thought, among other possible examples.

There remains the general necessity of *reading* Du Bois anew and of situating him as a thinker, rather than simply or primarily as an activist and political figure (even if now the figuration is under the heading of a cultural politics), which is still the overwhelming mode of approaching him. For one does not disavow the political inhabitation of Du Bois by approaching him under the heading of thought, instead one radicalizes and deepens it (simultaneously specifying his discourse and freeing it).[56]

At such a juncture—that is, another order of reading—the original openness of being in, or as, thought is given an unfungible announcement as historical possibility, it simultaneously accepts a legacy and bequeaths one, or perhaps more than one, indeed by way of this irreducible singularity. However, the plane or order of other possible examples cannot and should not be understood as one comprised of simply exchangeable samples in a series. Rather, or instead, the practices in question should be thought as maintaining within their texture, warp and woof, a certain tractable path of historicity, perhaps in unique or distinctive exemplification.

A parallel, more commonly acknowledged domain of practice within all that is usually called African American may be apposite here. Thus, I propose that if, for example, I seek to understand the conditions of thought, existence, and an always incipient demand for a renewed genesis in creativity that has been set afoot in an "African American" inhabitation of what is usually called music, it might be a necessary stage of formulating such an inquiry to simultaneously appropriate and disabuse the heading of composer by refusing the supposed finality of its assumed contemporary distinction from performer. At such a juncture of thought, the question of a certain "example" arises. One would not be remiss to give a single proper name: Cecil Taylor.[57] Or, in turn, it could be equally radical to offer a serial enumeration of incommensurable figures: Betty Carter, Sun Ra, John Coltrane, Thelonius Monk, Charlie Parker, Billie Holiday, Duke Ellington, Louis Armstrong.

Must not singularity be recognized in each instance and in a way that nonetheless can also accept the status of the example?

In this light perhaps it may become distinctly legible that my deeper concern, proposed by way of this tracking, is to expose and disturb some of the encrusted layers of presuppositions that restrict our recognition in the practice of thought of the possible places wherein new soil can be turned up on old ground.

Disturbing the layers of sedimentation that hold the figure of Du Bois in his accustomed place in the history of thought might set loose new soil that can be used not only for preparing the way for a new thinking of the problem of the Negro but also for another kind of inhabitation of the problem of thought as such in our time, one that would be resolutely recognized as differential in both its origin and becoming.

Delimitation

The aporias that arise at the movement of enunciation for Africanist figures (in truth, for anyone who would participate in the discourses of the Negro) are not simply historical. They arise at another level of existence. They should be understood as part of the conditions of existence, of thought, as such. Or they mark, perhaps, the unconditional conditions of the operations of thought. That is to say, thought is always an inhabitation of the problem of essence. But, specifically, in the situation of "the Negro" in the Americas, this problem as a self-reflexive question of identity or identification (in all its dispersed forms), with all its paradoxes, is announced not only as the condition of thought but as its very object or theme. Thought, existence, is always already thematized as a problem for this figure; historical existence is always already this thematized problem of existence of being in thought. The difficulties that attend such inhabitation cannot be resolved by way of declaration any more than to ask a question about the possibility of question can avoid presupposing that very possibility in the asking. It is in this sense, of thought as inhabiting its own premises in such a way that it cannot simply leap outside of them to some other ground, that I have proposed the concept-metaphor *economy* to account for a problem or problematic for those who would think the problem of the Negro as a problem for thought.[58] In the formal sense, and unavoidably in our time, I have in mind those aspects of this concept-metaphor that draw on Greek conceptuality in which this term combines the sense of *nomos* (as rule or law) and *oikos* (of hearth, domesticity, of the circular or diurnal) to name a kind of ordering and systematicity. The systematic character of the problem of the Negro as a problem for thought is what I have tried to address with this formalization. In another sense, a sense that I will place under the heading of historial, I have in mind with my formalization of this term, an ultimately inadequate analogy, catachresis if you will, of the kind of force or, better, violence, that is in play in the domain of this problem—the violence by which the historical conditions of the emergence of the Negro or African American as such makes the very historical emergence of this entity the scene of an ontological question. The conditions of the historical emergence of this entity and the ontological question of possibility, as an unconditioned condition of thought, are folded one inside the other, each displacing the other, as conditional moments in the history of the Negro as a problem for thought. The remains of this historical genealogy of violence in the problem of the Negro show forth each time one would respond to such violence and seek to limit or overturn its bearing. In each gesture of practice as thought, in the historical field of the Negro or African American, or the African diaspora, the ontological paradox of the problem of essence that arises carries within its bearing the lineaments of this historical violence. Thinking this question, then, means that one cannot move under the heading of innocence or neutrality. I have proposed, by way of the itinerary of W. E. B. Du Bois, that one must engage this situation by responding *simultaneously* to its premise and its conclusion: (a) one must respond to the unavoidable premise of essence by thinking beyond such, and (b) one must also think short of the conclusion that essence is not given by affirming the possibility of a difference, not just difference in principle, but *this difference, this one, here, now.* This possibility at stake in this present. This complicated situation is an economy, a system of the same, or of difference, of origin or end. And yet one must think otherwise than its absolute givenness.

The discourse of antecedent Africanist figures in the discourses of the Negro, for example, heterogeneous and multiple, both within each enunciation and across the whole taken as an ensemble, can yet be understood as announcing and elaborating this situation or problem for thought (of *habitus*, of the historically given in every sense and of *eidos*, of project, of futural possibility, in every sense). Thus, their work should not so much be understood first or ultimately as the hypostasization of some final or fully given entity. One thinks, for example of the question as it comes from Phillis Wheatley's marvelous pen: "That from a father seiz'd his babe belov'd: / Such, such my case. And can I then but pray / Others may never feel tyrranic sway?"[59] Or, one thinks of Sojourner Truth's question to Frederick Douglass within the century following Wheatley's: "Frederick, is God dead?"[60] The discourse incipits here by way of that *long* middle passage, a passage that is historical but in such a way that it can never resolve itself as such, not only for the Negro or African American, but taken as the orientation to a problem, for a common historicity and thereby for thought as such. This discourse, of antecedent figures, such as Walker or Stewart for example, in the heart of the antebellum period, elaborates a dispersion of markings, an ensemble of traces, that can be understood as a certain tracking of the irruption of the problematization of existence that is the very historicity of all that we might call our own—the "our" here exceeding all the borders or boundaries that we might wish to draw and the "own" here as confounded by the opening of this question. Thus, Du Bois can say in the "Forethought" of *The Souls of Black Folk*, when writing of "the strange meaning of being black here at the dawning of the Twentieth Century," that "this meaning is not without interest to you Gentle Reader." We see here this double gesture that moves according to a certain necessity, a simultaneous configuration (or gathering) and delimitation of an Africanist problematic, which by way of this double inhabitation or inhabitation of the double moves from and remarks, or makes possible a remarking, of a certain exorbitance.

To think this "strange" situation certainly requires thinking its incipit according to a kind of nominalism ("fate" as instituting rather than determining) and a thinking of its devolution by way of the tracking of its immanence.

The study of the Negro or African American, or the African diaspora, must begin with the problems announced for thought within its own historicity. This would be the fundamental epistemological bearing of Du Bois's felicitous definition of the field of African American studies as the "study of the Negro problems," as in the title of his 1897 programmatic essay. That is, it cannot and should not presuppose the object of its concern, the object given to it, as a simple transcendental entity, whether hypostasized as an object of a discipline of knowledge (such as society or culture) or as a discrete social entity (such as a racial or ethnic or cultural group or a "national identity" or some derivative thereof).[61] Rather than attempt to name the African American as acceding to some supposedly pure status, "something like" a "racial" group, or a "cultural" group , or an "ethnic" group, or a stable sub-"national" identity, it demands that we rethink the premises of all concepts of historicity and sociality by which such entities are demarcated. Relation must be thought under the (non) heading of passage, of "between," the agonistic movement of the *apeiron*. Further, rather than attempt to name African Americans as relatively unperturbed or undetermined by the great systems of modernity (and the impulse here remains strong to defend those understood as African American from the great denigrations of social science as pathological figures and in a certain sense this practice cannot and should not be voided), this situation requires that we rethink the idea of system such that structurality appears under the heading of dissemination.[62] This must be a thought of the nonlinear concatenation of the movements of force. That is, we must rethink problems of power and authority anew. At that juncture, then, we can begin to reinscribe the devolution of system under the figure of the so-called minor term, "Negro" for example, as a kind of hyperbolic proposition.[63] Along this track, for instance, Du Bois's elaboration of the colloquial term of the "color-line" can be understood as a kind of theoretical practice, whether or not it is named as such by him. Reinscribing his thought in such a manner might make it possible to resituate the way we narrate the history of capital or the devolution of modern systems of authority. Accordingly, this reinscription might radicalize the thought that not only is system only possible in and through its limit, but the limit, the outside, would appear within system. To think the possibility of system would require, in a certain way, that one think both sides of the limit as other than the hypostatization of a possible present, otherwise than as "structure" or "idea" susceptible to figuration as a future present, other than a logic of the pure analogy. Something like the figure of the double in the situation of the African American would or could maintain another kind of attention, if not something wholly new, in thinking of the problem of relation, system, totality, structure, or idea. System, for example, might be understood to find its pertinence (which may also be a nonpertinence) only at the level of subject and subjectivation in and through the movement of dispersal and dissemination (in which spacing or another temporality sets afoot something otherwise and perhaps new) that is at stake in something like a Negro or African American as the heading of a general problem.

This exploration has also necessarily formulated a problem of strategy, of practice, of methodology in the general sense. I have summarized it under the heading of a *double gesture* and, in the explicitly theoretical sense, of a *redoubled gesture*. In the first instance, I mean the thematizing of the figure of the double at the root of the problem of the Negro American; that is, the necessity to both mark or name a difference while simultaneously inhabiting the necessity of elaborating an understanding of this difference as other than pure or simple. In this sense, Du Bois's naming of the African American as a figure of double identification, "an American," "a Negro," neither of which one disavows, both of which one maintains, in a certain way, can be understood (to the extent that it is never simply or only double, if the double could ever mean that) to name the heterogeneous gathering that attends any formation or postulation of identity or figure of sameness. Du Bois's formulation would be an example of the double gesture. In the second instance, such a thematizing act would recognize the necessity of the African American *both to be and not to be*. One thinks of the preacher in the prologue to Ralph Ellison's *Invisible Man*: "Now black is . . . I said black is . . . an' black ain't."[64] However, the pivotal aspect is that one then inhabits this recognition as a theoretical practice. Such practice can take its measure, if at all, only as part of a grouped or ensemblic textual field or scene of discourse or practical-theoretical labor dispersed across numerous semiotic, symbolic, social, and political strata. It would be the work of a kind of elaboration. This latter kind of gesture or practice, a theoretical path, can only come on the scene late, always too late, after a decision will have already been made. Or it will always be too soon, before the arrival of another horizon of freedom, in which the problem of the Negro as a problem for thought is no more one.

In practice, this would require at least the apparition of a certain tactical nominalism. And, although this formulation necessarily crosses the threshold of judgment from practice to critical reflexivity, it should not simply be lifted out of the specific labor of this essay, or any discourse such as this one, or the practical theoretical work of engagement where something is at stake, and deposed into a realm of pure speculative anticipation or deduction. It should not be simply appropriated to a theoretical disposition or vocative position that one might hypothesize as pure or situated at the level of a transcendental or of science in the broad sense of thought in general. One must begin from where one is situated. One cannot, in fact, be commensurate with one's protocols, either at the inception of one's gesture or in the realization of an intervention. This circumstance, however, does not lessen the claim of a certain unlimited responsibility in the face of the unbearable demands that it poses for thought and practice. One cannot *simply* choose, even if one *must* choose, make a decision. The problems given to thought, of being as a problem for thought, maintain within the movement of their formation and devolution a freedom that would exceed all decision or action or judgment, as such. Yet, one cannot not choose. Practice then is a certain inhabitation of necessity in the space or spacing given of freedom. For, in the interval, the space or spacing that opens between tactic and end, arises the possibility of something other than what has been, something other than the simple repetition of the past in the future. It would be in such an interval that the problem of the Negro as a problem for thought becomes something other than simply or only the problem of the Negro, if there is such.

The Negro or African American as a problem for thought is both *from* an exorbitance, otherwise than according to the classical determinations of metaphysics, and *about* an exorbitance, as a problem within metaphysics as it tries to situate the Negro as within knowledge, according to philosophy as science. In this way or along this track we see the *general* pertinence, certainly for all that we call "America," or that which has been called "Europe," and for what has been called the modern epoch, or modernity, or its aftermath (including the historicities that have been called the stages of the history of capital), of a consideration of the problematization of existence that opened the scene and space of the work of antecedent Africanist thinkers in the discourses of the Negro. The African, the Negro, or African American, or the African diaspora in general, the Africanist figure in the Americas, as a problem for thought is *of* exorbitance.

Coda

At this stage, this late conjuncture, in terms of the discourse that I have proposed in this chapter as a whole, perhaps a certain kind of annotation would be apposite, enfolding thereby, the figure of an X, in a graphic rhetoric, in relation to the epigraph that has been placed at its opening.

On the one hand, Du Bois, in his practice with regard to the question of "Negro freedom," as he once put it, was exceedingly thoughtful, precisely with regard to the history of questions that philosophy has long sought to claim as its own.[65] If I have made, or attempted to offer, any understated suggestion in this essay with regard to that practice, it is that Du Bois, rigorously, even astringently, practiced a strategy of practical theoretical intervention with regard to this inherited ensemble of questions as a whole. Adduced early on in my critical engagement with his thought, this perspective on Du Bois has guided my own reception and address of his work and itinerary for some three decades. Yet, while already thinking with Du Bois, so to speak, from the turn to the 1980s according to my own hypothesis of the structure of Du Bois's practice, and while undertaking from this sense the reading of Du Bois that is adumbrated in this essay and elaborated throughout my engagement with his work, it was not until the early spring of 2011, while I was living in Kyoto, Japan, and while I was working on the question of his relation to Asia, Japan and China in particular, that I came across what to my scholar's readerly ear rang out as a somewhat remarkable and utterly succinct statement by Du Bois of the complex critical sense that he maintained on the question of his supposed identification and its implication as a matter of premise and strategy (the latter formulated primarily on a register that is predominantly political, but which is also and thereby necessarily epistemological), wherein he formulated an enmeshment such that the negotiation of this problematic can be understood only as at once a philosophical practice and a practice of politics. It is a statement that Du Bois wrote most likely in the midst of the late winter of early 1937, within weeks of his return to the United States from a worldwide research, study, and lecture tour. The tour had taken place during the last six months of 1936. Reading through his weekly column in the *Pittsburgh Courier*, I came upon a formulation that adduces his engagement of the question of strategy in a distinctly legible manner—precisely on the order of the problem of the Negro as a problem for thought, as I have sought to bring it into relief herein. Du Bois was writing just as he entered the last year of his sixth decade.

> I was unconscious until a few years ago of any contradiction in my ideas or in the ideas of most Negroes concerning segregation. Recently I have realized this vividly. For many decades I was pursuing two partially contradictory lines of thought. On the one hand, I was what we were fond of saying a "race" man: that is, I believed passionately in Negroes, I wanted to associate with Negroes, I defended Negroes as Negroes, I planned for their future development and future self-assertion in the world. This point of view I assumed unconsciously as a matter of course. I can remember the blue eyed, black haired maiden of my German university days. I was surprised that she was thinking of possible marriage. I told her very frankly, not simply of the difficulties of intermarrying and living in the United States, but of my own very clear plan of marrying no one who was not of Negro descent. One of my first published essays was on the conservation of races, in which I argued strongly for the preservation of racial traits and successful competition with all other races.
>
> On the other hand, just as earnestly and just as wholeheartedly I was absolutely opposed to race discrimination and segregation, disfranchisement based on color, Jim Crow cars, separate sections of the city; all that called for my fierce denunciation. It was to my mind undemocratic and illogical and called for organized and continuous opposition. I looked upon separate schools as an evil to which we submitted only because of force, and I went first to the separate school, Fisk University, because a scholarship had been offered me there and I didn't have money to go to Harvard. I went back to Harvard as a triumphant vindication of my demand for universal education.
>
> I began to be conscious of a paradox in these two attitudes when I saw the way in which these two philosophies acted upon my fellows. Those who agreed with me in race loyalty were apt not to accept

segregation, but desire it, and be lukewarm in their fight against discrimination. Those, on the other hand, who fought discrimination and segregation were apt to be ashamed of colored people, bitter because of their identification with them, and desirous of living, and working, and thinking just as far from them as possible. Having made a curious synthesis of this contradiction and paradox in my own life and thought, I could not understand why the same synthesis did not meet in other souls. (Du Bois 1937; Du Bois 1986)

While, in this passage, Du Bois proposes that the apparent "contradiction" in his thought and practice came into a certain theoretical or metatheoretical relief for him at almost seventy years of age, it can be shown that it was already at stake and formulated within his thought—precisely astride the years of his writing of the "conservation of races" in the late 1890s—some forty years previous.[66] What set in motion this apparitional contradiction—for in all truth it is such only from within the dispositions of a traditional metaphysics and a traditional politics (a supposed or proposed sovereign form of intervention in the world)—is the kind of *economy* that I have adduced with regard to the problem of the Negro as a practical theoretical problem for thought and traced by way of Du Bois's practice. In a word, I have sought in this chapter to outline the fundamental order of the necessity of this "curious synthesis" in the address of the problem of Negro freedom, or better, the problem of the Negro as a problem for thought. It remains for contemporary theoretical inquiry to accede to the accomplishments of Du Bois's practical theoretical itinerary. Too, I have thus also sought to propose the implication of this whole problematic for the contemporary address of the horizon of problems of historical and social difference among humans on a global scale—both its implacable, and at times seemingly intractable, necessity and the ways in which an exemplary tarrying with—a patient, seemingly indefatigable, negotiation of its terrain in the itinerary of a remarkable figure, W. E. B. Du Bois—might offer resource for our own endeavor on the horizon of new forms of *mondialisation* and globalization.

On the other hand, as I have suggested from the outset, with reference to a discourse that would for all appearances be from another horizon, Jacques Derrida's elaboration of a grammatology, or general science of the mark, under the heading of "*archi-écriture/archi-writing*"—an intervention staged on the terrain that the sciences of the human have claimed as their own (even or especially in the concern of this intervention to produce a displacement of the anthropological reduction of the *question of existence*) since the advent of a critical transcendental thought in the latter half of the eighteenth century—it proposes the theoretical order of address that I have come to consider necessary in the engagement with the problem of the Negro on the order of its most profound metaphysical, especially philosophical, organization.[67] (Yet too, for example, so is the work of Cecil Taylor announced on this horizon beyond horizon.)[68] Working on this order of difficulty for thought would always demand a kind of paleonymic practice. It should be understood then that I feel no need to diminish what I have long understood as the originality of Derrida's meditations on the problem of strategy in his work of the 1960s (the essays "From Restricted to a General Economy" and "Violence and Metaphysics," for example), the accomplishment of which is summarized, in part, in the interview quoted in the epigraph to this chapter.[69] Likewise, I consider his itinerary of work in general as one of the most remarkable in contemporary thought. Yet, given the ease with which an old and racialized frame can be placed on the interwoven questions of my relation to the work of Derrida, by way of a hasty or presumptive reading of the structure of citations in this chapter, and likewise on the question of Du Bois's relationship to philosophy in general, perhaps by way of a nonreading or superficial reading of the latter's texts, several annotations may be apposite here. (I am reminded here of those critics who, in their engagement with the fundamental music of Cecil Taylor reference Béla Bartók, Edgard Varèse, or Olivier Messiaen—as if such reference in his work would mark a limit to his originality, whereas a similar reference is usually taken as a mark of belonging to a brilliant lineage for Iannis Xenakis, Pierre Boulez, or Karlheinz Stockhausen—but have little purchase on the place of Duke Ellington, Billie Holiday, Thelonius Monk, or James Brown, in his musical practice (not to speak of Budoh, Kabuki, or Noh performance traditions, for that matter, and so on). It can be said then, that I have attempted to carry out a certain practice of intervention in discourse, to enact a certain politics of theoretical discourse. I have remarked it here and elsewhere as a kind of desedimentation. I specifically propose this concept-metaphor here as otherwise than a procedure that might be primarily one of recovery or return. I think of it as a kind of resetting, a setting afoot or apace, a destablization that is at once architectural and otherwise than architectonic in its attention to the orders of the example and exemplarity. In part, my formulations have taken reference to the work of Derrida, especially his earliest work, a translation and introduction of an enigmatic late essay fragment by Edmund Husserl (on the genetic historicity, the transcendental opening, of the possibility of mathematics, in which geometry is the exemplar, from 1962) wherein he tracked the latter's idea of a desedimentation of the "origins" of science, subsequently developing the thought in his own additional directions and attuned to an order of concerns throughout the 1960s that might be understood as supplemental to those of the older scholar, while not relinquishing that inheritance.[70] Yet, there is in the question of desedimentation as it has acquired its coherence as a concern for me an ineluctable and intractable movement of force as a massive violence which remains, despite all manner of dissimulations, the very terms of the announcement of existence or being as a problem for thought. By way of such incipit, all discourse, any mark, or all marks, that one might think to mobilize to produce a radical questioning of the problems that ensue in the precomprehension of essence undergo an incessant and ceaseless diacritical rearticulation. In this torsion, one cannot even pretend to speak of the "pure," such as the "pure trace," even as one must speak of the difference that is nothing in itself. Desedimentation brings this paleonymic problematic to bear as a distinct order of concern and would announce thereby the simultaneous reproblematization of both an ultratranscendental order of attention and a new thought of immanence. Working along these lines, I have proposed that with regard to *our* contemporary thought, Du Bois, then, should be understood, instead, *first* in parallel to *his* contemporaries, such as Husserl , Weber, Durkheim, Boas, or Freud (the first figure being one of those who opened the pathways along which Derrida's thought took its first movements), much prior to Derrida's formulation of his own questions in the 1950s and early 1960s. The question then remains as to whence Du Bois in an itinerary such as Derrida's and, further, in contemporary thought in general. For example, it may likewise be said that the questions afoot in this study that resonate with those of Foucault were first raised for me in the reading of Du Bois. All this leads one to wonder whence Du Bois in Foucault's itinerary (which is not to gainsay the question of the status of Weber in that same itinerary, as well)? With regard to my own development, as I began to read the texts of Professor Derrida in the late 1980s outside of the classroom, so to speak, while I was at the University of Chicago, it was Du Bois's thought which more often more fundamentally than any other opened for me *in this reading* the spaces by which Derrida's discourse acquired its resonance for me. On the other hand, I can recall first hearing about Du Bois (and later reading the opening passages of *The Souls of Black Folk)*, through the guidance and teaching of a relative, at my father's church, during my grammar school days.[71] It was during Black History Month, perhaps when I was six or seven years of age. Of course, Du Bois's death in Accra, Ghana, would have occurred just a few years earlier. A consideration of all of this would require further work in desedimentation and the practice of another kind of paleonomy.

CHAPTER TWO

THE FIGURE OF THE X

An Elaboration of the Autobiographical Example
in the Thought of W. E. B. Du Bois

For Dwayne Hoskins, am memoriam[1]

I n some considerations on what is given in *The Souls of Black Folk:*
*Essays and Sketche*s, John Edgar Wideman adduces the order of the
problematic that we must bring into focus when we approach the matter
of the autobiographical in the writing of W. E. B. Du Bois.

> Like Freud's excavations of the unconscious, Einstein's revelations
> of the physical universe, Marx's explorations of the economic foun-
> dations of social organization, Du Bois's insights have profoundly
> altered the way we look at ourselves. The problem of the twentieth
> century is the problem of the color-line. With this utterance the
> unconscious, relativity, class warfare are all implicated. Du Bois pos-
> its a shift of cataclysmic proportions, demanding a reorientation of
> consciousness as radical as that required by physics at the atomic
> level.[2]

Perhaps it is appropriate to suggest that Du Bois's discourse *should* alter
our self-understanding. If it carries such capacity, such force, it is not only
because it specifies an historical generality, that is, a mundane or ontic
generality, for example the historical modalities of "the problem of the
color-line," of the concept of race and the practice of racial distinction,

{ 68 }

that could find its pertinence as the field of an historiographical inquiry, for example as that which Du Bois once described as the "problem of the twentieth century," but also because Du Bois's discourse broaches an investigation of the terms by which we would attempt to render a theoretical disposition on the constitution of social and historical identity and forms of identification, as such. And, perhaps I should add that I do not think that Wideman's formulation leaves the question to rest at an order that would be relative in the epistemic sense. The suggestion contained in his formulations might well be considered radical. Indeed, following the path that has been suggested by Wideman, perhaps I would render this thought as concept-metaphor by reference to the subatomic—the subindividual—in all senses.

For what emerges at the very inception of Du Bois's discourse and remains afoot throughout his entire itinerary is his conception of the necessity that in order to think the possibility of something like an African American subject one must be able to think not only the actual social practices that give our historical modernity its specific character, for example, the operation of practices under the sign of race, but the most radical infrastructural possibility of identity and identification. In this chapter I shall simply, but strategically, call this the question of difference or the question of the other. This possibility would entail not only those practices that organize our general but specific historicity, for example the practice of racial distinction in all its modalities—conceptual, political, economic, theological, among others, for example. For, although we cannot avoid a passage through the constitutive deployment of racial distinction in the historical field proper to the African American subject, and although in one sense our modernity cannot rigorously be thought as something other than a historicity marked by *the very idea of* race, a mundane or ontic elaboration of the force named by Du Bois under the heading of "the problem of the color-line," of the practice of racial distinction by itself, simply, would not attain to the full depth of the order at stake here. The same could be said, for example, of the concept of the commodity or the concept of the unconscious. We must also give an account of that structure of ontological possibility in which the practice of racial distinction opens, and to which the concept of race, and hence racist practice, is a certain kind of response, indeed, a violent, destructive, response. This possibility would be the general possibility of difference—we could even say that there *is* difference. In another discourse one might propose the heading of *the question* of being or the movement of *différance*. As our way, here, now, perhaps the thought of the possibility of the other, in its apparent simplicity, should suffice.

Yet the particular richness of Du Bois's discourse must be continually and hence gradually (re)emphasized.[3]

The innovation of Du Bois's approach was perhaps first opened by his manner of proceeding. We might summarize the pathway of Du Bois's innovation in the following terms. His thinking of historicity in general was developed entirely according to a methodological protocol that required him to attempt to think the particulars, the minute historical specifics, that which we often call the micrological, of a specific historicity, the history and status of that which we call African American (or Negro) in America, especially in what has become the United States. Yet, it seems to me, his concern was also to specify, at all levels of generality, the systemic site or structures that organized the emergence of the African American or Negro as subject. This concern to think the micrological, while remaining preoccupied with the most general possible formulation of the question of the Negro, led Du Bois to ask the question of the status of the historical example. That is, he was led to pose the question of the status of the Negro or African American, in every sense, the question of foundation, or of general possibility: to imagine, perhaps, that such might never have been, or might not ever be, such.

A concern with the question of the *status,* or the ontological ground, of the African American subject, both collectively and individually, rather than only the question of the ontic and empirical modes of existence, remains as the decisive meditation of "The Conservation of Races" and emerges as the distilled and organizing ground of the problematic of "Strivings of the Negro People," even as the register of thematic attention shifts from one to the other.[4] We note simply in passing here and now that both texts were written in 1897, a year that was pivotal for Du Bois. It was his concern with the question of status, his manner of rethinking this question, that opened the way for Du Bois's central innovation in the question of the Negro as a problem for thought, one that is both conceptual and theoretical, at once pertaining to matters epistemic in general and questions of ontology, in discourses on the Negro or African Americans.[5]

In trying to formulate the problem of the status of the African American subject, Du Bois was led to the question of how to think the status of the problem of that which we call race and, beyond (yet in part on the basis of) this particular historical problem, the problem of the status of difference in general. Beyond simply empirical or so-called real history, at the core of the question of race and our historicity was another question, one for which Du Bois never proposed a proper name in the register of discussion such as that I am attempting, and which I call, in this chapter, for reasons of strategy and economy, the question of the other, of the general possibility of difference. However, according to another mode of reflection, his persisting and ex-foliating formulation of the "problem of the color-line" across his entire itinerary, in particular a certain motif therein, can be understood to offer resource for the engagement of this question. (In the closing chapter of this study, I offer some considerations along this line.) The problem formulated in simple and somewhat prosaic terms was how to situate the question of difference, how to situate with respect to each other the relation of sameness and difference.

This led Du Bois to raise the question of how our entire historicity and "our" world is constituted, in both an historical and a certain transcendental sense. This question was similar—given its full elaboration—as the order of problems for thought posed by the itinerary of Marx and Freud; for, it is from this standpoint that we must approach Du Bois's avowed discovery of the discourses of these two thinkers in the later part of his itinerary. Most fundamentally, Du Bois is best approached on the order of his discourse which can recognize him as an incipient thinker on the path of reopening a question about the very fundament of historial possibility.[6]

For we must recall the generality of the problem of racial distinction for Du Bois. In its innermost interstices, the structural economy (a certain oppositional logic or principle) at stake here is such that, even if not called by the name of "race," its pertinence extends, at least, to all that we can call modern or modernity.[7] And beyond that, to all discussions of difference in general, among human social groups certainly, but also to thoughts about genera as such, including their possibility. That is to say, in its full implication it would solicit the very inception of the critical discourse that would delimit the possibility of knowledge, of the concept of the human, and the horizon of the human sciences. It pertains to the very way in which the itinerary of the question of the transcendental and the question of being, respectively, are announced within modern thought.

Although a more fulsome elaboration of the formulation of this thought in Du Bois's discourse is necessary, perhaps it can be remarked here even if in an adumbrated form.[8]

On the surface its guiding thematic is historical. Yet, as Du Bois explicitly suggested on more than one occasion and across several decades, the theme or question of race, the movement of the strange and powerful economy that organizes the movement of the practice of racial distinction, takes us close to the root of that which we consider constitutive of our world, of our modernity, of our common colonial nexus. Thus, the implication of an elaboration of this question will remain excessive to all the particular or microhistorical domains in which we might seek to simply situate it. For example, the most general and decisive implications of perhaps the most commonly cited of Du Bois's formulations of this question, and to which we have already referred, are seldom made the focus of a thematic questioning.

We can open this annotation by reference to the beginning of the second chapter of *The Souls of Black Folk*, which is a meditation on the aftermath of the Civil War and the project that was summed up in the Freedmen's Bureau (the thesis of which, that the question of Negro slavery and the question of Negro freedom were the principal issues of the Civil War and Reconstruction, respectively, came to magisterial fruition Du Bois's great study *Black Reconstruction* from 1935).[9]

In that chapter, which inaugurates and situates the historiographical and ethnological itinerary through the post-Emancipation South developed across the following twelve essays of *The Souls of Black Folk* as first and foremost a reflection upon a historical *problem*, Du Bois writes that "the problem of the twentieth century is the problem of the color-line— the relation of the darker to the lighter races of men in Asia and Africa, in America and the islands of the sea." This sentence is oft-quoted. However, and decisively, the next sentence (not often quoted and seldom thought) opens with a formulation that recontextualizes the entire problematic with regard to the United States and its relation to a larger horizon: "it was a *phase* of this problem that caused the Civil War" (*Souls*, 13–14, chap. 2, para. 1).

Perhaps the problem of the color-line was *the* problem of the twentieth century for Du Bois, but its structures far exceed the limits of that horizon. In this formulation a rethinking of the contextual status of the problem of race, in every sense, and a gesture to resituate the American

Civil War in the context of the historical unfolding of modern, global, colonialism, in particular the promulgations of European states (then at the moment of consolidation in Africa, for example) and the United States (then at the inception of its most expansive initiative up to that time), as nodal moments in the history of modern imperialism was simultaneously proposed.[10]

Forty years later Du Bois repeated the formulation, this time with a spatial valence. Despite its functionalist conceptualization and its restriction to a particular form of social practice, given a certain concern with the implications of the discourse of Marx at that moment in his itinerary (and the dominant readings thereof at the time), its continuity and faithfulness to a question should be remarked. "The economic foundation of the modern world was based on the recognition and preservation of so-called racial distinctions. In accordance with this, not only Negro slavery could be justified, but the Asiatic coolie profitably used and the labor classes in white countries kept in their places by low wage" (*Dusk*, 103). No single structural domain or practice can situate, or, that is, simply reduce, the heterogeneous pertinence of the problematic adumbrated in these lines for the entire historicity that we might call modernity. This heterogeneous problematic can only be made the topic of a thematic questioning, the only justification of which is a strategic calculation. That is to say, while historical in its reference, its value lies in its capacity to stand as the heading of a problem for thought and not, in the final instance, as the name of a simply given and ready to hand actuality. That is to say, its yield is not simply the gathering of historical reference, but the itinerant exploration of an epistemic horizon such that it might then be able to suggest possible domains of critical theoretical production.

Moving from within the horizon of an historicity given to him as by instituting fate, so to speak, at the very inception of his itinerary, Du Bois undertook such a calculation (or enacted a practical solution that in its eventuality took on the retrospective organization of a form of calculation) and formulated a strategic line of questioning by which he could desediment some of the structures buried, in the American context, around an axis of denial (in every possible sense of this word) with regard to the ensemble of practices and concept-metaphors organized around the sign of race. The strategy, developed by Du Bois, that I have thought to privilege in this chapter is that which focuses specifically on those processes that fashion the subject of sense, of sociality, of a certain inhabitation of the world as a social being. Du Bois called it the "autobiography of a concept."

Our reference to the articulation of such a revisionary historiographical sense may allow us now to recognize a certain thickness in the perspective that is Du Bois's and which we are seeking to adduce. For, in all truth it opens upon the historical form of a certain kind of metaphysical query: What is man, what is the human, and how such difference? While this question lies in the background, so to speak, of the historiographical inquiry, it is precisely the given, historical terms of this perennial form of question about the existence of the so-called human that is everywhere at stake in the discourse of Du Bois on the problematic of the practices of distinction by way of the idea or concept of race and his formulations of the "problem of the color-line."

This conjunction of the historical and the transcendental, eventually construed in a manner that we may with justification remark as a certain kind of "ultratranscendental"—both short of any traditional idea of the transcendental, in its resolute concern with immanence, and yet beyond such, in its persisting refusal of a reduction to the same, the simple, or the pure—organized and motivated, with a certain rigor, a decisive contribution of Du Bois's discourse. This was his description of the movement and force of the practice of racial difference as simultaneously revelatory, on the one hand, and productive, on the other hand, of the difference that is (the chance, or the possibility, or) the movement of the constitution of subjectivation in general, pursued in alternating contexts on theoretic levels of individuation that could account for both collectivity and the autobiographical. Du Bois was thus led to think the originary moment in the constitution of racial distinction (or racialized social difference), thought as a subjective practice that is not reducible to the intentionality of the subject, and in the constitution of the African American subject, thought in terms of its concept or possibility (hence in terms of subjectivation in general) as a unique structure of repetition. An analytical formulation of this structure recognizes each "originary" or inaugural moment as a reinauguration. The supple precision and paradoxical rigor with which Du Bois's discourse can be understood to desediment and sift into relief this originary structure out of the play of the ensemble of relations that is our racialized "modern" subjectivities and the historicities that set them afoot remained unsurpassed, it seems to me, in twentieth-century thought.

I submit that Du Bois decided that these questions could be thought in no better way than by thinking in as exact and thorough a manner possible the questions posed by the actuality of the African American subject, the history of the experience of African Americans, the structures of historicity which are the histories of African Americans. These questions, as formulated in Du Bois's discourse in all their specificity, I am suggesting, can be succinctly and powerfully gathered up into the question of the general possibility of a being, specifically a subject, like an African American. Thus, Du Bois was led to return to that with which he began, but in a new way.[11] According to his own exigencies, then, his own protocols, Du Bois, perhaps in a manner that was not ordered simply by intention, in trying to give an account, an empirical account that would also be an account of that which we sometimes reference as the meaningful or the symbolic, of the social and historical marks of the mode of being of those who for so long have been understood as African Americans in the United States, formulated a strategic method for thinking along with the question of the subject, the historical question of racial distinction and the "ultratranscendental" question of difference. Under the force of palpable necessity, the abusive practice of racism, and for strategic reasons whose economy this chapter elaborates (in a word, having to do with the status of heterogeneity or what I call the problem of purity or pure being in the Negro-Black-Afro-Afra-Colored, or-African American case), Du Bois took the status of the African American subject as an exemplary path by which to trace the theme (or develop the topic) of the problem of racial distinction, and hence, the problem of difference in general.

For similar practical and strategic reasons, in this regard, Du Bois could do no better than to question himself, to critically and reflexively inquire back into the genealogies and histories by which he was organized as such a putative subject.[12]

Late in his life, writing at the end of the 1930s in a discourse that was eventually gathered and published in 1940 under the heading of *Dusk of Dawn*, Du Bois called this strategy the "autobiography of a concept," specifically the "autobiography of a race concept." Indeed, the text was subtitled, "An Essay Toward an Autobiography of a Race Concept." Du Bois wrote:

I seem to see a way of elucidating the inner meaning and significance of that race problem by explaining it in terms of the one human life that I know best. I have written then what is meant to be not so much my autobiography as the autobiography of a concept of race, elucidated, magnified and doubtless distorted in the thoughts and deeds which were mine. (*Dusk*, viii)

Let us note that in the formulation as just given, Du Bois does not seem to consider here that this "concept" or "conceptual problematic" might not be, as such, except *as* the "thoughts and deeds," or more generally, the practices of a particular subject or the devolution of such an order of subjectivation in general, in all of its contradictory modalities (for example, that of a subject socially and historically understood as "White"), even as it would not be reducible to (the intentionality of) those thoughts and deeds or practices. Such a consideration might allow one to think the possibility that the structures that make possible the emergence and functioning of this concept (or any concept, any practice, indeed historicity in general) might not have any other phenomenal status than as such is given in and by way of such "magnifications and distortions" as those registered in the order of historicity remarked in his "autobiography." Hence three annotations that would help to situate an ambivalence in Du Bois's text can be placed here.

First, we note that the opening of Du Bois's autobiography that we quote here is called an "Apology" (*Dusk*, vii–viii). He was simultaneously hesitant or reserved about its objectivity and insistent on its capacity to render for thought and inhabitation a certain kind of fundamental critical truth.

Secondly, this may be juxtaposed with the thought that a decisive post-Enlightenment epistemological problem, a problem given by the sedimentations of an Enlightenment concept of objectivity, has been how to account for the production of a general concept or objectivity (in an epistemological, that is, an already reduced frame, we might say "truth") that nonetheless is or must be constituted in a subjective genesis.[13]

Third, as a specific example, both of the two points just summarized can be recognized in Derrida's tracing of the problem of genesis in Edmund Husserl's itinerary in a manner that can place it proximate to the inception of Du Bois's discourse. For, within a certain dimension of Husserl's path of problematization, a persistent questioning of the subjective and historical genesis of mathematical truth can be adduced, even as he withdrew from any naive historicism or psychologism in an account of such genesis, according to Derrida's engagement.[14] Indeed, the latter figure made this question his own and it became the very site for the emergence of that most fundamental opening for all of his subsequent discourse (just as it had, in another sense, done the same for Heidegger at an earlier moment). It is a rethinking of the transcendental (where the distinction transcendental-mundane cannot be absolute) that Derrida undertakes there. For me, the essence of the accomplishment of the work summarized there is Derrida's elaboration of the absolutely interlaced necessity of history for the *logos* and of the logos for history. The critical edge for philosophy of course is Derrida's insistence on the necessity and risks of the "historical" status of the *logos*, indeed in the very movement of the production of ideality, such as mathematical truth. This posed, long ago now, a new thinking, a rethinking, of that which has been called materiality or empiricism in general, which remains somewhat new on the order of an epistemic horizon.

Thus, I have ventured this chapter on the "autobiographical" problematic of Du Bois's thought under the general aim of one guiding question: Is it possible for the most particular or "subjective" history to tell the most general of truths, perhaps precisely because such histories do distort, or magnify, and so on in particular sorts of ways? No doubt this is the thought of a certain "nominalism" whose pertinence can only be given if it is maintained this side of the transcendental or the ontico-ontological difference (that is, one that affirms the difference that is nothing by which a thought such as the transcendental can be posed). Derrida proposed a thought that he famously called *différance*, understood as a certain movement of the trace, as he also put it, among others. Here, I am simply tracking the movement of an X, which is not *simply* nothing (or, rather, not absence), and for the always provisional situation of discourse, here we have accepted the given appellation "Du Bois" and likewise the heading "African American," or to put it more in the terms that arise in the discourse under the name Du Bois, an "autobiography of a concept." In a certain way this thought, this side of the transcendental elucidation, is certainly a maintenance of thinking as practice within the irruption that is materiality; a philosophical name might be immanence.

I emphasize, however, that one of my central suggestions in this chapter in terms of Du Bois's own development is that the deployment of the methodological strategy for thinking the status of our socius that he called an "autobiography of a concept" was first broached in the opening paragraphs of the first chapter of *The Souls of Black Folk* or, more precisely, in the essay produced in 1897 and that would then be redeployed as the opening chapter of the collection of essays five and a half years later.

> Between me and the other world there is ever an unasked question: unasked by some through feelings of delicacy; by others through the difficulty of rightly framing it. All nevertheless, flutter round it. They approach me in a half-hesitant sort of way, eye me curiously or compassionately, and then, instead of saying directly, How does it feel to be a problem? they say, I know an excellent colored man in my town; or I fought at Mechanicsville; or, Do not these Southern outrages make your blood boil? At these I smile, or am interested, or reduce the boiling to a simmer, as the occasion may require. To the real question, How does it feel to be a problem? I answer seldom a word.
>
> And yet, being a problem is a strange experience,—peculiar even for one who has never been anything else, save perhaps in babyhood and in Europe. It is in the early days of rollicking boyhood that the revelation first bursts upon one, all in a day as it were. I remember well when the shadow swept across me. I was a little thing, away up in the hills of New England, where the dark Housatonic winds between Hoosac and Tagkanic to the sea. In a wee wooden schoolhouse, something put it into the boys' and girls' heads to buy gorgeous visiting-cards—ten cents a package—and exchange. The exchange was merry, till one girl, a tall newcomer, refused my card,—refused it peremptorily, with a glance. Then it dawned upon me with a certain suddenness that I was different from the others; or like mayhap, in heart and life and longing, but shut out from their world by a vast veil. I had thereafter no desire to tear down that veil, to creep through; I held all beyond it in common contempt, and lived above it in a region of blue sky and great wandering shadows. That sky was bluest when I could beat my mates at examination-time, or beat them at a foot-race, or even beat their stringy heads. Alas, with the years all this fine contempt began to fade; for the worlds I longed for were theirs not mine. But they should not keep these prizes I said; some, all, I would wrest from them. Just how I would do it I could never decide: by reading law, by healing the sick, by telling the wonderful tales that swam in my head,—some way. With other black boys the strife was not so fiercely sunny: their youth shrunk into tasteless sycophancy, or into silent hatred of the pale world around them and mocking distrust of everything white; or wasted itself in a bitter cry, Why did God make me an outcast and a stranger in mine

own house? The shades of the prison-house closed round about us all: walls strait and stubborn to the whitest, but relentlessly narrow, tall and unscalable to sons of night who must plod darkly on in resignation, or beat unavailing palms against the stone, or steadily, half hopelessly, watch the streak of blue above. (*Souls*, 1–3, chap. 1, paras. 1–2; Du Bois 1897b)[15]

In a 1904 commentary on *Souls of Black Folk* Du Bois himself called attention to its ground in a certain autobiographical organization.[16] Of the textual changes from its initial 1897 publication to its revised 1903 version as the opening chapter of *Souls of Black Folk*, only one change was introduced into these opening paragraphs: the addition of a letter. The phrase "the world I longed for" in the second paragraph was changed to "the world*s* I longed for." Although richly significant in one sense (introducing a semantic inflection that, as a description, both retains and displaces an oppositional structure), by its minuteness this change does not contest, but rather, tends to affirm the suggestion I am proposing here: that Du Bois was not led to question the general path of inquiry, a certain sort of autobiographical inquiry, adumbrated in the opening paragraphs of this early text. I would suggest as well that across the multiple and heterogeneous movements of Du Bois's itinerary over some six and a half decades he never questioned the approach he put forth in these opening paragraphs.

Indeed, this formulation, this reflection upon the autobiographical, was a decisive aspect of Du Bois's entire itinerary and of all the subsequent diverse problematics he approached. Not only is it affirmed through his practice in other essays in this early volume, *Souls*, but his subsequent writings return to this approach again and again. At the time of his death, Du Bois was yet still pursuing the writing of the autobiographical. The historian Thomas C. Holt touched a major chord, one with which any reading of Du Bois should reckon or resonate, when he wrote that Du Bois's "own life became the text, the point of departure, for each of his major explorations of race, culture, and politics."[17]

It is the implication of a confirmation of the fecundity of Du Bois's strategy, relating to how *we* understand *our* entire modernity, that is to say how we situate ourselves in some reflexive or redoubled manner to such, that motivates the itinerary of reading that I am following here. Which is also to ask—who is this we of which we portend to reference?

Situating the Example: Concept

In order to properly situate the strategy of this methodology of Du Bois's, for he had many others, it must be recognized that the autobiographical *example* in Du Bois's methodology is approached at a level of distinctive generality. I have chosen, in this chapter, to elucidate this question of the example, if possible, with one example from Du Bois's discourse: from the 1940 *Dusk of Dawn* text, I will attend to a passage of some fourteen pages in the pivotal chapter, "The Concept of Race" (*Dusk*, 97–133, esp. 103–17). The passage in question is principally concerned with Du Bois's address of his family genealogy. This desedimentation is at once a certain kind of investigation of the history and possibility of an African American subject, such as Du Bois, of the concept and practice of racial distinction, and of the general possibility of difference as it is announced in the form of the human.

The first theme that I wish to underline is that the elaboration of the autobiographical in *Dusk*, as well as elsewhere in Du Bois's work, is nothing less than a radical formulation of the status of the example, bearing implications for any methodology of interpretive practice. It formulates, with regard to the subject in general, what I call here, by analogy, the subatomic. To formulate this theme I will, initially, proceed through a reading of the five-page opening chapter of *Dusk*, which Du Bois enigmatically calls "The Plot" (*Dusk*, 3–7).

In a general sense Du Bois's "autobiography of a concept" does not offer a reduction of historicity to the (individual or collective) subject, nor a simple elimination of the subject from the production of historicity, but rather resituates the structure of subjectivity; it resituates (the) intentionality (or consciousness) (of the subject). Du Bois's production operates in a domain that Louis Althusser and Michel Foucault, and others following them, later claimed as their own: (1) the subject is *only* possible in the space or spacing of a system of distinctions or practices, however, (2) likewise, the system itself does not simply precede, in its root possibility or opening (and above all analytically), the constitution of the subject or subject position.[18] Thus, according to Du Bois's account all that concerns this autobiographical figure can be shown to articulate itself in the formation of a certain movement of "between"— as this "between"—of the movement or structure of the constitution of the subject.

If Du Bois has to justify the choice of his example with reference to a certain empirical order as an indispensable guardrail against saying anything whatsoever, and if we must note that this empirical order is always privileged by Du Bois throughout his many different projects (as in the *Philadelphia Negro* study and its related projects and in the projects and texts related to the Atlanta University Conferences on the Study of the Negro from 1898 to 1910), we should not understand this privilege as claiming a simple first-order or ultimate status for such an order of phenomena or a first-order truth for our knowledge of such an order of phenomena.[19]

In the passage from *Dusk of Dawn* quoted above, we must not understand Du Bois's reference to "the one human life I know best" as claiming a first-order truth for his self-knowledge. If Du Bois explicitly followed a method of reflection upon himself, of reflection upon his constitution as an individual subject, his stated intention, in this passage, is anything but *simply* the elaboration of a self-possessive and self-possessed narrative subject, although there is certainly a subject at work or play here. Thus Du Bois writes, "I have written what is meant to be *not* so much *my* autobiography as the autobiography of a concept of race" (*Dusk*, viii, emphasis mine). I call it the autobiography of a (conceptual) problematic (conceptual here is anything but *simply* ideal or mental). We should note what Du Bois wrote to Paul G. Partington in a letter dated March 31, 1961: "*Dusk of Dawn* was not an autobiography. It had a great many autobiographical notes, but it was distinctly the story of a theory of race and how it had developed in my own life."[20]

Moreover, Du Bois explicitly distinguishes the order of intentionality or subjectivity organized by the self-conscious motivations and practices of the subject (here marked as individual) from another order of "intentionality" or subjectivity (if it still makes sense to call it by this name), which is not reducible simply to the order of subjective intention, but is also organized as a certain kind of structural domain that I propose to try to think by way of the heading "between." In such a thought the structural, or better infrastructural, is anything but static; a rethinking of the concept of structure may be posed here.[21] Thus, Du Bois explicitly indicates that his intention as (an individual) subject does not *constitute*, pure and simple, the phenomenon being described (the *experience* of an individual subject). Rather, this subjectivity, this experience, the organization of intentionality, as well as sense in general— insofar as it is the specific object of Du Bois's inquiry—is itself situated in terms of a systemic possibility. However, if this is so, Du Bois practices a recognition, if he does not *name it*, of the necessity that in order for distinction by way of a social idea or formal concept of race to operate as an iterable distinction, as a system of repetitive marks, it can only do so in the making of subjects—*in* the making and not before. It is not given in the thing itself whatever is such. Du Bois analytically positions the relationship between these two orders of intentionality, the experiential and the systemic, in such a way that one (the latter) is "elucidated, magnified and doubtless distorted" in the other (the former): the order of "thoughts and deeds" was interpreted in terms of how it was situated in relation to another order, the order of a "concept" of racial distinction. Yet, the concept acquires its possibility only as a *text* we might say, as system of *practices*, the actual *making* of subjects. At the level of the subject, the unnameable movement of between that one might follow as a problem for thought, can, perhaps, be most specifically and generally elucidated, at once, in the demonstrative (that is, performative) style of the autobiographical.[22]

The order of "concept" put forth by Du Bois in *Dusk of Dawn* might be situated just a bit more precisely: just as it responds to the so-called immanent or material, it is not simply empirical, but neither is it simply ideal. It pertains to the dynamic process of the subjectivation of the subject as subjectivity. Du Bois's epistemological concern responds, it seems to me, to a problematic similar to that which led Edmund Husserl to elucidate that which he came to call the phenomenological.

I suggest, if only by analogy here that the problematic that Derrida (in his early work) has so carefully situated as organizing Husserl's early work, is similar to that which was at stake and decisive in organizing Du Bois's formulation of the domain of which he wished to inquire here, although it is proposed in a distinctly different way in the discourses of these two thinkers. It remains only an analogy because a detailed exploration of the relation of Du Bois's and Husserl's respective problematics stands apart from the principal concern of this chapter (even as it has not yet been considered, for the most part). Derrida wrote of Husserl's concern with the discourses of mathematics and formal ideality.

> Husserl . . . [sought] to *maintain* simultaneously the normative autonomy of logical or mathematical identity as concerns all factual consciousness, and its original dependence in relation to a subjectivity *in general*; in general but *concretely*. Thus he had to navigate

between the Scylla and Charybdis of logicizing structuralism and psychologistic geneticism (even in the subtle and pernicious form of the 'transcendental psychologism' attributed to Kant). He had to open up a new direction of philosophical attention and permit the discovery of a concrete, but nonempirical, intentionality, a 'transcendental experience' which would be 'constitutive', that is, like all intentionality, simultaneously productive and revelatory, active and passive. The original unity, the common root of activity and passivity is from quite early on the very possibility of meaning for Husserl. And this common root will ceaselessly be experienced as the common root of structure *and* genesis, which is dogmatically presupposed by all the *ulterior* problematics and dissociations concerning them. . . . [This was] the problem which is already Husserl's, that is the problem of the *foundation of objectivity.*[23]

Derrida goes on to trace how this problem of Husserl's overran its epistemological frame to become the question of the foundation and emergence of phenomenality in general, of the phenomenality of the phenomenon.

Du Bois's problem, of course, was to specify a distinct orientation of description of the social. This concern might be construed as primarily epistemological. Yet, this problem was produced, we must emphasize, not as an abstract question or as a term of a philosophical exposition, but as a pivotal moment of a practical effort to think, which is not simply to describe, simultaneously the order of the constitution of the African American subject and the order of the phenomenon of the systemic practice of racial distinction. Thus, Du Bois was concerned with concrete social practice; concrete but in its most general implications. In the closing paragraphs of the first chapter of *Dusk*, a chapter in which Du Bois maps out the questions that organize, for him, the discourse that follows, he specifically remarks this motif of the general: "Negroes must eat and strive, and still hold unfaltering commerce with the stars" (*Dusk*, 7).[24] His trajectory was moving in a direction precisely otherwise than that of Husserl. Yet, to the extent that the question of the foundation of objectivity, especially as Husserl raised it, proposed that such is possible only by an irreducible passage through history and the subject it broached the question of the structure of the subjectivity that might account for such production.[25] And Du Bois's question of the possibility of the radical difference of the subject, raises not only the social question of "the scope of chance and unreason in human action," as given in Du Bois's phrasing here, but the question of chance or freedom in general, in which the question of truth would assume its pertinence.[26] Thus, a discreet crossing and intermixing of the respective problematics and itineraries, of Husserl and Du Bois, can be recognized.

In a certain specific sense, Du Bois's question concerned the roots of phenomenal being from its inception. Two specific questions arise, already in 1897, and remain at work throughout his entire itinerary; for example, in 1940: Who, or what is, an African American or Negro?; What is race? Whence the authority of the practice of racial distinction? But the form of these questions, not only their frame as the epistemological question of science, "what is . . . ," but the autobiographical mode of their elaboration, perhaps paradoxically, may be understood to put at stake the "ultratranscendental" question of the status of difference or sameness, of the possibility of freedom and of truth. What Du Bois's discourse points to again and again, in part as a result of this double preoccupation of his thinking with specific historical questions along with the general problematics embedded within them, is an order of constitution in which the subject is neither the beginning nor the end of historicity. Yet, without the subject, historicity, which is the very matrix of the example, would in turn have no example itself, and hence no bearing.

Since Du Bois does not state this proposition literally as a theme, I propose it as an interpretation, support for which I rely upon Du Bois's practice—that is to say, his consistent preoccupation with the example, specifically the autobiographical example. The autobiographical example, at least as it is given in Du Bois's staging, the responsibility it demands as a demonstration, seems to insist that the recognition of meaning in history in general can only be announced in the unavoidable passage by way of the micrological or the subatomic.[27] The subject is situated in history and historicity; yet, the very possibility of historicity is *situated in* the structure that opens the possibility of subjective practice. (Later in this chapter I will propose to recognize this structure, at the level of the subject, under the heading of what Du Bois early on called "second-sight.") In the opening chapter of *Dusk of Dawn*, Du Bois poignantly situated this autobiographical register of the orders of subjectivation.

> In the folds of this European civilization I was born and shall die, imprisoned, conditioned, depressed, exalted and inspired. Integrally a part of it and yet, much more significant, one of its rejected parts; one who expressed in life and action and made vocal to many, a single whirlpool of social entanglement and inner psychological paradox,

which always seem to me more *significant for the meaning of the world today* than other similar and related problems. Little indeed did I do, or could I conceivably have done, to make this problem or loose it. Crucified on the vast wheel of time, I flew round and round with the Zeitgeist, waving my pen and lifting faint voices to explain, expound and exhort; to see, foresee and prophesy, to the few who could or would listen. Thus very evidently to me and to others I did little to create my day or greatly change it; but *I did exemplify it and thus for all time my life is significant for all lives of men.* (*Dusk*, 3–4, emphasis mine)

In a general sense, then, we can say that Du Bois's concept of the *example*, of the autobiographical, of the "autobiography of a concept," specifically the "autobiography of a race concept," is precisely other than a reduction of history or historicity to the subject (individual or collective), or of the subject (in whatever empirical modality) to the (a)historical. It should be understood to retain each inflection of these apparently opposed terms in a noncategorical way.

In order to further clarify the status of the *example* in Du Bois's discourse we might follow and attempt to give the general sense of the "autobiography of a concept" just outlined specification along two interwoven pathways. Here, I retain the path opened in Derrida's early work and invoke a thought of the "ultratranscendental." The other, in a manner that I hope to render as complex, we may call historical.

First, Du Bois's discourse seems to recognize that in order to *give an account of* himself, he must give a critical account of the specific historicity—the "particular social problem," "the problem of the color-line," "the worldwide domination of white Europe"—that organizes this autobiography, he must ask about its possibility and engage its reference within a metaphysical horizon and its apparition on the horizons of an ensemble of metadiscourses. To give such an account is the only way to avoid simply assuming this historicity and, hence, analytically presupposing that which is descriptively found. This historicity, this particularity, must itself be situated in terms of its general possibility. In order to think the question of this historicity, to give an account of it, in its root, the question of its general possibility must be formulated. In Du Bois's discourse, this question leads to the formulation of a question that, in its radicality, broaches a questioning of the status of the relation of identity and difference as such. We can call this the question of difference. We can also call this the question of identity. Further, we can call it the question of the possibility of difference and sameness among humans. We are within rights to remark therein a transcendental theme. Yet, it is not simply a transcendental question. Hence, I suggest that we can elucidate a discourse in its interstices that I have already adumbrated as "ultratranscendental" by way of an analogy to Derrida's effort to render thematic such a dimension of problem for thought; a rendering that he proposed by way of a reference, in turn, to the interpolation of the twentieth-century phenomenological tradition with the thought of the transcendental elaborated in modern thought across the eighteenth and nineteenth centuries. Du Bois himself can be understood to have formulated the problem of a transcendental sense as simultaneously practical and theoretical. Thus, we can reinscribe his formulation of question, perhaps, among the sheaves of our own discourse as a question of the "ultra" transcendental.[28] Du Bois may be understood to formulate the question in the following terms:

> What now was this particular social problem which through the chances of birth and existence, became so peculiarly mine? *At bottom and in essence it was as old as human life.* Yet in its revelation, through the nineteenth century, it was significantly and fatally new: *the differences between men*; differences in their appearance, in their physique, in their thoughts and customs; differences so great and impelling that always from the beginning of time they thrust themselves forward upon the consciousness of all living things. Culture among human beings came to be and had to be built upon knowledge and recognition of these differences. (*Dusk*, 4, emphasis mine)

The question in its root concerned the implication for human experience, for what we may perhaps call, in this discursive context, subjectivity in general, of the general possibility of the experience of difference (in this domain all terms become unstable), here specifically as marked by Du Bois's discourse as *difference* within all that might be understood as *of* that which has been called *man* or *the human*. It can be said in another register: the question in its root concerned how humans understand, or make sense of, the general possibility of difference. Let us for the moment not assume the given or already justified status of a claim for the moral unity of the human. If that is so, what is the ultimate status of such differences? Whence difference (itself or in general)? How does one situate its pertinence—difference as such or, let us say, with a certain apparently mathematical implication, the project of definiteness itself, but one that goes beyond, even, any mathesis as such—with regard to the problem of the human? What would then appear as at stake would be an immanence in which the possibility of existence can always be understood as simultaneously life and death. Such would be the premise of a discourse of the ultratranscendental, as I propose to translate and reinscribe it here. In a discourse that would respond to such demands, one cannot only historicize the eruption of a form of existence; nor, could one only remark on the transcendental. Rather, one must do both and then go beyond such ostensible distinction to an understanding that might announce another historicity of the transcendental or another approach to a transcendental history. It is in the space of this general problematic that the particular historicity that is our own, and that aspect of it which occupies Du Bois's horizon of question opens.

Secondly, Du Bois's discourse sketches a brief history of the unfolding of the question of difference *in* our historicity and *as* our historicity. Thus, as Du Bois puts it, although operating throughout human history (indeed, perhaps as history or historicity itself) the question of difference "in its revelation, through the nineteenth century," as a "particular social problem" of our modernity, our common imperial and colonial nexus, "was significantly and fatally new."[29] Continuing his twofold elaboration (in terms of the concept of race and of the African American subject) of the status of his "autobiography of a concept of race" in the passage quoted in extenso above, Du Bois develops an historical schema for situating the problematic that I have begun to adduce therein.

> But after the scientific method had been conceived in the seventeenth century it [the scientific method] came toward the end of the eighteenth century to be applied to man and to man as he appeared then, with no wide or intensive inquiry into what he had been or how he had lived in the past. In the nineteenth century however came the revolution of conceiving the world not as permanent structure but as changing growth and then the study of man as changing and developing physical and social entity had to begin. But the mind clung desperately to the idea that basic racial differences between human beings had suffered no change; and it clung to this idea not simply from inertia and unconscious action but from the fact that because of the modern African slave trade a tremendous economic structure and eventually the industrial revolution had been based upon racial differences between men. (*Dusk*, 4–5)

If we recall that the question for Du Bois is *how* difference is understood, we can recapitulate three statements, thus far, from his historical schema

and take note of a certain sort of conceptual ambiguity. (1) Du Bois suggests that eighteenth-century European discourse produced a static (perhaps hierarchical and typological) conception of "differences between
men," based upon a certain reading of the way humans "appeared" at that
time in a sort of global scenography. (2) Du Bois also seems to suggest
further that this conception could and *should* have been challenged by a
thinking of the world as historical that was affirmed in the nineteenth
century. (3) In the passage, as quoted so far, Du Bois suggests that this
conception of differences as static persisted, despite this challenge, due to
its ability to function in the production of modern systems of privilege
and subordination. We should also note here a certain ambiguity in Du
Bois's usage of the terms "culture" and "racial" to describe the problem
of human difference, in the three paragraphs quoted in extenso above.

Du Bois's analytic and political usage of the concept of race was
strongly and decisively inflected with a social valence that situated the
concept as a distinction of meaning, the ambiguous descriptive value
of which, in Du Bois's discourse as well as any other, derived from its
status as simultaneously *"real" as a meaningful distinction* (with brute,
potentially murderous, effects) and as *other than "real" as a meaningful distinction* (the ontological order of possibility on which it functions
and the force of which is such that it is not necessarily limited by what
we may take to be sensible, as fact, including supposed scientific truth
functioning in its existence as also a social fact). It is this social valence
in its historicity that is most at stake for Du Bois and is consistently and
rigorously elucidated by him over the course of his entire productivity. At
this point, however, it seems to me that Du Bois's discourse suggests that
the problem of human difference formulates the specific historical site of
the problematic that he wishes to elucidate. While recognizing the apparent ambiguity in Du Bois's usage of the term race, I suggest that what
was decisive for Du Bois was the way in which difference was situated.
Differences, Du Bois seems to suggest, were taken as signs of an essence
or an identity (pure or homogeneous) that is as primordial or ultimate.
Although Du Bois's schema implies that (what we now often call) cultural difference became 'racialized,' in a strict sense his formulation
suggests that the question of whether difference was conceived, respectively, under the concepts of "culture" or "race" (or, even "civilization")
would not be decisive. The radical question, Du Bois's discourse seems
to suggest, is whether or not difference is conceived in an oppositional

or categorical manner. Du Bois thus describes our racialized historicity as one premised on "the idea that [there are] *basic* racial differences between human beings" (emphasis mine).[30]

This structural distinction, Du Bois goes on to suggest, was elaborated into an apparently simple but exceedingly complex social *hieroglyphic*. It is at the nexus of the play and the production of this organization of mark—at once historical and social, ontological in its possibility—that Du Bois locates the systemic site of his emergence as an individual subject.

> This racial difference had now been rationalized into a difference mainly of skin color. Thus in the latter part of the nineteenth century when I was born and grew to manhood, color had become an abiding and unchangeable fact chiefly because a mass of self-conscious instincts and unconscious prejudices had arranged themselves rank on rank in its defense. Government, work, religion and education became based upon and determined by the color-line. The future of mankind was implicit in the race and color of men.
>
> Already in my boyhood this matter of color loomed significantly. My skin was darker than that of my school mates. My family confined itself not entirely but largely to people of this same darker hue. Even when in fact the color was lighter, this was an unimportant variation from the norm. (*Dusk*, 5)

According to Du Bois's text this social hieroglyph sediments, as an organization of mark or an ensemble of signs, as a meaningful distinction, reference to an entire social order and the organization of subject position therein. Du Bois's text specifies the *constitutive* force of the *practice* of distinction. It is not the ostensible referent of the sign itself or its status as a sign that is decisive, but rather how it is situated within a general order of distinction. First, Du Bois outlines the general pertinence of the sign of skin color to the entirety of the specific historical field in which he was born: an "abiding and unchangeable fact" inscribed in and inscribing "government, work, religion and education." Secondly, and this point is crucial to our reading of Du Bois, he indicates that the distinction in question, skin color distinction as a sign of racial difference which is understood in turn as a sign of fundamental human difference, was not of the ultimate importance: "even when in fact the color was lighter, this was an unimportant variation from the norm." Although a distinction among humans according to skin color has its own specific functional effects and modes of meaningful signification, for Du Bois it was not the color itself that was crucial, but rather the way in which color was understood. What mattered was the idea that differences of lighter and darker skin color could be determinately grouped as one kind or type, that is to say that what is constitutive in this social field is the force of a distinction premised on the idea of the oppositional or singular coherence of one kind or type in relation to another. What matters is not the potentially faulty application of the line but the insistence that it was possible to establish and maintain such a mark, to render it effective in the social instance and in the configuration of historicity in general. Du Bois suggests that the "norm," the distinction or difference in question, was organized as an oppositional distinction. It gave constitutive sense to this social field. What we must highlight here is that, in the process of his description, Du Bois outlines how, according to a certain kind of distinction, an oppositional distinction, social or subject position was produced. His examples are the social arenas of "school" and the "family." What Du Bois's text literally describes in this opening chapter of *Dusk* is the concrete or empirical social embeddedness, the sedimented meaningfulness, the specific historical pathway of this sort of distinction in his "life" or "experience."[31]

Having thus specified the levels of generality on which Du Bois situates the strategy that he called "autobiography of a concept," we can now turn to the example of this strategy in Du Bois's work that I have chosen to privilege in this chapter.

Situating the Example: Autobiography

Over the course of the three chapters preceding the fifth chapter of *Dusk of Dawn*, Du Bois gives a narrative account of his coming of age in the United States at the end of the nineteenth century. The chapter headings are, respectively, "A New England Boy and Reconstruction," chapter 2; "Education in the Last Decades of the Nineteenth Century," chapter 3; and "Science and Empire," chapter 4. What is distinctive is that this is an account specifically guided by the theme of a *racial* coming of age, rather than the somewhat more common motific guides of autobiography such as the becoming of a religious, political, or class-defined subject. In these chapters Du Bois describes (1) the familial and communal matrix by which he was situated as a racial subject from his "youth" (chapter 2), (2) the all pervasive conception of evolutionism that coordinated not just his formal "education" but also a social conception of human difference quite generally operative in the United States in the late nineteenth century (chapter 3), and (3) his response—both institutional and conceptual—to the limits of general scientific conceptualizations of human difference and social practice as such were organized in an "age of empire" (chapter 4).

In each case, Du Bois outlines, in the first person, a structure of experience that he does not name, as such, in *Dusk*, but which, in its operative coordinates, is the same as that which he very early on in his itinerary, in the opening chapter of *The Souls of Black Folk*, called "double consciousness" and remarked its irruptive and productive effects for reflection as "the *gift* of second-sight" within the horizon of a sense of historical world (*Souls*, 3, chap. 1, para. 3, my emphasis). A certain sense of inhabitation, of a sense of self, within the general movement of the distinctions in question, a sense called into formation by a certain experience of (or position in) the practice of racial distinction, which Du Bois called "double consciousness" in that text, would then be announced as a certain form of experience of that general social structure and is the pivotal recognition in this coming of age narrative. It is a sense that is produced as an eventuality—at stake in the formation of subjectivation and produced in dynamic form of that production and not simply a given form of being.

> Had it not been for the race problem early thrust upon me and enveloping me, I should have probably been an unquestioning worshiper at the shrine of the social order and economic development into which I was born. But just that part of that order which seemed to most of my fellows nearest perfection, seemed to me most inequitable and wrong; starting from that critique, I gradually as the years went by found other things to question in my environment. At first, however, my criticism was confined to the relation of my people to the world movement. I was not questioning the world movement itself. What the white world was doing, its goals and ideals, I had not doubted were quite right. What was wrong was that I and people like me and thousands of others who might have my ability and aspiration, were refused permission to be part of this world. (*Dusk*, 26–27, and see also 13–15, 51–52, 54)

Oblique and limited in this initial formulation, the unfolding and specification of this space of structure or space of critique is the central theoretical or guiding motif for the elaboration of the narrative of *Dusk of Dawn*. That is to say, it is this movement of transformation retrospectively recalled and affirmed on multiple levels of experience and reflection that adduces the order of attention and understanding that is the devolution of the narrative itself, not only as the recollection itself but also the proposition of an intervention in the limits that are thereby revealed. In the context of the present chapter I only name here two key aspects of the text as headings for thought (for this book and even this motif in it can sustain and deserves much more attention and thought than this chapter can elaborate specifically on this question), and then name its general order of intervention. As one cross-cutting formulation of heading, we can note that Du Bois explicitly goes on in the narrative of *Dusk* to develop a deep and far-reaching motif of the self-reflexive sense of oneself as "white," culminating in the masterful sixth chapter, "The White World."[32] On the terms of another and further statement of heading, as I suggest below in this chapter, Du Bois elaborates this space of critique as a question of the ground of the very terms of human distinction, especially in the pivotal fifth chapter, "The Concept of Race."[33] However, the decisive matter in general theoretical terms here is that it was this structure of experience, self-consciously and strategically apprehended as a path of inquiry and understanding by Du Bois, that opened for him a critical (or desedimentative) space within the system of racial distinction.[34] As such, this structure of experience, operated epistemologically according to a methodology that Du Bois called the "autobiography of a concept," makes possible in this text the demonstration, the desedimentation, of the presuppositions of the concept of race and the practices that produce or operate it. This is the performative dimension of the production of the account Du Bois gives in the telling of his family genealogy. Situated in the interim between Friedrich Nietzsche and Michel Foucault, Du Bois's discourse here is certainly a kind of "genealogy" *avant la lettre*, shall we say, as we inherit it in the contemporary scene of theoretical practice.[35] We shall try to take a step toward recognizing the innovations of Du Bois's approach as we attempt to retell his telling.

Du Bois opens the chapter titled "The Concept of Race," a title whose enigmatic relation to the narrative has seemed almost to escape critical remark, with the following statement:

> I want now to turn aside from the personal annals of this biography to consider the conception which is after all my main subject. The concept of race lacks something in personal interest, but personal interest in my case has always depended upon this race concept and I wish to examine this now. (*Dusk*, 97)

His concern is "the history of the development of the race concept in the world and particularly in America" (*Dusk*, 97).

Du Bois begins by mapping out the "conceptual" context or the racial problematic (in every sense: political, economic, epistemological, and so on) into which he was born. There was one central and decisive aspect of this problematic. Racial distinctions were considered to be absolutely original, primordial, determinate, fixed, permanent, eternal, in the order of things, natural. Ultimately, the difference that was called racial was conceptualized as radically decidable as one thing or the other. In setting the stage for his desedimentation of his racialized biography, Du Bois describes his inscription into a racial logic of opposition thus:

> So far I have spoken of "race" and race problems quite as a matter of course without explanation or definition. That was our method in the nineteenth century. Just as I was born a member of a colored family, so too I was born a member of the colored race. That was obvious and no definition was needed. Later I adopted the designation "Negro" for the race to which I belong. It seemed more definite and logical. At the same time I was of course aware that all members of the Negro race were not black and that the pictures of my race which were current were not authentic nor fair portraits. But all that was incidental. *The world was divided into great primary groups of folk who belonged naturally together through heredity of physical traits and cultural affinity.* (*Dusk*, 100, emphasis mine)

As the denouement of his genealogical demonstration and at the inception of his formulation of the question of his relationship to Africa, Du Bois reemphasizes the oppositional character of the system of racial distinction in the Americas (and Europe and its colonies in general, perhaps) at the turn of the century.

> I was born in the century when the walls of race were clear and straight; when the world consisted of mutually exclusive races; and even though the edges might be blurred, there was no question of exact definition and understanding of the meaning of the word. (*Dusk*, 116)

In terms of logic and metaphysics, that is philosophy and science, and I wish to emphasize this context, which has no strictly delimitable margin, the distinction was considered to be oppositional. The schema that organized its deepest conceptual resources, involving we might say a certain understanding of being was formulated in Aristotle's *Metaphysics* as the so-called law of contradiction (or noncontradiction) and restated, for example, in one entire aspect of Hegel's project, that which insists on its virtuality, even if such is always belied by way of its own promulgation.[36]

Du Bois indicates that he initially accepted the logic of this system of distinction; although he never accepted the specific historical teleology derived from it, which placed a European "race" at the pinnacle of civilization, and eternally so.[37] Indeed, the "uplift" of the "Negro" race, according to the terms of this logic, provided the ground for the early conception of his life work.[38] Yet Du Bois also records that he early on began to question this system of distinction. His privileged example, that by which he was led to question this racialized logic, recognized through a mode of reflection that we are certainly within rights to remark as "second-sight" (*first of all existential and given in the form of an autobiographical reflection*) was the problem of *intermixture*. I thus would remark this latter term here. In so doing, I propose to reinscribe it in a theoretically provisional, apparently strategic, manner, which yet follows a certain necessity entailed in any practical theoretical intervention that would solicit the whole of the epistemic (or apparently ontological) structure that is at stake here.[39]

Along with the first theme of Du Bois's concept of the example, which we have explored above, the character and implication of the concept of intermixture, is the second theme that I wish to emphasize in this chapter.

Du Bois describes two provocations that lead him to question the logic of racial opposition. First, citing a shuttling instability of the grounds claimed for the distinctions proposed by social Darwinism, phrenology, and degenerationist speculation, Du Bois notes that he began to question the scientificity or truth claimed for the object of description. "The first thing that brought me to my senses in all this racial discussion was the continuous change in the proofs and arguments advanced" (*Dusk*, 99). The persistent change in the *epistemological* grounds claimed for the object, at the very least, made the object itself, something understood as "race," problematic (ambiguous, not readily susceptible to evidence). Second, and far more important, according to the emphasis of his elaboration in this text, this epistemological ambiguity, when combined with a certain *experience* brought the concept of race into radical question for Du Bois. "All this theory, however, was disturbed by certain facts in America, and by my European experience. Despite everything, race lines were not fixed and fast" (*Dusk*, 101). Du Bois specifies this nonoppositional heterogeneity in two ways. (1) There is the motif of internal differentiation, or internal dissociation, the subatomic, if you will. "Within

the Negro group especially there were people of all colors" (*Dusk*, 101). Du
Bois elaborates, in the sentences following the one just quoted, an acute
recognition and negotiation of the paradoxes that lay in wait for anyone
who would attempt a coherent response to the logic of racial distinction. A
simple declaration of neutrality with regard to a "racial" distinction (and all
social distinction would be at least symbolic and hence semiotic) *without a
systematic strategy for challenging the existing hierarchy of value* would both
(a) leave that hierarchy in place, and (b) intensify its force by reinstating its
governing schema, the logic of homogeneity, without recognizing it as such,
because racial distinction of any kind (no matter how pragmatically fluid)
is founded, in its deepest epistemic root, upon the logic of opposition and,
hence, is always hierarchical. (Even its semiotic operation, although susceptible to displacement, takes resource to the *effectiveness* of a distinction in
the *instance*, with or without proclaimed scientific authority.) In order to
bring such a system into question, according whatever purpose or in terms
of whatever order of generality, a difference, and especially the irreducible
radicality of the possibility of such, must be adduced. "Then too, there were
plenty of my colored friends who resented my ultra 'race' loyalty and ridi-
culed it. They pointed out that I was not a 'Negro' but a mulatto; that I was
not a Southerner but a Northerner, and my object was to be an American
and not a Negro; that race distinctions must go. I agreed with this in part
and as an ideal, but I saw it leading to inner racial distinction in the colored
group. I resented the defensive mechanism of avoiding too dark companions
in order to escape notice and discrimination in public. As a sheer matter
of taste I wanted the color of my group to be visible. I hotly championed
the inclusion of two black schoolmates whose names were not usually on
the invitation list to our social affairs" (*Dusk*, 101–2).[40] The set of paradoxes
inscribed in this passage mark the coordinates of an ethical challenge that
frames all of Du Bois's formulations of the problematic of racial distinction.
This ensemble of "racial" paradoxes also inscribes a quite general problematic.[41] (2) There is also the motif of external association, of the crossing of
boundaries (in every sense of the word), a form of interlacing. "In Europe
my friendships and close contact with white folk made my own ideas waver.
The eternal walls between races did not seem so stern and exclusive. I began
to emphasize the cultural aspects of race" (*Dusk*, 102).[42]

Du Bois inaugurates the telling of his family history with this phrase:
"There is, of course, nothing more fascinating than the question of the various types of mankind and their intermixture" (*Dusk*, 103). Yet he suggests in

this text published in 1940 that in the Americas, "where we have had the most astonishing modern mixture of human types, scientific study of the results and circumstances of this intermixture has not only lagged but been almost non-existent. We have not only not studied race and race mixture in America, but we have tried almost by legal process to stop such study" (*Dusk*, 103). We do not have to assume that only a utilitarian motivation is at work in the process of racial distinction to recognize (1) the distinct historical generality that Du Bois attributes to its functioning, pertinent to our entire modernity, and (2) the way in which he understands it to inscribe scholarship in its folds as well as to be susceptible to description by scholarship. Du Bois writes:

> Ever since the African slave trade and before the rise of modern biology and sociology, we have been afraid in America that scientific study in this direction might lead to conclusions with which we were loath to agree; and this fear was in reality because the economic foundation of the modern world was based on the recognition and preservation of so-called racial distinctions. In accordance with this, not only Negro slavery could be justified but the Asiatic coolie profitably used and the labor classes in white countries kept in their places by low wage. (*Dusk*, 103)

Although he never explicitly makes a declaration in the terms we are proposing here, the strategic importance for Du Bois of the problem of intermixture in the desedimentation of the problem of racial distinction is registered in every inflection of the passage just quoted. In the context of a global system, colonialism and its aftermath, of proclaimed oppositional (racial) distinctions, intermixture as the very organization of all that we may call "modernity," calls into question the logic of that system.[43]

Although phenomenally ubiquitous, in the Americas recognition of intermixture has been suppressed, by, for example, whites *and* blacks. "On the one hand, the white folk have bitterly resented even a hint of the facts of this intermingling; while black folk have recoiled in natural hesitation and affected disdain in admitting what they know" (*Dusk*, 104). Du Bois then marks this response and a counterresponse in his autobiography:

> I early began to take a direct interest in my own family as a group and became curious as to that physical descent which so long I had taken for granted quite unquestioningly. But I did not at first think of any but my Negro ancestors. I knew little and cared less of the white forebears of my father. But this chauvinism gradually changed. (*Dusk*, 103)

Given (1) the operability of (oppositional) racial distinctions in the modern world, (2) what Du Bois considered to be the paucity of studies of "racial" "intermixture" relative to its phenomenal ubiquity, and (3) especially, the capacity of "intermixture" to overthrow the entire oppositional logic by which racial distinctions were conceptually organized (certainly in America) at the turn of the century, Du Bois considered the study of intermixture of signal importance. But, to arrive at such an insight or recognition, Du Bois had to first desediment his own inscription within the logic of racial distinction. He had to formulate a conceptual change with regard to himself. As we have noted above, the pivotal pathway by which he was able to produce such a formulation was a form of "experience" that I have described as "second-sight," produced by a certain position within the practice of racial distinction. It led him to recognize the nonabsoluteness of racial distinction in practice. The innovation of Du Bois's in-sight or double sight was that he not only took it as a basis for resituating his personal understanding and behavior, but also he recognized its general relevance for the way in which the entire system of racial distinctions were organized in the "modern" or "colonial" world. To recognize and situate the heterogeneous structure of the Americas, the modern world, and identity as such, Du Bois had to first recognize and situate his own heterogeneous origins, the nonreducible heterogeneity of his own constitution.

It is at this multiply layered juncture that Du Bois situates the telling of his autobiographical problematic, as a telling example. Du Bois proposes a genealogy of his family. "It is for this reason that it has occurred to me just here to *illustrate* the way in which Africa and Europe have been united in my family" (*Dusk*, 103, emphasis mine). Then, the crucial claim of the *value* of *this* example, its phenomenal generality, with regard to the *historical* field in which it operates: "There is nothing unusual about this interracial history. It has been duplicated thousands of times. I am, therefore, relating the history of my family and centering it around my maternal great-great-grandfather, Tom Burghardt, and my paternal grandfather, Alexander Du Bois (*Dusk*, 104)."[44] This narrative provides a genealogical account of Du Bois's family for five generations on his maternal side and eight on his paternal side.[45] What is distinctive about this narrative in terms of the strategic method and problematic that we have been mapping in this chapter is that Du Bois has recalled his paternal genealogy, which he had formerly set aside because of its heritage of intermixture. In this recollection he places it alongside his maternal genealogy, the genealogy which records the matrix of kinship in which Du Bois was actually raised. As early as the fourteenth chapter of *Souls*, Du Bois had privileged his maternal line, emphasizing both maternity over and against

W. E. B. Du Bois—Paternal Genealogy

1600

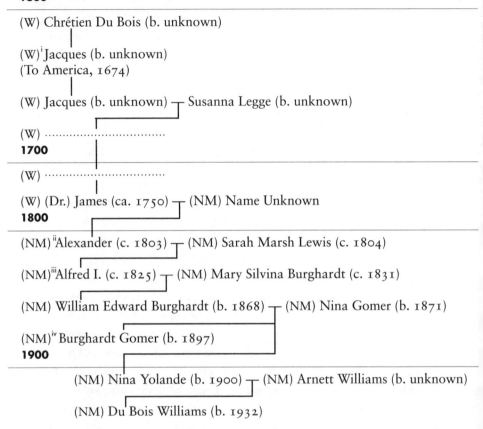

(W) Chrétien Du Bois (b. unknown)

(W)[i] Jacques (b. unknown)
(To America, 1674)

(W) Jacques (b. unknown) ⟶ Susanna Legge (b. unknown)

(W) ....
1700

(W) ....

(W) (Dr.) James (ca. 1750) ⟶ (NM) Name Unknown
1800

(NM) [ii]Alexander (c. 1803) ⟶ (NM) Sarah Marsh Lewis (c. 1804)

(NM)[iii]Alfred I. (c. 1825) ⟶ (NM) Mary Silvina Burghardt (c. 1831)

(NM) William Edward Burghardt (b. 1868) ⟶ (NM) Nina Gomer (b. 1871)

(NM)[iv] Burghardt Gomer (b. 1897)
1900

(NM) Nina Yolande (b. 1900) ⟶ (NM) Arnett Williams (b. unknown)

(NM) Du Bois Williams (b. 1932)

Footnotes:

i Apparently a brother Louis also removed to America (from France), but his subsequent family line is unknown.

ii A brother John was also born from the same parentage. His birth year is unknown and he died young, in his twenties, with no known progeny.

iii An elder sister, Augusta, was born in 1823, from the same parentage.

iv Du Bois does not indicate his son, Burghardt Gomer Du Bois (1897–1899), on any of the family genealogical notes or charts that he produced during this time period, the late 1930s.

Legend Note:

"W" indicates "White" person; "NM" indicates, Negroes or Mulattoes, per Du Bois's annotations; and note that the term "mulatto" may be understood to indicate African, European, and Native American ancestry.

Acknowledgment: These charts are adapted from a hand-drawn family genealogy of W. E. B. Du Bois dating from the late 1930s which can be found in the Papers of W. E. B. Du Bois, Special Collections and University Archives, Series 3, Subseries C, MS 312, W. E. B. Du Bois Library, University of Massachusetts Amherst. (A copy of this handscript can also be found in the microfilm edition of these papers, *The Papers of W. E. B. Du Bois, 1803 (1877–1963) 1979*, Sanford, N.C.: Microfilming Corp. of America, 1980, on Reel 89, Frame 609.) It serves as a reference here by the kind permission of the David Graham Du Bois Memorial Trust, all rights reserved.

W. E. B. Du Bois—Maternal Genealogy

1600

1700

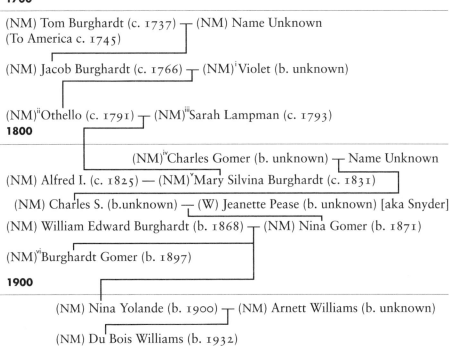

(NM) Tom Burghardt (c. 1737) ┬ (NM) Name Unknown
(To America c. 1745)

(NM) Jacob Burghardt (c. 1766) ┬ (NM)[i]Violet (b. unknown)

(NM)[ii]Othello (c. 1791) ┬ (NM)[iii]Sarah Lampman (c. 1793)
1800

(NM)[iv]Charles Gomer (b. unknown) ┬ Name Unknown
(NM) Alfred I. (c. 1825) — (NM)[v]Mary Silvina Burghardt (c. 1831)

(NM) Charles S. (b.unknown) ── (W) Jeanette Pease (b. unknown) [aka Snyder]

(NM) William Edward Burghardt (b. 1868) ┬ (NM) Nina Gomer (b. 1871)

(NM)[vi]Burghardt Gomer (b. 1897)

1900

(NM) Nina Yolande (b. 1900) ┬ (NM) Arnett Williams (b. unknown)

(NM) Du Bois Williams (b. 1932)

Footnotes:

i W. E. B. Du Bois's maternal family lore claimed that this person was either born in West Africa or of African parents only recently arrived in the colonies. She is usually understood as the source of the "African" song to which Du Bois famously refers in *The Souls of Black Folk* (Du Bois, 1903: 254, chap. 14, para. 7). Elizabeth "Mum Bett" Freeman (c. 1742) is noted by Du Bois in *Dusk of Dawn* (see next footnote) as the second wife of Jacob Burghardt, but the eventuality of a second marriage remains uncertain.

ii From the same parentage (Othello Burghardt and Sarah Lampman), the siblings of Mary Silvina, Du Bois's mother, produced many offspring, as did the offspring of her paternal uncle, Ira Burghardt. Several extensive hand drawn lists of this maternal genealogy for Du Bois can be found in the Du Bois Papers as previously cited. Du Bois describes briefly the size of this kin network in chapter five of *Dusk of Dawn* (Du Bois, 1940: 112–14).

iii Du Bois describes her in *Dusk of Dawn* as "probably the child of a Dutchman perhaps with Indian blood" (Du Bois, 1940: 112).

iv The Gomer line is the paternal line of Du Bois's first wife, Nina Gomer Du Bois.

v Mary Silvina gave birth to a son, Adelbert Burghardt, born in 1862, most likely with a Charles Craig, who was probably a Great Barrington resident, as later claimed by Adelbert (Lewis 1993: 24). He was thus an elder brother of W. E. B. Du Bois. However, he is indicated by the latter only in the unpublished genealogical lists of the Othello Burghardt line, under his mother Mary Silvina, in the same generation as W. E. B. Du Bois and not in the published chart included in *Dusk of Dawn*.

vi Du Bois does not indicate his son, Burghardt Gomer Du Bois (1897–1899), on any of the family genealogical notes or charts that he produced during this time period, the late 1930s.

paternity and the supposed African provenance of that line. He repeats this "African" reference in *Dusk* (*Dusk*, 114–15). Yet it should be noted that Du Bois approaches both the maternal and the paternal line under the heading of patriarchy. On the one hand, we recognize here the replication of an old and tenacious sexist kinship discourse, that must be brought into question. On the other hand, part of the value of Du Bois's narrative is its ironic effect, its paradoxical desedimentation of paternity, in particular that form which would appear within a horizon marked in the Americas by the idea of race as unmarked, so-called White paternity. By desedimenting his "mixed" paternity, he raises questions about any so-called pure genealogy (especially as such might be understood across the history of the American South, the Caribbean, and South America, in the wake of the history of modern slavery, under the hegemonic notion of the paternal as a figure of "whiteness"), and ultimately any notion of "pure" origin in general.[46] Hence, because the desedimentation of Du Bois's paternal genealogy allows us to negotiate all the effects to which we have been alluding, for reasons of strategy and economy, I focus in a thematic sense in the reading that follows on that aspect of his narrative. Perhaps ironically, because although my reading is partial, I believe that the implications of the track it outlines or follows in Du Bois's discourse are quite general. Its effects are not partial. Indeed, it is not a disavowal of the maternal that leads us to focus on the paternal, for it is precisely the force of the maternal in the paternal line, marked by a certain absence, a certain X perhaps, that may be remarked and can lead us in the elucidation of the effects that we are attempting to bring into relief.

Du Bois focuses the inaugurating moment of his narrative around his paternal great-grandfather, Dr. James Du Bois, a physician, landholder, and slaveholder, based in Long Cay in the Bahama Islands, who was a fifth-generation descendant of a French Huguenot from near Lille in the north of France, whom W. E. B. Du Bois has come to know as Chrétien Du Bois. Let us read a bit of the narrative:

> My paternal great-grandfather, Dr. James Du Bois was white and descended from Chrétien Du Bois who was a French Huguenot farmer and perhaps artisan and resided at Wicres near Lille in French Flanders. It is doubtful if he had any ancestors among the nobility, although his white American descendants love to think so. He had two, possibly three, sons of whom Louis and Jacques came to America to escape religious persecution. Jacques went from France first to Leiden in the Netherlands, where he was married and had several children, including

a second Jacques or James. In 1674 that family came to America and set-
tled at Kingston, New York. James Du Bois appears in the Du Bois family genealogy as a descendant of Jacques in the fifth generation, although
the exact line of descent is not clear; but my grandfather's written testimony establishes that James was a physician and a landholder along the
Hudson and in the West Indies. He was born in 1750, or later. He may
have been a loyalist refugee. One such refugee, Isaac Du Bois, was given a
grant of five hundred acres in Eleuthera [in the Bahamas] after the Revolutionary War. The career of Dr. James Du Bois was chiefly as a plantation proprietor and slave owner in the Bahama Islands with his head-
quarters at Long Cay. Cousins of his named Gilbert also had plantations
near. (*Dusk*, 105; interpolation mine)[47]

The first pivotal reference of the narrative occurs here. Dr. James Du Bois
"never married, but had one of his slaves as his common-law wife, a small
brown-skinned woman born on the island" (*Dusk*, 105). Du Bois does not
know a proper name for this woman, who would in its eventuality become
his paternal great-grandmother. Du Bois records, marks, but does not explicitly re-mark this absence. She appears, if she can be said to appear at all, as an
absence, or under the sign of absence, an invisible X, perhaps.

Even as we cannot and should not try to simply narrativize her into existence, and Du Bois's text is noticeably reticent on this level, we must and
should remark the effects of this apparently absent figure within the organization of the entire problem, problematic, and problematization that we
are following in Du Bois's discourse, that is the track that we seem to find
therein.

It requires us to step back from the text for just a moment and remark this
juncture within our discussion.

Without producing itself as an arche or being susceptible to such a proclamation on the part of one who would follow it, or for one who might attempt
to outline its trace(s), it nonetheless renders a solicitation that cannot be
simply evacuated in fact or in concept. We can recall here that the figural
figure that is no figure, which thus might perhaps best be remarked by way
of the difficulties it poses for even a metaphoric approach—as beneath and
between the ocean and the bottom, or as perhaps the remains of a burning,
to interlace the tracks of multiple histories and historicities of "our" epoch,
of the modern—apparent absence can still solicit. For, even sedimentation at
its most ponderous can only proceed by way of a dispersal of forces along its
fault lines, relations of force, whether genealogical or geological, and whatever the patience of the duration. Even if only traced by way of "the elbow

to get to the thumb," the figural effects of lability within paternity would always bear their mark, that is give, even in withdrawal, perhaps.[48] Here I will circumstantially colloquialize this as the X of the chromosomal kind. And most certainly we can also speak of subatomic force here. Or, alternately, we can recall that X of the shuttling signature that remains of the unnamed and unnameable Negro or African American slaves of the four centuries up to the nineteenth, only iconically recollected at the juncture of emancipation when the ex-slave soon to become the so-called freedman, could mark only X for a name, to indicate or proclaim her, or his, status.

It is thus that Du Bois's form of quotation of the "sorrow songs" (as he calls them in the closing chapter of *Souls*), wherein only graphic marks, signaling pitch and cadence, with no "words" as such, verticality with the most minimal horizontality, nonetheless, marks the production of resonances of cavernous or reverberating capacity. And, here, in this context the work of Cecil Taylor can assist us, for it adduces an unheard order of resonance for us—even as the diss-harmonic harmonic "sound" of "one" note to which we referred above in the Anacrusis to this study—as a protocol of writing practiced as a thinking. The way of this gesture of "quotation" by Du Bois might then be understood to respond to this force and its exigency. On a whole other register, so to speak, we can now remark that we must respond to a measureless silence that sounds without sounding, which, yet and *thereby*, can be resounded. For it solicits our letting be of the passive in generation as the general possibility of genesis. For such is at the very emergence, the unconditionality of its form of announcement, of the African American problematic. In this way, it can also be understood to place at stake a certain exorbitance to thought that takes as its simply privileged guide the aegis of being. It is in this order of practice and work that Taylor's example guides us here.[49]

With these generous precedents in practical theoretical affirmation of possibility in mind—Du Bois's and Taylor's—we can now return to the letter of the text at hand.

For, according to the narrative, this unnameable, invisible difference can be understood to produce a radical displacement of identity. Two sons were born, Alexander and John.

> Alexander, my grandfather, was born in 1803, and about 1810, possibly because of the death of the mother, the father brought both these boys to America and planned to give them the education of gentlemen. They were white enough in appearance to give no inkling of their African

descent. They were entered in the private Episcopal school at Cheshire, Connecticut, which still exists there and has trained many famous men. (*Dusk*, 105–6)

We could remark this unmarked phrasing "gentleman," to perhaps amend it to read "[white] gentlemen." For, at this moment the second pivotal event of the narrative occurs. It accentuates the motif that we are following in Du Bois's narrative. "Dr. James Du Bois used often to visit his sons there, but about 1812, on his return from a visit, he had a stroke of apoplexy and died. He left no will and his estate descended to a cousin" (*Dusk*, 106). The boys were removed from school, bound out as apprentices, and cut off from the "white Du Bois family." That connection was never renewed.

These two narrative moments set the stage for a richly paradoxical meditation by (W. E. B.) Du Bois focused on the process of racial inscription borne by his paternal grandfather, Alexander Du Bois.

> Alexander Du Bois thus started with a good common school and perhaps some high school training and with the instincts of a gentleman of his day. Naturally he passed through inner turmoil. He became a rebel, bitter at his lot in life, resentful at being classed as a Negro and yet implacable in his attitude toward whites. . . . If Alexander Du Bois, following the footsteps of Alexander Hamilton, had come from the West Indies to the United States, stayed with the white group and married and begotten children among them, anyone in after years who had suggested his Negro descent would have been unable to prove it and quite possibly would have been laughed to scorn, or sued for libel. . . . Alexander Du Bois did differently from Hamilton. He married into the colored group and his oldest son allied himself with a Negro clan but four generations removed from Africa. (*Dusk*, 106–7)[50]

We will not follow this paternal narrative any further except to note two facts that we consider pertinent. First, in the part of his narrative that immediately follows the passage that I have just quoted, Du Bois describes his grandfather's negotiation of the system of racial distinctions in the United States. Initially, it seems Alexander attempted to maintain a position of openness in the negotiation of his "racial" identity. For example, he joined a nonsegregated church, but eventually he left this congregation to join a segregated church movement, perhaps, Du Bois surmises, due to some extreme racial insult. Second, of the account of the maternal side of Du Bois's genealogy, beginning with his maternal great-great grandfather Tom Burghardt (whom Du Bois describes as "an African Negro"), the central fact that bears upon our analysis is that, as Du Bois writes, "I was brought up in the Burghardt clan and this fact determined largely my life and 'race.' The white relationships and connections were quite lost and indeed unknown until long years later" (*Dusk*, 109–15).

Du Bois's narrative of the inscription of his grandfather as a supposed racial subject offers references useful for reflection with regard to the inflections of racial distinction that it sediments in its telling. I focus all to briefly on two aspects that I consider decisive: the relationship between choice and system or classification and displacement of classification. Du Bois's discourse itself remarks these aspects for us.

First, choice is only coherent as system or structure. Du Bois suggests that Alexander, by emigrating to the United States, could have had a certain limited flexibility in his negotiation of the supposed lines of race or the so-called color-line due to his physical appearance. Yet theoretically we can propose quite generally that even this apparent choice is governed by the system of racial distinctions operative at the time. At this juncture we can recognize the operation of the structure, the logic of a system of racial distinctions that Du Bois describes—it takes reference in the presumed fundamental depth of an oppositional distinction. For, we can recognize the systemic governance of Alexander's apparent choice in this paradoxical truism. The decisive question is not whether Alexander ostensibly had a choice. Rather, what matters for our considerations, the problem of the Negro as a problem of theoretical reflection, is that the choice is between being socially understood as either one or the other, that one cannot coherently, according to the operative systemic practices, simultaneously assume a position that would claim to be both. And then too, perhaps even more radically, that one—such as Alexander Du Bois—could not and still cannot be socially and historically understood as neither.

Secondly, however, we must yet affirm, again in a theoretical register, that the operative categories do not simply preexist the immanent formation of the subject position, or even the putative subject, of such distinction. Alexander had to be produced as a certain subject. For example, he had to be either "schooled" (as a "[White] gentleman" or as a "[mulatto] apprentice [shoemaker]") or de-schooled (as a prepubescent mulatto boy or as a "former" White-gentleman-in-the-making). He had to be made, and in this making the historicity of the "system" is marked. It is rendered by way of its constitutive iterability both reproductive and yet open to a movement of possible transformation or contestation. This latter capacity acquires its performative possibility, and a certain transformation is indeed irreducible, because the system of distinction or practices that announce it must constitutively shutter itself from its own most original properties, its very possibility. This originary organization is the structure of intermixture—to maintain this insufficient metaphor here as a form of paleonymic theoretical practice—which is always already afoot, always previous. For no mark, no social reference, and certainly no supposed social and historical form of *identity* or *difference*, can be rendered, nor can such appear as coherent—that is, manifest at all—without this constitutive detour through the other. Even for the most self-reflexive claim to repleteness this must occur for such gesture to consolidate and reproduce itself. That is to say this structure of intermixture remains operative and functioning, sedimenting its irreducible difference, its X, in the very space of supposed or projected purity.

It is the paradoxical play of this X that Du Bois, in a figure of irony, desediments in his autobiographical genealogy. Hence the desedimentative force of Du Bois's narrative is such that it has the logical force to overthrow the very concept of race that appears to coordinate its problematic. The possibility of his genealogy and the structure that organizes it, the structure of intermixture, indicate that there is no stability of distinction at the root. There is no absolute criteria that would delimit Du Bois's grandfather as either black or white. Such is likewise for Du Bois.

The further paradox is that socially defined as a Negro, Du Bois was somehow led to recognize not only the ultimate nonpertinence of that specific form or register of social designation, but of all such social and historical designation. As he tells it, he was guided by a kind of "second-sight."[51]

Thus, by its fidelity to its theme and the form of its telling, the autobiographical, Du Bois's discourse, it seems to me, comes upon a rather profound and profoundly original structure. Stated at the level of the subject, and this mode of thematizing its constitution, Du Bois desediments the fact that according to his most intimate genealogy *the other* is, quite literally, *himself.* And, this is *true* in a double sense: (1) he is other than himself, his subject position fashioned through the other, by the structure or play of a certain X; and (2) that which he thought was *the other, is he, himself.* This originary structure would be *as true for a white as for a black* Du Bois.

Although Du Bois is concerned to specify the relevance to the Americas of his autobiographical exploration, it would, by analogy at least, question any notion of hereditary or genealogical purity regardless of the historical domain in which such was proposed. From this standpoint, an understanding of the social implication of this metaphoric theme of intermixture would not be historically delimitable to only the Americas or to a discrete idea of colonial context. Further, I have been suggesting in this chapter that Du Bois's discourse also formulates a structure, one that we have provisionally called "intermixture," following his discourse, which would be general to the operation of identity or difference as such, and hence not simply delimitable to any particular historical field.[52] Rather, it would allow that historical field to open, as such, and with the configuration original to it.[53]

The Figuration of the Example

There is a valence in Du Bois's discourse that encourages, to the extent that it does not state, the generalization I am proposing of the formulation of the problematic that I have outlined therein. Indeed, if we return to the opening chapter of *Dusk*, with regard to the *historical* generalization that I have proposed (the suggestion that the problematics of the constitution of the African American subject might be relevant to the constitution of colonial subject positions in general, and those operating in their historical wake, and in particular to a "white" or "European" or "Euro-American" subject or position), Du Bois explicitly highlights this distinctive valence, in a way that in itself could authorize our preoccupation with the generalizing aspects of his discourse. We must note here that this generalization is produced in an autobiographical writing that proposes to situate—that is, to some extent give an account of—the status of the autobiographical. Du Bois outlines an itinerary of desedimentation and affirmation that remains the fecund site of our responsibility.[54] *I would propose no name for such a position or disposition, as such.* Our responsibility remains as the rigorous thinking of the generality described therein.

> As I grew older, and saw the peoples of the land and of the world, the problem changed from a simple thing of color, to a broader, deeper matter of social condition: to millions of folk born of dark slaves, with the slave heritage in mind and home; millions of people spawned in compulsory ignorance; to a whole problem of the uplift of the darker races. (*Dusk*, 5)

The palpable effects of the force of this social distinction ("the problem") as Du Bois describes it is enough to blight the eye, to render the spirit jaundiced, to set conviction on a path of forceful revenge. Yet we must tease out an implication that would authorize an overrunning of all the embedded oppositions of our racialized socius while nonetheless positioning our sense of possibility at the fecund conjuncture of responsibility and generosity. What we may find is that the *same* structures that position certain historical subjects under the back-breaking and discouraging violence of enforced racialized subordination (for example, that of an African American or Negro subject), the devolution as "ultratranscendental" structure that marks its possibility and the historical structures that organize its specific motivation (and the distinction of these two structures would not be a true one, whose functioning could be logically regulated), *also* produce another experience of violence, another distinctive historical subject positioning (for example, that of a Euro-American or white subject), whose most distinctive sign may be that it unfolds under the cloak of normalcy, that is, as an unmarked sign.[55]

The thought here can be schematized, perhaps too elliptically, in the following way: if one would mark the force inscribing the first historical experience of (racialized) violence by the name the force of the double, then that force which inscribes the second historical experience of (racialized) violence is what may be remarked as the double force of the force of the double. If there is such a movement as the force of the double, then it is, itself, most precisely, at least, double. And if at least double, never only double. (This thematic is traced along a different ridge in the closing chapter of this study.) What is registered here is the strange and powerful play of a certain asymmetry and symmetry.[56] The point is that while retaining the historical specificity of its topical concern with the experience of African Americans, a demonstration like Du Bois's also demonstrates the processes through which a Euro-American or White subject is constituted.[57] The crucial distinction, of course, is that they are historically positioned differently with respect to those structures, particularly the specific character of the *violence* of this process. Yet they nonetheless are marked and constituted as they are in their very emergence by *the very same process*, in the movement of racial distinction. By this theme we can recognize two generalized implications of Du Bois's demonstration. The structural aspects of the process that is brought into relief by his discourse, those aspects constitutive of his subject position as an African American, (1) are certainly generally relevant to discussions of *any* modern historical identity or form of social existence as it acquires its specification under new forms of differentiation or renderings of sameness, and (2) provide a rigorous pathway for the elucidation of a heterogeneous structure as operative at every level of generality of such figures of difference, of the organization of their identity, or the forms of lived existence. Hence, his thought proposes the possibility and necessity of a desedimentation of the root presuppositions of canonical philosophical conceptions of identity, or a traditional interpretation of them (still widely afoot even when categorically and hence naively disavowed). Likewise, it could overthrow the current simplistic engagements with the hegemony of an essentialist understanding of difference or sameness, when elaborated with respect to *the openness of its style*, that is to say, its autobiographical mode, its strategic decisions and negotiations, that is, its affirmation of the passive in generation, that is, as given here, the implication of the general possibility of "intermixture."[58]

I have tried to give an account of that peculiar problem of the double, of the enigmatic movements *of* between we might say, at work in Du Bois's text, the specificity of this conjuncture, at once individual and general, historical and (ultra) transcendental, Afro and Euro (black and white), to which he calls attention when he writes on the one hand of "my problem of human difference, of the color line, of social degradation," and on the other hand of the unavoidable force of the practice of racial difference "for me and many millions, who with me have had their lives shaped by this course of events" (*Dusk*, 6, 7). Both this problem and this force are simultaneously historical and "(ultra) transcendental," inscribing, in this way, if they mark any part thereof, an entire historical field without partiality. Thus, as I have suggested, the persons whose form of being is implicated in such a manner surely could not be limited simply to a *given* identity. Although the differences of specific inhabited subject positions must always be given an account. Du Bois's methodological practice, his strategic choice of an "autobiographical" account of a concept, of the practices organized around a concept of race, proves remarkably resourceful in elucidating and elaborating such a general account.

What is striking is that this familial demonstration produces effects at all levels of conceptual generality: it displaces on a theoretical level a logic of racial distinction pertinent to our entire historical modernity, but it can also be shown to displace more formally the proclaimed governing pertinence of a traditional philosophical schema, a logic of opposition, by which identity and difference in general have been understood in their pertinence to man or the human and, in this order of generality, which I have called the "ultratranscendental" in this chapter, it would by analogy be conceptually pertinent to the way we talk of any identity or difference (for example, gender, religious, political, and so forth, and perhaps especially "cultural").

Thus, although we are, so to speak, looking at Du Bois, looking at his own constitution as a subject, this is anything but an itinerary in simple self-reflection. It refers to what Gayatri Spivak once called for as an act of "de-identification": a sort of self-reflexive account that is precisely a referring of the subject to those structures that mark and organize its active emergence. In her own autobiographical gesture that remains timely, it seems to me, in our own untimely time, Spivak writes:

> I'm interested in a sort of deconstructive homeopathy, a deconstructing of identity by identities. . . . I believe that the way to counter the authority of either objective disinterested positioning or the attitude of there being no author (and these two opposed positions legitimize each other) is by thinking of oneself as an example of certain kinds of historical, psycho-sexual narratives that one must in fact use, however micrologically, in order to do deontological work in the humanities. When one represents oneself in such a way, it becomes, curiously enough, a deidentification of oneself, a claiming of an identity from a text that comes from some-where else.[59]

Spivak can be understood to perform her own masterful "reformation of mastery" in an interlocution with Derrida's discourse, to borrow and performatively operate a phrasing put forth in Houston Baker's thought of African Americanist practices.[60] Spivak generalizes an appeal here, recalling, in a contemporary discourse the order of generality that we have tried to elucidate in Du Bois's autobiographical practice.

> A mother tongue is something that has a history before we are born. We are inserted into it; it has the possibility of being activated by what can be colloquially called motives. Therefore, although unmotivated its not capricious. We are inserted into it, and, without intent, we "make it our own." We intend with in it; we critique intentions within it, we play with it through signification as well as reference; and then we leave it as much with out intent for the use of others after our deaths. To an extent, the way in which one conceives of oneself as representative or as an example of something is this awareness that what is one's own, supposedly what is proper to one, has a history. That history is unmotivated but not capricious and is larger in outline than we are, and I think that this [such self-representation] is quite different from the idea of talking about oneself.[61]

Indeed, I have intended to suggest just how different from simple self-reflexivity, from solipsism in general, is such an elucidation of the autobiographical example.

Yet, within this vortex, as Hortense Spillers has so ably and decisively outlined for us, the historicity of a figure such as Du Bois—white, black, Negro, American, European, African, Caribbean, continental, descendant of slaves, descendant of free persons, and so forth—must be placed within the great network of the historicity of the Atlantic basin that marks the incipit of an originary modernity. Within that reference the material symbolic terrain in which one can be announced to oneself takes shape as a treacherous horizon of inhabitation. As was the case for Du Bois's paternal ancestors of two generations before his arrival, there is often in the historicities of modern slavery "a hideous paradox"— of the male progenitor of children with an enslaved mother, as the owner of slavers, thus attenuating in the extreme the "cultural courtesy" that is the practice of fatherhood. However, at a deeper register still,

> Because African American women experienced uncertainty regarding their infants' lives in the historic situation, gendering, in its coeval reference to African-American women, *insinuates* an implicit and unresolved puzzle both within current feminist discourse *and* within those discursive communities that investigate the entire problematics of culture.[62]

It is here then that one places the infamous "'*partus sequitur ventrem*'"—the legal principle according to which "the condition of the slave mother is 'forever entailed on all her remotest posterity.'"[63] It is in this sense perhaps that one should notate Du Bois's avowed reserve toward his paternal line at the inception of his itinerary (as noted in *Dusk of Dawn*). For, buried within that line, as it were, was this originary text of disavowal, of the slave mother, as the figure of his great-grandmother—and we cannot say that it would not be so further back still, if there is such. So, across his itinerary Du Bois can now be understood to have performed a complex practice of a general affirmation: to at once deny and affirm, respectively, a father right and a mother right, across the early stages; to also affirm and deny, respectively, a long deferred mother right and an always already claimed and yet disavowed father right of the great-grand ancestry, across the later stages (within the long temporality of the torsion that makes of this gesture a slower than slow realization, perhaps always for any of us). That is to say, his way effects a denial of a disavowal by way of a strategic affirmation. I propose this gesture as radical.

We may thus reinscribe Du Bois's passage of reflection here with the diacritical annotations rendered available to us by Spillers, that is, offer a certain affirmative response to a certain form of bequest given within this historicity as radical in our time. With the setting aside of the *pater* as given "mimetic" horizon, by both violence and disavowal, and the apparition of the *mater* as such, by way of its projection toward another possible practical synthesis of world in which the maternal might be the name of possibility, this historicity offers for progeny understood under the sign of the masculine (but, this may also be understood to supplement such functioning under the sign of the feminine), "the specific occasion to learn *who* the female is within itself, the infant child who bears life against the could-be-fateful gamble, against the odds of pulverization and murder, including her own."[64] Yet this would be true for either a black or white Du Bois, or for one announced or reannounced within any of the *given* forms of engenderment, or a figure announced as of this historicity who might yet be understood according to another heading or other headings altogether.

Thus the paradox of becoming other, of becoming oneself as even an encompassment of the other, that takes shape as the way of existence, thought, and practice in this domain, is not produced by way of a speculative disposition toward an idea or an ultimate whole. It is rather in fact a referral to a constitutive order of the possibility of sensibility, being, and existence. This complex passage and way of inhabitation remains for us, here, now, only by way of this mark, this remainder, perhaps, *of* X.

If so, we can now notice on another register of discourse that Du Bois's practice should be understood to resolutely resist the reduction of the subject of historicity to a figure of the simple same. This is so even if only by the form of his reflection, for the form of the autobiographical is variegation itself and as given here is the very claim of its content. Du Bois seems able to recognize by this general style, far better than some interventions since his time: that there is only a field of historical determination if there is such a *problem* as an "overdetermined" subject or movement of subjectivation.[65] Du Bois recognizes by his practice if not by a declaration, that sense, historicity, especially as epistemological sense, that which is often called truth or understanding, may *remain* only because it is at risk and open in something like the problem of subjectivation or the rendering of the problem of the formation of a putative subjectity. As example, of a problem, Du Bois's practice solicits *us*—whomever might be such—to look at ourselves in a radically *other* way.[66] This is the figure of the X. In the apparently most simple, yet, in all truth, exceedingly complex terms, this remains *the line* for contemporary thought in our time.

CHAPTER THREE

THE SOULS OF AN EX-WHITE MAN

W. E. B. Du Bois and the Biography of John Brown

For Herbert and Fay Aptheker, am memoriam[1]

The Sight of Death

Death always comes at least twice to one whose life is marked by greatness, once in life and again in biography. And, more radically, if death is at least double, then it most assuredly is never only double. One death always begets another death. If death, however, is understood first of all or only as loss, then the rich drama, the generosity, of this incessant doubling will most assuredly remain closed up and withdrawn. The difficulty of tracking some of the modalities of this irruptive doubling of death always shows itself in the scene of biography.

There is perhaps no better example of this generosity of the double, of the excessive giving that arises within the space of absence, than the narrative of the death or deaths, or lives, of John Brown. It is this enigma that sets the stage or scene of W. E. B. Du Bois's telling of this tragic and beautifully difficult story.[2]

It is this second death, of course, that must occupy our attention, for it is within its unfolding that the first is named, maintained, and given meaning or a kind of livelihood. John Brown, at least, will always lead a double life within the space of this second death, the death of biography: once as a friend of the Negro in life, and again as their martyr in death. Both stories are wont to be told enough. For, the telling of the story of Brown's friendship with the Negro is also the story of the death of a "White" man. And the telling of the story of the martyrdom of John Brown is also the story of his life as icon of the possibility of a new beginning, the story of a social being formed within the idea of belonging simply and purely to a "White" race who yet came to recognize himself as configured within the movement of an unsettled question, one that he, perhaps strategically, continued to call by the name of the "Negro question." This latter movement, of course, would be one in which neither reference, "White" or "Negro," could be easily set aside. For this reason, the story of John Brown can only be a story with a double reference. For this reason, it is enigmatic and difficult of telling.

Yet, of the many biographers of John Brown and of the incessant and ceaseless retelling of his life's story in almost every genre of literature, including song, we and ensuing generations have W. E. B. Du Bois to thank for bequeathing to us the story or narrative of the *double* soul or souls of John Brown.

What we know is that John Brown was a "White" man who died to achieve the freedom of the Negro. What we do not yet realize, or really know, is the extent to which he already lives again, through death, as some historical being that is yet to come. Of course, he survives as an icon or as an ideal—a monumental, even if oft-denigrated, figure who stands as an appeal for the future. Also, however, he survives within the risk and loss of living as a flesh-and-blood man, configured within the very limits and frame of the world into which he was born. He survives, that is, as an example of a flesh-and-blood man whose character acquires its peculiar force only in and through the limits of his being, rather than because he transcended them. This survival is, thus, not absolute; rather, it is always at stake in the struggle toward another liberty or liberation; it is always at risk of giving up or reproducing that which it seeks to overthrow, perhaps due to the very force with which it seeks to carry out this overturning. This latter thought is the lesson, the historical inscription, both obvious and subtle, that W. E. B. Du Bois's *John Brown* can teach us. It is a telling of something within the frame of what we think we know, in such a way that the unknown within it begins to acquire a certain unstable and enigmatic legibility. This is the performance of Du Bois's narrative. How is this so?

First, we might surmise that it is, perhaps, because he was not absolutely decided on the moral bearing of his tale, unlike so many studies of the life of this man, that Du Bois did not fail to recognize that, even if named primarily as an apocalypticism, one often articulated in the idioms of evangelical Christianity, death was the central meaning of life for John Brown. Du Bois's narrative is positioned within the space of a certain horror, one that we may usefully describe as metaphysical. In the turning folds of Du Bois's narrative of Brown's boyhood, maturity, marriage, fatherhood, violent militancy, and martyrdom, Brown seems unable to inhabit the present in any simple fashion. Moved perhaps by the theological position of death within Christianity, or perhaps by a sense of chance and fate within a young and expansive society—one marked strongly by a sense of the frontier that was nineteenth-century America—Brown developed a profound sense of disjunction from the world into which he was born, as Du Bois describes it, especially the institution of slavery. This disjunction was marked by a sense of the way in which the possibility of absolute loss remains open within the most mundane and secure activities of living. Herein, it seems, Du Bois positions a certain question as open within the consciousness of John Brown: Is it only the Negro American—for whom slavery as violence can be considered to open a movement of metaphysical horror or withdrawal with each inscription within the flesh, the body, the way of being of the slave—is it only such a being who can live within death, upon its jowls so to speak, and yet give rise incessantly to stark, originary, perhaps meaningful life? It is this question or one like it, we might suggest or hypothesize, that forms itself somewhere in the shadows, the dark recesses, of this melancholic Du Boisian narrative. The response, Du Bois's or Brown's, formulated by Du Bois through Brown, is that it is not simply or only the Negro American.

Du Bois describes a melancholic John Brown, compelled to challenge the very terms of his fate or death. In doing so, the narrative that his life and precipitate death makes possible outlines a tear in the fabric of providence, and thus marks his struggle with the limits that have been bestowed upon him as privilege. It moves in some tenacious relationship of maintenance or affirmation, as well as a sense of loss, of the sense of possible being that has been withdrawn, the ways of being a "white" man that have been marked as beyond the acceptable or the normal, that is, the ways of being other than a "White" man. This struggle, marked so tenaciously within the life of John Brown, we might call the melancholic movement or structure of whiteness.

Perhaps because he senses or realizes that Brown's melancholia is rooted in his uncertain struggle over the possible meanings of his own death, Du Bois was able to recognize that the uncertain outcome of that struggle motivated and organized the life and practice of John Brown.

To Begin Otherwise

There is a second register of Du Bois's telling of this story, however—one that gives it historical and intellectual uniqueness. And, we might suggest that herein, Du Bois reveals the secret that so many writing on the life and death of John Brown have been unable to discover or to recognize. Du Bois, I suggest, recognized within the life of John Brown a simple, but fundamental and radical orientation. In addition, Du Bois found a means by which to bring this radical orientation of John Brown into renewed relief. What was this orientation? John Brown seemed to understand that, to the extent that in America of the nineteenth century, especially at the end of the antebellum era, he was socially and historically understood as "white," as a "White" man; that in order for him to live he must give this socially granted life over to death (or not to live, or to maintain himself only within a kind of death by living as a "White" man); or rather, we might say, that in order to live, he had to take this socially and historically granted life and dispense with it, kill it, destroy it, give it up to the risk and possibility of absolute dissolution. This meant that, within the circuit of his own experience, he had to die twice: once as that ordinary historical being called a "White" man and, again, as that flesh-and-blood being who can only be given a "proper" name: John Brown.

Within this death of John Brown "proper" opens another movement of the double, one whose possibility and bearing is already set loose in the first movement of double death. This second movement of the double, of course, is the figure of the double with which I opened this preface and under whose heading I have placed the question of biography. This complicated figure of the double arises because the "proper" name can never have an absolutely proper reference; that is, it can have no proper birth or death, cannot come into being on the basis of some true reference, or dissipate with the absolute loss of such a reference. With regard to "whiteness," Brown, for example, realizes that it has no true or simple ground. It remains an open question as to whether he realized fully the implication of the possibility that it had no true or simple death. With regard to the first death, the death of John Brown in flesh and blood, John Brown "proper," the radical impossibility of the proper as such means that this extraordinarily proper physical death must be relived, recreated, rebirthed incessantly, in discourse, biography of one kind or another; this is precisely because there is not, nor can there be, any absolute referent or absolute loss or absence of such. Hence, John Brown must be an example that stands only for itself or himself, an historical monstrosity or dream that our discourse or words cannot fail to produce. We are compelled, then, to make up for this ineffability of the proper, its reclusiveness. We try to do it in discourse, in narrative, in biography. As such, John Brown is condemned by history, not only to live *or* die again, anew, with each generation, but to live *and* die, again, anew, perhaps always. Du Bois, it seems to me, practiced a recognition of this enigma.

If John Brown seemed to live this necessity of a double cathexis, of the death of the "White" man and the death of John Brown "proper," did he in fact maintain some actual recognition or reflection of such? Certainly, he understood both necessities, but it must remain a question as to whether he understood both together. It is Du Bois's narrative that weaves these two questions together in discourse. This is the enigmatic line of originality in Du Bois's elaboration. This is perhaps what it means for Du Bois to say in the preface to the first edition that the only "excuse" for his study is a "new emphasis," a "different point of view." How does this unfold, if we follow Du Bois?

The recognition on John Brown's part that, I have suggested, set in motion this movement of the double was not simple or pure; it was not sui generis. We must not forget that the imagined thought of such a possibility—that of an absolute repleteness—was the ultimate reference of cathexis for the nascent discourse and practice of "whiteness" in mid-nineteenth-century America. Thus, it must be underlined here that this recognition of the necessity of a certain disjunction from the given moorings of his identification as a "White" man, and through it his struggle with the coming meaning of his death—a meaning that by necessity preceded for him his death—that this recognition was itself achieved or produced by the strange movement of a "White" man becoming "otherwise," other than simply "white," perhaps. We will not try to name all at once what he became—avoiding, first, the idea that he became something else all at once or finally, and also, secondly, the idea that he became, simply, Negro, or Black. We can instead rest with Du Bois's formulation in the preface to the first edition of this study, that Brown, perhaps of all "Americans has perhaps come nearest to touching the real souls of black folk." Of course, it is only meaningful to rest with such a thought if we also follow its path of implication, the path followed by Du Bois in the narrative itself. In this narrative, that "touch" is always a response, a mark of a passion, carried bodily, invoked by a call or gesture, a solicitation that is otherwise than a simple or passive invitation. Within the narrative, whether by a particular figure or as the slave in general in America, it was the Negro American that, according to Du Bois, solicited the recognition of John Brown. We can underline that this solicitation was not passive by considering what it set in motion within the movement of self-identification of John Brown: a movement of becoming other. On the one hand, becoming "otherwise" for Brown was both to become other than a "White" man, while yet unavoidably reproducing that very figure of being, even in the movement of becoming other, of becoming other than simply "white." On the other hand, this movement, this becoming other, is also to become what one "is" through or by way of the other. It is, thus, this risk of self in the detour or passageway through the other that remains the scene of the production of the deaths and lives of John Brown. It is the historical form of this passage to self by way of the other that Du Bois takes as a palimpsest for the inscription of his own narrative of John Brown "proper." It is the history of this passage by way of the other in the production of John Brown that Du Bois's narrative seeks to tell.

A Second-Sight

Du Bois writes in his first preface that "the viewpoint adopted in this book is that of the little known but vastly important inner development of the Negro American." What exactly does Du Bois mean by reference to something he calls the "inner development" of the Negro or African American?

Nearly every commentator on Du Bois's study of John Brown, since its first publication in 1909, has remarked or called attention to this passage. Yet, it seems to me, most have not succeeded in providing a convincing account of the structure of this "viewpoint"—that is, the organization and pertinence for historiographical study of the "inner development of the Negro American." Yet, the position that a reader takes concerning this formulation will affect, to some extent and in a decisive manner, almost every other aspect of one's interpretation of this great study. To the extent that this formulation remains inscrutable or simply opaque to a reader, such an interpreter would be hard-pressed to recognize or trace the lineaments of Du Bois's elaboration and its most decisive gestures. The central bearing of Du Bois's approach is not in and of itself substantive or primarily substantive; that is, it is not first of all or ultimately about particular or specific empirical or concrete matters. Rather, the meaning of this reference to the "inner development of the Negro American" is primarily an epistemological one, having to do with the very way in which the object of critical reflection comes into view or being. This is what Du Bois means when he refers to "point of view" as the site of the originality of his study. In particular, this epistemological frame has certain theoretical effects, we might say, having to do with the orientation of an interpretation, or of the explanations put forth in this biography. It does not have so much to do with a particular substantive insight, or set of such insights or revelations. It should almost go without saying that still less does this originality have to do with the production or circulation of facts. Indeed, we know from Du Bois's own statements that his is a study produced almost entirely on the basis of previously published sources, entailing, thus, no archival investigation by him. What Du Bois enacts, as he says that he has sought to do, is quite simply to study John Brown from the point of view of the Negro. Yet this, as I have already suggested, is where the simplicity ends concerning this narrative.

This point of view that arises within the "inner development of the Negro American" concerns the consciousness, or more precisely the self-consciousness, of the Negro. What scholars and other commentators on this study of Du Bois's have yet to realize is that Du Bois formulates and carries out his approach to his study of John Brown on the analytical premise of the relevance of the double cathexis of the Negro, of the double reference of the Negro, to both an Africa and an America, to the interpretation of the life story and deaths of a "White" man, John Brown. What is this relevance?

Du Bois had already proposed the enigmatic bearing of a double reference within the social and historical identification of the Negro American in "Conservation of Races" (1897) and "Strivings of the Negro People" (1897) (Du Bois 1897a; Du Bois 1897b). In the revised version of the latter that stands as the opening essay of his classic *The Souls of Black Folk: Essays and Sketches* of 1903 this formulation emerges as titular for a narrative of such subjectivation (*Souls*, 1–12, chap. 1).[3] For Du Bois, in the historical and existential sense, this movement of double identification was set loose within, or as the formation of, the self-consciousness of the Negro American through the palpable force of a limitation or mark (often, but not always, of exclusion) which would distinguish one social figure from another under the heading of race. Within the movement of this double cathexis, Du Bois describes a sense of "double conscious-ness" as the sense of being, the relation to self, or the self-consciousness of the Negro American. It is to this structure that Du Bois refers when he speaks of the "inner development of the Negro American." In that essay, Du Bois had famously written:

> After the Egyptian and Indian, the Greek and the Roman, the Teu-ton and the Mongolian, the Negro is a sort of seventh son, born with a veil, and gifted with second-sight in this American world,—a world which yields him no true self-consciousness, but only lets him see himself through the revelation of the other world. It is a pecu-liar sensation, this double consciousness, this sense of always look-ing at one's self through the eyes of others, of measuring one's soul by the tape of a world that looks on in amused contempt and pity. One ever feels his two-ness,—an American, a Negro; two souls, two thoughts, two unreconciled strivings; two warring ideals in one dark body, whose dogged strength alone keeps it from being torn asunder. (*Souls*, 3, chap. 1, para. 3)

What is first of all important here is to recognize something of the archi-tecture of this formulation by Du Bois. We might consider what Du Bois calls "second-sight" as a sort of general historical structure of reflection (one which of necessity refers to the possibility of reflexivity in general, even if that is not its primary idiom of elaboration here by Du Bois or our primary concern). Within the frame of this historically situated reflec-tion and reflexivity, we might consider, then, a sense of this reflexivity, a sense of being, to arise for a particular historical and social figure. The figure is the Negro. This sense of being Du Bois describes as a kind of "double consciousness." Secondly, what must also be remarked is something of the kinetic force of this formulation for Du Bois. For him, this movement of double consciousness, although appearing or motivated in its appearance under the heading of the negative, also appears under the heading of the affirmative. Du Bois names the structure of "second-sight" as also a "gift" in the very locution of his announcement of its formulation. And despite his concern for the difficulty—the violence and paralysis—that can attend this movement of the double, within the very next paragraph of this essay, Du Bois refuses to disavow (or affirms, to put it precisely) either term of the double reference that configures this movement of "double consciousness," even if he affirms each differently.

> The history of the American Negro is the history of this strife,—this longing to attain self-conscious manhood, to merge his double self into a better and truer self. In this merging he wishes neither of the older selves to be lost. He would not Africanize America, for America has too much to teach the world and Africa. He would not bleach his Negro soul in a flood of white Americanism, for he knows that Negro blood has a message for the world. He simply wishes to make it possible for a man to be both a Negro and an American, without being cursed and spit upon by his fellows, without having the doors of Opportunity closed roughly in his face. (*Souls*, 4, chap. 1, para. 4)

For Du Bois, in this essay, the difficulty of this double reference did not mean that the Negro should reject one term or aspect of its identification for another. Rather, this doubling was the very future or possibility of its becoming. It marked out the very space and possibility of desire and that which is yet to come.

Within the gesture of this affirmation of the bearing, the legibility, the heterogeneity, of a double reference is situated the conceptual resource on which he draws to illuminate the question of John Brown.

This affirmation sets loose within Du Bois's conception of the African American a profoundly rich understanding of the possibility of a new way or new ways of social being, ways that would be excessive to the simple and oppositional divisions that would dominate the social field in which the Negro American arises. This figure of the double gives rise to an excessiveness within the American context in a twofold manner. On the one hand, it maintains the social being of the Negro in a domain of identification that refuses to abide by the oppositional logic or categories of racial distinction; one *can* be both a Negro and an American. It confounds the ultimate premise of racial distinction, a categorical or oppositional logic of distinction or identification. On the other hand, it affirms a difference as operative in America, one that Du Bois, perhaps strategically, perhaps anachronistically (and perhaps not) names as "African." This difference produces a heterogeneity within the general social field of American life and history, one that would be organized according to a racist logic of categorical distinction and be given over to a narrative of purity, of the self-repleteness and historical becoming of a white subject, an historical and social being supposedly arising of its own initiative, unmarked by any sign of difference. Such a subject would be understood to realize the purity of its own self-image in every form of historical and social activity. For this reason, we might suggest, Du Bois considered the reference to Africa, or a difference that could not be simply dissolved, an essential reference in the recognition of the position of the Negro in America. He would not let the mark of such a reference or difference be erased from the historical ledger in positioning the African or Negro in America. He maintained such, even as he resolutely insisted upon the identification of the Negro as also American, also in a manner that could not be simply dislodged or dismissed.

It is this double reference of the Negro American that Du Bois uses, critically and affirmatively, to reopen the question of the meaning of the death and the life of John Brown. How does he do this? It is at the precise site, in a conceptual sense, on the ground of the conceptualization that he has already formulated with regard to the African American, the conceptualization of an historical difference that Du Bois has already named as "African" in the 1890s, as we saw in the passage from *The Souls of Black Folk* quoted above—it is with reference to this difference that Du Bois begins to tell, or retell, the narrative of John Brown.

Du Bois begins this biography, not with a statement of when and where John Brown was born in America, but with a first chapter, titled "Africa and America," about the contribution of Africa to the making of America. Let us recall the epigraph and opening two paragraphs of this opening chapter. In so doing, we may be able to make legible the analytical bearing of Du Bois's formulation of the heterogeneous reference of the Negro American in his biographical study of John Brown.

"That it might be fulfilled which was spoken of the Lord by the prophet saying, Out of Egypt have I called My son."[4]

The mystic spell of Africa is and ever was over all America. It has guided her hardest work, inspired her finest literature, and sung her sweetest songs. Her greatest destiny—unsensed and despised though it be—is to give back to the first of continents the gifts which Africa of old gave to America's father's fathers.

Of all inspiration which America owes to Africa, however; the greatest by far is the score of heroic men whom the sorrows of these dark children called to unselfish devotion and heroic self-realization: Benezet, Garrison, and Harriet Stowe; Sumner, Douglass and Lincoln—these and others, but above all, John Brown. (*John Brown*, 15)

Du Bois thus situates John Brown squarely within the folds of the productivity of Africa in America. However, both terms of this double figure are essential for the formulation of Du Bois's argument, for this positioning of the Negro American and John Brown to be coherent and attain analytical force. If there is no reference to Africa, only to an America, then analytically one is hard put to remark the distinctiveness of the role or function of the Negro in the development and making of American history, or of the great historical figures in American history. If there is no reference to America, and the Negro is understood as essentially and definitively as something other than American, as African in a simple and primordially given sense, then the Negro in Africa might conceivably have a place in human history, perhaps even tangentially in America, but there could be no analytic or historiographical recognition of its position within the great maelstrom of historical becoming that was the making of the American project (for some four centuries by the turn of the last century). In order to recognize the bearing of the "inner development" of the Negro on understanding the death and life of John Brown, this essential doubleness of the Negro in America must be affirmed at every level of generality. This affirmation of the double stands at the root of Du Bois's interpretation of John Brown.

Du Bois frames this question first in a global manner, as "Africa's" relation to "America." America's "destiny," its great future, is, for Du Bois, to be responsible to the great legacy of ancient Africa. This ancient legacy is borne out in American history through the inspiration to greatness that the history of the Negro in America sets loose or calls forth in America. Within this global and broad social frame, Du Bois positions the telling of the story of great figures. It is here, positioned within the broad sweep of world historical movements, that Du Bois situates the telling of the story of one individual. If the ancient legacy of Africa is moving in America, it is through the striving and passion of the Negro American. Exactly how such inspiration is produced in the life of John Brown is the prime and motivating question of this biographical narrative.

With the economical and deft formulations of his opening two paragraphs, then, Du Bois sketches the entire frame of his study and begins his narrative. We must remember and maintain in heightened relief the fact that this narrative does not begin in New England, in Connecticut, where John Brown "proper," so to speak, was born in the flesh, but by reference to Africa, to another beginning.

Another Telling

As the telling of the narrative, as such, bears no proper substitute, I will only remark, as a question, the way in which Du Bois's discourse accomplishes or fails to accomplish its task. It is the concern of this chapter simply to formulate and bring the character of this task into a certain relief.

As it were, comprising thirteen chapters in sum, the narrative develops according to what can be described as four stages.

Across the first four chapters, the initial stage of the study, Du Bois offers a presentation of the development of a certain moral rectitude on the part of John Brown, from his boyhood through full maturation, into the early part of his fifth decade. This rectitude is a disposition with which Du Bois maintains a persistent affirmation. In the second staging of the narrative, the five core chapters of the story of Brown's life, proper, as it were, Du Bois proposes an account of the development of John Brown's expressed and active opposition to slavery, by way of this figure's engagement with the question of the Negro and his direct relations with Negro Americans. The third stage brings to its conclusion the story of John Brown's life in two sharply drawn episodes, by way of its telling of the event of the aborted insurrection at Harper's Ferry and its aftermath.

And then, almost as a kind of coda, in the final stage of the text the narrative proper undergoes a kind of metamorphosis, wherein its central question up to this point in the narrative of the comprehension of the terms, motivation, and commitment of John Brown in his decision to act toward the violent and revolutionary overthrow of American slavery gives way to (or, better, is enfolded within) a far-reaching theoretical proposition of the articulation of the global-level "problem of the color-line." On the one hand, such purview does allow an understanding of the eruption that was the initiative of John Brown proper. Yet, too, on the other, the maintenance, persistence, and commitment to the extension of slavery within the American context and the assent to modern colonialism on a worldwide basis (that is, the worldhood of Europe and America, in particular), of which Atlantic slavery both marked its incipit and became a nodal expression, was likewise rendered tractable. Here, taking reference to the final chapter of the biography, the world historical extension of Du Bois's perspective and its relation to the African American example—moving from Brown's *then* of the 1850s then to Du Bois's *now* of the 1910s, on the eve of the First World War, from American slavery *here* (in the so-called New World) to European and American imperial colonialism *there* (in the supposed Old World)—may be given a distinct legibility.

> We are, in fact, to-day repeating in our intercourse between races all the former evils of class distinction within the nation: personal hatred and abuse, mutual injustice, unequal taxation and rigid caste. Individual nations outgrew these fatal things by breaking down the horizontal barriers between classes. We are bringing them back by seeking to erect vertical barriers between races. Men were told that abolition of compulsory class distinction meant the leveling down, degradation, disappearance of culture and genius and the triumph of the mob. As a matter of fact it has been the salvation of European civilization. . . . The same is true in racial contact. Vertical race distinctions are even more emphatic hindrances to human evolution than horizontal class distinctions, and their tearing away involves fewer chances of degradation and greater opportunities of human betterment than in the case of class lines. On the other hand, persistence in racial distinction spells disaster sooner or later. The earth is growing smaller and more accessible. Race contact will become in the future increasingly inevitable, not only in America, Asia and Africa, but even in Europe. The color line will mean not simply a return to the absurdities of class as exhibited in the sixteenth and seventeenth centuries, but even to the caste of ancient days. This however, the Japanese, the Chinese, the East Indians and the Negroes are going to resent in just such proportion as they gain power: and they are gaining the power, and they cannot be kept from gaining more power. The price of repression will then be hypocrisy and slavery and blood. This is the situation to-day. (*John Brown*, 381–83)

It is then by way of this epistemological perspective that Du Bois turns to propose the principal question of his study, enunciated here as two distinct and yet inseparable locutions, two forms of the same vocative register, comprising the last two chapters of the study, respectively. The penultimate chapter, construed as an account of his trial for treason, which in turn is a trial of the principle of justice at stake in the American law of slavery, poses the question: "What is the meaning of John Brown?" And, here the question of justice is no longer subtended by the ontological question—the idiomatic question or riddle of the ages, that is "the riddle of the sphynx," given as an interrogative—"What is man?" which could then be extended within legality as a proposition that the enslavement of the human is without justification and hence such practice can be adjudged as wrong or morally corrupt; not only that, but rather the whole problem of justice has become distended by the question what is to be done in the relation of human to human, let us say, in the care for the other?[5] It is thus that the closing chapter, in the form of the question "What is the legacy of John Brown?" is able to unfold a question about futurity, in which death is something other than simply loss, and which may perhaps be thought also as a name for possibility, for that which gives, for generosity. Du Bois invokes the possibility of a temporality that extends both before and after the time of American slavery—"beyond this narrow Now," as he frames the death of his still-infant son in the penultimate paragraph of the chapter devoted to his passing in *The Souls of Black Folk*—stretching the limited frame of the historicity that would indict John Brown for his actions at Harper's Ferry beyond its holding points. The persistent refrain of the narrative—that the "cost of liberty is less than the price of repression"—now comes into its own. The cost of war, we can now adjudge could be dissimulated for a certain time, and perhaps place, in history, but so long as such an organization of relation as fundamental violence were maintained, the exorbitance of its "price" would in its eventuality become the very terms of future historial possibility.

     If such an organization of violence were to remain the definitive terms of historial existence, death, then, in its capacity to give, on all levels of historical generality, would remain closed up and withdrawn.

     In this sense, it can be said that in this study, Du Bois not only offered an account of the inner moral and ethical development of John Brown, referred as it were, to the moral and ethical development of the Negro

as American in the United States, but likewise the coming into crisis of
the inner moral and intellectual development of the so-called American
nation. Let us now fold this description of the outward face or form of
this narrative reference back, across, and through its own textured frame,
of a life both within death and yet beyond, otherwise than a simple mark,
so that we can come to recognize the lineaments, the lines of intersection
and contoured relief, another form of fold, that may show therein, if not
now, then, otherwise than now.

Another Beginning

Another beginning, or a beginning otherwise, made it narratively or
interpretively possible for Du Bois to construe John Brown as configured
in a double cathexis, just as Du Bois had already described himself and
the Negro American in general as configured by way of a double reference, to both Africa and America. That is to say that Du Bois described
for John Brown, a man socially and historically understood as "white,"
a structure of double reference, a kind of reference that he had already
described for the Negro American as a kind of "double consciousness."
Thus, in a theoretical sense—that is, with regard to its angle of interpretation—Du Bois's study is a sustained inquiry into the structures of
"double consciousness" of a "White" man, understood by Du Bois to be
configured as such by way of his being with reference to the Negro in
America.[6]

Yet, what is of equal importance is a structure of possibility, a general epistemological condition of Du Bois's narrative that is sedimented
everywhere, but remains almost just beyond legibility: namely, that the
essential condition of possibility of Du Bois's own narrative, of his "new
emphasis" in the telling of the story of John Brown, of his "different point
of view," is the structure of double cathexis, of "double consciousness,"
that configures the ground of his own social being and, for Du Bois, the
Negro or African American in general. He, Du Bois, is only able to tell
the story of John Brown from this "new" standpoint, that is, of recognizing John Brown's production and self-identification as a social being by
way of a double reference to both the Negro (or Africa) and America, by
way of his own inhabitation of a certain double reference. Du Bois's own
"double consciousness" is the condition of possibility of his narrative of
John Brown's "double consciousness." As Du Bois will write of himself

just a few months after the publication of *John Brown*, in a radical and groundbreaking essay, "The Souls of White Folk," he is both a Negro and a "White" man, formed within the movement of the production of each; hence, he can claim to see and understand each from the "inside," so to speak.[7] Du Bois, perhaps, wrote that later essay on the basis of the accomplishment of the narrative of *John Brown*. The thesis of the later essay, to which I have just referred, might well be taken as the ultimate thesis of the biographical study, *John Brown*.

What should be added here is that, for Du Bois, his study was exemplary—exemplary in every way: of the position of the Negro in America, both in the past and in the future; of the possibilities for rethinking the history of America from this standpoint; of the place of a great individual in the life of a nation; of the passion necessary for the historian or biographer to recognize the meaning of history (to offer a few examples). It is perhaps for this reason that its title is iconic, standing for the man, the book, the symbol—each, in a movement of reference that has a shuttling instability, with the final meaning of this title resting simply with none. This instability, of course, is part of the instability of the proper in general, and thus part of what opens the question of John Brown, incessantly, to the future.

What Du Bois has accomplished here is the study of the production and dissolution of "whiteness" by way of an account of the history of the position of the Negro as a problem in America.[8] Du Bois delivers John Brown to us, and to the future, by situating the meaning of John Brown as a figure arising within or through the meaning of the Negro, the African, in the history of America and, by implication, the modern world. This we might say is a certain formulation of the Negro as material idea, the Negro as a problem for thought, a figure of exorbitance, in the modern epoch. This is the uniqueness and enduring legacy of Du Bois's study. In this regard, it stands as a monument to the position of John Brown within the historical consciousness of the Negro in America.[9] Yet it also stands as an exemplary testament to those "White" men who, over the centuries past and in those yet to come, have discovered from the "inside" out the enigmatic difficulty of living on the basis of a kind of death, one that entails "two souls, two thoughts, two unreconciled strivings, two warring ideals," configuring the meaning, for oneself and thus for history, of one's own body, one's own flesh. For we must remember or recognize that it is ultimately of John Brown's relationship to himself, his sense of himself, his self-consciousness, that Du Bois so persistently and carefully seeks to give an account. We can perhaps recognize the form or movement of two "souls," one bending into the other, one moving inextricably within the other, in a statement of John Brown's given near the end (John Brown "proper," the one who has already sought the death of John Brown the "White" man), the statement with which Du Bois closes his study: "You may dispose of me very easily—I am nearly disposed of now, but this question is still unsettled—this Negro question, I mean. The end of that is not yet."[10] Who knows but that perhaps this *John Brown*, this biography, this story that begins from a death, is the living proof of this statement, or last testament, of John Brown, "proper."

CHAPTER FOUR

ORIGINARY DISPLACEMENT

Or, Passages of the Double and the Limit of World

For Hortense Spillers[1]

Preamble

It is widely believed that a real thing called "America" exists. Yet, it is precisely this idea *of* America in itself that we should not accept without examination. Is "America" in its truth the anchorage point that supports the social-cultural practices of African Americans? Or, is it rather a complex idea formed inside the (historical-transcendental) movement of the constitution of the African American as material idea? Perhaps it can be shown how this idea of "America" took form in different operations of power and the definite role it played in them.[2]

I can restate, in a more explicit fashion, the stakes of the question that will organize itself somewhere near the core of this chapter by annotating the salience of an epistemological suggestion offered by Ralph Ellison: "It is possible that any viable theory of Negro American culture obligates us to fashion a more adequate theory of American culture as a whole."[3]

With this reference in mind then, I can state the central theoretical proposition of this chapter: that, in a certain way, we should generalize and therefore radicalize W. E. B. Du Bois's formulation of the African American sense of identity as "a kind of double consciousness," reckoned as experience under the palpable force of the practice of racial distinction, to all forms of an identification that might stake itself as American, as such, and even to the formation of forms of subjectivity in all that we might henceforth name as modern historiality in general (*Souls*, 3, chap. 1, para. 3).[4]

Although this central suggestion is primarily theoretical, it is necessary that it simultaneously encode a methodological decision and implication. Thus if all critical reflection must proceed by way of example in order to maintain within its elaboration a responsibility to the historicity of its problematic, the orientation that I wish to give to Du Bois's formulation is that the study of a particular example of the *problem* of identity or reflexive identification in the modern era—that of the African diaspora in general—might well serve as an exemplary guide in rethinking some essential determinants in our contemporary theorizations concerning the grounds of historical identification. Even more precisely, my own methodological focus is primarily on the African American in what has historically become the United States. I propose, following Du Bois, that this problematic identity, or identity that is a problem, is a good example, "good to think with."

Developing this proposition will lead us to challenge certain theoretical formulations under which the question of African American subjectity has been thought. It is time that we systematically expose the pervasive operative presumption that general theory or conceptual reflection is formulated elsewhere than in African diasporic (American) studies, and that it is only applied here. We will have to bring this presumption into question for two reasons.

First, we must question this practice because those theoretical positions have been formulated in disciplines of knowledge that have themselves been marked by uncritical presuppositions about African American identity, principally through the itinerary of the concept of race (or the conception of purity that organizes it) within their formation and development (since the sixteenth century). There is no contemporary discourse that is free or independent of the itinerary of the concept of race.[5]

It is at this precise juncture that I wish to articulate the questions that I am following here with some of those posed around the itinerary of Michel Foucault and its relation to the problematic just named here.

Certainly, it is of theoretical interest to notice several formulations adduced by Homi Bhabha on the question of race and the discourse of Foucault just prior to the initial publication, in French and later in English, of the latter's lecture courses from the Collège de France during the last decade of his work. For while the point of interlocution is Foucault's *The Order of Things*, Bhabha's formulation references a larger discursive tapestry—one that extends beyond the question of the implication the discourse associated with that name and toward what is at stake in it at its furthest reaches. We can both affirm and supplement Bhabha's formulation. If the problem of post-Enlightenment anthropologies "is to think the unthought that falls between the empirical and the transcendental . . . that which is not given to consciousness," Bhabha suggests that we can place a certain new question in this schema. Precisely to the extent that they are practices, "what is the structuring principle of that in-between intertextual and interdisciplinary space" of the knowledges of "race" (as concept or ensemble of concepts and theories) and racism (as both concept and practice of racial distinction)—and the gap between "race" and racism here is nothing if not immeasurable—in the field of the general deployment of racism? Affirming Bhabha's recognition of the excessiveness of this "new question" to Foucault's established discourse, we redeploy Bhabha's questions while marking the fact that if nowhere else, Du Bois's discourse inhabits this between, soliciting and calling forth solicitation. "What is the specific nature of the unthought or unconscious of race? What figures of ambivalence structure the authority of race/racism as a form of knowledge and as a practice of discursive power? How do the social hierarchies and cultural representations of Western civility coexist with the consciousness of their own history of colonial and postcolonial metropolitan racism?"[6]

Referencing transcriptions from lecture courses by Foucault that remained unpublished at the time which address some aspects of this problematic—that is to say, lectures from the winter and spring of 1976 at the Collège de France, first published in France in 1997 and now widely available in English translation— Ann Laura Stoler's leading study from the early 1990s had already noticed several discussions within Foucault's lectures that propose an intervention in this domain.[7] However, across these lectures as since published, even if more remains to come, the fundamental character of the idea and concept of race, and too the practice of racial distinction as such—or, what Du Bois called the "problem of the color-line" on an epochal level of generality—still seems to be understood there as a secondary, or derivative question within the epistemic horizon (however one names it) that has taken on a distinctive shape since the middle of the eighteenth century and the historically coextensive irruption of the new critical project within science and philosophy, on the one hand, and the idea of a new kind of political order, that is a liberal and democratic one, on the other. The problematic in question seems to remain in these lectures a controlled and subordinated question in Foucault's overall discourse. While it is certainly an original extension of thought moving along the lineaments of Foucault's discourse, Stoler's early reading does not seem to clearly delimit this positioning. The difficulty here seems to me to arise precisely in the domain of the relation of our contemporary problematization of the idea of sovereignty and the contemporary radicalization of a problematization of the idea and concept of race. The difficulty arises on a fundamental level and for profound reasons. In the key texts of the mid-1970s, both the signal closing section of his introduction to his new problematization of the history of sexuality and lectures under the heading of "society must be defended," which are essentially not only of the same discursive fabric, but even of the same intermeshed vocative breath, as it were, Foucault was primarily concerned to distanciate a juridical understanding of sovereignty by way of a renarrativation of European modernity. The key to that new narration is a movement from binary hierarchy to a horizontal dispersal or (what Foucault called) normativity. The complex manner in which racial distinction as the practice of something that Foucault is first beginning to call "biopower" in this moment of his itinerary might set afoot another hierarchy within the movement that produces the normativity that Foucault narrates, that is the maintenance of an essential commitment to an idea of the pure, to the thought of a possible purity, and purification that would nonetheless always work to preserve a status quo of hierarchy, cannot be recognized at the depth of its pertinence within the theoretical preoccupation that governs his 1976 lectures. In this regard, I am not certain that the terms of Stoler's early reading of this passage of Foucault's thought can account for the profound paradoxes that the ontological claim implied in racial distinction, *no matter how indirectly*, presents for global modernity.

This may also well be the root of Foucault's, and then Bhabha's, conundrum. The domain that Foucault wishes to address is not that of a history of representations or behaviors or attitudes, but rather the way in which being gives itself to be problematized. It can be suggested that the problem of racial distinction or the "problem of the color-line" is constitutive of a global modernity as such a form of problematization.[8] Yet it is the formulation of problematic in the work of Du Bois that is our fundamental guide here. For, from the turn to the twentieth century Du Bois had already offered a narrativization of the formation of a new organization of hierarchy, a new global order, as "the problem" of that century, and he continued to elaborate this thought throughout his long itinerary, especially in the magisterial *Black Reconstruction: An Essay Toward a History of the Part Which Black Folk Played in the Attempt to Reconstruct Democracy in America* (1935), *Color and Democracy: Colonies and Peace* (1945), in *The World and Africa: An Inquiry into the Part Which Africa has Played in World History* (1947), and, of course and indeed even in the narrative of the novel *Dark Princess: A Romance* from (1928) (Du Bois 1935; Du Bois 1945; Du Bois 1947; Du Bois 1928).

In this regard, my solicitation of the discourse of these thinkers, Foucault's and Bhabha's, and perhaps Stoler's, would be lateral, recalling and respecting an excessive configuration, according to which the figure of the African American or Negro remains the mark of the excessive itself, especially for thought. (How could it be otherwise in "America," even Foucault's America? In "America," for example, the problem of sexuality, or the problem of racial distinction, retains everywhere and always the question of the "African American" or "Negro.") Hence, perhaps it can be said, these questions, Foucault's and my own, Bhabha's and my own, Stoler's and my own, displace each other as movements of a discourse. Therein, one can name the necessity of a fundamental reengagement with the initiative in thought posed by the practice of Du Bois on this common terrain, this common horizon, this colonial and postcolonial nexus.[9]

Secondly, a certain essentialist privilege in theory in ethnological discourses (history, sociology, anthropology), philosophy, and literature has tended to preclude a thinking of the paradoxical centrality of "marginal" examples (in our case African American) to any theoretical formulation of a general problematic.

This paradoxical structure must be remarked. This centrality occurs because theory is only as good as its "worst" example. Theory (*theoria, theorein*) holds within it a double concern. This double reference makes its worst example also its best. On the one hand, theory is always about something, phenomena, perhaps. There is some structure of reference. It attempts, on the other hand, to formalize some aspect or aspects of phenomena, to articulate some relationship entailing the objectivity in question, ideal or otherwise. The generality, or limits, of this formalization is less marked by what it claims as its most typical example or object than by those phenomena that seem to exceed its borders or boundaries, exceeding the borders either of the concepts employed within this formalization or the relationships construed to hold between certain key concepts or described phenomena (within this ensemble). Hence, to the extent that the commitment of any inquiry is to develop, at whatever level of generality, the most comprehensive understanding possible (and every inquiry, whether under the heading of science or interpretation, is enfolded, from the moment it formulates a question, in a speculative, and hence philosophical, discourse), the good (or best) example, that which makes "good" theory, is the "bad" (or difficult) example.[10] If this is so, it must nonetheless be emphasized that the example as proposed and elaborated in this chapter attempts to suggest a thinking of the structure of exemplarity such that an irreducible nominality sets in motion a lability within the figuration of the exemplar.[11] In other words, we might say that we are always called on to rest with, if not simply go by way of, the specificity of the example. Epistemologically, the irreducible importance of the example for theory indicates the irreducibility of the particular, the specific, the apparition of the nominal. We not only cannot, but should not seek to rid ourselves of the limits of the example as ensconced in its specific and particular context. Methodologically, although we can never resist formalization in order to read a text, social or otherwise—for we are always interpreting, never simply describing—due to the particularity of the example, we can never formalize absolutely or completely.

It is not a question of rejecting the kinds of studies of modernity or of the making of America that have been justly definitive in a general sense in contemporary scholarship. Indexing exemplary work in the wake of the 1960s that had proposed to revise fundamental narratives—in retheorizing the making of the modern world, such as the work of Immanuel Wallerstein, or in study of the making of early North America, such as the intervention of Rhys Isaac, to name just two examples—analysts have remained unable to recognize just how paradoxically central to all that we might wish to name as modern is that which appears to lie at its periphery, that which seems to flow along marginal passageways, that which seems to have its origins, in every sense, elsewhere. What must be rendered fully available for theoretical discussion is the thought that the system(s) into which these histories and experiences—that of the making of a situation, subject position, and form of existence that one might mark as African American—were apparently simply inscribed may in fact have only begun in the most fundamental sense of their historicity, or had another beginning, by way of the paradoxical dynamics of the force that has for so long been understood to simply induce their subjection. Perhaps this is the premise that Cedric Robinson had in mind two generations ago in the middle stages of his signal study of the formation of modern Europe and a world economy in and through the "transmutation" of the African diaspora. This would be otherwise than those perspectives that, although salutary, such as that offered in some of the work of Stuart Hall, tend to emphasize the matrix of a system into which the histories of the African diaspora were inscribed or submerged. The significance of the methodological suggestion I am proposing should be emphasized here: the study of the making of African American subject positions, identities, or histories, as you like, is one of the best historical sites of study for clarifying the most general social processes of our time. As is now perhaps more readily acknowledged than in the past, such exemplarity pertains to how we theorize historical processes such as those entailed in the making of "American" identities in general. Yet, in a more epistemologically general formulation, I suggest that the consideration of some of the most particular and micrological aspects of the making of these identities, may make possible some of the most general analytical insights and sustain some of the broadest theoretical inquiries.[12]

In order to recognize the salience of the formulations I have just adduced, I will concern myself with the suggestion of the possibility of a general desedimentation of a traditional conceptual premise that organizes the interpretation of the African American subject in the United States. Bringing this traditional interpretation into question may assist further in opening a new way of thinking the question of the African American or African diasporic subject, the implications of which might bear force on our understanding of the modes of constitution of any historical subject that might be called American, especially for all that has been called "White" American, and likewise for those we have called

modern or placed under the heading of modernity in general. Proposing a certain reading of an early narrative in the African diaspora, *The
Interesting Narrative of the Life of Olaudah Equiano,* I outline below some
motifs of another way, if not an entirely new one, that we might pursue
in the thinking of the question of the African American or American
subject.[13]

Theoretical Disjunction

At this juncture, however, two kinds of distinction must be remarked
in order to suggest the distinctiveness of the orientation proposed here.
The first concerns the specificity of the analytical point of view I am proposing; the second concerns the structure of the historical problem in
question.

First, the approach proposed here follows and brings into relief the
traces of the ways in which the attempt to account for the formation of
an African American social or historical subject produces an account of
structures that are constitutive in a general sense of subjectivity and subjectivation, especially within the historical frame in question—modernity, especially an American modernity. As such, I should note that this
orientation marks a difference within contemporary efforts to give more
nuanced accounts of the production of subordinate and supraordinate
forms of subjectivity and subjectivation, even if the approach proposed
here remains complimentary to other practices. One premise that is fundamental to most current efforts to rethink subjectivity in the social field
is that the supraordinate subject configures itself by way of reference to
an other, figured in the US context along an axis referencing the ethnological in general as Native American, Asian American, or Latino American, as well as African or Negro American, and so forth. Thus studies of
"whiteness" have proliferated in recent years to establish such a thesis as
general to the production of modernity or America.[14] In the wake of this
work, a considerable amount of discourse has flowed. However fundamentally necessary and valuable such studies are, and I underscore my
solidarity with them both practically and theoretically, if taken up all in
one go, so to speak, the theoretical risk remains that they tend to reproduce a fundamental limitation of the perennial discussions of difference
both within the horizon of "America" and in a key sense on a global level
when the address concerns the problem of "whiteness." What almost all

of these projects seem more or less unable to displace, or, to put it more radically, to desediment (as in to make tremble by dislodging the layers of sedimented premises that hold it in place), is the privileged orientation toward the very texts and historiographical subjects that are themselves the products of the very social hegemony that the scholarship seeks to question or render relative.[15] In contradistinction to these approaches, the one offered here follows the accounts of the formation of a subordinate subject, an African or Negro American, as the titular object of inquiry. It proposes that another heading be given for the inquiry into the configuration of the historical and social subject if the account of the formation of a supposed "White" or supraordinate subject by reference to the other is not to remain an enigmatic consolidation of the same. It may be that the status of a putative subject of whiteness can be reauthorized with even more hegemonic force by the narrative of its heterogeneous reference if that narrative is recast simply or primarily as its capacity— whether realized or "ostensibly" failed (and hence potentially recuperable by way of the arrival of a certain liberal dispensation)—to become other, as simply describing the plurality of the ideals that it can encompass. To provoke a different inscription or reinscription of the desedimentative force of such accounts, one must strategically elaborate the way in which the figure of the subordinate, the figure of the other, gives rise in the movement of its production to the figure of the hegemon—in this case, to the subject of whiteness. I emphasize the formulation "in the movement of" as opposed to a formulation such as "on the basis of." The differential structure at issue here is not derivative of a figure but is the "origin" of figuration as such within the social field in question. Thus the account that follows adheres to the enigmatic trace of the other within the formation of an African American subject, a track whose marks are such that the coherence of the figure of the "African American" and the other of such is rendered relative.

Secondly, even before formulating the conceptual problematic in question, let me, however abstractly, formulate the structure of the historical problematic in which the question of the African American first appears as such. I place it under the heading of displacement. In a radical sense, the only descriptive position that addresses the difficulty of naming this heading is *atopos*. The subject position of the African or Negro American is atopic in the sense that it is outside of spatiality as a given. This historical moment is the inauguration of slavery in the Americas.

(A) Thus, in a strict historical sense, the question of African American identity was broached with the inception of the enslavement of Africans in the Americas. Configured even prior to that which is often called the "middle passage," the question of African American or Negro American identity was raised for the captured on the shores of West and Central Africa. And, I wish to proceed precisely here, for a conceptualization of origin is what is most at stake. Even on these shores (of Africa), the question of identity would not be so much a question of relation to origin, for that, perhaps, was not the relevant concept. Rather, the experience or sense of difference or differences that specified identity as the difference recognized in or as a relationship would be decisive. (B) In a conceptual sense, that which might be called origin, or identity, became such only in the configuration of these new relationships. As I have just suggested on the basis of a specific historical reference, an origin is constituted as such only as an effect of displacement. Its status as origin is determined only by a repetition that then specifies it as its origin, or at least in a reciprocal and "simultaneous" sense, although the concept of time here is rendered, or rended, in this movement, it is not given absolutely or in the form of a "before." But if such logic is its mode of appearance, then the origin of the origin is this repetition, that is to say, a certain nonorigin, and so on.[16] What matters for our analysis here is not only that this formulation (1) in a general sense assists in gathering up into analytical view the essential predicates of the structure in which African American history is opened, but that (2) the order of generality would pertain to all levels at which historiality could be proposed as at stake, from the mundane to the ontological. Hence the pertinence of African American experience (even habitation, if you will), as example, for how history, origin, and identity in general is understood, can be made quite legible within the history of philosophy and general theory in the human sciences if we propose a certain solicitation of that history.[17] It would be an exemplary example. Without, perhaps, anticipating everything that is at stake in this chapter, then, I can suggest that taken as exemplary, it suggests the fecundity and necessity of a rereading of American history in general from this viewpoint or, better, from this horizon of problematization of existence. A certain experience offers, then, another view of system or the systemic. And this would remain so even if its exemplarity dissipates within the view of that systematicity. (C) In this conceptual-historical sense, the experience of identity as difference for African Americans, we might say, was made operative during slavery as habitual practice. And, leaving the limits of the "we" unspecified here, for it may well overrun all boundaries and distinctions, we can also say that "we" are still within the forms of that experiencing. This historical experience, then, of enslavement and the operative practices of slavery, formulates our problem, which we can trace according to two alternative and interwoven pathways: the problem of difference, that is, heterogeneity (in every possible sense), and the problem or question of origin. I call this a form of double displacement: displacement of origin and displacement from habitus.[18] This problem of heterogeneity or originary displacement, we might remark in anticipation, has the capacity to defy the privilege of (traditional) ontology.[19] Given a certain attention, the thought of the double, of double displacement in particular, renders the movement of history and historicity as radical in its delivery of an irreducible nominality within the very production of system and structure.

The Historiographical Sovereign

The General Schema

If we might anticipate the possibility of such a thought, it remains that within African American studies, a still dominant traditional interpretation of this historical problem grounds itself on certain conceptual presuppositions that would preclude it.[20] First, this approach tends to presuppose a determined historical identity or origin as its ground, a certain "America" and (often presupposed in turn as a ground of this "America") a certain "Euro-American," or better "White," subject. Secondly, it also, almost universally, presupposes the question of the ground or possibility of such an identity or origin.[21]

We need to rethink this traditional understanding of the African American problematic. An interpretation founded on such presuppositions cannot be general; it cannot give an account of the general system or possibility (historical or transcendental) in which a subject emerges (however its nominality is modified, as Euro or Afro, or some other such heading). In a sense, an interpretation, such as the traditional one, presupposes what it must explain; that is, it presupposes the system (historical or transcendental) in question. It does this by presupposing an origin of the system. In order not to operate this way, on the basis of such a presupposition, we must rethink the status or possibility of origin. In our discursive context, this means rethinking the status of a certain Euro-American subject. To undertake this rethinking, we must recognize a certain continuity of the structure of the constitution of a Euro-American subject with the processes operative in the constitution of an Afro-American subject. Let us be clear—not a simple continuity of subjectivity, but rather of the processes by which subjectity is constituted. What we will discover is that although there are differences, there is no stable ground for marking an inside and outside. Or, we can say, while there is no stability to any mark that would claim to register or recognize an inside and an outside, the yield of the processes in question is a differential deployment or dispersal of position in relation. We will not be able to undertake this rethinking unless we rethink the problem of identity or origin in general.

If one considers discourses about African Americans, their historical and contemporary experience of social subordination is mirrored in discussions of African American identity, American identity or identities, and American society in general. What happens here is a strange tale, stranger still for its ubiquity, for the fact that it remains both so legible (I will not say obvious) and so hidden. For in those texts, often under the guise of recognizing the agency of African Americans in the making of some social text, it is the constitutive force of the African American subject(s) that is most precisely blunted, dulled, or denied. These discourses have yet to comprehend (rather, they precomprehend) the ground on which they stand or, shall we say, pretend to stand. The unthought in these discourses is always, more or less, the status of a Euro-American subject. Herein lies the enigma: in trying to explain the relativity of this Euro-American subject, its constitution in relation, these discourses still presuppose this (Euro-American) subject. How does this occur?

If the autonomous status of the Euro-subject is not presumed directly, it is presupposed because these writers assume that, in one way or another, the system (of whatever sort—economic, political, cultural, religious, and so forth) begins and, hence, ends with the inaugural actions of this subject. Typically, the procedure is something like this: the system in which the subordination occurs, because it exists, is analytically presupposed, and then the subjects are inserted into this preestablished matrix to engage in their functional articulation of the permutations prescribed therein.[22] The general, and salutary, concern has been to formulate, in the most balanced and sustainable manner, an account of the simultaneous production of the position of the subordinated subject as nonoriginary and displaced, *and* as resistant to subordination and creative in practice. Yet in producing such an account, the constitution of the general system or structure in which, and by which, that (African American) subject is gathered or constructed has remained analytically presupposed or unthought, if not simply assumed. In this traditional schema, a certain preconstituted or nonconstituted subject is placed at the origin, as the origin, of the system in question. Which is to say that the system is not thought, that the system itself is approached within the circuit of analysis as preconstituted, that the system itself is assumed or presupposed. It is as if, then, we were simply trying to recognize a certain form of pre-determination. It is only then, more or less, and the discourse seldom exceeds this circuit, a question of calculating and plotting the functional distribution of the operations of this system. The matrix sketched out by the conjoined resourcefulness and limitations of this conceptualization, the aporias that are incessantly produced within it, effectively constitutes what we may call the problematic, the order of questions, that must concern us when we ask about the African American subject.[23]

If this schema that I have just outlined seems too general, I will now take notice of how it is produced and specified in a major text, first published in 1974, Eugene Genovese's *Roll, Jordan, Roll: The World the Slaves Made.*[24]

The Genovesan Example

Genovese's *Roll, Jordan, Roll* is a now-classic example of the traditional interpretation of the African American problematic, which is yet still contemporary in its articulation of an epistemic order of questions, more than a quarter of a century after its first publication.

I have chosen Genovese's study in part because the writings of Du Bois are invoked rather consistently and broadly throughout his discourse. It is almost as if the structure at stake in my chapter is produced here by Genovese's quotations of Du Bois. However, I have also chosen Genovese's work because it has been so widely influential, not only in discourses concerning the African American in the United States and the Americas but in discourses concerning the subordinated subject in general. Moreover, I have chosen Genovese's work because it represents an entire generation of scholarship that signaled its difference from earlier scholarship by its commitment to represent the point of view of the African American, and especially the African American in slavery, the fruits of which have indeed been magnificent, despite the limitations that I will seek to bring into relief here.[25]

The central problem with Genovese's investigation is its conceptualization of the relation of slaveholder and slave as a relation between an undifferentiated, essentially homogeneous subject position (or historiographical entity) and a differentiated, essentially heterogeneous subject position (or historiographical entity). The former would be the slave owner; the latter would be the slave. The entirety of Genovese's analysis is organized around this coupling and this conceptualization of its structure.

The conundrum is that Genovese's text is an analysis that is understood to have the primary burden of historiographically producing the "world" or, we might say, the "subjecthood," of the slaves, that which, in a certain sense, would be common to those inhabiting the subject position of a slave in this system. Genovese determines that which is common to those in this position as precisely the tenuousness, absence, or lack of a self-determining homogeneity (collectively, especially, and individually). Up to a certain point, of course, I do not have any quarrel with this line of analysis. Although I am not persuaded by certain emphases and analytical decisions with regard to the historiographical interpretation of the practices of these slaves, this is not the only or primary concern I wish to formulate here. Rather, I want to focus our concern on Genovese's conceptualization of the subject position of the slave owner and, hence, draw our attention to the conceptual and rhetorical effects that this conceptualization produces in his history of the "social system as a whole," which he calls the "Old South" (Genovese 1974, 661).

Articulated in the narrative, Genovese's discourse produces a static conceptual opposition, which is also, as we shall see, a certain conceptual hierarchy, a schema—and I emphasize that the two work hand in hand, as two faces of the same conceptualization—that functions as the decisive or operative conceptual grid in *Roll, Jordan, Roll*, beyond or despite Genovese's stated intentions or explicit declarations. Thus I formulate two thetic statements. (1) In this text, Genovese's discourse produces an oppositional distinction between its principal "units" (or "elements") of analysis, slaves and slaveholders. He begins and concludes his analysis as if these two respective positions had (historiographically speaking) already been accomplished, conclusively established. Hence, processes of fundamental transformation could not be recognized as operative *within* the system, even if such "actually" occurred. This means, further, that Genovese's account is functional; it is an account of the functional operation of a system. Moreover, it is an insufficient functional account. Insufficient because, although transformation is certainly a functional aspect of any system, Genovese's discourse does not seem capable of acknowledging such a motif in a history of the Old South.[26] (2) This oppositional distinction is hierarchical because it has to presuppose that one element of its units of analysis is atomic, homogeneous, and replete in order for the oppositional distinction to hold; yet if both are such—that is, truly or radically atomic—there is no system, no relation, no history, nothing to explain. The presupposed homogeneous, or pure, element is understood, hence, according to the logic of this schema, as a preconstituted term in the analysis. It is understood to acquire its coherence, its essential predicates, prior to the relationship in question. Yet there must be a system for there to arise the form of a problem that solicits historiographical analysis. The preconstituted term, however, could not then be understood as *subject* to the system in any fundamental way. Rather, in this inquiry, the system, *if it is to include this term at all*, has to be analytically built on the presupposition of this term's preconstituted identity. It would be understood to mark the opening or closure (or both) of the system in question. This element or unit, then, predetermines the theorization of the direction of operation of the system by specifying its origin and, hence, its telos. In the narrative, it makes the entire teleological movement ultimately (and this intensifier is intended to specify that rhetorical and conceptual register in which all the decisive questions of Genovese's text are decided) the working out of the project of one of its subjects, a white, male, Euro-American slaveholder. The other subject, in this staidly dialectical account, is seen as a priori limited in its accomplishments of its own desire or projection. In fact, accomplishments actually made by this other subject, a slave subject, are always recuperated or recuperable in Genovese's narrative as part of the teleology announced by the practices of its other, a slaveholding subject. In the decisive moments of this text, this entire schema is understood quite literally as operated by the law of the (white) father (*master, lord, padrone, patron, padrón, patrão*) (Genovese 1974, 5–6, 166–67).

This returns us to the originating move of Genovese's analysis and the problem that we have noticed therein. Genovese's analysis proceeds as if— fait accompli—the historical structure of which he is concerned to give an account should be understood as an epistemic given. He writes too often as if, historiographically, the historical system that he is analyzing is complete, finished, resolved in its movement. Yet according to the most secure and resolute protocols, those that allow us to recognize the very opening of historicity and those that allow us to formulate the project of historiographical interpretation, we know that historical systems are irreducibly open, unfinished, and irresolvable in their movement. In a fundamental sense, not only is their end yet to come, but so too is their origin (or better, the value and pertinence of the structure of their genesis). For the latter is always undergoing its own unfolding according to the impress of what has become possible and stake in a never foreclosed sense of futurity. At the level of its narrative, Genovese's discourse seems unable to remain fully open to these protocols.

I will trace one example of this problematic in this great book, Genovese's description of the "law" of slavery. And, I should underscore that the term and concept of "law" used here is from Genovese's discourse; as I hope to suggest, law in that sense acquires its organization within the movement of becoming that is excessive to simple operability. ("Law" in any sense, but especially in the sense that Genovese names it in this chapter, would always appear within the movements of force, of power, of the trace of the other—in the conceptual metaphoric sense proposed at the outset of this chapter—in the constitution of any subjectivity. In the specific sense that I am proposing, following Du Bois, its devolution is only or by way of the movement of the double, by way of the force of the double, of the production of a reference for subjectivation that is always at least and never only double. In the analytic sense, in an inquiry such as Genovese's, "law" can only be after the "fact." My suggestion is simply that historical discourse in general, *if it would be a critical one, must* take this epistemological moment of its inscription within metaphysics into account.) I wish to make legible two interwoven presuppositions within his account.

First Presupposition: Genovese begins his chapter "The Hegemonic Function of the Law" with a functional demarcation of the historical period in question.

This functional orientation of this entire analysis of law is in part due to its borrowing its principal conceptual orientation from Antonio Gramsci's brief notes on the function of law in the essay "The Modern

Prince" and the notes on "The State and Civil Society." The functional
reduction occurs in part because Gramsci is formulating a prescription for the operation of law by the state in a revolutionary situation
and Genovese is attempting to develop a description of the operation of
the law of slavery in the antebellum South. To the extent that Genovese
reproduces Gramsci's prescription as a description, law appears simply as
the pivotal instrument in the slaveholding class's self-initiated reproduction of the system of slavery.[27]

He writes that although Gramsci's concept of hegemony implies class
antagonisms, "it also implies, for a given historical epoch, the ability of
a particular class to contain those antagonisms on a terrain in which
its legitimacy is not dangerously questioned" (Genovese 1974, 26). The
operative concept here is "danger" or "dangerousness." Anything less is,
more or less, simple reproduction. This is because "danger" or "dangerousness" has already been understood in terms of a preconstituted idea
of what is the relevant historical "period."

Second Presupposition: Genovese then goes on to reduce the functioning of law to an instrumental value, reproductive of planter rule in
all its transformations. Although he proclaims a dialectical identity of
the slaveholding class, that "the slaveholders arose and grew in dialectical
response" to the other classes in the society, that the law was an "active
partially autonomous force, which mediated among the classes and [even
that it] compelled the rulers to bend to the demands of the ruled," the
system of law of the slave South is understood in this book to both begin
and end with the inaugural actions of the slaveholding class.

At the very least, Genovese is unable to respond fully to his own proclaimed protocols. Although I cannot give full notice here, I note that
his narrative is marked by several rhetorical gestures that indicate its
circumscription by its presupposition of the slaveholder as the "origin"
of the system in question. The most prevalent marker is the location of
the subject of key sentences at the head of paragraphs and chapters or the
play of pronouns, which indicates that the analysis is proceeding from
the point of view (that would analytically be that) of the slaveholding
class.[28] At the very beginning of the chapter on law, Genovese writes,
"The slaveholders as a socio-economic class shaped the legal system to
their interests" (Genovese 1974, 27). Near the end of this chapter, comparing the slave code of the American South to those of Brazil, the various
Caribbean colonies, and Spanish South America, he writes that, contrary

to the fact that in those other societies where the slave codes were drafted by metropolitan elites who were not slaveholders, in the United States, the slave codes "came from the slaveholders themselves and represented their collective estimate of right and wrong and of the limits that should hedge in their own individual power" (Genovese 1974, 48). What is important is that for Genovese, the law issued not only from the slaveholding class as a whole but more precisely from an "advanced fraction" of that class. Herein we can recognize the orientation around a homogeneous, self-constituting subject. Genovese asserts that a certain gesture took place within the slaveholding class.

> [A] political center arose, consolidated itself, and assumed a com-manding position during the 1850s. The most advanced fraction of the slaveholders—those who most clearly perceived the interests and needs of the class as a whole—steadily worked to make their class more conscious of its nature, spirit and destiny. In the process it cre-ated a worldview appropriate to a slaveholders regime. For any such political center, the class as a whole must be brought to a higher understanding of itself—transformed from a class-in-itself, react-ing to pressures on its objective position, into a class-for-itself, con-sciously striving to shape the world in its own image. (Genovese 1974, 27)[29]

To the extent that Genovese recognizes that the law of slavery is founded on a radical incoherence or exorbitance and yet insists on the line of analy-sis quoted above, he cannot analytically be responsible to an insight that he recognizes as his own: that the law of slavery is opened as a problem only in the relationship of slavery, we might say, due to the force of the slave, due to the effects of the capacity of the slave to intend or to will; that the system itself is opened only in its possibility and its particular historical configu-ration in the infrastructural movement that announces this irreducible capacity of the slave to act or choose otherwise. He recognizes that the law of slavery inscribes an aporia: the premise of the idea of slavery in America and thus of the American law of slavery is the denial of the humanity of the slave—that is, within a system of value and authority where the essential mark or sign of the human is the capacity to be or become a subject—yet the slave can be made subordinate to the law only by recognizing his or her capacity to transgress it. Thus, the law in its reflex must recognize—even if under the heading of a denegation—the will and, hence, the subjectity or position of the slave as one of a putative subjecthood, notwithstanding the necessarily relational and differential announcement of such a figure. Hence, the law of slavery "had to" recognize precisely that which has been understood in the dominant discourse of right in Europe and America since the sixteenth and seventeenth centuries as the basis for a recognition of humanity.[30] Genovese reduces this problematic to a functional modality within the system instead of recognizing that it opens the system itself. The law of slavery is constituted in this difference, this abyss; the law of slavery is of this structural exorbitance, both issuing from it as well as portending to determine its implication; the law of slavery is a formation constituted by the operation of this movement, produced under the force of its disjunctive impress, stretched across the abyss of a grounding fault line. As such, it is also always unwriting itself even in its gesture to write itself.[31] In this sense, it is always in danger.

We can sum up the effects of this conceptual misplacement by noticing Genovese's closing statement in this chapter. The force of the slave as subject or as constitutive dimension of a general form of subjectity that is operative in and as this scenography is utterly evacuated in statements such as the following:

> Since the slaves knew that the law protected them little and could not readily be enforced even that little . . . [f]or protection against every possible assault on their being they had to turn to a human protector—in effect, a lord. They had to look to their masters for protection against patrollers, against lynching, against the strict enforcement of the law itself, as well as against hunger and physical deprivation. And they had to look to some other white man to shield them against a harsh or sadistic master. Thus the implicit hegemonic dual system of law conquered the quarters. (Genovese 1974, 48)

While it is hard not to give privileged attention to the absolute denial of any lateral solidarity among slaves in terms of the concept of a collectivity under the heading of which an account of a sense of world could be given (as a social class, in Genovese's dominant theoretical reference in this study) what we should note about this passage is its summary statement of the presupposition that, as principle, guides all terms of the whole account given in this study, which yields an interpretation of the slaveholder as the originator of the movement of power, of the play of difference.

I have tried to briefly remark here some of the conceptual and theoretical limits that I summarized above as a general problematic in discourses concerning African Americans in the United States and to trace some of their effects in one key aspect of Genovese's interpretation of the African American subject in slavery. Motifs that run parallel to those just outlined with reference to legality as such could also be adduced in his discussion of African American religion during slavery, taking particular notice of the reduction of the origin of slave practices to a certain "Europe" or "Euro-America" and the subsequent placement of the slaveholder as the metonymic figure of "God-the-father," as a singular, self-possessed, and all-encompassing paternal figure (or origin) in relation to a dispersed, self-divided, plurality of subordinate subjects, among whom there is no lateral or horizontal identity, and whose only functional common ground stems from their subordination to the same figure (Genovese 1974, 161–284).[32]

Here, let me add two notes. First, the functioning of this schema remains more intractable than one might think. The task of its critical disruption remains an ongoing epistemic conundrum. A more careful rethinking of its premises may indeed give a more fundamental basis for shifting the dominant orientations afoot in African American and American studies, of all Americans, and of the very concept of America itself. It promises to help us get beyond simple declarations of essentialism or nonessentialism, while not giving up the force of the critique that opened the way for the recognition of the figure of the subordinate in discourses concerning the African American. Secondly, it remains, however, that the dissolution of this schema is more difficult, enigmatic, and uneasy than one might imagine, and mutations or transformations in the logic of its functioning are always at risk of falling back into the old logic or of locking gears under the myth of the neutral.[33]

I suggest a different approach, one that marks the force of the subordinate, even as it recognizes a double or redoubled valence at the heart of the critical response to subjection. In an inimitable fashion, Hortense Spillers has formulated the concept-metaphor of "ambivalence" to describe the African American as subject in relation to all that is called America. She suggests that this concept-metaphor can describe the historical-ontological, or "cultural," situation of this subject. She writes, "If by ambivalence we might mean that abeyance of closure, or *break* in the passage of syntagmatic movement from one more or less stable property to another, as in the radical disjuncture between 'African' and 'American,' then ambivalence remains not only the privileged and arbitrary judgment of a postmodernist imperative, but also a strategy that names the new cultural situation as a wounding."[34] All this subtends an "abeyance of closure" of the Negro subject within an order that is grounded in or oriented by a metaphor of the pure or the simple. When the necessity of this ambivalence is recognized within the infrastructural organization of systems of domination and exploitation, and its bearing thus becomes generalizable in a certain way, then a certain hyperbolic force operative within this movement that configures the subordinated subject acquires a certain relief, and thus so does its originary bearing in the production of symbol and value. I will attempt to track the edges of this legibility below by following certain motifs of Olaudah Equiano's narrative of enslavement, slavery, and freedom. I suggest that this formulation, perhaps Spillers's and certainly my own, finds its most poignant resonance if not its absolute resource in Du Bois's pivotal formulations. It is to that resource that I now, briefly, turn.

Theoretical Conjunction

> After the Egyptian and Indian, the Greek and the Roman, the Teuton and the Mongolian, the Negro is a sort of seventh son, born with a veil and gifted with second-sight in this American world,—a world which yields him no true self-consciousness, but only lets him see himself through the revelation of the other world. It is a peculiar sensation, this double consciousness, this sense of always looking at one's self through the eyes of others, of measuring one's soul by the tape of a world that looks on in amused contempt and pity. One ever feels his two-ness,—an American, a Negro; two souls, two thoughts, two unreconciled strivings; two warring ideals in one dark body, whose dogged strength alone keeps it from being torn asunder. (*Souls*, 3, chap. 1, para. 3)

We can recall here that I have proposed that the traditional schema that governs discourses on the Negro American has presumed the possibility of a certain replete figural position as the inaugural moment in the organization of the field that has been called America. Claiming to recognize relation as the general shape of this field, it has nonetheless understood relation as an overdetermined hierarchy in which—in both an historiographical and theoretical sense—the figure of the subordinate issues only within the dispensation made possible by the figure of the supraordinate. While force and domination and exploitation by force may well be actual, most emphatically so, it remains that it would be too quick to assume thereby the productivity of this relation as simply a direct and overdetermined yield. While the process of such productivity is precisely the terms of the common, such continuity at once also issues as an order of discontinuity. This formation, paradoxical in its apparition as a form of presence, acquires this tensed configuration most fundamentally because there is no simple outside to this relation. There is not nor can there be any stable historial term—as position or subjectum—outside, before, after, or beyond this relation. Any configuration that can be remarked is produced only in and through the dynamic torsions of such relation. As we will see, it sets afoot a peculiar asymmetrical symmetry.

At this juncture, I can now begin to reposition the still perennial presumption and traditional schema that has governed in discourses concerning the African American by remarking its logic on a more general register and thereby finding an initial way to position the generality of the effort in theoretical reconceptualization that I propose.

First, I recall my assessment in the previous section of this chapter that the thesis of the singular continuity of dominance in all its modalities with hegemony in all its registers—forming what is in the end a unitary and smooth whole, in virtue or ideal, if not already as a direct and actual apprehendable fact—has been the governing premise in the discourses concerning the Negro in America in general. And, I recall too that this has meant the presumption that there is a sovereign figure somewhere that might subtend this smooth dispensation made possible by dominance (and even exploitation).

Previous theory, as exemplified in this still exemplary initiative in scholarship (the work of a post-1960s generation in historical scholarship), has too often and too easily assumed a given figuration of "mastery" and sovereignty. In such an assumption, the formation of the figure of the supraordinate, no matter its diacritical remark, has been understood in a conceptual and theoretical sense to acquire its ontological status, its pertinence as an existent for an analysis, prior to the relation of slavery. Or if somehow it is put in a fungible manner, that in fact such figure of dominance should be seen in relation, it is still too often understood under the heading of a presence that has already arrived at a certain fullness (even if a conservative and reactionary one).

Along the line of the discussion of the previous section of this chapter, we have recognized this premise in a now classic and still commanding account (according to modification and theoretical amendment) of the organization of slavery on the North American historical terrain, taking the statement given in the account of "the world that the slaves made" as the nodal point of a whole itinerary, both before and after, in the work of Eugene Genovese.

Secondly, however, while I have already begun to question the logic of this schema, by way of the example of that classic projection in discourse, I can now begin to remark the matter more generally and thus also begin to name more directly the character of my proposed reformulation and elaboration of its broader implication.

For, within the discourse that has been perennial for more than a century—especially within the once emergent but now overwrought disciplines of a general sociology or ethnology (historiography, ethnography, demography, economy, psychology, and so on)—with regard to the provenance of the practices of African Americans on the historical terrain of what has become in the North American context the United States, this premise—and the terms of the debate that it has put in motion—has taken on a distinct and definitive organization. Such practices—Afro-Afra-Negro-Colored-Black-African-American—have been understood as either homogeneous with the dominant order (under the sign of the hidden sovereign produced by way of supposed critical thought itself), in which the constitution of that order as it has been understood has its essential inauguration prior to and apart from any reference to the announcement of such practices as an historical configuration. Or, such practices have been understood as a pathological deviation therefrom, as a pathological form in relation to such an understanding of dominant order (legal, political, cultural, theological, linguistic, literary, familial, and economic). And while there are exceptions to such resolute theoretical disposition, their status as such, variable and yet productive as they may remain, proves the rule and the norm.

The idea that the very possibility of the practices of such an apparent historical form known as African American might be understood to offer the terms by which to name an originary organization of historial irruption that might be general to an entire historicity which has for a long time gone under the name of "America" has remained at best an ambiguous and indifferently proposed thought. Thus, while I have begun to question the theoretical premise of this whole schema—by formulating a thought of a founding violence, which would disavow or dissimulate the terms of its own initiation, which encodes, nonetheless, a certain lability into its own supposed foundation—it is the implication of such rethinking as opening the space of this general thought that is of foremost importance for theory in this domain.

The already incipient form of a retheorization has led me to begin to propose that we recognize relation as the originary instance, in a theoretical sense and in a certain manner (or a sense in which spatiality and temporality would incessantly displace each other as the idiomatic marks of emergence), of the constitution of respective subject position. As such, at the level of an ontological constitution of a social or historical field— the historial, that is to say—a fundamental mutuality of position can be understood and remarked. And this bearing of relation is decisive no matter the character of the violence or force entailed in opening the field of possibility for the production of such historial emergence and formation of historical order. Hierarchy, then, is produced in and through this originary configuration and not beforehand. This relation does not issue from hierarchy and a putative pure position of origination. Rather, hierarchy and origination, in their original configuration, acquire their form in, by way of, and from, this relation.

This theory of the continuous discontinuity of dominance and hegemony must be elaborated, even if only in a provisional manner, searching and remaining open to finding its way in multiple futural registers.[35]

Thus, third, we can recall here that the lability of the founding violence of the colonial projection—in which slavery in what has become North America was originarily announced—and its aftermath may be most assiduously recognized on the order of the profundity of the demands it puts to theoretical sense by following the track of the constitution of the subordinate subject in formation.

Fourth, if the latter threshold premise holds its practical theoretical value as guide, it is because we can notate there a certain figuration of ambivalence, a motif of double marking, even of a redoubled consideration.

This is to say that we can now begin to render thematic as a theoretical proposition that the subordinate subject in the context of what has come to be known as "America," the slave if you will, is produced as a figure of ambivalence, a figuration of a certain thought of the double, as a figure whose inaugural reference of subjectivation is that of double identification, at once an identification and a disidentification. Let us say more generally that in the historial sense this figuration of emergence is more properly understood as an instance of originary double displacement: that is to say, displacement from both origin and habitus. In such a devolution, this here and this now can only be simultaneously the requisite of an affirmation—a way out of no way—and the mark of a limit that must remain only as the form of an institution given as fate or providence— "Why must God make me an outcast and a stranger in mine own house?" (*Souls*, 3, chap. 1, para. 2).

The movement that marks the itinerary of this constitution of the subordinate will paradoxically allow a return to the scene of origination—the scene of an originary displacement—to remark its organization and originary order of productivity.

Our privileged example here is given in the work and itinerary of W. E. B. Du Bois—for he both names this movement in the historial profile of the African American, in multiple specific itineraries, as slave, as freed person, as the so-called New Negro (of multiple generations), and as the subject of a new order of civil rights—as he outlines the path of the production of a certain "double consciousness" and a distinct possibility of historical "second-sight" (*Souls*, 3, chap. 1. para. 3).

The ensemblic forms of subjectivation entailed arise by way of the forceful and destructive productivity of the practices that Du Bois placed under the heading of "the problem of the color-line," the manifestations of which in the "American" context of the United States he placed, in turn, under the concept-metaphor "the veil." What must be annotated and emphasized here is that this form of historicity is not first of all or in the end a simple mode of exclusion but the actual and historically irreversible titular form of the production of *the horizon of historial order*, of historicity most generally and of all those symbolic orderings of practice that have been named by way of the concept of culture, but especially of the sense of possibility as it has been announced within the limits of existing technologies for the making and remaking of self-as-becoming-other than the given. This is a way, perhaps the way, in which impossibility *and* possibility in the form of historial limit *is produced* as existence.

Yet the force of this production, of a subject perhaps, of a subject position no doubt, as of ambivalence, of double reference, renders legible for critical thought the mark and seam of a founding liability within the schema of any proposed hierarchy within such configured relation. It yields as Du Bois's account offers it to us, "a second-sight." This is to say that within and by way of such "second- sight," the fictionality of the historical order in general can be recognized ("this American world," for example) as one that is announced only within and by way of the institution of this violent hierarchy and organization of difference, and yet as also an instituting formation which in that very movement opens within its devolution, simultaneously as it were, the dissemination of any proposed limit of historical possibility.

Still more, within this general scene, of historicity, this peculiar sense, this doubled remark of the world, allows one to recognize the fiction at the root of the constitution of the subject position of the claim to a certain form of dominance and thence a proposed hegemony. A mobile distanciation can be adduced beyond the fiction of self-constitution, self-authorization, or sovereign domination, and the claim to a unique origin and telos of historical becoming.

In the gesture to gather itself and proclaim itself to the world, to the world community of nations as Thomas Jefferson put it after the fact of the formal-legal inaugural claim of a "declaration of independence," the doubled sight remarks the originary constitution of position as putative subject—even of world historical status—as taking shape *only* in and through (by way of historial passage) the relation of slavery and the promulgation of an imperial colonial order. We note that the figurative dominance proffered as titular was one that pursued the mercantile destruction of indigenous orders of whatever lineage (no presumption of a simple anteriority or antecedent purity, in the event) on both sides of the Atlantic basin, in this specific historical instance. And we note that likewise, in its centuries-long eventuality, it participated in the destructuration of the organization of those forms of historicity that would have subtended it at the base (the supposed metropole) of the imperial projection. The forms of world-hood that might be named as modern within this historicity can in no instance of their essential configuration be understood apart from the global-level promulgation of what Du Bois placed (and we retain it here in a theoretical sense not only despite but precisely with all of its metaphoric instability, which remains productive for critical or paleonymic thought) under the heading of "the problem of the color-line." On this order, the supposed supraorigin is understood quite simply as a derivation of a specific kind and implication.

It is here that we can index and annotate the admirable and telling question posed by Ranajit Guha in his meditation on the structure of

the production of a "dominance without hegemony" in the colonial theater. "Why," he asks, are there "two paradigms" of "political culture" in
the eventuality of colonial organization and its aftermath in the Indian
subcontinent, for example? These two paradigms can be described
simply: one of an indigenous reference (even if borrowed in the main
from a somewhat moribund past, in Guha's schema) deeply marked by
religious premise; another of foreign reference, that was imposed by a
form of power that in the act and its ongoing maintenance contravened
its own claims of a universal dispensation, encoding that very mark as
the ground of the claim for its supposed authority. In this context, the
colonial state failed to generate a hegemonic authorization for its presence—as indicated, for example, by the incessant forms of insurrection,
mutiny, organized rebellion, and eventually a certain form of revolution
in the direction of a supposed independence—because it could continue
only by failing to fulfill its universalizing claim. We can extend and
reelaborate this suggestion by recognizing, through an attunement to Du
Bois's thought of a global-level problem of the color-line, that with the
advent of the modern imperial colonial eruption the idea of a singular
or unitary whole as a practical theoretical projection has, in its eventual
unfolding, been rendered obsolete. As such, all theoretical efforts to project another thought of the whole under the heading of an idea of the *singular*—the replete and distinct figure of the one, even in the form of the
singular example—will be confounded by this difficulty. Only concepts
of relation, otherwise than a dialectic, that is, a radical thought of the
subatomic, if you will, might allow the elaboration of another thought
of whole, which as an eventuality rather than an instance, in its realization and as its accomplishment, could only always reopen the question of
relation. Form, if there will ever have been such, would remain distended
in its becoming. This new thought affirms such sense of a reference—one
that is always at least and, hence, never only double—as the most fecund
sense of possibility. By way of this thinking with the supposed constitution of the subordinate we propose to address on a fundamental order
the question of the general form of historial possibility as it shows forth
in existence.[36]

   And too, certainly, within all of its limits and possibilities—that is the
American scene, for example, or the modern historical world in general,
for another order of such—the subordinate figure is here recognized as
an originary figure in the production the historial. While a constitutive

figure in the order called "America" as the putative exemplar of the modern form of social order, for sure, but it is even more so articulated generally in the postcolonial horizon as itself a certain potentially radical mark of the existing futurity of the global order. This production is by way of the mode of its constitution in and through the irruption of an always previous originary displacement. And, in the instance of the African or Negro American in the North American context, I have diacritically attended this genesis as a form of double displacement—from both any ostensible simple figuration of origin and from habitus.

It is with this double implication of the example—of the subordinate in general, the African American in specific, and the slave in particular—of subjectivation as arising only in this torsion of a doubled reference that a certain sense of possibility can begin to be remarked. For the narrative account of this process if tracked by way of the figure of the subordinate always maintains within its devolution a profoundly reflexive and recursive configuration. It always affirms within its terms *a possible rethematization* of the path of subjection. Its very articulation as subjectivation as subjection opens a distanciation within the institution of the mark allowing thereby a turning back onto the ground of its own production an attention that solicits, or renders thematic, the disjunctive form of the constitution of both position and subject as position. The sense of this path of subject constitution, if there is such, as a movement of ambivalence, makes possible in turn a naming of an operation or process moving within the system that exceeds, or remains exorbitant, to any projection of the historial as a realized structure, and perhaps announces both its possibility and limit.

It is in this sense that we might reformulate our opening question in terms appropriate to our discourse as it may appear to us here in the midst of an effort at epistemic desedimentation.

Can the production of a social being in subjection, as an irreducible "double," be understood in an analytical sense, but with irony not far from our vocative utterance, as the titular subject of an account of the movement of subjectivation—a titular figure that would be general in its bearing—with regard to the structure of its subjection? Can such a thought be made general here, in the sense of an ironic deployment? I have suggested the general conceptual resource available in the orientation of Du Bois's formulation that the African American subject as always figured as a subject only in and through the force of a limit, or the other.

If this is so, is it general to the African American as such, throughout the historicity that becomes announceable in the formation of such a subject? What of the other through which the African American subject is marked, in particular in the horizon of the legal and formal general subsumption that was the institution of Atlantic-basin slavery, a so-called master, or a "Euro-American" or "White" subject? Does such a subject, the supraordinate subject, escape this movement of the double that Du Bois describes for the Negro American? How might these formulations be rendered in the general field of the colonial and the postcolonial? Might not this formulation of Du Bois's prove "good to think with" in an uncanny manner? I have tried to pose, here, in a certain theoretical register, the value of thinking with Du Bois, by way of Du Bois, working with his formulations of the problem of the "double," of "double consciousness," toward a thought of a general understanding of the production of historical subjectivity across the expanse of our common colonial nexus since the inception of these modern practices—of imperial projection in and as slavery and colonialism of the most recent past centuries.

The Paradoxical Emergence

Now then, following upon the orientation that we have formulated by way of reference to the discourse of Du Bois, pursuing it in tracking another discourse, let us expand our canvas and briefly consider a text, *The Interesting Narrative of the Life of Olaudah Equiano, or Gustavus Vassa, the African, Written by Himself*, first published in 1789.[37]

I am concerned to ask: To what extent, across the nearly one and a half centuries between Du Bois's formulation and the narrative of Equiano, and during slavery, can one find a resonance among these Africanist articulations of modernity? Is there a resonance in such an early moment of the problematic that Du Bois formulated as a movement opening the processes of subjectivation of the Negro American in the United States? Might Du Bois's formulations help us in considerations of the foundations of authority within the opening stages of the itinerary of a certain "America," and of our common nexus in modernity, in the general social field as well as in those domains that fall under the heading of law and politics? Equiano's narrative can rightfully be invoked as belonging to several different canons (both the Hispanic and English Caribbean, West African, British, and North American). We consider this text precisely because it sits at so many crossroads, at so many junctures in which our contemporary modernity takes shape.

This text was produced in that historical moment when slavery was at its height, when capital acquired its position of an irreversible consolidation within a key part of Europe, and thereby a certain world economy, and began to distribute its effects globally. It was the doubly configured moment when, on the one hand, the social institutions of the market and the industrial organization of capital that dominate our time took their first definitive shape, and, on the other, the colonial expropriation of wealth took on a renewed and global dynamic, precisely as a modern form and as constitutive in that modern reorganization of wealth and power. On the one hand, it should be noted that this thought stood at the root of Du Bois's thematization of the modern horizon already from the turn of the century and was then fully articulated in his magisterial study during the 1930s of the limits of reconstruction in America in the aftermath of the American Civil War. On the other hand, certainly this conjunction marks the scene of an ongoing problematization for contemporary thought as it would propose to account for the productivity and legacies of the history of Atlantic slavery in the making of the modern global order.[38]

As such, Equiano's is a text that articulates the problematic of African American or diasporic identity with the very presuppositions of all that we call modernity. This is to say, Equiano's text is selected here, according to the theoretical judgments I have just noted, precisely because it confounds all essentialist grounds for its inclusion or exclusion from our purview and yet sediments such densely interlaced layers of the social realities in which it acquires its configurative character.

While the excavations of the inimitable Arna Bontemps prepared a presentation of the text in the wake of the dynamic reengagement with the history of matters African American set in motion by the movements of that fateful decade of the 1960s that could place it in my initial purview, it was Houston Baker's discussion afoot the emergence of a new theoretical discourse in advent of the 1980s that annotated the mercantilism of Equiano in this narrative and as such provided the first provocation for my efforts to recognize the other register of telling that I propose here.[39] In this regard, I consider my reading as a contribution simply interwoven with Baker's reference. As such, it can be said that our common discourse of that latter half of the twentieth century and the turn to the next, in its turn, is simply a punctuation in the nodal irruption that is registered both within the eighteenth-century text as given and its afterlife as a practical engagement with the torsions of this most modern of histories, stretching not only to remark its past but also to address its futures across the coming decades and centuries.

Narrative Figurations

Against the surface grain of a narrative that represents itself as outlining the workings of the hand of Providence in his life story, Equiano's text sediments another telling. First, let us give the heading.

> I was from early years a predestinarian, I thought whatever fate had determined must ever come to pass; and, therefore, if ever it were my lot to be freed, nothing could prevent me, although I should at present see no means or hope to obtain my freedom; on the other hand, if it were my fate not to be freed, I should never be so, and all my endeavors for that purpose would be fruitless. In the midst of these thoughts, I therefore looked up with prayers anxiously to God for my liberty; and at the same time used every honest means, and did all that was possible on my part to obtain it.[40]

Yet, this story, as one can note in its phrasing "at the same time," portends itself as something other than an account simply of beneficence, divine or otherwise, and a receptivity appropriate to such. As such then, secondly, we can already note the possibility of an atheological dimension that could show forth within the interstices of this text. Or, to extend this thought just a bit further still, however, I propose not only that it marks a "self-conscious, mercantile self-evaluation" and the self-initiative implied therein, but that almost beyond the order of intention that it ascribes to itself, it registers the play of a general organization of force, which I will call the force of the double, in the articulation of the relationship of lord and bondsman. In such an organization, disruptive maintenance of an ambivalence that paradoxically hinges on the bias shows forth under the figure of irony.

With such headings in mind—our own positioned here as economic, philological, and historial and our narrator's figured as theological—in the most simple and limpid fashion then, we can now take a somewhat more sustained reference to the text of Equiano's evocation of his passage and its narrative (of) accumulation.

After a year of labor with a new owner, Robert King, whom Equiano describes as kind, the slave begins to recognize his value to him.

He writes, "I became very useful to my master, and saved him, as he used to acknowledge, above a hundred pounds a year" (Equiano 1969, 73; Equiano 2003, 103). He then generalizes this recognition: "I have sometimes heard it asserted that a Negro cannot earn his master the first cost, but nothing can be further from the truth. I suppose nine-tenths of the mechanics throughout the West Indies are Negro slaves; and I well know the coopers among them earn two dollars a day, the carpenters the same, and often times more; as also the masons, smiths and fishermen, etc. And I have known many slaves whose masters would not take a thousand pounds for them" (Equiano 1969, 73; Equiano 2003, 103). Then as an example, he notes, "My master was several times offered by different gentlemen, one hundred guineas for me, but always told them he would not sell me, to my great joy" (Equiano 1969, 73; Equiano 2003, 103–4).

In this self-evaluation, Equiano, a slave, comes to recognize that it is his relation to property that organizes his relationship to humans, both to himself and to others.

The abstract character of this relation can be outlined as follows. First, this structure includes his relationship not only to things as property but also to humans as property. Secondly, this relation entails his relationship to his "self," "himself," as property. Third, and further, this relationship to self entails his status as a free or autonomous (in will or intention) subject, according to social convention, especially law. This specific idea of an abstract organization of relation to self within the social field acquired its terms of value or presuppositions within an unfolding transnational horizon of social order marking the Atlantic region at the time of Equiano's inscription into slavery and his production of the story of this process. It registers thus the mark of an evolving social practice general to the imperial expansion of European nations at this time, the mid-eighteenth century. As given in the philosophical discourse from John Locke to Immanuel Kant we can name three motifs, dimensions of a contractual horizon: (1) one does not own something, property, if one is not free to do with it as one pleases (one owns something only if one can do with it as one pleases); (2) one's negotiation of transfer of property (or participation in a contract) is considered binding only if one is considered autonomous in such transfer or participation; and (3) a slave, as property himself, cannot transfer property, including himself, or enter into contract, in his own name.[41]

The narrative illustration of this relationship is organized as a series of ironies arrayed around one central and embedded irony. That is, if

Equiano, as property, acquires property (albeit small), he can transform his relationship to humans, including himself.

The story line of events is quite simple. First, Equiano begins work aboard his owner's sloop. Shortly thereafter, Equiano begins to think that traveling on board the ship might provide a means to freedom either by allowing him to earn wealth through trading or by providing him with opportunities to escape. In the narrative, Equiano considers each option, turning down escape and pursuing the accumulation of capital. At that point, there arises in the narrative a statement of self-activity by a slave that seems prosaic but can be rendered to attest to a quite stunning force within the interstices of its economy and the apparent simplicity of the force of its articulation, for within the context of the narrative it might be shown to lace together in the gesture of one locution so much of the moral and social order unfolding around him:

> After I had been sailing for some time with this captain, at length I endeavored to try my luck, and commence merchant. I had but a very small capital to begin with; for one single half bit, which is equal to three pence in England, made up my whole stock. However, I trusted the Lord to be with me; and at one of our trips to St. Eustatius, a Dutch island, I bought a glass tumbler with my half bit, and when I came to Montserrat I sold it for a bit, or six pence. Luckily we made several successive trips to St. Eustatius (which was a general mart for the West Indies, about twenty leagues from Montserrat), and in our next, finding my tumbler so profitable, with this one bit I bought two tumblers more; and when I came back, I sold them for two bits, equal to a shilling sterling. When we went again, I bought with these two bits four more of these glasses, which I sold for four bits on our return to Montserrat. And in our next voyage to St. Eustatius, I bought a jug of Geneva, nearly about three pints in measure. When we came to Montserrat, I sold gin for eight bits, and the tumblers for two, so that my capital now amounted in all to a dollar, well husbanded and acquired in the space of a month or six weeks, when I blessed the Lord that I was so rich. (Equiano 1969, 84; Equiano 2003, 116)

The epistemic richness of this rather prosaic account will have to be adduced, for the narration of this activity can be shown as marked by several interwoven figures of irony.

Narrative Configurations

The first irony is the conjunction of luck (as in speculative venture and risk) and trust (as in Providence, telos) in a single gesture or reflection upon such a gesture. On the one hand, Equiano will "try his luck" in this mercantile venture. On the other hand, he states that he "trusted the Lord" to deliver his freedom. Although it raises an entire structure of theological questions, we should note that to "try" Providence, to calculate Providence, is at least to supplement the will of God. Hence, we should wonder as to the both the narratological forthrightness and the entrepreneurial naivete of our intrepid sea-goer.

The second irony is that Equiano's embarkation on mercantile trade, while apparently the most normal of practices in even the most mundane forms of economy of exchange, one certainly highly developed not only at this *time* in some general periodization but within the specific *place(s) and temporalities* of Equiano's Atlantic travels, still yet beneath this prosaic presentation, offers an account that entails a conceptual monster for the rising forms of contract theory in Europe and the Americas. It is the case of property transacting property. This is monstrous to the presuppositions of ascending liberal market conventions, the authority of which was then in the process of being consolidated in Europe and in its colonial and imperial theater. Let me specify those presuppositions a bit more: First, there is the idea of "the non-contracted and non-contractual capacity of individuals to be treated as beings entitled to rights."[42] Secondly, there is the idea that for there to be proprietary rights of an individual over property, that is, possession, use, and alienability, ownership must be considered free and complete. According to these presuppositions—in Locke, Rousseau, Kant, and Hegel—how could a slave, whose status as supposed nonbeing and as proprietary object is understood as determined by an exchange between two others (men, "white" men, owners of slaves), engage "legitimately" in the exchange of property (legitimacy being the socially conventional way of referring to Equiano's private commitment to earn his freedom by "honest and honorable" means)? Yet in fact, or in fiction, property exchanging property seems to be occurring at this juncture in Equiano's narrative.

The third irony is that a slave is gaining freedom on the back of the slave trade, quite literally on board the same ships and along the same pathways by which others are being transported to be enslaved. Equiano's narrative brackets this; it cannot seem to account for the risk to which its own force exposes it. It always risks simply reinscribing precisely that which it wishes to overthrow. At its best the silence of Equiano's text is ironic. Yet to give up his quest would just as assuredly reproduce that same structure. There is no abstract and risk-free position in the economies, in every sense, in which the problem of the Negro, or of the African diaspora, arises, which I have schematized as a movement of between.

What is outlined here are a series of questions specific to the making of an African diasporic subject, for we must recall the historical moment, the ascendance of capital, for example, of this making. An extraordinary process is represented here, one excessive, it seems to me, to what we have come to consider canonical literature, philosophical or imaginative, of its time. As Houston Baker writes, it registers the "ironic transformation of property by property into humanity."[43]

Unfolding within this series of ironic narrative figurations, and at the core of the central irony (that is, that behind this prosaic story of interested but putatively indifferent accumulation, an indifference implicitly proposed by an accession to providential belief), is a simple and yet paradoxical motif: the transformation of Equiano's relation to property will change his relation to humans.

I propose as a theoretical concept-metaphor in general and abstract terms a thought of the play of the force of the double. It is a thought put forth as a name for one way to track the implication of relation in the formation of figural position and the reflexive gathering that comprises subjectivation within the social and historical field. In this thought, there is no absolutely singular gesture *of* or *for* the self. Certainly every self-referential gesture will have always already acquired its inauguration within such configured relation. Yet, even more, in such movement no principle of sovereignty, old or new, could maintain its pertinence. It is thus that tracking the figure of the *un*sovereign—a putative subject that would appear only in the reflex and recoil of the torsion and toil of its engagement with its own always already in motion becoming, as other—may open the way to the most fundamental account of the dynamis at the heart of the possibility of the subject in general. It proposes a tractable and yet dispensable name for the constitutive force of the relation to the other, as primordial shall we say, including the possibility of the self, as such.

In the context of Equiano's story, we can name it the paradox of donation or credit, or, alternatively, the paradox of recognition.[44] On the one hand, African American discourse, writing, and subjectivity seem to emerge on the basis of an originary grant or credit of a kind of recognition of the African American slave by a political or legal authority of some kind. On the other hand, might not this recognition also mark the possibility in the general sense, and the terms of an analytical responsibility in the space of discourse and theoretical practice, of a space of reversal in the systems of domination and exploitation that organize the scene of production of the African American subject, especially as a writing subject? I will now outline a structure of ambivalence that, although not producing an absolute reversal, should demonstrate in this context—the relationship of lord and bondsman—an irreducible space, an opening, a paradoxical structure, in which and on the basis of which (a basis that is also a kind of nonbasis) a reversal is always (in a conceptual and theoretical sense, that is in principle) possible.

As annotation, I emphasize here that this is an infrastructural organization of the situation in which the Negro American as subject, captive or perhaps "liberated," arises. Whereas above, following Spillers, and, further, Du Bois, I recalled its movement in the production of the sense of being of the Negro American subject, here I emphasize that this organization has a systemic and structural bearing, implicating every order that could be called economic, as well as other systems, within this historical-ontological situation.[45]

First, we must mark the actual dependence of the slave owner on the slave. We recall that King did not want Equiano to travel on the sloop without his supervision, but as Equiano tells it, he was too valuable on board for King to restrict him. We also recall that King's dependence on Equiano led King to grant Equiano credit. King grants Equiano the initial (capital in the form of) goods by which he could begin to trade. The point in the narrative at which this grant of credit occurs is important. It occurs after a considerable discussion between King, Equiano, and the ship's captain as to whether or not Equiano would try to escape (Equiano 1969, 92–93; Equiano 2003, 124–26). King states that he will manumit Equiano if he earns forty pounds, and then he grants Equiano the credit to get started. Yet, here, it could also be remarked that although it is not directly stated by the text, this "capital" that is lent to him by the owner was most likely just part of the yield that King had already accrued from the previous labor by Equiano. At the time he extends this "loan," King requests and receives Equiano's assurances that he will not try to escape.

Secondly, I want to suggest that the grant of this credit registers an unavoidable and irreducible force structuring the relationship of lord and bondsman. This force is the double of the will of the master.[46] Control, especially "absolute" control, over the will, perhaps an intention—the capacity for action—of another being, even if understood as nonhuman, requires recognition of that capacity. There is no need to control that action, will or intention, the general possibility of doing otherwise, which has no force or apparition of force. This suggests that the apparent possibility of absolute control is a kind of transcendental illusion.[47] Ultimately, this illusion presents itself as an aporia within the system of legality that ostensibly derives from it. Here, in the text bequeathed to us, both the general field of the social and linguistic dimension thereof, this force, the force of a will or intention other than that of the slave owner's, is signified practically by the risk of flight or escape. The slave can always choose to escape or attempt to escape, including the choice of death or suicide. Equiano continually declares, in the first person, "If I am 'ill used,' I will leave." It is this force—as the operations of a structure that can be adduced by abstracting it as a flexible, supple, recursive relation, if you will—that organizes the symbolic and conceptual significance of the technical or practical dependence of the slave owner on the slave. The dependence is real and has practical effects. Namely, the owner makes money, a profit from the labor of this enslaved being—from his technical capacities in particular. But only because another will or intention can come back to haunt the slave owner must the latter acknowledge this dependence, that is, act (as in will or intend) according to an acknowledgment of this dependence. Thus even when King "grants" Equiano manumission, the text records the risk for King. Equiano's action by his will or intention might lead the slave to take any choice in the matter completely away from King, as the owner. When King hesitates to manumit Equiano, the ship captain, a free white man who works for King, intervenes. He first suggests that Equiano has returned King's investment several times over. He then proposes that if King manumits Equiano, the former slave will then continue to make money for King, "as he will not leave you" (Equiano 1969, 102; Equiano 2003, 135). The key phrase implies, all the more tellingly because of its ellipsis in style, the risk of absolute loss for King that is posed by Equiano's capacity for will and perhaps intention. The paradox is that Equiano is more likely to leave if *not* manumitted. So Equiano is manumitted by King, in order to maintain (the latter hopes) some measure of control over the former slave's intentions, as wage laborer.

This force that I have just outlined is the "double" of the will of the master. It not only delimits his will but specifies it as his, as that of a slave owner. It also organizes and directs it, in the quite specific sense that it forces him to act in the interest of another in order to act in his *own* interest, although we have just complicated any notion of exactly what the form of intimacy suggested by this word of self-possession could mean here. Again, we can come to a distinct recognition of the construction of a Europeanist subject by following the particular and quite specific story of the making of an African American or diasporic subject.

The play that is set afoot is the movement of something that we can position under the heading of "double consciousness" as Du Bois formulated it—seeing "oneself through the eyes of others"— although we might be obliged to say at this juncture that the movement in this case occurs as a kind of double unconsciousness. Not privy to the incipit of its own position in relation, it would too yet disavow the *force* of the other— the affirmative and active bearing of its practice—within that relation. And the matter would take on an even darker hue—a form of redoubled unconsciousness—as one can theoretically name that the positive existence of the discourse of the free individual in the rise of the modern text of the Atlantic basin is itself a putatively coherent proposition only if such is resolutely presupposed as secondary to an originary and always previous singular whole.

Yet, as we have begun to see, something else has already announced itself here in the text of the modern. Hence this credit, or apparent donation, is anything but outright philanthropy.

What is distinctive here is that if we focus on what I have proposed to call the movement of between, following Du Bois, we can see in the most direct manner by way of Equiano's narrative something of the way in which subject position is constructed in relationship and not before. There is no "monopoly of power" here. More generally, there is no such thing as force—there are only differences of force.[48] There is no absolute or radical stability to any given understanding of a distinction between an inside and an outside in the constitution of the system of domination in slavery or, perhaps, within the production of systems of colonial organization in general, even if there are relative positions that arise within its structures. There is the movement of "between" at or as the opening of the law of slavery in "America," at or as the opening of the colonial order, at or as the opening of our common modernity in the aftermath of the contemporary articulations of such systems of subjection.

Refigurations

This movement of between, and the figures eruptive and emergent within its interstices, remarks that domain or zone, which is also nowhere as such, a topos that one can describe as historical-ontological, and the reflection upon it, which is ineluctably a discourse (heterogeneous to itself), that we might describe as historical-transcendental, as the scene of an implacable problematic. This problematic, as I have sought to adduce it, concerns two aspects simultaneously. On the one hand, it concerns the question of the Negro or African American as subject, which, in the elaboration proposed here, entails this question as a general one, invoking the question of an ensemble of subject positions within the historical field in which something like the Negro American acquires its coherence, as well as bearing the sedimented leitmotiv of the question of the subject as such. On the other hand, it concerns the question of the configural production of system and structure, the general form of the economies by which any historical process acquires its shape. As such, that which I have strategically begun to track under the heading of the movement of between—or, that which we can now limn as passages of the double, marking the limit of the idea of world—following the pathways recognized by a certain tracking of Du Bois's discourse, elaborates itself as or within the kinetic and volatile disjunction of the empirical and the transcendental, of the mundane and the ontological, issuing thereby as a historical yet structural affront to systems of subjection, even as such systems configure the subordinate and supraordinate alike within its devolution. Operating just beyond the schema of presentation announced as the titular guide or heading of metaphysics, this movement of between names a path of impression, articulation, and resonance that is always strategic and historical, situated, in the last instance.

The pertinence of the African American example construed here, by way of Du Bois and Equiano, is that it makes possible a certain attention, tactile and deliberate, in tracking the organization of subjectivation and subjection. Du Bois's formulation of the figure of the double as the Negro, as what the Negro is, embeds the question of the humanity of the

Negro, of the human, of the subject in the classical European sense, in the question of the experience of being such a kind of human in such a way or manner that the question of the human or subject (or what we have understood that to be) is reopened, reinaugurated. Thus both of the questions—Who or what is the Negro? and What does it mean to be a Negro?—entail the fundamental question of the kind of being that is the Negro. This surely means by way of answer, at least, that the Negro is a human and, more precisely, a particular kind of human. However, it places at the root of the question of status the question of the sense or experience of being such a human. This sense certainly arises from or as a structure of reflection. In this regard, it articulates the capacity of an ensemble of beings. Yet, further, that this reflection concerns itself and thus articulates a capacity for consciousness of itself proposes that it may mark especially that kind of being that is human, possessed of spirit, or capable of being possessed of spirit (to articulate one with the other of canonical formulations within the European discourses and the African diasporic traditions of the inhabitations of the spirit).

However, it is the character of this sense, the way in which it arises and develops, as well as the structure that it exposes or makes thematic, risible, legible, for this specific kind of human being, the Negro or Negro American, that becomes decisive in Du Bois's formulation. As he proposes it, the capacity for reflexivity marks only the conjunction of a general ontological structure and its always necessary elaboration in or as a historical practice, a form of historicity: a "second-sight" within an "American world." What makes this general capacity so decisive or transformative within the movement of living as such a being is that this order of reflection opens within an historical experience (that is not contemplative and placid) of violence and an order of domination in such a way that the sense of self can be understood only as grounded in an originary complication, as other than simple. What must be emphasized here is not only that the sense of self is not simple, and that it cannot even be formulated in a commensurate manner in the language of description—the language of the third person (and the logos and science in general)—but that it is experienced in such a manner that a sense of the nonsimple, of a founding complication, is the sense of being itself, and thus to be is to be in or as this sense of being. Being such a being, a Negro American, is to originate with a historical movement in such a way that the sense of being Negro, which is what it means to be, to be human, is to exist as an originary complication, in Du Bois's phrase, as the double. (Who knows, for it may well maintain therein an originary complication of the very idea of human?) However, not only does this complication mark the origin or reference to origin as nonsimple, but the orientation toward the future or that which remains yet to come, telos, also remains ineluctably complicated, double in its affirmation. The putative punctuality of a present inhabitation unfolds according to both this ineluctable retreat of the origin as future in general and this always irruptive reorganization of loss as otherwise than simple or given. This double displacement from origin and habitus is thus originary.

To that extent, I have suggested that we can follow Du Bois's account of the constitution of the African or Negro American as radically and essentially at least double as an exemplary pathway by which to raise not only the question of that social being but the question of the European American subject and of that which we call American in general.[49] And more generally, folded back into the system and scene of its historical production, by way of the movement of the double that configures it, such an understanding of this figure participates fully in the ongoing transformations of thought that has solicited or made tremble the most deeply embedded canonical formulations of subject, of systemic pertinence, and of subjectivation. This figure of the double, as a given or particular inhabitation of being, nonetheless remarks, thereby, the general pathways by which subjectivation and the bearing of historical process unfold.

The analysis I have presented here is offered as an example of how we might (re)think the question that I posed at the outset of this chapter. "Now, it is precisely this idea of an America in itself that we cannot accept without examination. Is not 'America' rather a complex idea formed inside the (historical-transcendental) movement of the constitution of the African American as material idea?" Hence, we might reformulate our question. Could we not conceive, according to a certain alogical logic, one that I have positioned above under the heading of the concept-metaphor of the movement of between, that the thought of a certain "Afro or African or Negro America" best situates that which is really the "anchorage point," if there ever were such, that supports the social and cultural practices of all that we call "America"?[50] This was already the perspective of Du Bois as we know. He writes in the penultimate paragraph of the closing chapter of The Souls of Black Folk: "Your country? How came it yours? Before the Pilgrims landed we were here . . . " Something quite otherwise than a paean about exclusion, it should be understood rather as a presumption of a whole order of historial productivity. In any case, a certain account of the historicity of that which is called African-or-Negro-or-Colored American, for example, could show how this idea of America took form in different strategies and operations and the definite role it played in them.

PARENTHESIS

For Aaron Eisuke Chandler[1]

There is no given horizon of thought or critical practice that is, or can be rendered, in its contemporary formation, commensurate with the problematic named under the heading of the problem of the Negro as a problem for thought.

In a word, this conundrum has yielded what may be called the problem of theory with regard what has often been called by the names—Afro-Afra-Negro-Colored-Black-African-American—or that is to say, if we allow to stand in here, an even more brief short-hand annotation, the so-called African Diaspora.

Within my own formation—which is to remark the privileged problematic and the discourses that have constitutively marked my own possibility in enunciation and as put forth across the whole of this study, which is also to say other itineraries and signposts could be privileged—four signal references on this terrain of discourse must be remarked.

In his 1915 text *The Negro*, expressing an achieved perspective that he had won across the opening decade and a half of the twentieth century, W. E. B. Du Bois essayed what should be understood as an epistemological conception of "the Negro" as a global diasporic ensemble, that is, a "serious synoptic view of Africans around the world." Du Bois had noted at the head of the closing section of his little book, titled "Suggestions for Further Reading," that "there is no general history of the Negro race."[2] It is in all truth in light of this epistemic conception that Du Bois would subsequently develop (in tandem with many others) a far-reaching political conception of a global Africa—in the pan-Africanist movement of 1919–45 and in his conception of "worlds of color" (already from 1900, but especially from the end of the First World War) in which he conceived of colonialism as the twentieth century's broadest articulation of the "problem of the color-line."[3] Yet, it must be remarked in this context that for Du Bois in his 1915 text (as earlier in his itinerary), there was no stable criteria by which to consistently name the terms of the supposed object of his analysis—for, he explicitly disavowed the concept of race, even as he had no other term by which to bring into view the ensemblic whole in question. This problem remains our own, despite and beyond all manner of disavowals.

It is in this context that one might understand the penultimate challenge of Harold Cruse's *The Crisis of the Negro Intellectual* of 1967 (beyond his ultimate strident categorical challenge to American democracy) as a call for a new theorization of the African American situation.[4] It was a problematic that in fact was exploding in the moment in historically spectacular form with worldwide implication as a matter of political representation, only to reopen in a new way, in its eventuality across the ensuing decades, as a somewhat more intractable dimension of this problem that is as a question of epistemic possibility (of power as both resource and economy, of institution, and of techniques of thought).

Initiated in this same historical unfolding, yet elaborated in the immediate wake of the 1960s, Cedric Robinson's monumental effort and tremendous, indeed historic, accomplishment in *Black Marxism: The Making of the Black Radical Tradition*, first published in 1983, posed at its core the necessity of a retheorization of modernity as a whole—specifically the figure of a supposedly replete Europe and a certain dominant discourse of radical thought attendant to it (a radicalism claiming a "European" lineage) and a replacement of the thematization of slavery as located at the root of capital accumulation in its modern form. This led him to announce a complex and enigmatically difficult figure, or hypothesis, of a certain "black subject" as a theoretical guide for a renarrativization of contemporary historicity and the possibilities encoded therein. Further, and finally, challenging the "black radical tradition," even as he avowed it, he can be understood to have also posed the demand for a new theorization of the problematic of the African Diaspora.[5]

Unfolding into our own moment, in a parallel or proximate but distinct manner, the work of Hortense Spillers, in particular as documented in the remarkable project placed in 2003 under the heading of *Black, White, and in Color: Essays on American Literature and Culture*, has for more than three and a half decades been carrying out the patient, difficult, and insurmountable work of clarifying not only the terms of the announcement of a new subjectivity, or its possibility—especially under the exemplary guidance of the situation of the African American woman—but of simultaneously carrying out a retheorization of the terms of the production of theoretical work. In this latter sense, Spillers has above all called attention to the task and responsibility of theoretical labor as a problem of the terms of epistemic representation as distinct from, although already implicated within, the still dominant sense of the problematic as one of political representation.[6]

It is at this conjuncture that the problematic as it has come to me can now be formulated. I propose that we are amidst the transformation of the problematic named under the heading of the African Diaspora from a question of presentation, or representation (encoded most often in a theory of leadership, above all a political leadership, but also as an epistemic figuration within knowledge as an organization of power), toward a question of the cultivation of possibility (as both chance and freedom, but beyond both, and especially, as the illimitable).

I offer then the following further formulations—in light of, in the wake of, in resolute receptive companionship with, the work and example of these exemplary antecedent practitioners.

I.

The practice of theoretical labor is the forging of a bequest to future generations of creative intellectuals—artists, activists, academics, writers, political representatives. That is to say—it is the form of the maintenance of a responsibility to generations to come.

Yet, theory in itself is not an end, but a means, to the production of possible end(s). In this sense, theory is always practical. By its maintenance, we pursue the practical theoretical.

II.

In light of the epistemic clarifications that have been set afoot in previous critical work on the question of the so-called African diaspora, it must now be understood that the African Diaspora is not a thing—at least, not a given thing, an actual existent.

Rather, it is a name—a theoretical object—for thought.

We can understand it as a necessary theoretical fiction. The disposition that there is a normative order of precept in terms of which an objectivity can be named for thought cannot be simply set aside as if it were a decision to be made by the individual practitioner. Rather, no sense of a claim to account for where one is located can be given without the gesture to name in principle the limits of one's purview. Thus, the term "African Diaspora" is the name of a problem that has taken shape for a certain historical practice of critical, or self-reflexive, work. This kind of work may be notated as—the practice of critical thought, the practice of self-reflexive thought, the practice of thought that accepts the ethical demand (as the very opening of—the path—toward *sophia* or wisdom) to give an account of oneself, or rather of one's own possibility. It is this sense of an always unstable whole that must be proffered as a sense of the norm of critical thought that cannot be simply voided. Yet, the most crucial matter is that it sets the mark—not of inclusion or exclusion, of an inside and an outside, but—of the perhaps possible transformation of world, yielding the sense of possibility beyond the limit of given world (of horizon, of civilization, of forms of social and historical existence in general).

The problematic at stake, then, is (nothing less than) the possibility (and necessity) that a new "civilization" will arise within the historicity of our own formation. And we leave open, delimited, the sense of the "we" in question.

This is all to say that, if, as Fred Moten has taught me, Cedric Robinson has proposed that "Black studies is the critique of western civilization," then I am proposing its affirmative extension—by way of reference to the radicalism of his practice in thought, his example of generous irreverence, that is a generosity without limit—as the opening toward another form of "civilization" altogether.[7]

That is to say,

— beyond all problems of *remembrance* (although an unfungible, necessary reference);

— beyond all existing *forms of limit* (which must yet be ceaselessly
   engaged, challenged, displaced, and dismantled); and even,
— beyond what we can yet inhabit as *imagination* (which must
   still be affirmed without reservation, even in the form of desire
   [the twinkle in the eye]);
— the "African Diaspora" or, better, the general problem of the
   Negro as a problem for thought may be taken as a theoretical name for the possibility (and necessity) that a new organization or constellation of historicity (across the centuries to
   come) will have been inaugurated in the ceaselessly redoubled,
   disseminated, practices by which a certain (mobile and strictly
   undelimitable) *we* has been constructed for itself and for
   others.[8]

III.

Those histories that we can chart, then—that is, to offer a cartographic
practice (and I annotate and affirm here the principled and reserved
considerations of a "cultural demography" in the work of Hortense Spillers as she put it in the early 1990s; likewise, the pro-genitive, generous,
and passionate gathering of contemporary thought by Tiffany Ruby Patterson and Robin D. G. Kelley in order to propose for consideration a
certain sense of a "unit" of analysis within a global frame of references
in their signal reflection of the late 1990s; and also, the philosophical itinerary outlined by Lewis Gordon in his pathbreaking work on the possible genealogies of—if I may put it thus, a future horizon of philosophy
beyond philosophy, and not only that practiced under the heading of
"Africana," in his work recently presented at the end of the first decade of
this century)—while in themselves susceptible to the ruses and productions of forms of power as knowledge (many of which can and should
be affirmed, even when severe limits for understanding can be noted
therein), are also, and at each juncture, yet the remark of that which is
otherwise than within limit, not reducible to the simple form of limit.[9]
Within this formulation, the gesture or resonance is toward the demand
within historicity that *possibility* be honored without reserve—let us call
it here after Ronald A. T. Judy's work of the early 1990s, the *"inhuman."*[10]

IV.

The African diaspora—whatever is such—is set afoot as a re-mark of history in which the Negro as a problem for thought is simply a name for this general problem for thought and for critical practice of all kinds. Too, then, practice is something otherwise than discipline; it will always have been an art, within and through, yet, still, beyond both science and imagination, as such.

We can turn then to the *strophe,* for example—in song, in sermon, in prayer, in the oration, in poem, in the story, in the graphic in general, in the organization of space and sight line, in the gesture and the voice, from the practice of Phillis Wheatley to the work of Cecil Taylor, from the work of Ella Baker to the practice of W. E. B. Du Bois, in the passage of those whose names remain for us as simply the sign of absence (the interminable figure of the X)—for remembrance, for transcendence of a given mark as limit in historicity, for the subtle and difficult attunement of pleasures (even as desire), but more fundamentally we turn, or we are turned, toward it for the radical challenge that it proposes as a solicita-tion beyond existence as given in any and all senses. In this thought, in my own intellectual generation, the practice of Fred Moten remains my singular guide.[11]

This is the problem afoot under our contemporary shuttling forms of heading of the African American, the African Diaspora, the problem of the "Negro" if you will—noting too therein a certain continental inheri-tance (Africa, that is to say)—as a problem for thought.

For, it is the problem that opened, has always already opened, when "the stranger knocked at our gate," to take the formulations offered by Rabindranath Tagore to W. E. B. Du Bois and presented in the pages of *The Crisis: A Record of the Darker Races* in 1929, and thereby also to "the American Negro" as a whole (as the recipient might have put it, and whatever is or might be such).[12] Or, in all truth, it gives the threshold mark by which thought may yet recognize the incipit of a whole other possible epistemic horizon, such as that which is announced in the theo-retically transformative work of Denise Ferreira da Silva or exemplified in the fundamental historiographic gathering of Louise Young. For, if we recognize herein a necessity at once theoretical *and* historical, it is the problematic that has always reopened in such articulation: for, too, once you have announced yourself as the stranger knocking at the gate, what you have hitherto called home has henceforth ceased to belong only to you.[13]

V.

Across the centuries from 1442, when that first historic group of thirty Africans from the west coast of the continent were landed in Lisbon, to 2442, the turn of a millennium to come, and in all the registers that can come to mind—economic, political, theological, legal, philosophical, epistemological, for example—the practical-theoretical problem of historicity, that is how to engage the very production of *life*, began to turn on its axis from a theoretical disposition that privileges the question of the production of power by repetition (hierarchy, accumulation, capitalization), toward a theoretical imagination that will always have only recognized itself in the production of *possibility as an iterable practice* (democratization, dissemination, dispensation). And too, this will only and always have been, without, otherwise than, or beyond a dialectics. For just as hierarchy, accumulation, capitalization are not ends in and of themselves, neither is democracy, dissemination, or dispensation. For the mark that would distinguish community (in any register of reference, economic, political, epistemological, and so on) has no absolutely original or final status. Instead, all such motives of historical practice remain subject to the illimitable that is the very announcement of the possibility of a new organization of historicity.

It is this difficult and somewhat fragile, almost intractable, thought— of a possibility yet to come—that we may understand as named under such headings as we have offered herein. Or, perhaps we should just call it "X," that is the problem of the Negro as a problem for thought.

Notes

1. **Dedication:** More than any other, and for more than a quarter of a century, Cecil Taylor's work has been my most constant companion in the journey of thought. The singular capacity for the transconfiguration of the limits of existence in our time that shows forth in his work of more than half a century may yet be understood as epochal. The gift of the capacity to give, perhaps that is the greatest of gifts. For such a giving, in the example of his practice, and his friendship, even to give "thanks and praises" is no restitution. For his is a work of freedom. Thus, I offer here both the simple and the absolute, in acknowledgment and respect, for his example and his friendship, never enough, always yet to come.

2. Two decades on, the question of the future is even more implacable and at stake. The question of what is to be done is also necessarily the question of how shall it be done. So, too, across an earlier turn of the centuries, the eruption of such a question in the form of brutality also marked the experience of W. E. B. Du Bois. In his 1940 text, *Dusk of Dawn: An Essay Toward an Autobiography of a Race Concept*, in the chapter titled "Science and Empire," he wrote, "At the very time when my studies were most successful, there cut across this plan which I had as a scientist, a red ray which could not be ignored. I remember when it first, as it were, startled me to my feet: a poor Negro in central Georgia, Sam Hose [*sic*], had killed his landlord's wife. I wrote out a careful and reasoned statement concerning the evident facts and started down to the Atlanta *Constitution* office, carrying in my pocket a letter of introduction to Joel Chandler Harris. I did not get there. On the way the news met me: Sam Hose [*sic*] had been lynched, and they said that his knuckles were on exhibition at a grocery store farther on down on Mitchell Street, along which I was walking. I turned back to the University. I began to turn aside from my work. I did not meet Joel Chandler Harris nor the editor of the *Constitution*" (*Dusk*, 67). Historiography

has now rendered available to us that early in April 1899, Sam Holt, "a black farm laborer of Palmetto, Georgia, [was] accused of murdering his employer in a quarrel over wages." He escaped, and while still at large was accused of raping his employer's wife. After his capture, following a sensationalized two-week manhunt in central Georgia, "he confessed to the murder but refused even under duress to admit to the rape charge. He was lynched, burned alive, and mutilated, with a mob of nearly 2,000 men, women, and children looking on; the tree on which he was hanged was chopped up by souvenir salesmen" (Huggins 1990, 226). This event marked the inception of a tide of lynching throughout the state, at least nineteen of which occurred between May and November of that year (Brundage 1990, 235–36). At that time, the spring 1899, Du Bois was living in Atlanta, Georgia, where he was a professor of sociology and history at Atlanta University. He was in the final stage of preparing his study *The Philadelphia Negro* for publication. As memorialized in that most poignant chapter of *The Souls of Black Folk: Essays and Sketches*, "Of the Passing of the First Born," his son would take ill and suddenly and tragically die on May 24, in part because of being refused proper medical attention in the Jim Crow South (from both sides of the color-line, so to speak), just a week before Du Bois would sign off on the preface of that landmark study. At Atlanta, he had begun to carry out a program that he had devised across the second half of 1897, while in Philadelphia, to pursue a comprehensive study of the social and historical life of African Americans in the United States, in both rural and urban contexts. Some eighteen months later, in a 1901 essay that would be redeployed as a referential chapter in *The Souls of Black Folk*, "Of the Black Belt," at the very beginning of that discourse Du Bois placed these events in an allegorical frame: "And a little past Atlanta, to the southwest, is the land of the Cherokees, and there, not far from where Sam Hose [*sic*] was crucified, you may stand on the spot which is to-day the centre of the Negro problem,—the centre of those nine million men who are America's dark heritage from slavery and the slave trade" (Du Bois 1903b, 111; Du Bois 1901b). All this would come to stand as the mark for the bearing of a whole era in the life course, not only of a scholar, researcher, thinker, and writer, but of a self-reflexively identified people. For my own discourse, and its inscription within this overwrought frame, in particular its relation to the reading of Du Bois, the surreptitious work of memory—which yielded this reference to lynching—is perhaps not arbitrary. In those months, around the time of the event of "Los Angeles," Thomas C. Holt helped to recall and thus focus my attention on the passage from *Dusk of Dawn* noted above during a fall 1991 meeting of the Workshop on the Politics of Race and the Reproduction of Racial Ideologies at the University of Chicago.

3. One might recall at this conjunction the movement of work placed under the heading of the composition "Olim" by Cecil Taylor recorded April 9, 1986, live during the "Workshop Freie Music 1986," Akademie der Künste, Berlin, Germany. "Olim—an Aztec hieroglyph meaning movement, motion, earthquake" (quotation from CD back cover) (Taylor 1987). Yet, we may be allowed to also take reference the Latin word "olim," which avers to "at that time," such that it may refer to the past as in "formerly," "recently," or "once," but also to the present as in "for a long time now," and then even to the future as in "hereafter," or "one day."

4. I was invited by a friend and colleague, Sue Hemberger, to speak at the annual meeting of the Law and Society Association, as part of "a round table on the Los Angeles brutality trial and its consequences," entitled "No Justice, No Peace?" The conference was held May 28–31, 1992, in Philadelphia, on the borders or just in the Seventh Ward where Du Bois undertook his first major empirical research project, a study of the Philadelphia Negro community. He probably wrote the passage we quoted above in the spring of 1897 while he was living with his wife of less than a year in a room above a settlement cafeteria; it was most likely just a few blocks away from what was our 1992 conference site. The preceding paragraphs follow from the opening remarks of my contribution to that discussion. Also, I thank my friend and colleague Sarah Diamond for the hospitality that enabled this writing on that occasion.

5. On this specific point, as a way to indicate a certain order of our proposed intervention, the contribution by Martin Heidegger as given in his considerations "On the Grammar and Etymology of the Word 'Being,'" is apposite (Heidegger 2000, 55–78; Heidegger 1998, 40–56). So, too, I recall here Jacques Derrida's elaborations of these considerations (Derrida 1976, 22ff.; Derrida 1967a, 35ff.). Yet, even as I would still affirm along with Derrida a recognition of the decisiveness of Heidegger's intervention with regard to philosophy in its inheritance of Greek conceptuality, I also highlight a certain requestioning of that contribution in the work of the younger scholar, among others. And so too, I affirmatively recall as signal the early appearance in Derrida's work of what became an ever-growing reserve toward the older thinker's way, in particular all that subtended his ethical retreat and abusive gestures complicit with the most massive violence in the face of the other, astride the interregnum that gave way to the Second World War (Derrida 1989; Lacoue-Labarthe 1989, 267–300).

6. "How many ways/ can one note/ its re-resonances/ physically impelled/ to produce a myriad of/ inflections timeless/ intheglareofanobsidianblade?" Cecil Taylor asks in the chanted "anacrusis" to his composition "Charles and Thee" on the recording *In Florescence* (Taylor 1991). (The specific tone[s],

dynamics, pacing, and emphases of Taylor's voicing are in their own inscriptive effects as voice excessive to diacritical marks of graphic technics. Hence,
I simply remark that which writing—as graphematics—must pass over in
silence.) Or, we could cite the interwoven meditation on "anacrusis" in the
"notes" to his *Unit Structures* (Taylor 1966a). In the spring of 2001 during a
seminar on his work while he was an artist in residence under the auspices the
Humanities Center and the Program for Comparative American Cultures at
John Hopkins University, in a discussion of notation and composition, for
example, Taylor said of Thelonius Monk in a manner that is apposite here,
and I quote from my own memory: "Monk is the only pianist who can play
one note and you hear what for a long time was often called harmony." Or,
again, Taylor might, perhaps, just offer a proper name, "James Brown." Here,
my thought is of the hyperbolic character of African American practice, of
thought as practice, of being as given in performance, if there is such. This
might be understood as the radical opening for thought and practice that
is formulated and elaborated by Fred Moten in *In the Break: The Aesthetics
of the Black Radical Tradition* (Moten 2003). Sometimes I hear the rustle of
chains and the sway of the ship, as in the "Middle Passage," perhaps, in the
next "composition" on the 1990 recording noted above. It is titled "Entity."

7. Reading the *New York Times*, on November 2, 1992, I came across a
statement, a quotation that, if tracked in a certain manner, can set afoot a
desedimentation, for it marks and remarks the site of Cabrini Green: "'Out
of 10 of my friends, seven have been locked up,' Henry said. 'It gets worse
around here as you get older.' Jimmy added, 'But to me this is not a war
zone. This is a poor neighborhood, but its home'" (Terry 1992). There is a
saying of African American provenance: "Another [man-child] done gone,
do you know his name?" Now the refrain of the spirituals or the blues, both
sacred and profane at once, which named the loss of a "man" under the back-
breaking impress of enslavement in the old American South is here replaced
with that of a "man-child"— and I leave it as an unstable paleonym, with
an explicit remark here of both its purchase and its limit, the gendered lexicon of the ancestral reference. It was October 13, 1992: Dantrell Davis; seven
years of age; Cabrini Green; seven thousand people; seven miles south of my
home—during the autumn of 1992; killed by sniper fire while walking—to
school. Later, astride the first decade of the new century and a new millennium, one recalls with a start the headline article "Killing Time: Rival Gangs
Rap with a Cop Who Walks a Different Beat" from the November 1992 issue
of *Streetwise: A Non-Profit Monthly Newsletter Empowering Chicago's Homeless Through Employment,* which records—including in the *double-entendre*
of its title—a momentary truce, in one dissimulating theater of this war,
after the death of Dantrell Davis (Whitaker 1992). I deposit here, and reserve

for another consideration, in another rhythm, notes made at the time concerning the *Chicago Tribune's* "Architecture Competition for Public Housing" and its aftermath, created in the wake of the death of Dantrell Davis,
the first responses, a key stage, in a nearly two-decades-long and still ongoing displacement of the primarily African American original inhabitants of
the residences and the neighborhood in general—which in fact was located
on some of the most choice property of the city, from a June 10, 1993, special
report in that newspaper (Kamin 1993a; Kamin 1993b). And, then, further,
one feels a solicitation toward a commensurate consideration on a theoretical level of the deep historicity of this event. For it has now issued, quietly
as it is kept, as one of the most massive and exemplary reorganizations of
public housing in the history of the United States. It has become a deeply
conflicted new chapter in an essentially tragic history and has centered for
the past generation on the displacement and appropriation of the residence
of the poor (Sharof 2000; Feemster 2003; Venkatesh and Celimli 2004; Kelly
2005; Hunt 2009). I hope to return to this scene in a future effort in critical
excavation and theoretical engagement.

8. I quote here the title of one of Cecil Taylor's gestures—which remains
radical in his practice throughout—in the wake of Thelonius Monk, recorded
at Nola's Penthouse Studios, New York City, June 9, 1958, and presented on
the album *Looking Ahead!* the following year (Taylor 1959).

9. And too, then, this history would connect to an aspect of language that
Jacques Derrida's citation of Baruch de Spinoza's reflections on the grammar of Hebrew brings into relief, when the former writes, in the context of
his discussion of the French *entre* that "Nous avons dit les «entre(s)» et ce
pluriel est en quelque sorte «premier»." In the translation of Derrida's text
by Barbara Johnson, this line reads, "We have spoken of 'betweens,' and this
plural is in some sense primary." I reference here "The Double Session," in
Derrida's *Dissemination* (Derrida 1981a, 173–286, esp. 211–24). The translated
sentence in remark here is given in a footnote (Derrida 1981a, 222n36). While
I would emphasize a paleonymic aspect of Derrida's quotation of the word
"premier," as in first principle or founding premise or first philosophy, in
which he both maintains it with reference to that philosophical appurtenance but yet displaces or disseminates the ultimate bearing of that reference, Johnson's translation of *"entre(s)"* by "betweens" seems to carry an
etymological resonance to the semantic histories that I am remarking here.)
Derrida then goes on in the same note to quote Spinoza's *Compendium gram-
matices linguae hebraeae* in French translation in a manner pertinent to our
considerations: "In truth this plural expresses not the relation between one
individual thing and another, but rather the intervals between things (*loca
aliis intermedia*)—in this connection see chapter 10, verse 2, of Ezekiel—or

else, as I said before, this plural represents preposition or relation abstractly conceived [cited by Derrida as *Abrégé de grammaire hébraique* (Spinoza 1968, 108)]." Although I had pursued a reading of Derrida's texts, concentrating on the early material, for some years, I first read this latter text in October 1992, nearly a year after formulating a thought of "between" as traced in outline here, with considerable surprise and pleasure, especially regarding the status Derrida adduces for *entre* and the alogical logic of *hymen* in a text of Stéphane Mallarmé.

10. In the work of Jacques Derrida, one finds too, a sense of the necessity of this form of the passage beyond limit. The "first" lexical appearance in his discourse of this specific analogical thought, the undecidable, might well be indexed here for it emerges in temporal or generational proximity to the work of Cecil Taylor that I have already noted above—for they are of the same artistic and intellectual generation. And Taylor's work had already begun to announce the most committed radicalization of a centuries-long eventuality in the historial practice of African Americans, from, let us say at least, end of the 1950s, as cited above (Taylor 1959; Taylor 1966a). Of Derrida's initial work, I reference "section three" (without section title) of his "introduction," first published in 1962, to Edmund Husserl's posthumously published fragmentary text "*The Origin of Geometry*," first published in 1939 (Derrida 1974, 37–51, e.g. 38ff.; Derrida 1978b, 51–62, e.g. 53ff.; Husserl 1954; Husserl 1978). There Derrida writes, "In its very negativity, the notion of the un-decidable—apart from the fact that it only has such a sense by some irreducible reference to the ideal of decidability—also retains a mathematical value derived from some unique source of value vaster than the project of definiteness itself." And then, in a footnote appended to the end of the parenthetical clause in the sentence just quoted, Derrida writes, "That the analyses of the *Origin* concerning the synthetic style of mathematical tradition serve as an example of tradition in general is thus confirmed. The very movement which enriches sense retains a sedimentary reference to the antecedent sense at the bottom of the new sense and cannot dispense with it. The intention which grasps the new sense is original insofar as the prior project still remains and the intention will simply not 'give way' to it. Thus, undecidability has a revolutionary and disconcerting sense, it is *itself* only if it remains essentially and intrinsically haunted in its sense of origin by the telos of decidability—whose disruption it marks." Might this not help to outline in some philosophical form, for another history of science if you will, that which would recognize the irruptive generality of that anonymous practice of generations, of the regeneration of generations, announced in the historial passage that has gone under the heading of African American since, perhaps, 1619, and which acquired a nodal rearticulation across the opening

decades of the twentieth century in the movement of sound as something once called, respectively, the spirituals or the blues? I prefer to note such historial movement as general, not restricted to art in any simple sense, where living and what has been called death is, too, the "making of a way out of no way," to turn an old and idiomatic phrase.

11. I mark here the resonance of *Silent Tongues*, a solo piano composition given in performance, by Cecil Taylor, recorded live on July 2, 1974, at the Montreux Jazz Festival. Its form is given the following notation: "Abyss (first movement); Petals & filaments (second movement); Jitney (third movement) (18:32)—Crossing (fourth movement) pt. 1 (8:36)—Crossing (fourth movement) pt. 2 (10:00)—After all (fifth movement) (9:39)—Jitney: no. 2 (3:25)—After all: no. 2 (2:50)" (Taylor 1975). For it remains the titular guide for this study. But, then, one must take resource to the whole of what I have come to think of as the "indent series" in Taylor's practice, taking the name from his first composition of an astonishing passage in the solo presentations of his art, from March 1973 to July 1974, which subsequently exfoliated into the group work, as well: *Mysteries*, March 1973 (later re-released under the title "Indent") (Taylor 1977b); *Solo*, May 1973 (Taylor 1973); *Spring of Two Blue-J's*, November 1973 (Taylor 1974); *Silent Tongues*, July 1974 (Taylor 1975); then too, *Dark to Themselves*, June 1976 (Taylor 1977a); and *Air Above Mountains (Buildings Within)*, August 1976 (Taylor 1978).

CHAPTER ONE

1. **Dedication:** I acknowledge here the customary generosity of the late Jacques Derrida. During the spring of 1996, upon receiving a copy of the published version of an earlier essay (which has now been enfolded into the present chapter), he telephoned across the Atlantic to offer his thanks and express simple and kind words of appreciation. As his death occurred during the time of the revision and elaboration of that earlier text (including the work of restoring original sections that were not previously published but which pertain in particular to its philosophical provenance), and since the theoretical gesture announced in the chapter at hand proposes, among other things, an interlocution; thus, to the extent that his example as an interlocutor in contemporary *philosophical* thought remains unsurpassed for me, I place this double affirmation, a certain form of appreciation, at the foot or head of this chapter. A thought, thus, of thanks, perhaps of many, yet to come, for an example and a friend from afar, whose departure remains both so old and yet still so new.

2. The quotation is from Jacques Derrida, *Positions* (Derrida 1981c, 41–42, emphasis in the original; Derrida 1972b, 56–58, emphasis in the original). Certainly one must look at the whole summary development of the thought

of *différance* that Derrida offers in the paragraphs extended before and after the quotation placed here as an epigraph. For example, preceding the passage quoted, Derrida introduces the problematic:

> What interested me then, that I am attempting to pursue along other lines now, was, at the same time as a "general economy," a kind of *general strategy of deconstruction.* The latter is to avoid both simply *neutralizing* the binary oppositions of metaphysics and simply *residing* within the closed field of these oppositions, thereby confirming it. We must proceed using a double gesture, according to a unity that is both systematic and in and of itself divided, a redoubled writing [*une écriture dédoublée*], that is, a writing that is in and of itself multiple, what I called in "The Double Session" a *double science* [*une double science*]: on the one hand, traversing a phase of *overturning* [*renversement*]. I insist much and without ceasing on the necessity of this phase of overturning [*renversement*], which one perhaps too quickly attempts to discredit. To do justice to this necessity is to recognize that in a classical philosophical opposition.... That being said—and on the other hand—to remain in this phase is still to operate on the terrain of and from within the deconstructed system.

This entire summary development schematizes what Derrida here calls "a kind of *general strategy of deconstruction*" in the inhabitation of metaphysics. He offers a more elaborate and complicated formulation of such a "general strategy," *which is not a method* as such, in "Hors Livre: Outwork, Hors d'oeuvre, Extratext, Foreplay, Bookend, Facing, Prefacing," a text published proximate to the interview noted above, and in a key footnote in the passage from *Positions* just quoted, he refers to an ensemble of his principal essays from 1967 to 1969 that elaborate the developments summarized here, especially the thought of a "general economy" (Derrida 1981a, 3–59; Derrida 1972a, 7–68). The strategies of a practice inhabiting the movement of deconstruction would attempt to produce in a certain way a discourse operating simultaneously in multiple dimensions. Derrida and others have sometimes outlined this as a twofold movement. Here, I will remark it as fourfold. It is (1) a methodical "solicitation." In his essay "Force and Signification," Derrida used this term in its Latinate sense to suggest a radical questioning of the whole, a critical interpretive engagement that is more than simply either a critique or an interpretation. In terms of a philosophical hierarchy, this gesture would question the "ground" upon which the dominant term is given its authority:

> One perceives structure in the instance of *menace,* at the moment when imminent danger concentrates our vision on the keystone of

an institution, the stone which encapsulates both the possibility and the fragility of its existence. Structure then can be *methodically* threatened [*menacer*] in order to be comprehended more clearly and to reveal not only its supports but also that secret place in which it is neither construction nor ruin but lability [*n'est ni érection ni ruine mais labilité*]. This operation is called (from the Latin) *soliciting* [*soucier ou solliciter*]. In other words, *shaking* in a way related to the *whole* [ébranler *d'un ébranlement qui a rapport* au tout] (from *sollus,* in archaic Latin "the whole," and from *citare,* "to put in motion"). (Derrida 1978a, 6; Derrida 1967b, 13)

Following Martin Heidegger in part, Derrida's formulation at the mid-1960s posed the most powerful institution of this ground as the determination of being as presence, most systematically elaborated in the tradition of Greek metaphysics, especially as inherited in European discourses. It is this "whole" that must be shaken. It is also (2) a process of "*overturning*" the systematic and axiological conceptual hierarchies of metaphysics (philosophy). One could say that the emperor must be shown to have no clothes. This would entail an elaboration of the devolution of the classical figure of the sovereign. It takes the disassembling of the presupposition of the simple unity of being as an opening, a *spacing* if you will, by which to locate the determinations of metaphysics as determined aspects of a more general question. Derrida considers this overturning absolutely necessary. The attempt to simply remark the instability of being as ground or essence in the domain of the subordinate, or the work that one does to prepare such an elaboration, if not accompanied by a simultaneous elaboration of the distantiation of the hegemon, can function principally to resituate tradition, or the given, as hegemon or authority. This is the locus of considerable ambivalence and limit in contemporary critical thought. The opening stage of this essay proposes this necessity on its own terms. What takes place or can take place in the movement of deconstruction or a strategy *of* deconstruction would also undertake or involve (3) a systematic "reinscription" (sometimes referred to by the phrase "placing under erasure," *sous rature*) of certain titular concepts that work according to the exigencies of the metaphysics of presence. That is to say, the practice of a certain kind of *paleonomy,* inhabitation of old thought in a new way, is necessary. Even if one cannot simply leap beyond certain premises of thought, not all inhabitation of such a limit is the same. The necessary nominalism here is not a simple empiricism. Rather, it is the very scene of engagement, theoretical and political, which one cannot simply choose by a philosophical—that is, scientific—anticipation. Thus, finally, a certain movement of deconstruction would also (4) mark or remark that "interval" between all the "moments" of deconstruction marked in those three ways ("solicitation," "overturning," "reinscription") and the "irruptive emergence" of a "new thought," a new way of thinking, of a new "concept" or an "aconceptual concept." This new "thinking" would acknowledge its dependence on metaphysics but would radically challenge metaphysics itself (displacing the recuperative operation of metaphysics, such as it functions in the Hegelian system of the *Aufhebung*). For example, see the entire 1971 interview cited above.

3. On the question of problematizations, of problems for thought, and of problematics, especially with regard to the question of "the problem of the Negro," please see my considerations on this matter in the opening sections of a forthcoming study (Chandler forthcoming).

4. To take only a few examples from the early wave, see works, respectively, by Kwame Anthony Appiah, Adolph L. Reed, Paul Gilroy, and Kenneth Warren (Appiah 1986; Appiah 1992b, 28–42 and see also 173–80; Appiah 1989; Reed 1986, 61–95; Reed 1992; Reed 1997, 93–126; Gilroy 1993; Warren 1993) .

5. In the move to gather oneself to question the logic of essence, one finds that one has already presupposed essence. Martin Heidegger, for example, formulates the necessity of what he calls the precomprehension of being in language in the opening sections of *Being and Time* and in another important text from early in his itinerary, *An Introduction to Metaphysics* (Heidegger 1962; Heidegger 2000). Early in his itinerary, Jacques Derrida reelaborated this problematic in a distinctive manner in many of his texts, for example, by way of a certain attention to the structure of Georges Bataille's relationship to the discourse of G. W. F. Hegel and in a consideration of Emmanuel Levinas's relation to the thought of both Hegel and Heidegger, but notably also to the work of Edmund Husserl, and returns to it on the terms that he adduced there throughout the rest of his itinerary, even or especially in the last years, for example in *Rogues: Two Essays on Reason*, both essays of which were written during the summer of 2002 (Derrida 1978d, 251–77, 79–153; Derrida 2005). Gayatri C. Spivak has succinctly stated the politics of such a limit in thought:

> It is not possible, within discourse, to escape essentializing somewhere. The moment of essentialism or essentialization is irreducible. In deconstructive ethical practice, you have to be aware that you are going to essentialize anyway. So then strategically you can look at essentialism, not as descriptions of the way things are, but as something one must adapt to produce a critique of anything. (Spivak and Adamson 1990; Spivak 1989)

This genealogy of an unconditional condition that is a complication for thought is perhaps announced in this form in European discourses in what

Immanuel Kant formulated as a necessary transcendental illusion that reason produces by way of its speculative "interests" in his elaboration of a transcendental dialectic in his first *Critique* (Kant 1998). Yet, I have resisted here such nominalizations as transcendental, ontological, grammatological, and so on, for the sake of the rhetorical force of the claim of the radical in this context alone.

6. For the North American context, Winthrop Jordan's classic study, *White Over Black: American Attitudes Toward the Negro: 1580–1812*, remains essential, among other virtues, due to its historical breadth (Jordan 1977).

7. For example, see the closing chapter of Appiah's *In My Father's House* (Appiah 1992b, 173–80). There he is compelled to affirm *by way of* Du Bois the possibility of a "non-racialist pan-Africanism." It is a position for Appiah that should have led to a deep hesitation in the stringent and headline denigration of the positions of Du Bois that is proposed at length in the opening of the book. It is thus only a surprise of circumstances to this practitioner that in its eventuality Appiah has now been led some two decades later to praise Du Bois as perhaps an exemplary "rooted cosmopolitan" (Appiah 2005). Moreover, one reflects with ongoing caution on certain aspects of Manthia Diawara's thoughtful call during the early 1990s for a new discourse on "a black good life society," a call that has been well heeded over the past decade and a half in the exponential projection of a "black cultural studies" in the North American context. On the one hand, I would doubly affirm, along with Diawara's initial statement, the necessity of the critique of essentialism, while also underlining his reclamation of the 1980s critique by the London-based cultural studies practitioners of the perhaps too easy displacement of the question of a Black identity in the Birmingham configuration of the 1970s, and acknowledge, thus, for example, Paul Gilroy's marvelous *There Ain't No Black in the Union Jack: The Cultural Politics of Race and Nation* from 1987 (Gilroy 1991). On the other hand, it seemed almost as if for some intellectuals writing from the late 1990s onward (perhaps Diawara too in that moment), in terms of popular culture, at least, the revolution had arrived. Such a position maintains within its premises a certain neutralism—in apposition to a fundamental or radical critique—about which I remain cautious. Too, it must be noted, for example, that what Diawara therein referenced as "oppression studies" had already called from its inception for a study of "performance," of the creativity of Blacks and the originality of their vision of the world, precisely under conditions of oppression (Diawara 1995). W. E. B. Du Bois, in *The Philadelphia Negro*, prepared from the autumn of 1896 through early 1899, consistently affirmed this dimension of African American practice even as he documented the oppressive conditions of their situation and the negative effects on their habitations at

that time (Du Bois and Eaton 1973). And then, in his pioneering and foundational essay from 1897, "The Study of the Negro Problems," he made the study of the *existential* (or *experiential*) order of African American life, one of the two epistemological frames under which African Americans should be studied (the other frame might be described as general *historial* or *systemic* order) (Du Bois 1898b; Du Bois 1982f). This essay is included in a new annotated collection of early writings by Du Bois (Du Bois forthcoming[c]). It is hereafter cited in text as TSNP followed by pagination and paragraph number from the latter edition. See further discussion of this essay below. I have proposed to trace the originality of this vision in "The Philadelphia Negro Project: W. E. B. Du Bois and the Program for a Study of the African American in the United States" (Chandler n.d.). See also the essay by Werner Lange (Lange 1983).

8. From an ongoing conversation on the history of modern philosophy, April 1993 and February 1995; the emphasis was given in his formulation.

9. Given Michel Foucault's intrepid manner of working over this ensemble of questions for more than two and a half decades, it may be apposite to specify our suggestion a bit in proximity to his contribution. For, whereas he might have insisted upon the nonpresent materiality of a discursive formation in his writings of the late 1960s and early 1970s, he resolutely sought the movements of irruption and freedom even at that juncture in his itinerary, and certainly he thematized this question in his later work. My thought is that what he calls the "archaeological" in that work—see, in particular here, his concerns to specify the theoretical terms for recognizing the formation of an epistemic discourse in the opening chapters of *The Archaelogy of Knowledge*—and what we might call the epistemological (which arrives on the scene as the domain of contestatory claims) in the terms that he elaborates therein are not so easily rendered even analytically distinct in the case of the discourses of the Negro (Foucault 1972, 21–50; Foucault 1969, 31–67). To enunciate at all, to gather oneself into the position of one who could speak, perhaps we might say at zero-degree enunciation, sets shimmers afoot along the fault lines of this discourse, even as the forces in play could promulgate a domination that would have to devolve and could not be divested in any immediate sense. We wonder here, for example, about a Phillis Wheatley as in her remarkable poem "On Being Brought from Africa to America" (Wheatley 1988, 18).

10. I would even insist that it must still name in our time the character of an originary "spiritual world" in the domain of the Negro as a problem for thought, taking reference, for example, to *The Souls of Black Folk* (*Souls*, vii–viii, "The Forethought," para. 3). Or we might also cite Eugen Fink when he clarifies the import of his mentor Edmund Husserl's project as recognizing

and elucidating that every consciousness proposes a "transcendental" and not just empirical "origin of the world" (Fink 1970). And, on one side, it would miss the boat to reject the radicalness of this "worldhood" under the heading of a commitment to the empirical or the material, for it is the very organization or bearing of the empirical that is at stake in the "worldhood" in question. Further, on the other side, the thought of "spirit" and the "spiritual" in Du Bois, as in his formulation "of our spiritual strivings," should not be too simply or readily understood as an already accomplished fact. While the enigmatic status of the major and decisive theme of "spirit" in Du Bois's discourse can only be named as a heading here, awaiting further elaboration elsewhere, it can be recognized that for him it is not a question of the Negro as the ultimate or final exemplar of the becoming of "spirit" in either the Hegelian or Heideggerian senses. On the latter, see Jacques Derrida's *Of Spirit: Heidegger and the Question*; perhaps especially apposite and on point here are sections five and six (Derrida 1989).

11. One thinks here of Cecil Taylor's practice and his critical meditation on something that can be only circumstantially placed under the heading of an old Greek name, *anacrusis* (Taylor 1966a). And, of course, here, perhaps inhabited in a certain relation to Thelonius Monk, it acquires a radically other construal than that given in the hegemonic traditions.

12. Building on the work of other contemporary scholars, including the interpretive work of both Ronald A. T. Judy and the late Emannuel Chukwudi Eze, but also the bibliographic and scholarly, as well as interpretive, contributions of Robert Bernasconi, I would propose Immanuel Kant as the singular exception during the eighteenth century with regard to systematicity, the concept of race, and the question of the Negro as a problem for thought (Judy 1993; Eze 1997; Bernasconi 2001). Yet, my approach, proceeding by way of Du Bois and so forth, has moved according to a different bias than those scholars. In this regard, in a general sense, I propose that due to the architectonic character of his conception of reason, especially the status of teleology there-in, and the transformative impact of this conception for post-Enlightenment thought, including thought in our contemporary scene, this singularity of Kant is other than simply an exception. In an inquiry that was originally part of the present study, but which demands its own elaboration, I have begun to develop this thought under the heading of the epistemic relation of the problem of the Negro and the concept of Man in the eighteenth-century thinker's discourse.

13. Certainly, this sense was established in some of the early transformative historical scholarship on the discourses of the seventeenth and eighteenth centuries which was brought to fruition during the civil rights decades (Davis 1966, 446–82; Jordan 1977, 269–311). Although privileging the

Caribbean and South America in their formulations, Roger Abrahams and
John Szwed have proposed a broad outline of different phases of writing
on the African diaspora in the Americas from the seventeenth century to
the first half of the twentieth century. Following their schema and adum-
brating it somewhat, we can mark out three different formations of a discourse concerning the Negro in the Americas from the middle decades of
the sixteenth century through the end of the nineteenth. From the latter
part of the sixteenth century through the early eighteenth, we can outline a
discourse dominated by travelers' accounts and slavers' journals. The central question that strikes one from these accounts is whether slaves were
human and, hence, whether their enslavement was justifiable. From the
early eighteenth century through the middle of the nineteenth, a mission-
ary and abolitionist discourse (often these were the same persons) developed that was principally concerned with the question of converting the
slaves to Christianity. A corollary question concerning the possible social
effects of emancipation also developed. Would the slaves remain in the
New World or go somewhere else? Whereas the slavers' and many travelers' journals of the sixteenth and seventeenth centuries reflect a doubt as
to whether slaves could be "civilized" or changed to accord with supposed
"European" behavior, the eighteenth-century discourse often maintained
that slaves were not savage, but rather should be considered as infantile
or childlike and, hence, capable of being taught. From the early years of
the nineteenth century through its last years and into the early twentieth
century, a variegated discourse developed. Abrahams and Szwed outline
two discourses: that of ex-slaveholders and their children, committed to the
idea that Negro slaves needed white tutelage, and that of a "native" middle
class, which attempted to agree with some elements of the ex-slaveholders'
discourse but also sought to claim "creative accomplishments" by Negroes.
The principal discursive positions in this debate were a range of degenerationist (or retrogressionist) arguments, on the one hand, and arguments
for the recognition of Negro capacity, on the other (Abrahams and Szwed
1975, 2–3; Abrahams and Szwed 1983).

14. Two generations ago, Henry Louis Gates Jr., proposed an argument
that has now rightly become presumptively ubiquitous: that the eighteenth-
century African American response to the discourses of the Negro was
to demonstrate proof of their mental ability or capacity and hence their
humanity through developing literacy, especially by way of the skill of
writing (Gates 1987). However, the question of ability or capacity should be
ultimately understood as determined on the basis of metaphysical commitments, that is, speculative premises, rooted in the presupposition of a teleological basis for a final adjudication of the question.

15. Aristotle formulates this principle perhaps most fully at 1005b11–34 of his *Metaphysics*:

> So that he who is to have such knowledge of being qua being . . . must be able to state the most certain of principles of all things. This is the philosopher, and the most certain principle of all is that about which it is impossible to think falsely; for such a principle must be known (for all men may be mistaken about things which they do not know) and be also nonhypothetical. For a principle which one must have if he is to *understand* anything is not an hypothesis; and that which one must know if he is to know anything must be in his possession for every occasion. Clearly, then, such a principle is the most certain of all; and what this principle is we proceed to state. It is: 'The same thing cannot at the same time both belong and not belong to the same object and in the same respect; and all other specifications that might be made, let them be added to meet logical objections. Indeed, this is the most certain of all principles; for it has the specification stated above. For it is impossible for anyone to believe the same thing to be and not to be, as some think Heraclitus says; for one does not necessarily believe what he says. If, then, contraries cannot at the same time belong to the same subject (and let the usual specifications be added also to this premise), and if the contrary of an opinion is the negation of that opinion, it is evident that the same person cannot at the same time believe the same object to be and not to be; for in being mistaken concerning this he would have contrary opinions. It is because of this that all those who carry out demonstrations make reference to this as an ultimate doctrine. This is by nature a principle also of all the other axioms. (Aristotle 1966, 58–59)

One should also note what is said of "being and unity" at 1003b20–1004a9 of the *Metaphysics*. While one can elaborate a thought of the limit as the unnameable itself, here I wish to recognize the pertinence of the principle that Aristotle formulates as formalizing a telic structure that would inhabit all practices of racial distinction at their limit, in the putative fullness of their realization, no matter their partiality in fact.

16. For Immanuel Kant, see not only his remarks of the precritical writings, notably the infamous passages of the *Observations on the Feelings of the Beautiful and the Sublime*, but especially the appendix to the discussion of transcendental reason in the *Critique of Pure Reason* of 1781, and his essay formulation of the problem of teleology from 1788 (Kant 2007a; Kant 1998; Kant 2007b; Kant 2001); see Ronald A. T. Judy's critique of some of Kant's considerations on the figure of the Negro (Judy 1993, 105–55); and then see

also Robert Bernasconi on the concept of teleology and the concept of race in Kant's work (Bernasconi 2001).

17. See the text from 1830–31, which is understood as an "introduction" for what has been assembled as G. W. F. Hegel's lectures on "world history" (Hegel 1975; Hegel 1994; Hegel 2011; Hegel 1996). Hegel concludes his discussion of Africa in a discourse usually placed as an appendix, in remarks under the heading of a supposed geographical articulation of world history, with a now infamous statement, rendered in translation as: "What we understand as Africa proper is that unhistorical and undeveloped land which is still enmeshed in the natural spirit, and which had to be mentioned here before we cross the threshold of world history itself" (Hegel 1975, 152–209, quote at 190; Hegel 1994, 187–241, esp. 234). Jeremy Pope has brought into relief a fundamental ambivalence in Hegel's actual enunciation, an ambivalence that points to the contradictions of a truly speculative teleological thought—that is, one organized as an architectonic—for such a thought must simultaneously proclaim and disavow its outside, especially as beginning (Pope 2006). Along this latter track specifically, Hans Saussy's formulations of Hegel's account of China would also be pertinent (Saussy 1993).

18. See Thomas Jefferson, *Notes on the State of Virginia* (Jefferson 1972 [1787], 58–63, 134–43, 162–63; or Jefferson 1984a, 182–88, 260–70, 288–89). I will take up this latter text presently. Hereinafter cited in the text parenthetically as Jefferson 1972 [1787] and Jefferson 1984a [1787], respectively, followed by page number(s). I leave aside here any elaboration of this problematic with regard to two other key passages of thought: the removal of the question of slavery from the American Declaration of Independence and the infamous three-fifths clause of Article 1, Section 2, of the United States Constitution (Jefferson 1999, 96–105).

19. Even though the profound metaphysical, specifically philosophical, organization of the discourses that he follows seems at best on the periphery of his concerns, see the still pertinent pathbreaking early work of George M. Fredrickson (Fredrickson 1987).

20. While it is the case that at this *specific* juncture in the approach that I am outlining, I move along the same trajectory as that proposed and demonstrated by Toni Morrison in *Playing in the Dark* and thus it should be clear that her project is one that I profoundly affirm—that is, her tracking of the effects of figures of "Blackness" within texts by "White" writers—in the larger horizon of the approach I am suggesting, I would situate a gesture such as that one as only one moment, and in no way a titular one (Morrison 1992). Indeed, if a titular heading is proposed at all, and there are still principled epistemological and political reasons for adducing one, then such a heading must be the originarily complicated movements of the formation of

the Negro American, or an African diasporic figure, as a differential production within the historical situation of modernity and the Americas. On this one might consider the opening sections of Chapter 4 of this study, "Originary Displacement."

21. Which is to say, we must recognize his disposition as simultaneously distinctive within an epistemic order of the discursive horizon that we are trying to remark here, and yet entirely representative of that same horizon. Whereas almost half a century ago, Jordan specified the former, ongoing scholarship has remarked just how much that exception was yet representative of that same problematic (Jordan 1977, 429–81; Miller 1977; Onuf 2000).

22. Although I reference this thought by distinct locutions here, it should be taken as a whole internally organized passage of thought (Jefferson 1972 [1787], 138–50, 59–60, quotes at 138, 139, 141; Jefferson 1984a [1787], 265–75, 183–92, quotes at 265–66, 267).

23. Under the title "A Genealogy of Modern Racism," Cornel West once proposed an inquiry that would render thematic the *teleological* sense of the ontological claims in this problematic, a question that remains at stake and still must be put fully at issue in contemporary scholarship (West 1982, 47–65; Chandler c. 1988; Curran 2011).

24. Here, I do not reproduce this list and the rhetorical violence that it maintains, for it is a representation that is properly an expression, a vocative, of Jefferson alone and not of the people or persons he would purport to describe; yet, I believe that my concern with its overall sense is still at least indirectly accessible (Jefferson 1972 [1787], 138–39; Jefferson 1984a [1787], 265–66). He then continues:

> But never yet could I find that a black had uttered a thought above the level of plain narration; never see even an elementary trait of painting or sculpture. In music they are more generally gifted than whites with accurate ears for tune and time, and they have been found capable of imagining a small catch. Whether they will be equal to the composition of a more extensive run of melody, or of complicated harmony, is yet to be proved. Misery is often the parent of the most affecting touches in poetry.—Among the blacks is misery enough, God knows, but no poetry. Love is the peculiar oestrum of the poet. Their love is ardent, but it kindles the senses only, not the imagination. Religion has produced a Phyllis Whately [*sic*]; but it could not produce a poet. The compositions published under her name are below the dignity of criticism. . . . His [the eighteenth-century writer Ignatius Sancho's] imagination is wild and extravagant, escapes incessantly from every restraint of reason and taste, and, in

the course of its vagaries, leaves a tract of thought as incoherent and eccentric, as is the course of a meteor through the sky. His subjects should often have led him to a process of sober reasoning: yet we find him always substituting sentiment for demonstration. Upon the whole, though we admit him to the first place among those of his own colour who have presented themselves to public judgment, yet when we compare him with the writers of the race among whom he lived, and particularly the epistolary class, in which he has taken his own stand, we are compelled to enroll him at the bottom of the column. This criticism supposes that the letters published under his name to be genuine, and to have received amendment at no other hand. . . . The improvement of the blacks in body and mind, in the first instance of their mixture with the whites, has been observed by every one, and proves that their inferiority is not the effect of their condition of life. (Jefferson 1972 [1787], 140–41; Jefferson 1984a [1787], 266–67)

We should note that this final sentence carries a contradiction endemic to racist and pro-slavery discourses in the Americas. It simultaneously claims that Negro character is modifiable (in a social order), and as such has received any good character from a "White" source, while concluding that their inferior character is fixed or permanently established (in a natural order). One wonders about the relation of this passage to those of Kant of a similar nature from the *Observations on the Beautiful and the Sublime* (Kant 2007a). Whereas in that text, and elsewhere, Kant denigrates what he thinks of as the American Indian in relation to his idea of the Negro slave, in the *Notes,* Jefferson defends his own idea of the North American Indian in relation to what he thinks of as the Negro or the "blacks." This specific scene of intersection has seemed so far unthinkable, but now calls in an urgent manner for a patient unfolding and elaboration.

25. This passage appears in the midst of Query XIV titled "Laws" (Jefferson 1972 [1787], 142; Jefferson 1984a [1787], 268).

26. Certainly indicative is the editor of a canonical edition of the *Notes* and the three widely recognized commentators cited earlier, William Peden, Winthrop Jordan, John Chester Miller, and Peter Onuf, respectively (Peden 1972, 286–88n6; Jordan 1977, 455; Miller 1977, cf. 12–18; Onuf 2000, cf. 1–18).

27. Historiographical research, and to a lesser extent ethnological research in general, has raced far ahead of philosophical research and fundamental critical thought in offering a contribution to a thinking of this question. For example consider the organization of this problematic, respectively, in the diverse works of Edward S. Morgan, Thomas Holt, and Orlando Patterson

(Morgan 1975; Holt 1992; Patterson 1982). Yet, it seems that historiography and ethnology are wont to ask the question of the condition of possibility of the *relation* of slavery, except as a mundane and resolutely nontranscendental one. It remains necessary to move through and beyond, while remaining within, the trancendental problematic, such that another thinking of immanence might occur. That is to say, the historical has this problem of the transcendental or its beyond already at stake in it, especially when the thematic problem is that of the condition and possibility of enslavement. However, it should be noted that this problem has the capacity to disturb most attempts to think the problem of sovereignty from a preoccupation with the established understandings of the inheritance of the Enlightenment, that is from the standpoint of a putative sovereignty. Even Michel Foucault who, in his projects of the 1970s and in the years just preceding his untimely death, goes far in helping us to desediment this problematic confronts paradoxes on this score (not to mention those who follow in his wake). See for example "Right of Death and Power over Life," the closing section of volume one of *The History of Sexuality*, the brief essay "The Subject and Power" (in particular the section therein titled "How Is Power Exercised"), and his Collège de France lectures of 1975–76 (Foucault 1980a, 135–59; Foucault 2000; Foucault 2003). These paradoxes no doubt can be situated with regard to his inhabitation of a problem given in Greek thought in a certain way; this way is a thought that understood itself as only at stake for free citizens, men, and not as such, slaves, nor, in essence women, in general, whether ostensibly free or enslaved, even though slaves in general were most likely a substantial majority of the inhabitants of Athens of the fourth and fifth centuries BCE. I simply note the latter here, reserving this question for a further elaboration elsewhere. See M. I. Finley's fundamental work in economic and social history in *The Ancient Economy* and elsewhere, as well as the recent contributions of Peter Garnsey in intellectual history (Finley 1973, 63–93, cf. 79; Finley 1960; Garnsey 1996, esp. 1–19) (Garnsey 1996, 1–19). One wonders about the relation of the American South and ancient or classical Greece. This is the scene of a future inquiry. In addition, I note here and reserve for consideration in another context the question of a certain reconsideration of this question as it is developed in the midst of Hegel's *Phenomenology of Spirit*, the subsection titled "Independence and Dependence of Consciousness: Lordship and Bondage" (Hegel 1977, 110–19; Hegel 1998, 127–36).

28. In the wake of the general historiographical revolution in African American history since the 1960s, and constitutional history and literary history was revised adjacent to it, contemporary scholarship certainly caught this theme. See, for example, the differently situated work of Dana Nelson and Paul Finkelman, literature and history, respectively (Nelson

1992; Finkelman 1996, 105–67). I propose here its rhetorical motivation not only as internal to Jefferson's discourse but as situated at the very root of his sense of the ontological or theological ground necessary for his claim for a right to intervene or announce himself (and all to which he belongs) in history.

29. "Among the Romans emancipation required but one effort. The slave when made free, might mix with, without staining the blood of his master. But with us a second is necessary, unknown to history. When freed, he is to be removed beyond the reach of mixture" (Jefferson 1972 [1787], 143, and see 138; Jefferson 1984a [1787], 270, and see 264–65). Winthrop Jordan underlines this commitment of Jefferson's. "Throughout his life Jefferson never deviated from his conviction that Negroes must be 'removed' when freed, nor from the ground for that necessity. Six months before he died in 1826 he closed the matter with an octogenarian's finality: 'The plan of converting the blacks into Serfs would certainly be better than keeping them in their present condition, but I consider that of expatriation to the governments of the W.I. of their own colour as entirely practicable, and greatly preferable to the mixture of colour here. To this I have great aversion; but repeat my abandonment of the subject'" (Jordan 1977, 546–47). One cannot but remark here the confirmed disavowal by Jefferson of his own progeny with common-law wife, we might say, Sally Hemings, who was also his slave (Gordon-Reed 1997; Gordon-Reed 2008; Miller 1977). Hortense Spillers's powerful formulation of such disavowal as introducing a root complication in the structures of identification for an African American subject position should be resolutely affirmed. And then, here in the context of the citation above of Jefferson's voice, we can remark a double disavowal: of both his progeny *and* of the unavoidable complication of the movement of his own subjectivation by way of this relation. This points to the extension of this problematic into the domain of the constitution of paternity in every sense, that is beyond any supposed parochialism of the bearing of either so-called sexual difference or so-called race difference (Spillers 2003a; Spillers 2003c).

30. As quoted above in note 14, a traditional formulation of such a difference is proposed in what has come to be called Aristotle's principle of noncontradiction, perhaps, most fully offered at 1005b11–34 of his *Metaphysics* (Aristotle 1966).

31. In this regard, apart from his massive and still fundamentally generative contribution to the field, perhaps Sidney Mintz's gesture in an introduction to a reissue of Melville Herskovits *The Myth of the Negro Past* of 1940, in which he placed Jefferson's call for a "natural history" that would include the study of "black" and "red" men as the incipiting moment of an anthropological tradition in African American studies, such a gesture would—if

taken uncritically—put us on the wrong path (Herskovits 1990, ix; Jefferson 1984a [1787], see Query XIV, 270).

32. The formulation in this sentence and the first sentence of the next paragraph has in mind the attempt by Michel Foucault in *The Archaeology of Knowledge* to elucidate by elaboration the enigmatic status of *"l'énoncé"* which I will in this context translate as utterance *or* legible mark, but which resists any stable elaboration by Foucault, not even to speak of a simple translation from one language or theoretical formulation to another (Foucault 1972, 88–105). It has a special mode of existence, as Foucault formulates it, by which it is related to "laws of possibility, rules of existence for the objects named, designated, or described within it, and for the relations that are affirmed or denied in it." I am not concerned here to make absolute ontological claims about this mode of existence, as such. Rather I want to point toward the problem of specifying the movement of the irruption of being as thought, the movement of the presencing of thought. In this regard, what Foucault says specifically of a "referential" aspect of *l'énoncé* can be quoted at length as way of proposing the order, or status, of the problem to be addressed here.

> The referential of a statement [*l'énoncé*] forms the place, the condition, the field of emergence, the authority to differentiate between individuals or objects, states of things and relations that are brought into play by the statement [*l'énoncé*] itself; it defines the possibilities of appearance and delimitation of that which gives meaning to the sentence, a value as truth to the proposition. It is this group that characterizes the *enunciative* level of the formulation, in contrast to its grammatical and logical levels: through the relation with these various domains of possibility the statement makes of a syntagma, or a series of symbols, a sentence to which one may or may not ascribe a meaning, a proposition that may or may not be accorded a value as truth. (Foucault 1972, 88, emphasis in the original)

Foucault then goes on to specify the relation of *"l'énoncé"* to "a subject" and to an "enunciative field," as well as to attempt to situate its "materiality," that is, its possibilities for "reinscription and transcription" and its "fields of use," its "strategic potentialities" which "constitute for statements [*les énoncés*] a *field of stabilization* that make repetition possible" (Foucault 1972, 103, emphasis in the original). The epistemological level of discourse and social practice would then appear only by way of the movements at stake in this "enunciative level" of generality in existence. It would be approached by way of a practice of inquiry that Foucault never ceased to affirm and which he called "archaeology." (And we may note here that the concept-metaphor of "archaeology" was most likely initially developed as a theoretical term for Foucault by way of his reading of Kant; the latter speaks of an archaeology of history in proposing a distinction between what he calls natural history and natural description, respectively, in his thought on nature and teleology, which in turn was initially proposed in his essays that proposed a concept of race; see, for example, Immanuel Kant's essay "On the Use of Teleological Principles in Philosophy," first published in 1788 (Kant 2007b).

33. Elsewhere, in a study in progress, I propose to critically elaborate the character and stakes—the *epistemological* interest—of Du Bois's commitment to a scientific study of the question of the Negro, especially as formulated in his programmatic statement "The Study of the Negro Problems" (Chandler n.d.).

34. I borrow and translate here a phrase formulated by Robin D. G. Kelley in another context. "Rebirths of African American Studies" was the title for a talk and discussion led by Kelley at Duke University in November 1994, as part of the W. E. B. Du Bois Lecture Series of its African and Afro-American Studies Program. Also, I reference Mae G. Henderson's opening remarks at the session entitled "The Politics of (Dis)Location: Black (Cultural) Studies in the Academy," at the 36th Annual Convention of the Midwest Modern Language Association, November 11–13, 1994, Chicago, Illinois, a context in which some of the considerations of this essay were first presented.

35. These texts are cited from the versions of these texts included in the recently edited and annotated collection of Du Bois's writings *The Problem of the Color Line at the Turn of the Twentieth Century: The Essential Early Essays* (Du Bois forthcoming[a]). As indicated in the Note on Citations at the head of this study, "The Conservation of Races" is cited in the text as CR followed by page number (s) and paragraph number; likewise, "Strivings of the Negro People" is cited as SNP, followed by page and paragraph number(s); and "The Study of the Negro Problems" is cited as TSNP, followed by page and paragraph number(s). In addition, I provide here reference information for two other reliable sources of each of these texts, details of which can be found in the Bibliography. The first, is the original publication (Du Bois 1897a; Du Bois 1897b; Du Bois 1898b). The second is the reprint, as applicable in the case of two of the three essays, in one of the volumes published under the comprehensive title "The Complete Published Writings of W. E. B. Du Bois," compiled and edited by Herbert Aptheker from 1973 to 1986 (Du Bois 1986a; Du Bois 1982f). ("Strivings of the Negro People," like almost all of the texts by Du Bois that he included in one of his published volumes, was not included in the reprint series compiled by Aptheker.) Finally, all citations to *The Souls of Black Folk: Essays and Sketches* refer to the first edition of 1903, as outlined in the general Note on Citations provided at the beginning of this study (Du Bois 1903f).

36. Among many texts and the vast terrain collectively indexed by the work of these canonical figures, one might consider here, for example, certain key writings that address precisely the question of understanding and interpretation (Dilthey 1977, 123–43; Simmel 1980; Weber 1964, 87–157; Durkheim 1995).

37. Thomas C. Holt offered a thoughtful meditation on this theme, which remains a touchstone in consideration of the political dimensions of the autobiographical aspect of Du Bois's affirmation. For Holt, Du Bois's reflections upon his own life was the exemplary path to this critical affirmation of the sense of double reference or projection (Holt 1990b).

38. By *historial* I wish affirm the thought of a kind of movement in the constitution of a sense of being which, even if it cannot and should not be hypostasized as an absolute or final example, brings into view the question of the sense of being in its most fundamental sense by tracking worldly— or, so-called mundane—problematics rather than simply the pure—or, the so-called or primarily transcendental—questions of being, as such. This is certainly the practice that Du Bois exhibits throughout his work, but which is exemplified, for example, in the narrative "Of the Coming of John," the penultimate chapter of *The Souls of Black Folk* (*Souls*, 228–49). However, the mention of several interventions on the inheritance in the modern era of Greek conceptuality in Europe from that diverse formation that took shape as phenomenology in the twentieth century may have the virtue of interpellating these canonical references in terms of the inquiry we are following here. With regard to this tradition, I note especially the thought of the transcendental in the work of Edmund Husserl, for example *Ideas I*; and, then precisely the elaboration of the "ontico-ontological" difference as it is often remarked in the aftermath of Heidegger's *Being and Time* (Husserl 1980; Heidegger 1962). neither of which can be simply set aside here. If we follow the opening chapter of part 1 of Jacques Derrida's *Of Grammatology*, we may at least remark therein an inscribed place for some meditations along this line under the heading of a thought of the ultratranscendental, or the "trace," which seeks to maintain both the worldly or empirical and the movement of the transcendental as the passage of becoming, of the devolution of being, perhaps (Derrida 1976, cf. 23ff.; Derrida 1967a, cf. 38ff.).

39. In the Anacrusis, given earlier in this volume, I proposed some elucidations of this motif. Frantz Fanon, some fifty years after Du Bois, will explicitly recognize this capacity as a form of necessity. At the very beginning of the justly famous chapter of *Peau noire, masques blancs*, the chapter best translated under the heading "The Lived Experience of the Black," Fanon writes, "In the Weltanschauung of a colonized people there is an impurity, a flaw that outlaws any ontological explanation [*une impureté, une*

tare qui interdit toute explication ontologique]. Someone may object that this is the case with every individual, but such an objection merely conceals a basic problem. Ontology—once it is finally admitted as leaving existence by the wayside—does not permit us to understand the being of the black man. For not only must the black man be black; he must be black in relation to the white man. . . . [T]he Negro has been given two frames of reference within which he has to place himself. . . . Consciousness of the body is solely a negating activity. It is a third person consciousness [*La connaissance est du corps est une activité uniquement négatrice. C'est une connaissance en troisiem personne*]. The body is surrounded by an atmosphere of certain uncertainty [*d'incertitude certaine*]. . . . A slow composition of my *self* as a body in the middle of a spatial and temporal world—such seems to be the schema. It does not impose itself on me; it is, rather, a definitive structuring of the self and of the world—definitive because it creates a real dialectic [*une dialectic effective*] between my body and the world" (Fanon 1967, 109–11; Fanon 1975 [1952], 88–89). In this last, he remarks an experience of oneself as "body" as an *example* of one moment of this problematic, a moment that is nonetheless irreducible, according to his analysis. Yet, not to gainsay my own considerations by way of a thinking with W. E. B. Du Bois, it may be that Ralph Ellison's thought of ambivalence and the radical deployment and extension of it that one finds throughout the work of Hortense Spillers can also effectively underscore the pertinence of this problematic for *contemporary discourses* on the African American in the United States in a way that may be translatable for contemporary critical thought in general (Spillers 2003a).

40. It is with this sense that we must recall that this was the era that was described by Du Bois's distinguished student who was also a scholar of that historical period, Rayford Logan, as the "nadir" of African American history (Logan 1997).

41. I attempt to account for the fullness and systematicity of this epistemological statement on its own terms and, in turn, to elaborate its contemporary bearing for research in this field, African American studies or African diasporic studies, my aforementioned ongoing study (Chandler n.d.).

42. *The Philadelphia Negro: A Social Study* is Du Bois's key work in the former mode (Du Bois and Eaton 1973). *The Souls of Black Folk: Essays and Sketches*, which in this context can be understood as a companion text to *The Philadelphia Negro*, is Du Bois's most enduring work in the latter mode (Du Bois 1903f).

43. This can be specified on two levels: one internal to Du Bois's own discourse; the other external to it and in terms of historiographical research generally. First, then, Du Bois's *Black Reconstruction* from 1935 should be considered the full realization and exposure of this order of attention at

the level of an accomplished historical narrative (Du Bois 1976). Virtually every major thought put forth by Du Bois in this book had been announced in his earlier texts. Yet these ideas are produced in this context under the impress of a guiding problem of reflection, the status in historiographical discourse of the project of the reconstruction of American democracy that was ambivalently attempted and ultimately compromised following the Civil War and the abolition of legal slavery. This titular problem makes possible a simultaneous compression and elucidation of Du Bois's principal ideas of historicity, especially with regard to something called America, and an expansion of implication, of the bearing of this example for thought in general. It is no anomaly then that this text has over the decades gradually emerged as Du Bois's single most accomplished statement of a re-vision of the world. Secondly, along another temporal track we see those studies that document the impact on historiography, especially during the 1960s, of a vision such as that of Du Bois's, even if the scholars in question seem uncertain of his full *epistemological* importance in particular for situating the ensemble of questions gathered here in the broadest and most fundamental sense. See for example (Davis 1974; Meier and Rudwick 1986, 239–76; Wood 1976; E. Foner 1982).

44. I offer here the results of only one aspect of a thinking through of "The Conservation of Races," as well as the other two essays ("Strivings of the Negro People" and "Study of the Negro Problems") named at the beginning of the discussion in this section of the present chapter. I propose an elaboration—that is, a critical rethinking, a kind of thinking with and through these essays, and several other texts by Du Bois that surrounds them—according to a whole other order of attention in a related study (Chandler forthcoming).

45. As I have already suggested, earlier by reference to the term *Verstehen*, I am referring to the later work of Friedrich Nietzsche and Wilhelm Dilthey as preceding the group that I have in mind, which would be principally Edmund Husserl, Max Weber, Émile Durkheim, Sigmund Freud, Ferdinand de Saussure, and Franz Boas in their work that unfolded around the turn of the century (Nietzsche 1998; Dilthey 1977; Freud 1965; Husserl 1970; Husserl 1999; Weber 1964; Durkheim 1995; Saussure 1986; Boas 1940, cf. 649–47; Boas 1989, cf. 57–77). Hans Georg Gadamer comments on this problem by way of a discussion of the work of Dilthey is of signal import (Gadamer 1979). Too the work in intellectual history, respectively, of George Stocking, specifically on Boas's contribution to an elaboration of a concept of culture between 1887 and 1911, and of H. Stuart Hughes, in particular his considerations on the generational character of the emergence of the work of the figures named here and its implication for a new thought of the human sciences, can help

remark the epistemic moment in question (Stocking 1982, 133–233; Hughes 1977).

46. I refer here to the developments of the second chapter of Derrida's *Of Grammatology*, in which the limits of a linguistic address of the profound metaphysical appurtenances of the concept of the sign is elaborated by way of a consideration of the formulations of the pioneering figure Ferdinand de Saussure (Derrida 1976; Derrida 1967a).

47. Consider here Boas's essays "The Outlook for the American Negro" and "Human Faculty as Determined by Race" and his book *The Mind of the Primitive Man* (Boas 1989, 310–16, 221–70; Boas 1911, 253–72; Stocking 1982). It should be noted here that Boas delivered the commencement address, May 1906, at Atlanta University at Du Bois's invitation, where the latter was then a professor of sociology. The two men eventually developed a deep mutual respect that lasted until Boas's death in 1942 (Zumwalt and Willis 2008). This is a question that I explore in "'The Occurrence of All These Arts of Life': W. E. B. Du Bois and Franz Boas at Atlanta, Georgia, May 31, 1906," an unpublished manuscript.

48. On this difference, the specific and complicated and overwrought history of the development of the *field* of African American studies from the years of the First World War through the reinaugurations of the field in the 1960s and 1970s and the relation of this development to the various *disciplines* of the human sciences in general, including here the humanities, in which the situation or problematic that I am outlining by way of the example of Du Bois would have its bearing, would explain in part—but only in part—this latter difference of Du Bois within this configuration. This "history" is yet to be fully thought and written.

49. To the extent that we both must, and should be able to, understand much more about the relation of the concepts and propositions of Du Bois's thought and those of other figures in this configuration, this question must be approached by not assuming that we already know in any determinate analytical instance either of the terms to be brought into critical relation. Each term shifts when configured in this way. Each discourse would have to be re-read and thought from this perspective. Karen E. Fields has offered a pioneering and rich gesture in this direction in "Individuality and the Intellectuals: An Imaginary Conversation Between W. E. B. Du Bois and Émile Durkheim" (Fields 2002). I have followed her lead in reading some aspects of the relation of the thought and itineraries, respectively, of W. E. B. Du Bois and Max Weber (Chandler 2006; Chandler 2007).

50. Consider here Edward Said's citation of Antonio Gramsci's notion of *"e-laborare"* in his signal essay "Reflections on American 'Left' Literary Criticism," which places it almost as an order of ontology.

First, to elaborate means to refine, work out (*e-laborare*) some prior or more powerful idea, to perpetuate a world view. Second, to elaborate means something more qualitatively positive, the proposition that culture itself or thought or art is a highly complex and quasi-autonomous extension of political reality and, given the extraordinary importance attached by Gramsci to intellectuals, culture, and philosophy, it has a density, complexity, and historical semantic value that is so strong as to make politics possible. Elaboration is the ensemble of patterns making it feasible for society to maintain itself. . . . Thus elaboration is the central cultural activity . . . it is the material making a society a society (Said 1983, 158–77, see esp. 169–72).

I further index Manthia Diawara's citation of the same, which may index Said's elaboration of a responsibility of the intellectual for a *critical* elaboration of this ontological order, but does not explicitly cite him. Diawara situates elaboration most acutely as the space of a critical practice (Diawara 1995). Antonio Gramsci's articulation of this notion can be located in his text "The Study of Philosophy" (Gramsci 1971, 323–77). I propose the term *elaboration* here with those references in mind (but with some hesitation about the way that Said's extension of the term implies an ontological generalization that is not in itself given a critical account in the text referenced earlier). Here, I have in mind the question of an open response to Du Bois's life and practice as a form of theoretical responsibility, according to which as a first protocol the critic engaging his work must first take up responsibility for the questions that are announced therein on the terms by which they are announced, if his work is to remain available to the consideration of any contemporary question. This would require a certain passage through the text of Du Bois's thought, if not always, or only, the letter. Not only that, for, as Gramsci first proposed, elaboration is necessarily collective, and cannot be accomplished in the work of only one thinker or the practice of a single individual. For an example of my effort to sustain such a practice, I follow a certain motif in the practice of Du Bois in the next chapter, "The Figure of the X: An Elaboration of the Autobiographical Example in the Thought of W.E.B. Du Bois."

51. The formulations about the abyssal structure of authority and problems of thought given here move askance from traditional promulgations in intellectual history and in the history of thought, especially in almost all modes of the history and philosophy of science. I would in particular index the perspective given here as taking shape in light of some elaborations by Jacques Derrida in his work astride the 1960s (Derrida 1978d, 79–152; Derrida 1967c, 117–228; Derrida 2011; Derrida 1967d). I reserve for another space

a consideration of these developments on their own terms, but one should note that elsewhere in the notes for this chapter and this study as a whole, I indicate the way in which the example and problem of Du Bois poses its own challenge to Derrida's contribution here. And, then, the figure of break proposed here is more about the terms of an elucidation of another necessity in thought than about some simple accomplished disposal or departure. Indeed, it might well be thought of as a kind of radicalization, turning, or revolution within an inherited situation. On this terrain of an interrogation of the modes of engagement with the historicities of thought, I also have in mind some formulations of Michel Foucault in the later part of his itinerary (Foucault 1997b; Foucault 1985, 3–32, esp. 3–13). I would note especially "part four" of Foucault's The History of Sexuality, Volume One: An Introduction, while recalling concerning the latter Gayatri Spivak's critical and originative annotations (Foucault 1980a, 77–133; Spivak 1996a).

52. Two wonderful examples of Du Bois's inhabitation of this situation can be followed in Dusk of Dawn: An Essay Toward an Autobiography of a Race Concept, from 1940, when he was seventy-two years of age (Du Bois 1975c). There, in a chapter called "The White World," which will be followed by a chapter called "The Colored World Within," Du Bois produces in the former chapter, respectively two different, but continuous, fictional dialogues about the concept of race, with two "White" male interlocutors (who are described as his friends, one given a fictional name "Roger Van Dieman," the other unnamed except described as "free, white and twenty one" (Dusk, 141, 153–54). He precedes the opening of these dialogues with the following summary statement:

> With the best will the factual outline of a life misses the essence of its spirit. Thus in my life the chief fact has been race—not so much scientific race, as that deep conviction of myriads of men that congenital differences among the main masses of human beings absolutely condition the individual destiny of every member of a group. Into the spiritual provincialism of this belief I have been born and this fact has guided, embittered, illuminated and enshrouded my life. Yet, how shall I explain and clarify its meaning for a soul? Description fails—I have tried that. Yet, lest I omit the most important thing in the life of an American Negro today and the only thing that adequately explains his success, failures and foibles, let me attempt its exposition by personifying my white and colored environment. (Dusk, 139–40)

Now two further quotations, respectively. First, here is a bit of a dialogue between the autobiographical narrator and his fictional friend "Roger Van Dieman":

"Of course," he says, "you know Negroes are inferior." I admit nothing of the sort, I maintain. In fact, having known with some considerable intimacy both male and female, the people of the British
Isles, of Scandinavia, of Russia, of Germany, north and south, of
the three ends of France and the two ends of Italy; specimens from
the Balkans and black and white Spain; the three great races of Asia
and the melange of Africa, without mentioning America, I sit here
and maintain that black folk are much superior to white. "You are
either joking or mad," he says. Both and neither. This race talk is, of
course, a joke, and frequently it has driven me insane and probably
will permanently in the future; and yet seriously and soberly, we
black folk are the salvation of mankind. (*Dusk*, 140–41)

Secondly, he offers a dialogue between the narrator and a young friend
who is confronted with the contradictions of a "code of Americanism," that
is "the Golden Rule of Christianity" and its democratic formulas, of human
brotherhood and equality, a code that nonetheless also "led directly and
inevitably to another code . . . found in unfinished assumption rather than
plain words, . . . [and] this code rested upon the fact that he was a White
Man," which eventually came to mean that "he could not conceive of a world
where white people did not rule colored people" (*Dusk*, 154–60, 163). Now the
dialogue:

"Well, I like America. Darn it! I *love* it. My father died for it, although
not in war—and I am reasonably willing to. There's no doubt about
it, lambs have got no business prowling about lions and—oh, Hell!
Honest to God, what do you think Asia and Africa would do to us,
if they got the chance?" "Skin us alive," I answer cheerfully, loving
the "us." (*Dusk*, 167)

And now finally, for another example, the scholar Karen Fields produces
her own brilliantly ironic pathway through these enigmas in a commentary on its relation to Émile Durkheim's engagement with the matter of
totemism (as a world in which "clansmen imagine their kinship to one
another in terms of animals, plants, and occasionally inanimate objects,"
as produced in the characterization of lineal groups in Australia by eth-
nographers up to the time of Durkheim's writing) in her essay "Durkheim
and the Idea of Soul" (Fields 1996, 194) the whole of which should be cited
here (and whose remarkable recent complete retranslation of Durkheim's
The Elementary Forms of Religious Life [Durkheim 1995], should also be
noted, along with her superbly ironic "Individuality and Intellectuals: An
Imaginary Conversation Between W. E. B Du Bois and Émile Durkheim"
[Fields 2002]).

One of Durkheim's footnotes wittily upends the notion that the Australians were truly ignorant of the connection between intercourse and procreation. It would be better to say that they truly ignored it. And that they ignored it was entirely in keeping with the protoscientific mode in which collective identities are made. Once established as real, their collective identities entailed theories of heredity in whose terms the biological facts of procreation were irrelevant. By this same route we arrive not only at black Australians who resemble white cockatoos but also at the peculiar sense of shock I create every time I inform my students, dead-pan, that Frederick Douglass, the son of a slave and a slave owner, was one of the most distinguished white Americans of the nineteenth century. (Fields 1996, 196)

53. And, paradoxically, Du Bois may yet remain the most reliable guide to recognizing the depth of the implications of this eventuality, as for example in his postmortem, so to speak, on his efforts to articulate an institutional form of his projections in knowledge as science (Du Bois 1982b, 216–41). For contemporary scholarship, as given in the major biography to date, as only one example, seems to remark this eventuality most often as matters of personality or the limits of liberal concern (Lewis 2000, 422–53). Ralph Ellison's astonishing essay on this topography, while still fundamentally pertinent, seems to this reader only to follow the purview adduced by Du Bois (leading one to wonder at the least why such a brilliant essay—written astride the 1940s—remained unpublished until after Du Bois's passing) (Ellison 1995a).

54. In this context, that of an ongoing critically affirmative engagement with the implication of the work of Jacques Derrida as it is proposed in the contemporary horizon, I would here take reference to a similar question that he posed in light of the later work of Michel Foucault (Derrida 1994, esp. 264–65). Might not Du Bois's thought in both its order of questions and its theoretical claim on our thinking propose such a problematic—or reproblematization—for how we might take responsibility for the implication of the thought of both of those contemporary thinkers in the time to come, to take responsibility for approaching the limits of their work by way of their own respective formulations of the need to engage the question of such limit under the heading of possibility?

55. These formulations address certain aspects of Du Bois's essay "Sociology Hesitant" from late 1904 or early 1905, a reading of which I elaborate elsewhere (Chandler n.d.). The original nine-page typescript can be found as "Sociology Hesitant," in the Papers of W. E. B. Du Bois, Special Collections and University Archives, Series 3, Subseries C, MS 312, W. E. B. Du Bois Library, University of Massachusetts Amherst. (A copy of this typescript can also be found

in the microfilm edition of these papers *The Papers of W. E. B. Du Bois, 1803 [1877–1963] 1979*, Sanford, NC: Microfilming Corp. of America, 1980, on Reel 82, Frames 1307–12. The original papers were compiled and edited by Herbert Aptheker. The microfilm edition was supervised by Robert C. McDonnell.) I simply note here that I brought the fact that this essay was available among the Du Bois papers to the attention of my close friend and colleague Ronald A. T. Judy in the spring of 1996, subsequently held several conversations with him by telephone regarding the essay after his retrieval of the text from the archive, and in the spring of 1999 agreed to forego my own planned publication and introduction of the essay, out of respect for his desire to do so. The occasion of the latter was a panel on "W. E. B. Du Bois and the Turn of the Millenium," as part of the Collegium for African American Research, held at Wesphalia Universität. Münster, Germany, held March 20, 1999. Professor Kevin Thomas Miles (coorganizer with me), and Professors Robert Bernasconi and David Farrell Krell, along with Professor Judy, were participants on that important panel. (In this regard, the conference at Villanova University organized by Professor Miles, which is cited in acknowledgment note for the present chapter, should be understood as a certain kind of inauguration of these conversations and as a key moment in the interlocutions that have set loose or set on a different course several key conversations on "philosophy and race" in the United States since the mid-1990s, which cross several different borders, analytic and continental philosophy, questions of "gender" and "race," and the divisions of the human sciences, social science and humanities, for example, as well as that border between earlier and later generations of post-1960s scholars.) As I recall, David Levering Lewis's listing of this text as "since lost" in the first of his two volume biography of Du Bois had led Professor Judy to understand that the text was no longer available (Lewis 1993, 202; Judy 2000). Also, I wish to acknowledge that prior to the dates noted above, I had engaged in correspondence and conversation with Professor Karen E. Fields regarding the manuscript, "Sociology Hesitant" and, in part, through her initiative, had made plans in to publish it in 1997. (On the latter, see correspondence of December 9, 1997, Nahum D. Chandler to Karen E. Fields).

56. I address the general necessity affirming another order of *reading* Du Bois, other than the dominant modes up to now, in the opening of another study and in the introduction and annotations for a collection of some of his early writings (Du Bois forthcoming[a]; Chandler forthcoming).

57. Nonetheless, one would be in rights to insist that therein remains a multitude, as both root and leaf, as both water and sand (Taylor 1975; Taylor 1982).

58. In a similar way, Derrida, in a critically affirmative reading of Emmanuel Levinas as the latter philosopher engages the thought of G. W.

F. Hegel, Edmund Husserl, and Martin Heidegger on the question of the other, formulates the thought of what might well be called a transcendental "economy" of the relation to the other (in the specific scene of a discussion of Husserl's *Cartesian Meditations*, and writes of a "transcendental violence" in such relation that is the necessary passage through the same in the recognition of the other as other) (Husserl 1960; Derrida 1978c, 129). Such necessity can be understood as a paradox of the same order and as arising from the same movement of force that announces the transcendental opening—that is, as the necessary passage through *the same* as it acquires organization as the problem of essence—in the situation of Africanist figures in the discourses of the Negro. Yet, even as it remains invisible for traditional thought, the relation of the Africanist problematic to the history of a transcendental thought opens in an obverse way: it is articulated as a nodal but disavowed ground for the very historicity of the production of a thought of the transcendental (Kant 2007b; Kant 2001).

59. See Wheatley's poem "To the Right Honourable William, Earl of Dartmouth, His Majesty's Principal Secretary of State for North America, &c." (Wheatley 1988, 73–75, quotation at 74). In truth the whole stanza should be read:

Should you, my lord, while you peruse my song,
Wonder from whence my love of *Freedom* sprung,
Whence flow these wishes for the common good,
By feeling hearts alone best understood,
I, young in life, by seeming cruel fate
Was snatch[']d from *Afric's* fancy'd happy seat:
What pangs excruciating must molest,
What sorrows labour in my parent's breast?
Steel'd was that soul and by no misery mov'd
That from a father seiz'd his babe belov'd:
Such, such my case. And can I then but pray
Others may never feel tyrannic sway?

60. I take the quotation deliberately from Du Bois's uncanny and symbolic intervention in this historical memory, especially when he continues after recalling Truth's question, and he writes "'No,' thundered the Douglass, towering over his Salem audience. 'No, and because God is not dead, slavery can only end in blood'" in *John Brown* (93). Nell Irvin Painter clarifies the extent to which this question has come to us as an appropriated and overdetermined one in American discourses (Painter 1996, 162–63).

61. Its supposedly impure "culture" might be considered one of the principal reasons that historically the discipline of anthropology in the United

States devalued the African American in the domain of North America as an object of study. Or, better, this question has always stood at the threshold of any inquiry in this specific domain in the general field of the African diaspora by this discipline. Perhaps for this reason, even Melville Herskovits preferred to study the African diaspora outside of the United States, undertaking no major ethnographic work in this North American domain. This latter fact is not well known and virtually unremarked in the scholarship on this important figure (Herskovits and Herskovits 1966, esp. 43–61). The hypostasization of a preformed America or "White culture" is at the root of such a theoretical disposition. Perhaps it can be shown that this assumption functioned both within the tendency known as Herskovitsian and among those opposed to it. For example, from his own complicated ground of disposition—that is, specifically, his concern to remark the depth of the denial of the violence that was American slavery and the concomitant concatenation of that violence as the persistent, generalized, enforced, and practically effective disavowal of both the moral and political status of the Negro American—E. Franklin Frazier, too, was led to tendency to write or speak as if the America or the "White" position of subjectivation in this domain was replete in the face of the problem (or problematic) that goes under the heading of the Negro (especially as a problem for thought) (Frazier 2001 [1939]). It remained a common ground of presupposition. This is not to diminish or set aside the fundamental work of Herskovits or his students. Nor is to turn aside from the truth maintained with Frazier's intervention. On the contrary, it is to deepen or radicalize the impulse that seemed to animate both Frazier and Herskovits during the 1930s. On the one hand, the richly irreverent contribution by Richard Price and Sally Price concerning the diaries of Melville and Frances Herskovits from their first field trips in the summers of 1928 and 1929 among the Saramaka Maroons of Suriname should be noted (Price and Price 2003, cf. 83–87). On the other, the readdress of the order of questions for a putative African Americanist sociology as they announced themselves to Frazier in the interwar period must be given a new and far more supple epistemic consideration along the lines proposed by Andrew W. Platt just over a generation ago (Platt 1991).

62. Robin D. G. Kelley's *Yo' Mama's Disfunktional: Fighting the Culture Wars in Urban America* can be cited here as indexing the relevant political horizon of this epistemologically seated problematic of denigration from the immediately past and contemporary horizon. Its epilogue "Looking B(l)ackward: 2097–1997," likewise proposes rich interventions (Kelley 1997).

63. This would be the practice of a kind of paleonomy. In another discourse, Jacques Derrida's elaboration of a grammatology, or general science of the mark, under the heading of "*archi-écriture/archi-writing*" is an

example and formulates the stakes of what I have in mind (Derrida 1976; Derrida 1967a).

64. See Ralph Ellison *Invisible Man* (Ellison 1989, 9). Too, the possible construal of the paleonymic de-citation of Shakespeare's *Hamlet* here (Act I, scene iii, lines 56–89), "To be or not to be . . . ," not only maintains this possible reference, but, if its pertinence can be proposed, in turn disposes that reference toward a desedimentation of consciousness that would somehow expose the "invisibility" of "form" in being or the "silence of sound" (Ellison 1989, 6, 13). The theme of a transcendental patience (which is interwoven with its other, a certain impatience) legible within African American practice. Du Bois somewhere quotes these lines from *Hamlet*:

> Must give us pause—there's the respect/
> That makes calamity of so long a life./
> For who would bear the whips and scorn of time,/
> Th'oppressor's wrong, the pround man's contumely,/
> The pangs of dispriz'd love, the law's delay,/
> The insolence of office, and the spurns/
> That patient merit of th' unworthy takes,/
> When he himself might his quietus make/
> With a bare bodkin? (Shakespeare 1982, lines 68–72)

The elaboration of such a thought would then require (a) another thought of the historicity exposed in the tragedy of *Hamlet* and (b) a futural gesture, perhaps at times theoretical, that would reencode the African American problematic as epochal: exposing the measureless depths of the aphonic sounds of an African American inhabitation of being.

65. Writing during the Second World War, astride his seventy-fifth year, at a juncture when he began to realize that his second great initiative to secure support for his conception of a national level project in an African American studies had been undermined, Du Bois proposed such a summary heading for his life-long double pronged approach – at once epistemological and political, scholarly and activist – in the engagement with what he had called from the turn of the twentieth century "the study of the Negro problems" (Du Bois 1982).

66. In another study, a companion to the present work, I track the formulation of the premises of Du Bois's perspective as it is announced on this horizon of problem in his earliest work (Chandler forthcoming).

67. It was the accomplishment of a certain coming to terms with this order of problem that marked the turning—still within the enfolding and engendering problematic, nonetheless—that allowed the subsequent exfoliation in Derrida's discourse (Derrida 1967a; Derrida 1976).

68. It now measures as a lifetime of creative practice—in all senses of this latter term. One can reference, for example, a sample of work across a generational length of time (Taylor 1966b; Taylor 1975; Taylor 1982; Taylor 1987).

69. Citation of these two essays by Jacques Derrida are given in the endnote to that epigraph, details for which can be found in the bibliography for this volume.

70. In all truth, I refer to the whole movement of Derrida's intellectual development across the first half of the 1960s, more or less, to the cultivation of the grammatological discussion proper, so to speak (Derrida 1978b; Derrida 1967c; Derrida 1976; Derrida 1967a; Derrida 2011; Derrida 1967d; Derrida 1981a; Derrida 1972a) .

71. And this relative, a grammar school teacher in her own right—that is, over several decades—was Janice Herring. And by this reference, I annotate a whole circle of teachers within my church and extended familial community—of whom my parents were the first exemplar, whose commitment to education and learning helped to set me on the path that has, most precisely, yielded the present work.

CHAPTER TWO

1. **Dedication:** A dear friend of just three and a half years—which enclosed a lifetime—who, almost unable to walk in the late autumn of 1992 due to the weakness of body that follows from the onset of full-blown AIDS, could still sustain his sense of the possibility of a friend's future, such that he could join me in my free-rental-football-field-long white Lincoln Continental with all leather seats to tool around Chicago's Near Northside and give me expert advice in finding a sport coat to wear for my first interviews for an appointment as a professor. And, it seemed, that it would have been impossible for me not to succeed, with my one-of-a-kind J. A. jacket upon which he had steadily insisted. Just eighteen months later, he would maintain until I could return to Chicago from the South and visit him in hospice, barely conscious, before releasing from these shores. As his family honored me and my father's tradition by asking me to pray over him in departed state as one among them, a privilege that I here acknowledge as gift, this elaboration is to join in responsibility for the name of their memory. From the depth of the ocean bottom, according to its intractable movements, this memory finds its path and its dissipation, in our own time; for the measureless sound of a turning for a friend in need, in his own time, I retain here this notation of a rite of passage.

2. Offered in the midst of the opening of the possibility of a new reception of the work of Du Bois, as a certain thinker, perhaps, Wideman's formulation may now be understood a generation on as both an affirmation of this new

listening for the more fundamental registers of that discourse and an ongoing challenge to existing limits in this new engagement (Wideman 1990, xii).

3. I should perhaps offer, as a form of generosity and a certain caution, an
overture of a kind to the reader. I have written in a manner self-consciously
concerned to encourage, at times, and according to a certain protocol, a
nonlinear reading of this essay, attempting at times to recognize that certain problematics cannot be rigorously formulated or thought declaratively,
but acquire their most sustainable formulation by indirection, delayed resonance, open-ended-return-traversal of passages, and so on. Patricia Williams once wrote of her own approach: "I am trying to create a genre of
legal writing to fill in the gaps of traditional legal scholarship. I would like to
write in a way that reveals the intersubjectivity of legal constructions, that
forces the reader both to participate in the construction of meaning and
to be conscious of that process. Thus, in attempting to fill the gaps in the
discourse of commercial exchange, I hope that the gaps in my own writing
will be self-consciously filled by the reader, as an act of forced mirroring of
meaning-invention. To this end, I exploit all sorts of literary devices, including parody, parable, and poetry" (Williams 1991, 7–8). Although I cannot
claim to fill any gaps by my style, nor is the range of rhetorical forms at
work in the essay at hand as richly multiple as Williams's text, the principle
by which I have written recognizes the same structures as operative in the
reading/writing of this essay. It doubtless should be noted that the problem
of style that I have just outlined is the space in which Du Bois made lasting
contributions. The form of the autobiographical, in all its heterogeneity, is
one such form or style.

4. These texts are cited from the recently edited and annotated collection
of Du Bois's writings, *The Problem of the Color Line at the Turn of the Twentieth Century: The Essential Early Essays* (Du Bois forthcoming[a]). "The Conservation of Races" is cited in the text as CR followed by page number (s) and
paragraph number; likewise, "Strivings of the Negro People" is cited as SNP,
followed by page and paragraph number(s). In addition, I provide here reference information for two other reliable sources of each of these texts, details
of which can be found in bibliography. The first, is the original publication
(Du Bois 1897a; Du Bois 1897b). The second is the reprint, as applicable in
the case of one of the two essays, in one of the volumes published under
the comprehensive title "The Complete Published Writings of W. E. B. Du
Bois," compiled and edited by Herbert Aptheker from 1973 to 1986 (Du Bois
1986a; Du Bois 1982f). ("Strivings of the Negro People," like almost all of the
texts by Du Bois that he included in one of his published volumes was not
included in the reprint series compiled by Aptheker.) Finally, all citations to
The Souls of Black Folk: Essays and Sketches refer to the first edition of 1903, as

outlined in the general bibliographic note provided at the beginning of this study (Du Bois 1903f).

5. Hortense Spillers may be regarded as singular among earlier generations of scholars in the consistency of her astute recognition and annotation of this aspect of Du Bois's practice across his itinerary (Spillers 2003a, 269ff.; Spillers 1991b, 63–64).

6. Taking some reference here to the threshold contribution of the twentieth-century phenomenological tradition from Edmund Husserl, Martin Heidegger, Emmanuel Levinas, or Jean Cavailles to Frantz Fanon, Tran Duc Thao, and Maurice Merleau-Ponty, perhaps we can construe this latter thought in the nonfoundational sense of the ultratranscendental elaborated by Derrida in the 1960s (Derrida 1976, 61ff.; Derrida 1967a, 90ff.)

7. Several superb essays by Cornel West mark the inauguration of a contemporary rethinking of this question (West 1982, 47–65; West 1987; West 1988). Although begun independently, my own initial efforts in this domain were subsequently encouraged by West's contributions (Chandler ca. 1988). In October 1991, a discussion around a presentation by David Theo Goldberg as part of the Workshop on the Politics of Race and the Reproduction of Racial Ideologies at the University of Chicago, convened by Thomas Holt and Kenneth Warren, contributed to my thoughts along these lines, for it remains that at the time of his first work, the question of the status of race in modernity has remained a closed and vexed horizon of question within the traditional philosophical discourses (Goldberg 1993). I wish to thank Goldberg, in friendship as well, for generously sharing with me his extensive work along these lines prior to its publication and beyond the workshop, work that helped to open this field for the thorough-going discussion that is now full-on a generation subsequent.

8. I first broached this genealogy of Du Bois's formulation of the color-line as a problem of modernity as it is outlined here in an early version of a section of this essay presented and distributed at the annual meetings of the American Anthropological Association in November 1991, as noted above in the acknowledgments. Elsewhere, I offer an initial elaboration of this question (Chandler forthcoming).

9. More than half a century after its initial deployment and a whole three generations beyond its 1935 summation, its thesis can be said to have allowed the culmination of a complete paradigm shift with regard to the study of reconstruction and its aftermath, as represented in the signal summations astride the post-1960s eruptions of historiographical scholarship of Leon Litwack and Eric Foner on the United States and in the work of Thomas C. Holt in a study of the same order but situated on the level of a problematic of the British empire in the Americas in the undulating aftermath of the abolitions

of slavery (Litwack 1979; E. Foner 1982; E. Foner 1988; Holt 1990a; Holt 1992). And it perhaps can be understood to name the epistemic ground of a more recent equally accomplished summation of the horizon of African American initiative in the remaking of America in the aftermath of the failures of reconstruction in the United States (Hahn 2003).

10. Here, I leave the reference to the second chapter of *The Souls of Black Folk* to mark the theoretical frame (Du Bois 1903c). However, elsewhere I open a more patient consideration of the genealogy of this fundamental aspect of Du Bois's thought; therein, I notate its decisive formulation in December 1899, but with reference to his first formulations of this thought across the previous half-dozen years (Chandler forthcoming).

11. This new way, I hope to suggest later, opened onto the historical question that in the past two generations have sometimes been placed under the heading of the problem of the "subaltern" in a global sense, following formulations of Antonio Gramsci (Guha and Spivak 1988; Guha 1997b). More recently, in some of her work, Gayatri Spivak has elaborated the figure of "the native informant" on this epistemic terrain (Spivak 1999, cf. 1–111, esp. 4ff., 34ff., 72ff.). Although it should be noted that I would propose no conceptual name as such.

12. "With the best will the factual outline of a life misses the essence of its spirit. Thus in my life the chief fact has been race—not so much scientific race, as that deep conviction of myriads of men that congenital differences among the masses of human beings absolutely condition the individual destiny of every member of a group" (*Dusk*, 139).

13. This was Gayatri Spivak's suggestion as one line of intervention in post-1960s theoretical production across the human sciences (Spivak 1990, e.g. 50–59). And then too, we could remark this form of problem from Kant through Hegel, from Husserl to Heidegger, and into its thematization in the earliest work of both Foucault and Derrida, by way of examples.

14. For Derrida in his engagement with Husserl in his early work, such was *the* way into this dimension of the senior philosopher's itinerary (Derrida 1978b; Derrida 1974).

15. I should cite the entirety of the first four paragraphs of this opening chapter of *Souls*. Moreover, a formal protocol of pronouns could be traced throughout the entirety of the text. Long ago, Robert Stepto provided some suggestions in this regard (Stepto 1979).

16. "*The Souls of Black Folk* is a series of fourteen essays written under various circumstances and for different purposes during a period of seven years. It has therefore, considerable, perhaps too great, diversity. There are bits off history and biography, some description of scenes and persons, something of controversy and criticism, some statistics and a bit of story-telling. All

this leads to rather abrupt transitions of style, tone and viewpoint and, too, without doubt, to a distinct sense of incompleteness and sketchiness. On the other hand, there is a unity in the book, not simply the general unity of the larger topic, but a unity of purpose in the distinctly subjective note that runs through each essay" (Du Bois 1977).

17. Along with and even prior to Holt's intervention, this is a dimension that Herbert Aptheker consistently called to attention (Holt 1990b, 307; Aptheker 1968). It can be said that the autobiographical runs throughout Du Bois's itinerary and likewise it might be shown that its sense guides sets the tone of the narrative and suffuses on the order of example and perspective even his most systematic historical work (Du Bois 1982a; Du Bois 1982e; Du Bois 1975b; Du Bois 1986c; Du Bois 1982b; Du Bois 1968). The definitive turn, or deepening, of Du Bois's inhabitation of this order of discourse would have been the construction of *Dusk of Dawn* in the closing years of the 1930s (Du Bois, 1975c).

18. I reference here, respectively, the critique of the subject in Althusser's thought of "interpellation" and Foucault's rethinking of the constitution of the subject as it was staged across his later work, from 1977 to 1984 (Althusser 1971; Foucault 2000).

19. Perhaps there is no way to translate the character of Du Bois's attention directly into the terms of a common theoretical lexicon. However, it may be useful to remark his order of attention as a concern with meaning and his sense of access to it as a matter of understanding and interpretation (Du Bois 1982f; Du Bois 1980b; Du Bois and Eaton 1973; Du Bois 1982g; Du Bois 1980c; Du Bois 1901a; Du Bois 1980a; Du Bois 1901b; Du Bois 1901c; Du Bois 1982d; Du Bois 1976; Du Bois 1982b). In this context, one must underscore *The Souls of Black Folk* (*Souls*, 103–34, chap. 7).

20. See the bibliography by Paul G. Partington (Partington 1977, 201). He was a pioneering scholar of the work of W. E. B. Du Bois; working as bibliographer, he prepared the first bibliography that was comprehensive in scale. He included a photocopy of this letter as an appendix to the typescript bibliography that he published in the late 1970s, after nearly two decades of research.

21. For the contemporary horizon of theoretical discourse, a parallel reference may be adduced to the movement of *différance* elucidated in Derrida's discourse (Derrida 1982b, 17–27, esp. 24; Derrida 1982c; Derrida 1976, 27–73). Such reference may suggest the ways in which Du Bois's interpretive disposition remains open to what is at stake for us today.

22. Although his emphasis occurs according to a different trajectory, in my own time, Derrida's formulation of his own affinity for the problematic of the autobiographical is apposite here. I state such ironically of course,

with a double edge, since with regard to the history of African American autobiographical practices, Derrida's contributions arrive quite late on the scene in which these practices have emerged, yet he remains a thinker whose work offers one of the strongest possible justifications for recognizing the remarkable resources of the autobiographical (Andrews 1986; Gates 1991; Bennington and Derrida 1993). In the course of trying to situate his work as giving up neither philosophy nor literature, "perhaps seeking obscurely a place from which the history of this frontier could be thought or even displaced," Derrida states in a 1988 interview: "'Autobiography' is perhaps the least inadequate name, because it remains for me the most enigmatic, the most open, even today" (Derrida 1992b, 34).

23. See Derrida's 1959 ruminations, later revised, on the organization of Husserl's breakthrough thought (Derrida 1978d, 158–59, emphasis in the original, and see 162–64). Derrida is writing of Husserl as the latter came into his own mature formulation of problematic amidst the late 1890s. The problem of how to situate such a unity was nothing other than the question of the constitution of objectivity as such and bequeathed the opening to the phenomenological path of inquiry.

24. Three referential lines of desedimentation may serve us here. (1) One might well understand this as an allusion to Thales of Miletus, held "traditionally" as "the earliest Greek physicist, or enquirer into the nature of things as a whole" (Kirk and Raven 1969, 74–98, quotation at 74). Plato in the *Theaetetus*, a dialogue concerning wisdom, or knowing in the most broad sense, has Socrates say at 174a to Theodorus, one of this two interlocutors along with Theaetetus, " . . . just as . . . a witty and attractive Thracian servant girl is said to have mocked Thales for falling into a well while he was observing the stars and gazing upwards; declaring that he was eager to know the things in the sky, but that what was behind him and just beneath his feet escaped his notice." Translation from the Greek given in Kirk and Raven (noted above, p. 78n74). In the passage that immediately precedes the reference to Thales quoted above, Plato has Socrates give a speech about the "philosopher," the lover of wisdom, saying that "only his body sojourns in his city, while his thought, disdaining all such things as worthless, takes wings, as Pindar says, 'beyond the sky, beneath the earth,' searching the heavens and measuring the plains, everywhere seeking the true nature of everything whole, never sinking to what lies close at hand" (Plato 1989, quotation at 173e). In this context, of a possible allusion, Du Bois's citation however would also address the other "traditional" understanding of Thales as a man of considerable practicality. Aristotle in his *Politics* writes of him that "when they reproached him because of his poverty, as though philosophy were no use, it is said that, having observed through his study of the heavenly bodies

that there would be a large olive-crop, he raised a little capital while it was still winter, and paid deposits on all the olive presses in Miletus and Chios, hiring them cheaply because no one bid against him. When the appropriate time came there was a sudden rush of requests for the presses; he then hired them out on his own terms and so made a large profit, thus demonstrating that it is easy for philosophers to be rich, if they wish, but that it is not in this that they are interested" (Kirk and Raven 1969, 78n75). It is reasonable to presume that both of these "traditions" are apocryphal, but they have no less bearing for us. Du Bois, one can suggest, coming to his own question by way of the resolute materiality of the situation of the African American, is affirming the thought of the infinite, of infinite possibility, while nonetheless insisting on a certain maintenance of both. Thus, the Negro must, as a matter of survival in a peculiarly acute sense, attend to the mundane, but yet keep "commerce with the stars." As he says in "Conservation of Races," he sought to "rise above" the immediate and mundane, to consider "the whole question" in the context of "philosophy." And, then two notes should be simply deposited here, in the context a discussion of the problem of the Negro or African American. Socrates goes on in the *Theaetetus*, elaborating his thought in which the reference to Thales occurs, to speak further of the man of the city and the philosopher, aligning the latter with "every one whose breeding has been the anti-thesis of the slave's" (Plato 1989, 174c–176a). Also, tradition has it that Thales visited Egypt and learned from the priests there (Kirk and Raven 1969, 76–78). (2) Too, one might also think of that most famous statement of Immanuel Kant's, with which he opens his "Conclusion" to the *Critique of Practical Reason*: "Two things fill the mind with ever new and increasing admiration and reverence (*Erfurcht*), the more often and more steadily one reflects on them: *the starry heavens above me and the moral law within me*." And I take note here only of Kant's initial continuing remark of the first motif: "The first begins from the external world I occupy in the external world of sense and extends the connection in which I stand to an unbounded magnitude with worlds upon worlds and systems of systems, and moreover into the unbounded times of their periodic motion, their beginning and their duration" (Kant 1996a, 269, emphasis in the original). I underscore that I am making no claim here that Du Bois is himself directly alluding to this passage from Kant. Rather, I propose the juxtaposition to suggest the character of a possible *horizon* of interlocution, if taken as a question for fundamental thought, Du Bois's concern might well be understood to interpellate a certain given hegemonic tradition of inquiry, to put it in a manner that is only an apparent paradox. (3) Yet, from another direction or tradition, one can take note of the figures of "falling stars," and "bright sparkles" in *The Souls of Black Folk* and suggest a possible "allegorical" "bridge" that could connect them to a medieval Jewish tradition, which reconfigured the import of kabbalah concerning "*shevirat ha kelim*" (the breaking of the vessels), which refers to "a stage in creation after God has contracted into himself in order to clear a space for the world," to account for the experience of exile after the expulsion of Jews from Spain in 1492. This is the line of thought proposed by Adam Zachary Newton (Newton 1999, 1–4). He construes a relation of "stars," especially "falling stars" in Du Bois to "*nitzutzot*" (divine sparks, or falling stars) which fall to earth, disseminated and dispersed as the "emanations" of divine light made possible by this "divine self-limitation." This light was so "intense" that it shattered the vessels (*kelim*) that would have precipitated and carried this light to earth. Newton writes that it is "the task of *tikkun* (redemption) that all creation strive toward the freeing of these sparkles from their earthly captivity." He goes on the suggest that two centuries later, "Levi Yitzhak of Berdichev, one of the early Hasidic masters, claimed, much like Du Bois, that the divine sparks have a role to play in exile, to flash here and there on earth, and in that flashing thereby illuminate creation; like the angels of Jacob's ladder, the *nitzutzot* can rise up to Heaven as well as rain down from above." Perhaps one can maintain Newton's thought here and speak of a double necessity in Du Bois's inhabitation of the mundane and an openness to that which is always yet to come. I thank Bruce Rosenstock for the reference to Newton's study.

25. Perhaps this approach was unlike the formulations of Kant in his prefatory efforts for his *Critique of Pure Reason*, for example, wherein the critical philosopher may be understood to affirm the authority of the architectonic over the historicity of the production (Kant 1998, Avii–Axxii, Bvii–Bxliv). Consider Derrida's elucidation of this question in the context of a discussion of Husserl's work (Derrida 1978b, 39–42).

26. See the opening text called "The Plot" (*Dusk*, 7). This is in fact one of the most deeply sedimented and most productive lines in Du Bois's theoretical disposition, even if it is nowhere given a systematic exposition by him, for in fact he raises this question throughout his career (Du Bois 1903f; Du Bois 1982f; Du Bois 1977; Du Bois 1975a; Du Bois 1982b).

27. Across the first half of *Dusk of Dawn*, as he sets the directly personal references for his narrative, one might recognize this order of attention in Du Bois's telling (*Dusk*, 18, 49, 51–53, 64–65–67, 95–96).

28. Most certainly, there are in fact quite specific forms in which this question arises for our narrator (*Dusk*, 3–4; *Souls*, 13, chap. 2, para. 1). Yet, recognizing a path otherwise than a naive empiricism or a protoleptic transcendentalism, one can thereby remark a dimensionless dimension (which is nonetheless not nothing) within existence that simultaneously opens as nothing other than immanence. It would be an immanence in which the

transcendental opening has already been announced, always (Derrida 1976, 61). It would be an immanence in which the possibility of existence can always be understood as simultaneously life and death. Such would be the premise of a discourse of the ultratranscendental. In a discourse that would respond to such demands, one cannot only historicize the eruption of a form of existence; nor, could only remark on the transcendental. Rather, one must do both and then go beyond such ostensible distinction to an understanding that might announce another historicity of the transcendental or another approach to a transcendental history.

29. The quotation is from the opening of the book (*Dusk*, 4). "A man lives today not only in his physical environment and in the social environment of ideas and customs, laws and ideals; but that total environment is subjected to a new socio-physical environment of other groups, whose social environment he shares but in part" (*Dusk*, 134–35).

30. Elsewhere, I track the complex moves of Du Bois's engagement in "The Conservation of Races" essay of 1897 with the idea of racial distinction, in which he both (a) subjects the traditional concept of race to a radical and irrefutable questioning of its logic and (b) attempts to formulate, in a paleonymic gesture, the historicity and ideals for Negro Americans under its heading (Chandler forthcoming). In the pivotal moment of the essay, in a formulation that is precisely relevant to the passage that we are reading here from *Dusk of Dawn*, Du Bois proposes that what he called in his specific sense "races" (or sometimes "nations") are fundamentally historical and changing, if not evolving. Also, see the general formulation of this argument adumbrated in Chapter 1 of the present study. Here one may recall Thomas C. Holt's notations on this line of problem in Du Bois's thought in the midst of a debate on this question just over a generation ago (Holt 1990b, 321n3, n5, n6). Herein, however, I have proposed to render this whole matter thematic.

31. We may recognize here Du Bois's valuable and, perhaps, pioneering role, articulated already in his earliest texts, for example in *Souls*, in describing the double structure of colonial and postcolonial geographic spaces, marked and shaped by way of a constitutive (or, founding) violence, such as the two-part character of the colonial town remarked in later scholarly and political discussion (Du Bois 1901c; Du Bois 1903d; Fanon 1961; Cohn 1987a; Cohn 1987b). And, of course one can find later ethnographic descriptions given of the American rural South the urban North that follow on the path taken by Du Bois here (Du Bois 1985; Du Bois ca. 1897; Du Bois 1898a; Du Bois and Eaton 1899; Hurston 1935; Drake and Cayton 1945). This is theoretically where a certain conceptualization of transnationality must disrupt the metaphor of geographical homogeneity that can be implied by the semantic

gathering of the word transnational; likewise, such a (re)conceptualization would question the presupposition of nation implied therein.

32. We must recall that this thematic appears under an apparently auto-biographic heading (Du Bois 1975c, 134–72). While the text at hand dates to the last years of the 1930s, as Du Bois enters his seventies, this theme is actually already announced in Du Bois's conception from the outset of his maturation and is developed into its first full articulation in the years just prior to the First World War (Du Bois 1901c; Du Bois forthcoming[b]; Du Bois 1909; Du Bois 1973; Du Bois 1910; Du Bois 1917; Du Bois 1915a). It becomes definitive for him in the immediate aftermath of that war (Du Bois 1920; Du Bois 1975b).

33. These matters (in which the problem of the empty or unmarked place of a supposed subject, the position of a putatively sovereign figure, one that would be the apparent manifestation of an idea of whiteness, on the one hand, and the idea and concept of race, on the other, are at stake) are each broached again, partially, in the closing two chapters of the present study and each comprise the headings for quite general investigations. And, on another track, it raises the whole question of what is to be done, which is the guiding motif of the second half of *Dusk of Dawn* in general, which is the special burden of the two closing chapters of that text. As it requires its own order of attention to detail and question, this latter motif must be approached differently than I am doing here. I hope to address it properly in another context.

34. Du Bois never seemed to *assume* the possibility of simply stepping outside or beyond systems of racial distinction. Which is not to say that one cannot fundamentally challenge them. An entire paradoxical economy, elaborated nowhere as richly as in the work of Du Bois with regard to racial distinction and, for example, in the work of Heidegger or Derrida with regard to philosophical distinctions of sameness or difference, would dem-onstrate that such an assumption is at best simply naive and at worst politi-cally suspect. This is contrary to many contemporary thinkers. I consider the early formulations of Anthony Appiah concerning Du Bois an example of this conundrum; yet nearly two decades later he was led to formulate more caution on these matters (Appiah 1986; Appiah 1992a; Appiah 2005). Below, in this chapter, I touch on the ensemble of paradoxes at stake here; as well, they are outlined further in a formal sense in Chapter 1 of this study. On a related line of discussion, the possibility of the partiality of one's situat-edness opening precisely the question of a radical reflection on the historic-ity by which one is instituted and in which one is inscribed, I wish to note Shamoon Zamir was led to address the passage just cited in the manner that I have formulated here as a key moment in the opening chapter and thus the

framing of his study of some of Du Bois's early writings by way of my sharing my reference to it in a then-unpublished version of this chapter (ca. 1991). I notate this reference simply as a matter of record (Zamir 1995, 2).

35. By way of this reference we may question the contemporary genealogy of a critical and metatheoretical thought of genealogy (Foucault 1977, esp. 80–83; Nietzsche 1998). That is to ask, for example, whence Du Bois in the itinerary of Michel Foucault's discourse?

36. The dominant tradition, even in its dissenting twentieth-century form, can be noted here (Aristotle 1966, 1005b, 11–34; Hegel 1977; Hegel 1969; Heidegger 1969). We can now question too, thus, the problem of the idea of categorical difference *among humans* in the work of this tradition.

37. Even as he affirmed a certain idea of Europe, such as questioning of it as the telos of human ideals emerged as a persistent theme of his work already from the turn of the century (*Dusk*, 51, 98–99; Du Bois 1982c). His questioning may be said thus to place his sense of the problematic on the bias, the strategy of which I propose to outline in the opening chapter of this study.

38. "When I came to Harvard [in 1889, at the age of twenty-one] the theory of race separation was quite in my blood. I did not seek contact with my white fellow students. On the whole I rather avoided them. I took it for granted that we were training ourselves for different careers in worlds largely different. There was not the slightest idea of the permanent subordination and inequality of my world" (*Dusk*, 101).

39. First, it must be specifically noted that this term does appear under this lexical heading directly on the surface of this text (*Dusk*, 103). However, I propose to annotate and reinscribe it here within my own critical discourse according to a disposition that is similar to my remarks on the term "between" in the Anacrusis to this study.

40. This passage should give pause to those who might read the following in the first volume of David Levering Lewis's biography of Du Bois: "This subtext of proud hybridization is so prevalent in Du Bois's sense of himself that the failure to notice it in the literature about him is as remarkable as the complex itself" (Lewis 1993, 148). Lewis is there making reference to Du Bois's self-reference in the handscript diary of his return to America from Europe by steerage in the early summer of 1894. He quotes Du Bois's original text as: "There are two full-blooded Negroes aboard and (including myself) 3 half [crossed-out] mulattoes" (Lewis 1993, 148, Lewis's interpolation in brackets). The word "half" is crossed through on the original text. Lewis had just previously quoted the text of Du Bois's *Autobiography* on this steerage scene as: "There are five Negroes aboard. We do not go together." In a note attached to these two quotations Lewis scores Herbert Aptheker for "editing" the original

handscript text such that it is reproduced only in part in the *Autobiography*, thus apparently obscuring if not concealing Du Bois's supposed "proud" reference to himself as "mulatto." While in his note Lewis credits the staff of the Library of America as calling this apparent editorial intervention to his attention, he does not provide direct reference to, or otherwise indicate, the existence of documents that would suggest or confirm that the specific passage of text as it is given in the published *Autobiography* was determined by Aptheker rather than by Du Bois (for we know that the latter was revising the text right up to the end) (Lewis 1993, 613 n. 91). On a semantic level, it should be noted that the crossed out word "half" implies a reference to a putative full term that it modifies, such as "blood" as in "half-blood." And this sense would match with Du Bois's earlier remark in the original handscript text of some twenty-two pages with regard to "the Prussian Pole[s]" that he sees on the ship as "not physically debauched" despite the difficulty of their historical social situation, amidst references and a perspective from Du Bois that I specifically annotate on other terms as pejorative toward this same group (Du Bois ca. 1894). Likewise, one should index here a rather persistent motif in Du Bois's writings regarding the historical condition of certain forms of the "intermixture" of so-called races, as one might put it, that he claims to recognize in the history of "the American Negro," for it is a motif at the heart of the kind of "autobiographical" reflection that we are following in this chapter. As can be noted in the opening chapter of *The Souls of Black Folk*, Du Bois often harshly remarks what he called the "forced concubinage of slavery" and "the red stain of bastardy, which two centuries of systematic legal defilement of Negro women had stamped on his race" (*Souls*, 9, chap. 1, para. 9). As will be noted below, it was exactly this historicity within his own family genealogy, in the restricted sense, that had led him at the turn of the twentieth century to stand at a distance from the deeper history of his paternal family line. We can now quote more fulsomely both the original handscript text and the *Autobiography* on the reference to Negroes on the steerage trip. The original reads: "There are two full-blooded Negro [*sic*] abroad [*sic*] & (including myself) 3 [*the crossed through word "half" is here in the original text*] mulattoes. We do not go together—indeed have not all spoken together, but I think all have had a pleasant voyage with little cause to complain of any prejudice. Of course [*the crossed through word "the" appears here in the text*] we awakened more or less curiosity with some & I fancy something of distaste in others. Yet I find [*the crossed through word "them" appears here in the text*] us all talking to the women & one especially from his good heartedness & [*an illegible word is here*] seems a general favorite; in fine in a graded line of individuals here the Blacks would by no means stand at the bottom of the row" (Du Bois ca. 1894, interpolations in brackets and emphasis mine). The *Autobiography* continues beyond where Lewis's quote of it given above breaks off with the same words from the second sentence onward of the original text as I just quoted it, with some variation in punctuation mark only (Du Bois 1968, 181). In the more fully quoted text we find here Du Bois placing himself with, not apart from, Blacks, in some general sense—a term that should be noted as distinctive in his usage in this passage, since he had already used the Negro as the collective reference.

41. See the opening chapter of this study, for therein, in conjunction with my own formulations, I annotate the way in which Derrida's work can assist in tracking such a problematic, especially in the formulations that he adduced in his work of the late 1960s (Derrida 1981, 207–8nn24–25; Derrida 1981c, 37–96; Derrida 1976, 27–73).

42. That Du Bois specifies "Europe" as distinct from "America" is both an act of generosity and a critique. To recognize an openness in "Europe" is to recognize a heterogeneity among "white folk" and, moreover, to respond in kind. To specifically leave aside "America" in this acknowledgment can be nothing less than the harshest of judgments. Du Bois had already stated this theme in the second paragraph of the opening chapter of *Souls*. Also, I wish to thank Professor Cheryl Wall for her suggestion in conversation of the term "association" as I have operated it in this paragraph, in October 2003 at a conference at Northwestern University, organized by Dwight McBride and Robert Gooding Williams, on the occasion of the centenary of *The Souls of Black Folk*.

43. From within the discourse of modern anthropology one can note the summative work of Raymond Smith on this theme (Smith 1988, e.g. 3–4).

44. There is now accomplished for perhaps two decades a general critique of the anthropological discourse on kinship that is pertinent, not only for discussions of the supposed African diaspora, but for how we think of kinship and intergenerational relation in general. Thus, we can certainly take reference to an autobiographical telling such we find in Du Bois (*Dusk*, 103). Along side it, however, one can situate quite diverse general considerations; and such pertinence remains, despite the fact that the way in which the unmarked concept of race appears therein cannot be considered a critical one (Smith 1988, 82–109; Gutman 1976; Gordon-Reed 2008; Schneider 1980; Schneider 1984).

45. Please see Figures 1 and 2, which present a genealogical chart of Du Bois's family. Also, note the one from Du Bois's *Dusk of Dawn* (*Dusk*, 113).

46. I shall only note and not dwell (here) on the *general* fact that Du Bois's account follows conceptions of kinship (such as tracing kin relation by way of bifurcated parental lines, use of common "English" kin terms, conceptualizing the notion of family around a nuclear unit, and so on) that has been

found to be quite common and general in the United States and the English-speaking Caribbean (Smith 1988; Schneider 1980; Schneider 1984). However, we must also note the quite *particular* fact that Du Bois's discussion records *both* (1) the tendency, where so-called intermixture occurs, to trace the general family line according to a racial bifurcation, through either one or the other racial category, leading to both (a) the forgetting of the other line, and (b) the polarization of the difference between these two lines, *and* (2) a deliberate questioning of the logic of this tendency as its central theme.

47. We must recall here, too obliquely, a simple and limpid insight of the late James Baldwin: that there is no such thing as a "white" person; that, "white" Americans *became* white only upon the construction of such a category in the United States, and in relation to the construction of "black" people and "red" people (Baldwin 1998). Many related insights offered in Baldwin's work along these lines could also be adduced (Baldwin 1985; Mead and Baldwin 1971). Moreover, Baldwin noted this crucial irony: these immigrants usually came to "America" because they were not "white" in their own country. And one can note other twists in this paradoxical structure (Orsi 1992). Above all, we must note here, for elaboration elsewhere, that it was Du Bois was one of the first twentieth-century writers to recognize this problematic and to make it a theme, long before the contemporary eruption of the now form of "whiteness studies" (Du Bois 1899; Du Bois 1973; Du Bois 1910; Roediger 1991; Morrison 1992).

48. I thank Elizabeth Morrison for providing me with this timely and pithy colloquialism, "to go by way of the elbow to get to the thumb."

49. Taylor's meditation under the heading of "Silent Tongues" remains as the exemplary, that is the most radical, reference for the present study (Taylor 1975).

50. Two interrelated annotations can be given here, one "cultural," the other "legal." First, in an historical geographical reference, Raymond Smith's work, for example, in Jamaica and Guyana, and to some extent the West Indies in general, which should be understood as both continuous and discontinuous with the United States with regard to the general domain that anthropologists have typically understood as "kinship," records several similar histories (Smith 1988, 82–109; Craton 1979; Craton and Walvin 1970; Craton and Greenland 1978; Higman 1984; Gutman 1976). Secondly, the question of legality is central to the structure of racial distinction. Law will always err on, or insure, the side of the disciplining distinction. Du Bois had already qualified his narrative at its inception with this statement: "Absolute legal proof of facts like these here set down is naturally unobtainable" (*Dusk*, 104). At the point in his text that we have broken off for this note, Du Bois gave a contemporary specification to what we might call the law

of racial distinction. "Indeed the legal advisors of the publishers of my last book could write: 'We may assume as a general proposition that it is libelous to state erroneously that a white man or woman has colored blood'" (*Dusk*, 106–7). Aptheker quotes from the correspondence of Du Bois with his editor at Holt and Company in early 1939, confirming the account of it that Du Bois provides here, noting that in the end "no change was made" (Aptheker 1975, 10; Aptheker 1989a, 262–63).

51. Also, see note 52 of Chapter 1 of this study.

52. But I have also strategically proposed several other names, none simply commensurate with the others, such as "between," "the other," and the (force of the) "double" (which, because it is first of all internal, is never only double, to turn a phrase, for the stability of the before or after or the inside or outside is thus not given and is irreducibly only relational). I maintain Du Bois's term "intermixture" here with regard to its local textual context of its enunciation as both a kind of paleonymic practice that does not presume the place of a theoretical elucidation is or can be neutral or pure or final in its accomplishment. I submit my practice to the labor of a reading. And, thus I seek to allow this term within this context of enunciation to offer possible effects of catechresis.

53. Again, I wish to put this thought by way of Du Bois in tandem with a certain thinking of structure, one that I have remarked as seeking to account for such on an "ultratranscendental" order of level of generality, following Derrida's 1960s considerations, one that he also called "grammatological" (Derrida 1976, 61; Derrida 1967a, 90). The crucial concern of Derrida's elaboration of his thinking of structure in *Of Grammatology* is the formulation of its structurality in such a way that system does not *simply* preexist iterable mark as an already constituted transcendental field. It attempts to propose a rigorous apparent nominalism or empiricism which can only function as such if it is thought this side of, in the aftermath or wake of, the thought of the transcendental or the "ontico-ontological" difference (Derrida 1976, 62–65; Derrida 1967a, 91–95). Working in the wake of the itinerary of question given in the work of Emanuel Levinas, Derrida in that text proposed the thought of the "trace" in relation to question of the sign and of the other.

54. In the critical thought on colonialism and its aftermath that has been produced since the 1960s, this site has been adduced as the domain or position of the subaltern (Guha and Spivak 1988; Spivak 1988).

55. We must position at this juncture both Du Bois's long answer to the question "What is Africa to me?" and his enigmatic yet profoundly transgressive response to his ("white") interlocutor(s) on the question of what the "us" is that comprises "America" (Du Bois 1975c, 116–33, esp. 116–17, and 134–72). Also, see note 52 in Chapter 1 of this study. Romantic, perhaps, in

the hope he has for the "uplift of the darker races," Du Bois could only be accused of maintaining a fundamental commitment to a concept of race as biological fact, or even a supposed categorical historicism, by a naive or willful reading. Although not motivated as a response to any particular discourse, indeed my reading issues from a first concern to assume a certain responsibility for the *questions* that motivated Du Bois's discourse, and not necessarily his answers, the reading I have outlined in this chapter suggests that as a still pertinent symptom Appiah's reading a generation and a half ago of Du Bois's response to the first question quoted above (What is Africa to me?) is a severe misapprehension of the questions that organized Du Bois's discourse and an unjustified and unacknowledged reduction of his answer (Appiah 1992a; Appiah 1986). For example, the genealogical desedimentation that I have traced in this essay precedes and prepares the stage for Du Bois's response to this question, yet Appiah's reading of it seems, paradoxically, to overlook or fail to refer at all to the de-essentializing or even deontological narrative of the paternal line or the discourse of the previous chapters that prepares us to follow its movement. Nor can such a strongly held reading open itself up to the movement of the dialogue that Du Bois goes on to elaborate between "himself" and a "white" interlocutor in the very next chapter (annotated in note 52 of Chapter 1 of this study) under the title of "The White World." For example, Du Bois writes: "[Interlocutor]: '—oh Hell! Honest to God, what do you think Asia and Africa would do to us, if they got a chance?' [Narrator]: 'Skin us alive,' I answer cheerfully, loving the 'us'" (Du Bois 1975c, 167).

56. And here an index of Derrida's remarks on Emmanuel Levinas's engagement with Edmund Husserl on the question of the other is apposite, as he simultaneously renders due respect and a questioning of the assertiveness of philosophy as metaphysics on the problem of the same and the other in the domain of ego as otherwise than simply a psychic figure of self (Derrida 1978c, 118–33).

57. Hortense Spillers has offered a brilliant reading of William Faulkner's *Absalom, Absalom!* along these lines (Spillers 1991a). According to Spillers, the analytic recognition of heterogeneity in the constitution of racialized subject position might be generalized to a hemispheric dimension, not only by way of a reference to the non-United States Americas, but indeed from within a critical thought of the hegemonic formation that the apparition of North America proffers. While, in her reading cited here, Spillers does not explicitly annotate the pivotal contributions of Du Bois, she does so elsewhere (Spillers 2003d). To the extent that her tracking of mestizo America is profound, one wonders in the context of the present discussion if, perhaps, a Du Boisian gesture might also be affirmed. In the opening paragraphs of Roberto Fernández Retamar's

essay under the figure of Caliban, and in the text of José Martí, whose classic 1891 text figures centrally in Retamar's, a similar privilege is in play (Fernández Retamar 1989; Martí 1891). Both Marti's and Retamar's discourses are central to Spillers's essay. That Du Bois had raised the question of intermixture persistently throughout his itinerary, that his 1890s writings overlap with signal productions from Marti on the one hand, and that the writing of Du Bois text under discussion here was so temporally proximate to the publication of Faulkner's text suggests, even on its own, the relevance of Du Bois's contribution to this reconstellated circulation of discourses (Faulkner 1936).

58. Here, as noted above, one should reference Aristotle's *Metaphysics* (Aristotle 1966, 1005b, 11–34). Even Hegel, in the *Science of Logic*, writes of the "presence" of A in the third, in his discussion of the "law of the excluded middle," even as his way—almost despite himself, as it were—is open to a much more supple reading (Hegel 1969, 438–39).

59. In this sense, Du Bois may well be understood as a certain kind of precursor for a fundamental dimension of Spivak's own thought and itinerary, such as it is indicated here (Spivak 1989, 130).

60. Here, we annotate another theoretical refiguration of Caliban, this time for a gesture that would acknowledge the necessity of the double reference in our common colonial nexus as not only a critique of the supposed sovereign privilege, but as also a step toward a potentially radical affirmation the more than one as the name of possibility in all measures of subjectivation and identification (Baker 1987).

61. In this further elaboration, given with reference to that order of the symbolic known as the linguistic, Spivak may well be annotated as elaborating upon Du Bois's reflection of his relation to the "Zeitgeist," as I quoted and remarked it earlier in this chapter (Spivak 1989, 130–31).

62. Indeed, one may say that Spillers offers a fundamental specification and thereby a certain radicalization of Du Bois's protoleptic recognition (Spillers 2003, 224, 221).

63. Following, thus, Spillers's still prescient and pressing intervention, we may annotate how Du Bois's metadiscourse on his own itinerary brings too a confrontation with this problematic (Spillers 2003c, 227; *Dusk*, 103).

64. Such opening would remain susceptible to announcement within this problematic even if it "misnames the power of the female regarding the enslaved community," as it most assuredly has been inscribed within general ethnological discourse on the Negro up to now (Spillers 2003c, 228).

65. I index here, for example, the various formulations of protocol that arose from the intervention of Louis Althusser in the wake of the 1960s and which remain so articulated in contemporary discussions (a remainder that one should not simply disavow here) (Althusser 1971, 170–76).

66. One not only can but perhaps should construe this thought on the level of the collective as a form of individuation. As such perhaps there could be a questioning of the idea of a putative "Europe" along these lines (Derrida 1992a). We might say, then, there is no such *thing* as Europe, unless it too could come to recognize that it is only possible as such in and through such a possibility as that which we have remarked herein under the name "W. E. B. Du Bois."

CHAPTER THREE

1. **Dedication:** The central thought of this chapter had been in gestation for some years when, in early February 1997, I was privileged to be the afternoon guest in the home of the late Dr. Herbert Aptheker and the late Fay Aptheker in San Jose, California. After a nearly two-hour conversation with Dr. Aptheker, in the course of which, among other matters, he shared some poignant autobiographical reflections with me, we shared a fine meal at their favorite restaurant. Upon my return to my home and study in North Carolina a few days later, the text offered here announced itself early one morning, "all in a day as it were." With one major exception, the addition of the fourth section drafted on another occasion and in order to specify certain terms of my reading within the narrative proper, and some bibliographic specifications, the heart of the original essay remains without essential modification. I dedicate it thus to the memory of Dr. Herbert Aptheker and to the memory of Fay Aptheker, together, in honor of their lifelong companionship, and with my deepest thanksgivings for their generous hospitality.

2. The first part of the present chapter was initially solicited as a new preface or introduction for a reprint edition of the original publication of Du Bois's biographical study of John Brown. It was delivered to the publisher in February 1997. For reasons unclear to me, that reprint edition was never published. I have left the marks of that aspect of the occasion of its preparation intact here. Since that time, two new editions of this biography have been released (Du Bois 1997; Du Bois 2001). Although distinctively helpful, respectively, neither of the introductions to these new editions was able to bring into thematic relief the central motif of Du Bois's approach as I attempt to name it in this chapter. In this sense, it seems to me, in both this particular case and in general, that the writing of Du Bois as a distinct and resolute practice remains—not only to be read but more fundamentally—to be thought more closely according to the protocols by which it solicits its own futural implication.

3. *The Souls of Black Folk: Essays and Sketches* is hereafter cited parenthetically as *Souls*, followed by page number along with chapter and paragraph numbers (Du Bois 1903f; Du Bois 1897a; Du Bois 1897b).

4. This quotation is from the King James Version of the *Holy Bible*, "The Gospel According to St. Matthew," 2:15. The locution of the biblical passage is dense, as it is the interpretive apostolic voice that follows upon the scribal voice that has just recalled the "angel of the Lord" appearing in a dream to Joseph, after the visit of the magi, directing him to "flee into Egypt" until the passing of King Herod, who would seek the death of the Christ child. It refers, among other texts, to Numbers 23:22, "God brought them out of Egypt," but especially to Hosea 11:1, "When Israel was a child then I loved him, and called my son out of Egypt." If the latter, especially, is so, then perhaps "Israel, therefore, the 'son' of the prophet's texts, prefigured the Messiah." The latter quotation is from the editor's notes to Matthew 2:15 in *The Jerusalem Bible* (Bible 1966). However, the locution of Du Bois's act of quotation is dense in a commensurate and, in this case, allegorical fashion. The quotation performs by way of Du Bois's placement, as it also references the double configuration of the prophetic voice—here by way of allegorical recollection of the ancient Jews of Israel, Egypt, and the prophecy of the coming of a Messiah, folding over this ancient and sacred account of deliverance (already an iterative account, which is both historical and spiritual, by the act of the inscription that is the Gospel of Saint Matthew) to reveal another structure of prophetic reference, one that is still yet to come, both fictively within the frame of the narrative of the biography that is yet to be told, and historically within the symbolic, specifically moral, horizon of the "America" that was the scene of existence for John Brown and for Du Bois in the time of his writing, and which, perhaps, remains for us. I leave aside, for now, other aspects of this densely embedded act of quotation.

5. The last two chapters of the biography are titled, respectively "The Riddle of the Sphinx" (Du Bois's spelling) and "The Legacy of John Brown" (Du Bois 1973, 338–64, 365–404).

6. In the third chapter of *Souls*, "Of Mr. Booker T. Washington and Others," Du Bois offers a capsule narrative of the development of African American leadership from 1750 to 1900, placing John Brown within this genealogy on a plane of continuity with Charles Lenox Remond, William Cooper Nell, William Wells Brown, and Frederick Douglass as key figures in the mid-nineteenth century who represented a new historical moment of the "self-assertion" of Negro rights "by himself" (*Souls*, 47–51, chap. 3, paras. 10–15). That placement must be understood with reference to the formulation of Brown's historical position, proposed by Du Bois in the biographical study. Likewise, Du Bois's genealogical placement of Brown in *Souls* affirms the orientation that I have followed in reading this biography.

7. First, published on its own, this essay was presented in a conjoined fashion with Du Bois's 1917 essay "Of the Culture of White Folk," as one long essay

in the his 1920 book, *Darkwater: Voices from Within the Veil* (Du Bois 1910; Du Bois 1917; Du Bois 1975b). *Darkwater* was originally published in 1920 to offer a perspective on the devastated horizon of a demoralized world after the First World War from a "veiled corner," a view from which, as Du Bois writes in the "Postscript" (presented in the usual place of a preface), "The human scene has interpreted itself to me in unusual and even illuminating ways" (Du Bois 1975b, vii). Du Bois titles the penultimate chapter of *John Brown*, "The Riddle of the Sphinx," and then in *Darkwater* includes his poem by the same title, "The Riddle of the Sphinx," as the "intermezzo" that follows the chapter therein called "The Souls of White Folk" (Du Bois 1975b, 53–55). The poem was originally published under a different title in 1907.

8. I offered a formulation of the distinctiveness of this approach with reference to our contemporary discussions in the opening stages of the next chapter. In this context, the fundamental character of Du Bois's formulation of the "half-named" Negro problem in the opening essay of *The Souls of Black Folk*, almost in passing, comes into tractable relief (*Souls*, 8, chap. 1, para. 9).

9. I restrict my reference to the vast literature on John Brown to these two venerable scholars, Benjamin Quarles and Philip S. Foner, on the grounds that they are among the relatively few scholars—along with the editors of two new editions of the biography indicated in the second note of this chapter—who grant to this maintenance the intellectual, as well as political, status that it demands (Quarles 2001; P. Foner 1975, 240–65). Such acknowledgment is necessary for the reading of Du Bois's study within the horizon of what it gives for addressing the problem of the Negro as Du Bois proposes it, that is as a constitutive problematic in modern thought.

10. This phrase calls to memory the words of Jesus of Nazareth issued on the Mount of Olives, after leaving the Temple in Jerusalem following a disputation there, as the account of these events are given in the New Testament. These words comprise an eschatological and apocalyptic discourse prophesying the second coming of the Messiah. Given in all three of the synoptic gospels, the prophesy is perhaps most fully given in the text canonically known as the "Gospel According to Matthew" in the 24th book, with the words of most direct resonance at verses 1-6, which I quote in full here:

> Jesus left the temple and was going away, when his disciples came to point out to him the buildings of the temple. But he answered them, "You see all these, do you not? Truly, I say to you, there will not be left here one stone upon another, that will not be thrown down." As he sat on the Mount of Olives, the disciples came to him privately saying, "Tell us, when will this be. And what will be the sign of your coming and of the close of the age?" And Jesus answered them,

"Take heed that no one leads you astray. For many will come in my name, saying, 'I am the Christ,' and they will lead many astray. And you will hear of wars and rumours of wars; see that you are not alarmed; for this must take place, but the end is not yet. For nation will rise against nation, and kingdom against kingdom, and there will be famines and earthquakes in various places: all this is but the beginnings of the birthpangs" (Bible 2005).

In the biblical narrative, Christ will be soon betrayed, by one amongst his own, pass through the suffering of his night at Gethsemane, to endure arrest, trial, sentencing, scourge and death by crucifixion. The prophesy on the Mount of Olives stands then at the inception of the decisive transformation of the dispensation of the teachings of Jesus of Nazareth on earth and the narrative that proposes it thus stands as the inception of a radicalized eschatology. Du Bois, it may be adduced, by way of his quotation of Brown's resonance or resounding of this biblical prophesy, not only recalls thus the way that Brown's voicing would place in question any or all forms of the worldly orders that would claim the sovereign right to judge him, but puts into rhetorical motion the possibility that future words, as action, might propose a supraordinate judgment—at once moral and ethical, worldly and divine—upon the time and situation of his own passing. On this register of a discursive recollection, both before Du Bois's own time and beyond the time of his recollection and republication of his biography of John Brown on the occasion of the centenary of the Emancipation Proclamation and then his own passing in August 1963, an African Americanist historial projection, at once theological and political-philosophical—the appeal and oratory, respectively, of David Walker at the end of the 1820s, and Frederick Douglass at mid-nineteenth century (above all in his speech "What to the Slave is the Fourth of July" in 1852), as well as the discourse of Martin Luther King, specifically on the occasions respectively of his" Letter from Birmingham Jail" in April, 1963 and his speech, "I Have a Dream," during the March on Washington in August 1963—might be understood to acquire a distinctive resonance (Walker 1965; Walker 2000; Douglass 1982; King 1964; King 1991).

CHAPTER FOUR

1. **Dedication:** This chapter was initially presented on January 28, 2000, as part of "A 'National Treasury of Rhetorical Wealth': A Symposium on the Work of Hortense Spillers," sponsored by the Center for the Study of Black Literature and Culture at the University of Pennsylvania. The high-octane general discussion across the whole of the event was given by way of both the capacity and the generosity of those present who also presented work on the occasion made this a historic experience: Farah Griffin, Saidiya Hartman,

Gina Dent, Michael Awkward, Tommy Lott, Ronald A.T. Judy, and above all
Hortense Spillers. As her work, simply extraordinary intelligence, and way
in thought named the very possibility of the occasion, this essay-chapter is
dedicated to Hortense Spillers.

2. I should note that I have just produced a paraphrase and revisionary
displacement of Michel Foucault's admirable question: "Now it is precisely
this idea of sex *in itself* that we cannot accept without examination. Is 'sex'
really the anchorage point that supports the manifestations of sexuality, or
is it rather a complex idea that was formed inside the deployment of sexuality [*du dispositif de sexualité*]? In any case, one could show how this idea
of sex took form in the different strategies of power and the definite role it
played therein" (Foucault 1980b, 152). ["Or, justement, c'est cette idée *du* sexe
qu'on ne peut pas recevoir sans examen. « Le sexe » est-il, dans la réalité, le
point d'ancrage qui supporte les manifestations de « la sexualité », ou bien
une idée, historiquement, formée à l'intérieur du dispositif de sexualité? On
pourrait montrer, en tout cas, comment cette idée « du sexe » s'est formée à
travers les différentes stratégies de pouvoir et quel rôle défini elle y a joué"
(Foucault 1976a, 200–201).]

3. It was proposed in his 1964 critical review of *Blues People* by Leroi Jones
(Ellison 1995b, 283; Baraka 1963).

4. W. E. B. Du Bois, *The Souls of Black Folk: Essays and Sketches* will be
hereinafter cited parenthetically, followed by page, chapter and paragraph
number.

5. Some of the earliest work of Cornel West, which can be recognized in
three essays, was pioneering in this domain: "A Genealogy of Modern Racism," "Race and Social Theory: Towards a Genealogical Materialist Analysis," and "Marxism and the Specificity of Afro-American Oppression" (West
1982, 47–65; West 1987; West 1988). Likewise, remaining as a signal gesture a
generation on, for a fundamental inquiry that also thematized the politics
and ethics of this problematic on the horizon of a thought about the modern
epoch as a whole, consider the first major work of David Theo Goldberg,
Racist Culture: Philosophy and the Politics of Meaning (Goldberg 1993). However, too, one must also note two other signal texts, both before and after the
interventions of West and Goldberg: from before, the opening chapters of
Cedric Robinson's address of this thematic from within antecedent radical
thought from the African diaspora in the opening chapters of his monumental study, first published in 1983, and from after, the pathbreaking study
by Denise Ferreira da Silva (Robinson 2000; Silva 2007).

6. This question registers a fundamental dimension of Bhabha's thought
(Bhabha 1992). However, even as we index the radical force of the question in Bhabha's address, we would be wont to forgo posing the rhetorical

affirmation: Does this not simply index in turn, and thus address without annotating the matter as such, what more than two and a half centuries of African American discourse has posed in an emphatic interrogative to modern Western thought as a whole, in both its theological and scientific forms?

7. See Stoler's *Race and the Education of Desire: Foucault's History of Sexuality and the Colonial Order of Things* and Foucault's lectures published under the title *Il faut défendre la société/Society Must Be Defended* (Stoler 1995; Foucault 1997a; Foucault 2003).

8. Elsewhere, I will consider some aspects of this matter by way of a certain treatment of the discourse of Immanuel Kant along with that of Foucault.

9. I note here the recent pivotal intervention posed in this domain by the work of Denise Ferreira da Silva, which arrived at a juncture following the formulations thus far offered. Given its importance, I will engage it in full respect properly on another occasion. Here, however, I note that the extent, scale, and implication of both Du Bois's itinerary in general and specific formulations of "the problem of the color-line," as they mark out indispensable terms for my own initiatives here, remain for a full or direct address within her principal line of discourse. This is the scene of a whole future fundamental interlocution (Silva 2007).

10. Gayatri Spivak's reading of the strategic and subversive exemplarity of the "subaltern" in the work of the Subaltern Studies Collective across the 1970s and 1980s specified a motif that retains its pertinence in the contemporary moment. She writes, "In the work of this group, what had seemed the historical predicament of the subaltern [its displaced, heterogeneous and, in a certain language, alienated consciousness] can be made to become the allegory of the predicament of all thought, all deliberative consciousness, though the elite profess otherwise. This might seem preposterous at first glance. A double take is in order" (Spivak 1988b, 12). Also see related formulations by Jacques Derrida and note Deborah Esch on the question of a subversive example both of the same moment as Spivak's statement in discussions of theory arising from the site of the humanities discourse of the academy within the North American horizon (Derrida 1988, 116–20; Esch 1993).

11. Perhaps Derrida can be understood to have written of such thought in a hopeful challenge to both an old idea of Europe and its potential emplacement according to another understanding of the very possibility of exemplarity. What if this new possibility unfolded as an "opening onto a history for which the changing of the heading, the relation to the other heading or to the other of the heading, is experienced as always possible" (Derrida 1992a, 17)? As Michael Naas writes in this context, concerning Derrida's figuration of Europe as an example, "It would not exist somewhere prior to any

manifestation. . . . [It] would always only appear as an example of itself, an example that would at once forbid and necessitate comparison and resemblance. Such an exemplarity could never function as a neutral or transparent model or telos for discourse or thought" (Naas 1992, xxxi–xxxii).

12. I annotate the work of these several scholars, Wallerstein, Isaac, and Hall, most especially, because the *general* premises that govern their work interventions, seem not only apposite but necessary for fundamental scholarship in this domain (Wallerstein 1974; Isaac 1982; Hall 1990, cf. 222). On the other hand, Robinson's question may be shown both to propose a shift in paradigmatic perspective that remains at stake; likewise, it may be shown to resonate more fully with the fundamental character of the epistemic interventions of W. E. B. Du Bois than an initial engagement with his critical assessment of radical theory might seem to allow (Robinson 2000, 70–120).

13. Cited from Olaudah Equiano, *The Interesting Narrative of the Life of Olaudah Equiano, or Gustavus Vassa, the African, Written by Himself,* in *Great Slave Narratives,* ed. Arna Bontemps (Boston: Beacon Press, 1969), 4–192 (Equiano 1969). The edition of Equiano's narrative edited, with extensive notes, by Vincent Caretta is also noted here (Equiano 2003). Hereafter, both works are jointly cited parenthetically as Equiano, followed by respective date of publication and pagination.

14. In a historiographical or ethnographical manner, examples of such work which marked a certain generational turn in contemporary projects include David Roediger, Theodore Allen, Vron Ware, and Ruth Frankenberg (Roediger 1991; Allen 1994; Ware 1992; Frankenberg 1993). Yet such work also takes reference, even if indirectly, in the earlier historiographical studies of Winthrop Jordan, George Fredrickson, Ronald Takaki, and Alexander Saxton that took shape in the midst of or in the wake of the 1960s social movements—which themselves had already begun to rewrite the narrative of American history (Jordan 1977; Fredrickson 1987; Takaki 1979; Saxton 1990). In a literary or philosophical manner, such work which also marked a certain turn include, for example, the quite heterogeneous projects of Toni Morrison, Eric Sundquist, and David Theo Goldberg (Morrison 1992; Sundquist 1993; Goldberg 1993).

15. This seems to hold true as well at least in the initial gestures of Stoler's account of "race" and the colonial field (Stoler 1995, 95–137).

16. Although I was put on the track of the formulations outlined here by the work of W. E. B. Du Bois on the historicity of the African American tradition of spirituals, it was the example of the compositional and performance practices, the poetics if you will, in the work of Cecil Taylor that most steadily guided my initial steps here (Du Bois 1903f, 250–64; Taylor 1959; Taylor 1966b; Taylor 1966a).

17. This path of thought one can find proposed by Jacques Derrida in a desedimentation of the traditional concept of origin within philosophy and metaphysics. In a word, one can suggest that it addresses what I have here called the nonorigin (Derrida 1976, 27–63, esp. 60–65; Derrida 1991). With regard to Derrida's discourse in particular, it is conceptually positioned in an order of generality whose pertinence would have no determinable limit. He formulates in its place a structure of the trace to account for the question of being in a way that would address all levels of generality in which science, knowledge, and fundamental discourse (metaphysics, philosophy, and theology) are implicated. Of course, the historical paucity of direct reference in Derrida's discourse to such an example or the problem at stake in it remains to be fully remarked. And there is no reason to withdraw from the idea that Derrida would have affirmed such remarking. The necessity of such a marking, however, maintains itself within the irreducibility of the historical in the opening of a "grammatological" discourse. Spivak has outlined some of the motifs that might mark out the track of any such remarking in her meditation, "More on Power/Knowledge." "Catachrestic nominalism," which proposes the thought that a "subindividual . . . or . . . random . . . space" might ironically position "preontological Being as [*Dasein's*] ontically constitutive state . . . [where] *Dasein* tacitly understands and interprets something like Being," follows, in a certain way, the track of the empirical or the material within the figuration of the ontological. While not new at all, it nonetheless remains radical, especially within the historical practice of thought within our epoch, leaving the open frame of the "we" in question here. This "catachrestic nominalism" is precisely the strategic desedimentative practice we are affirming here. Of course, irony itself is at risk in this thought or practice. As suggested in the preamble to this chapter, I would call this a Du Boisian practice. Whence Du Bois in a contemporary discourse such as that of Derrida? How to place its solicitation within or with regard to the discourse of Spivak (Spivak 1996b, 141–74, esp. 147, emphasis in the original)? Spivak references Martin Heidegger's discourse on "Dasein" in *Being and Time* (Heidegger 1962).

18. It can be noted W. E. B. Du Bois attempted a similar line of formulation at the very inception of his mature itinerary in an essay titled "The Afro-American," dating most likely from the late autumn of 1894 or the early winter of 1895, in which he formulates the historical situation of "the Afro-American" at the turn of the century as one in which he is "suddenly broken with his past and out of touch with his environment," in which both the immediate past and the long past are referenced and the environment is the peculiar one indeed of the rise of Jim Crow and the epitome of the social epidemic of anti-Negro lynching (Du Bois 2010; Du Bois, forthcoming (a)).

19. Both Ronald A. T. Judy and Saidiya Hartman have tracked the disjunctive structure out of which the discourse of the African slave in the New World arises in ways that are proximate if quite original and distinct from the approach that I propose here. Judy has marked the way in which writing in this context is a kind of thanatology, in which and by which the inhuman registers its force, precisely as a certain illegibility; the movement of the inhuman within discourse situates and delimits all projects of the articulation of an intentional consciousness (Judy 1993, 33–98, 275–90). Hartman has formulated a profound theoretical sense of the way in which narrative in the African American context acquires its distinctive force by the way in which it maintains a recollection not so much of the desire for freedom but of the institution of loss, breach, and the terror that opens the historical scene of such subjectivation in the New World (Hartman 1997, 3–14, 49–78, 171–75).

20. The central thought of this section of the chapter acquired its first shape in a seminar on "postemancipation societies" directed by Thomas Holt at the University of Chicago in 1988, in which he encouraged me to consider the Hegelian references in the work of scholars on slavery. Although different than either of us expected at the time, this following, in part, is my response to that problematic (Holt 1992). In this regard, Bernard Cohn's seminars, also at Chicago, and his related work on forms of knowledge as a decisive part of the practice and history of colonialism has also made possible some of the questions that I develop here (Cohn 1987b; Cohn 1996).

21. Certainly the questioning of this presumption in two early texts of Martin Heidegger from the late 1920s and middle 1930s can be indicated here (Heidegger 1962, 19–64; Heidegger 2000, 1–54; Fried and Polt 2000, xiv–xviii). With reference to this interrogation from within discourses of a certain "Europe," we might well situate a thought of a moving field of force(s). For such a thought one might consider in proximity to Heidegger's formulations those of Michel Foucault in the discussion of "method" in his turn to the projection of a history of sexuality, especially in his discussion of how to broach an inquiry into *"La volonté de savoir"* (Foucault 1976b, 121–35; Foucault 1980a, 92–102). Likewise, all that Derrida proposed by way of the thought of the movement of the trace can be noted here, but especially the early formulation under the heading of "Writing Before the Letter" (Derrida 1976, 6–93).

22. This conceptualization and theoretical disposition organizes and limits even the most responsible of contemporary discourses, scholarly or otherwise, concerning the so-called subaltern subject and more broadly concerning the status and historical experience of those subject positions that emerge and function in positions of subordination in general. This conceptualization dominates discourses concerning the status of the African

American subject in the United States, in particular studies concerned with the centuries of slavery and the immediate aftermath of emancipation. A good example in the domain of social history is the outstanding interpretive work of Charles Joyner. After constructing a model of Afro-creolization, Joyner somewhat belatedly began to develop the theme of the creolization of the Euro-subject (Joyner 1979; Joyner 1984; Joyner 1993; Joyner 1999). However, for an additional sense of this problematic and further references, see the closing section of this chapter.

23. I recall here Louis Althusser's discussion of the idea of an order of questions, in particular their materiality as symbolic forms, in *For Marx* (Althusser 1970, 62–70).

24. Hereinafter this text is cited parenthetically as Genovese 1974 followed by page number(s) (Genovese 1974).

25. Already within a generation of the 1960s watershed, a new accounting of the history of this historiography had been produced (Meier and Rudwick 1986, cf. 239–76).

26. Early on in the reception of this text, both historian Herbert Gutman and anthropologist Marion Kilson recognized such a limitation (Gutman 1976, 309–20, esp. 311ff.; Kilson 1976).

27. The bizarreness of the point of Genovese's theoretical application should further annotated here. For, it may be proposed, that Gramsci was most concerned to affirm the possibility of the transformation of a putative hegemony according to the initiative of historically subordinate groups or classes (Gramsci 1971, 195–96, 246–47).

28. For example, he begins his formulation of the paternalistic compromise in the manner to which I refer. "The slaveholders had to establish a stable regime with which their slaves could live. Slaves remained slaves. . . . But masters and slaves, whites and blacks, lived as well as worked together. The existence of the community required that all find some measure of self-interest and self-respect" (Genovese 1974, 5). If we consider that it is precisely the question of the possible analytical meaning of "stability" and "community," and all that a naive or traditional thinking of such questions might conceal, then the effects of the point of view and the grammatical subject that is placed at the head of this paragraph can be recognized. The entire problematic that is stated to be a compromise is in fact determined already to issue forth from the work or action of one subject (who is thereby at that analytical moment taken as autonomous). The same formulation is legible in the following passage: "The logic of slavery pushed the masters to try to break their slaves' spirit and to reconstruct it as an unthinking and unfeeling extension of their own will, but the slaves' own resistance to dehumanization compelled the masters to compromise in order to get an adequate level

of work out of them" (Genovese 1974, 317). Or when one watches the subtle movement of the pronouns in the following sentence on its own, one may not notice the effects of an entire conceptuality. But if such sentences recur, page after page, as they do in this text, it becomes legible. This repetition establishes a pronomial structure that situates the problematic of this book about "the world the slaves made" squarely in the position of the slaveholder. Genovese writes, "Slaveholders usually interpreted every kind of behavior among their slaves in such a way as to justify the status quo" (Genovese 1974, 646). With such locutionary formulations, Genovese is unable analytically to account for precisely what is most at stake in his study: the movement of relationship in which the respective positions entailed are produced. He presupposes the terms of the relation as constituted, hence he presupposes the status of the system in question and the subject that would be its titular and functional origin.

29. Gayatri Spivak's cautionary interventions in the midst of the 1980s with regard to the limits of the idea of a class-for-itself in a theoretical inheritance that takes reference to the interventions of Karl Marx seems apposite here. She writes, "Marx is not working to create an undivided subject where desire and interest coincide. Class consciousness does not operate toward that goal. Both in the economic area (capitalist) and in the political (world-historical agent), Marx is obliged to construct models of a divided and dislocated subject whose parts are not continuous or coherent with each other" (Spivak 1988a, 275–80, esp. 276). At the turn of the century, she returns to this problematic in a manner that can be understood to generalize both its caution and its critical edge with regard to scholarship of the colonial and postcolonial across the last half-century—since a global movement of formal decolonization: "To treat what is powerfully speculative [Marx's *critique* of political economy] as predictive social engineering, assuming a fully rational human subject conscious of rights as well as impersonal responsibility, can only have violent and violating consequences" (Spivak 1999, 67–111, quotation at 84).

30. For pertinent critical summary formulations, see the work of Seyla Benhabib and C. B. Macpherson, respectively (Benhabib 1984; Benhabib 1986; Macpherson 1962; Macpherson 1975). The classic statements contemporary to this development remain canonical for modern social theory (Locke 1988b; Rousseau 1994; Kant 1996b; Hegel 1991; Mill 2008). With regard to this question and slavery, one can still note the summary work of David Brion Davis (Davis 1966).

31. After this section of this chapter was prepared, I was able to hear Jacques Derrida read the second part of his essay "Force of Law: The 'Mystical Foundation of Authority'." As one can read in the published text, in

the course of tracking Walter Benjamin's thought of a "founding violence," Derrida writes, "This founding or revolutionary moment of law is, in law, an instance of nonlaw [*dans le droit une instance de nondroit*]. But it is also the whole history of law. *This moment always takes place and never takes place in a presence*. It is the moment in which the foundation of law remains suspended in the void or over the abyss, suspended by a pure performative act that would not have to answer to or before anyone" (Derrida 2002b, 269–70). I offer this citation then as a palimpsest for that which is yet to come in a reading. It follows on other statements, all of which in fact refer back to terms formulated by Derrida, in part by way of a sustained engagement with the thought of Edmund Husserl, at the very inception of his intellectual itinerary (Derrida 2002a; Derrida 2007; Derrida 1978b, 87–107; Derrida 1974, 83–110). For Derrida, it must be noted, the problem of the "intelligibility or interpretability" of such law is decisive. My own tracing of an X, inscribed in the discussion at hand by way of the movements that would constitute the figure of the slave, marks the path of an ongoing and still future reading.

32. Similar motifs could be adduced in the classic and quite rich essay by Sidney W. Mintz and Richard Price written in 1972–73 on the provenance of culture in the African diaspora (Mintz and Price 1992). Like Genovese's study, it is a product of the efflorescence of African Americanist studies in the late 1960s and early 1970s. In this study, Mintz and Price write of African slaves as more "crowds" than "groups" or "communities" (18); whereas they write of Europeans as "representatives of particular national traditions" (1–2). But the key issue is that they conceive the master as possessing, in slavery, the "monopoly of power," which therefore has the analytical effect not only of following their distinction of society and culture but of determining the latter, in the case of the slaves, simply by the former (which is understood to be a system, already constructed, to which slaves are acculturated). Like Genovese's account, everything is decided (in the direction of the master) in the register of the *ultimate* (and, by analogy, *final*) instance. See also Herbert G. Gutman's dilemmas on this issue in his signal book *The Black Family in Slavery and Freedom, 1750–1925*, notably taking reference to a distinction of "culture" and "society" of a social science of the immediate postwar decades (including the work of Sidney Mintz) and despite his criticism of Genovese therein, as noted above (Gutman 1976, 554–55). Along the track of the relation of intellectual generations, it may be noted too that the itinerary of contributions by Richard Price to date has accumulated as one of the most remarkable in scholarship of the African diaspora, hardly matched by anyone else of his intellectual generation, especially from within a practice of ethnography, and in light of the extraordinary intellectual partnership that he shares with Sally Price (Price 1983; Price 1990; Price and Price

1991; Price 2006; Price 2008). Yet, a theoretical proposition of the *general* "creolization" by which the supposed cultures and societies of the ensemblic *historial* domain in question have been constructed across the modern epoch—not only those of the "New World," in particular North America in what has become the United States, but throughout the entire Atlantic basin—has seemed somewhat unremarked, or underremarked in his work in any manner that might be commensurate with both its historicity and its epistemic value. It is perhaps for this reason that the apparitional "miracle of creolization" (to quote the title and to affirm much that he proposes in a thirty-year retrospective on the debate set in motion by his essay with Mintz noted above) at or as the genesis of an African America(s) or a diaspora, so to speak, seems to remain withdrawn from historiographical and ethnographical retrieval (Price 2005). Whereas, we might rather consider such an apparent "miracle"—even under the most extreme of conditions—as an articulation of the most ordinary historical exemplar of the order of genesis (or even regenesis, if you will) across the entire geographic dimension in question on the horizon of the centuries since the inception of a generalized slavery in the advent of the renaissances adjacent to the Atlantic basin across the early centuries of the last millennium. (Even the intellectual modes of inquiry that we use to ask about it may be understood to issue from it; modern anthropological scholarship, for example, is itself always already an articulation of the processes of creolization.) It may stand, thus, as the most common of roots of the inception of the historicity in this domain, old or new world, African or European, American or Caribbean, among others. My suggestion here is that only such a thought could begin to account within the study of the African diaspora for the horizon in which the ongoing and general retheorization of our common colonial and so-called postcolonial nexus is at stake on a planetary scale.

33. See the opening discussion of Chapter 1 above, "Of Exorbitance: The Problem of the Negro as a Problem for Thought," for an engagement with the question of the neutral in critical discourse concerning the African American in the United States.

34. This reference is taken from Spillers's incisive considerations of the complex negotiations of such ambivalence in the sermon within the African American Christian tradition and should be referenced in its entirety (Spillers 2003d, 262). See also her brilliant essay "Mama's Baby, Papa's Maybe: An American Grammar Book," which pursues a certain desedimentation of this structure of ambivalence specifically with reference to the historiography of slavery (Spillers 2003c). My own intuition here is that Ralph Ellison's thought of "ambivalence" might be Spillers's own most inimitable guide. For a few suggestions along this line see the "Prologue" in *Invisible Man*, and,

for example, Ellison's remarkable tour de force in the late essay "An Extravagance of Laughter" (Ellison 1989, 3–14; Ellison 1995, 628–37). On another order of reference, I note here that in my reading, Du Bois is the most overwhelmingly unremarked figure and guide for Ellison, a matter that I propose to address elsewhere.

35. During the autumn of 1989, Ranajit Guha visited the South Asian Studies Workshop at the University of Chicago and presented the just afoot—not yet published—version of his now classic essay "Colonialism in South Asia: A Dominance Without Hegemony and its Historiography," under the initiative of Bernard S. Cohn. Through the initiative of Professor Cohn and the intellectual hospitality of Professor Guha, I was able to participate in that seminar and later to discuss at length with the latter scholar the relation of the historiography of slavery in America to the problematic that he proposed in that essay and his ongoing respect for the example of Du Bois. The remarks that I offer in this section then register that interlocution a generation after the fact with the simplicity of a profoundly felt historical acknowledgment across the generations and local historicities for a work well done (Guha 1997a).

36. While Guha reads this problematic through a constellation of references to the thought of G. W. F. Hegel, Karl Marx, and Sigmund Freud, the latter reapproached by way of Jacques Lacan, I suspect that he would not be adverse to my interpellation of these discourses by reference to the thought of W. E. B. Du Bois (Guha 1997a, 61–65; Guha 2002).

37. Cited in the subsequent discussion as indicated in note 13 of this chapter (Equiano 1969; Equiano 2003).

38. It is the periodization offered by Du Bois—of the incipit of modern slavery as situated otherwise than within capitalism or within modernity, neither inside nor outside, but rather at and as its inception—in its interpolation with a critical discourse on capitalism that I intend to index here (Du Bois 1976; Marx 1977; Blackburn 1997).

39. The dates of these two publications mark out the trajectory of a reinscription of the slave narrative into the renarrativation of this history of the making of America, not only in its political and legal senses, but especially in its supposed cultural provenance (Bontemps 1969; Baker 1984, 34).

40. Citations for publications of this narrative are given herein, within the text, to both an edition prepared in the late 1960s by Arna Bontemps and published as part of an anthology and to the definitive edition prepared by Vincent Carreta at the turn of the century (Equiano 1969, 87; Equiano 2003, 119–20).

41. I propose that this entire ensemblic discourse, even within its variegations, may yet be taken as one epistemic locution (Locke 1988a, 283–302,

384–97, sec. 22–51 and 175–96; Kant 1996c, 401–52 [AA 6:245–308]; Hegel 1991, 67–132, part 2, sec. 34–104; Macpherson 1962; Benhabib 1984).

42. In this quotation, I wish to retain here, thus, a reference to the whole of Seyla Benhabib's recollection (Benhabib 1984, 162).

43. This seems to me to remain the profound theoretical proposition of Houston Baker's intervention on this order of reading (Baker 1984, 36). For, this might be a general phenomenon that has yet to be thought on a commensurate level of generality afoot in the New World or the contexts of modern slavery.

44. The question of legality arises in some richly paradoxical ways in the earliest African American texts, petitions; there, the question of donation or credit structures the question of writing from the beginning. For example, with regard to a petition dating from 1661, concerning the appeal to the "Noble Right Director-General and Lords Councillors of New Netherlands" (operating through a charter granted to the Dutch West India Company) by free godparents that their godchild, whose free parents are deceased, not be confined to slavery, one could argue that the ultimate signatory or countersignatory (making the petitioners' credit good) was God, rather than any ecclesiastical authority (Aptheker 1990, 1–2). In such a scene, God is the original donor. But even if God is the original grantor, and the slave must accept a Christian (in this case) jurisdiction in order to claim the protection of the law, the law can only claim its force by granting recognition of its subject. The purity of the original donation, as grant or philanthropy, is thereby at least compromised.

45. In the Anacrusis to this study, I have elaborated a formulation of this movement as nonspace under the heading of "between" in a reading of the opening of Du Bois's *Souls of Black Folk*.

46. Such a thought resituates the terms by which certain theorizations, even those ostensibly sympathetic to the productions of the enslaved, which proposed to think the empirical moment, the ongoing eventuality of enslavement, in such a way that the master's projection would ostensibly organize the historial incipit of this relation (Mintz and Price 1992, 40).

47. I would place Orlando Patterson's thought of a possible "social death"—by which the premise of mastery is understood as in the instance and ultimate or final sovereign—under this problematic (Patterson 1982).

48. This motif has also been rendered thematic in certain relatively recent attempts to think otherwise than the presumptive encompassment of difference proposed within the terms of modern philosophy as it took shape in a European horizon across the past two and a half centuries (Derrida 1982a, 17; Derrida 1988, 149–50; Deleuze 1983, 40–44; Foucault 2000).

49. I first proposed this thought under the title "Force of the Double: W. E. B. Du Bois and the Question of the African American Subject," a

paper presented at the annual meeting of the American Anthropological Association, Chicago, Illinois, November 20–24, 1991. The order of reading that I have proposed affirms those histories across the past two generations within the most traditional forms of the historiography of the "colonial" era which have come to propose that the relation of a supposed "European American" subject to a so-called origin in Europe is explicitly marked by the same structure of repetition that has been adduced regarding the Negro or African American. For in this historiography, the European American subject is irretrievably displaced and it recognizes a range of pivotal shifts in sites of theoretical explanation, which in its eventuality should amount to a reconceptualization of both history and America (Greene 1970; Greene 1988; Zuckerman 1977; Zuckerman 1987). This reconceptualization draws, of course, on the tremendous accomplishments in social history generally, in the history of women, and in African American history since the 1960s. If this reconceptualization is made radical, the various conceptualizations of America, which would marginalize or exclude the African American, are brought into question from an entirely other direction than that attempted by some commentators, across several generations: for example, in the work of Sterling Stuckey, the concept of a given "national" essence seems to both presuppose what must be analytically at stake, the provenance of an African American identity, and to give up too much, a constitutive claim on the whole of any projection that goes under the heading of America (Stuckey 1987); or, for example, a conceptualization such as that of Adolph Reed, whose de-essentializing orientation tends to presupposes a(n) (Euro-) American identity, a hidden form of homogeneity, precisely what is most at issue for theory in this domain (Reed 1992); or the interventions of Mechal Sobel, which tend to contain a potentially radical analysis by presupposing *both* a Euro-American and an Afro-American identity under the governance of a traditional concept of origin, which results at times in a kind of analysis where one presupposes the trait that one supposedly finds at the site of origin (Sobel 1987; Sobel 1988). On the other, in this same moment, scholars in both historiography and literature began to propose a rethinking of the European subject along these lines. Hortense Spillers is signal in this regard (Spillers 1991a). Stretching toward a whole other horizon of reference and problemati-zation, a new form of interweaving, but with an opening reference precisely to a rethinking of the place of the figure of the Negro or African American within the narrative of America, such juxtaposition as we find it in the work of Ronald Takaki may yet be understood as pivotal for the opening marked in that moment (Takaki 1989). Within this latter work, "America" as such, and perhaps even the possible meaning of the modern world as such, is not yet.

50. See the Anacrusis section of this study. Or it might do well to quote Ralph Ellison, again, this time as given by interlocution with the writer Alan McPherson: "'I don't recognize any white culture,' he says, 'I recognize no American culture which is not the partial creation of black people. I recognize no American style in literature, in dance, in music, even in assembly-line processes, which does not bear the mark of the American Negro'" (Ellison 1995d, 356).

PARENTHESIS

1. **Dedication:** Announced to me before he arrived, his genesis always of two lines, and always bequeathed of more than one generation, at least, but never only, the tensile strength of which arises from an interlacing (let us recall it as "a coat of many colors" as given from the ancients in verse), Aaron Eisuke Chandler, renamed for me the sense of the possible impossible horizon. In this, he is joined with his mother Ayumi Chandler. These words, written for him, "asleep in the next room," as it were, at Kyoto in Japan, during the early Autumn of 2011, announced themselves to me through his example. They are offered, thus, in turn, to him—which is to say, already—to "give thanks and praises," never enough, and more yet to come.

2. This statement appears in a place that is almost outside of the text proper (Du Bois 1915b). Yet, it was a formulation echoed by George Shepperson more than half a century later, in his 1970 introduction to a reissue of Du Bois's little book, as then still an appropriate judgment (Shepperson 1970; Aptheker, H. 1989b). This apparently prosaic statement seems to me to remark the fundamental breach within contemporary thought of world, and its limits, both old and new, not only concerning something called the Negro, or the African, or the African Diaspora, but in general.

3. It can be indexed across the whole of his itinerary (Du Bois 1900; Du Bois 1909; Du Bois 1915a; Du Bois 1920; Du Bois 1925; Du Bois 1928; Du Bois 1935; Du Bois 1945; Du Bois 1947).

4. And, we note that the discourse of this text took shape—in a sense, by necessity—outside of the academy of its time (Cruse 1967).

5. And this discourse was brought to its term and first published outside of the United States, astride the simultaneous efflorescence and impasses of progressive thought in the wake of the denouement of that long decade of the 1960s (Robinson 2000).

6. This work, the gathering of which takes in the whole of the historicity from the 1960s to our own contemporary moment, may be understood as the first order of theoretical discourse to which the present work has proposed to offer a certain reception (Spillers 2003a).

7. I must annotate here that Cedric Robinson, upon hearing some of these remarks, clarified for me that this thought and this formulation was in its turn given to him by way of the work and example of C. L. R. James.

8. I index here a thought that I have begun to develop elsewhere as another theorization of the movement of historicity under the formulation of an alogical logic of the second time, in which supposed originary genesis arises in the form of an elliptical movement of repetition. Certain annotations throughout this study are on this track; however a companion study offers additional developments in an address of the work of W. E. B. Du Bois by way of a certain practice of elaboration. Too, though, I have proceeded by some fundamental reference to the work of Cecil Taylor and to the discourse of Jacques Derrida (Taylor 1966a; Taylor 1966c; Derrida 1967a).

9. Within this parenthesis, we are noting three diverse interventions that collectively address themselves to the whole ensemblic field of the human sciences, announcing themselves in a form of punctuation that crosses the whole time-span of the immediately past intellectual generation (Spillers 2003b; Patterson and Kelley 2000; Gordon 2008).

10. Announcing the coming of age of a whole new generation of thought, this text remains a principal solicitation of the first order in the constellation of thought from which the study at hand issues (Judy 1993).

11. As such, I would propose to recognize the work of Fred Moten as fully and equally generative as both poetry and theory, not only poetical theory (as if could ever be only that), but of such capaciousness that it is now also theoretical poetry (Moten 2003; Moten 2010).

12. The full note, "penned in the poets own hand" as his secretary wrote to Du Bois, reads, "What is the great fact of this age? It is that the messenger has knocked at our gate and all the bars have given way. Our doors have burst open. The human races have come out of their enclosures. They have gathered together. We have been engaged in cultivating each his own individual life, and within the fenced seclusion of our racial tradition. We had neither the wisdom nor the opportunity to harmonize our growth with world tendencies. But there are no longer walls to hide us. We have at length to prove our worth to the whole world, not merely to admiring groups of our own people. We must justify our own existence. We must show, each in our own civilization, that which is universal in the heart of the unique" (Tagore and Chakravarty 1997; Tagore 1929).

13. I take reference here to exemplary work of two scholars of my generation that maintains within its very announcement a reference, oblique or declared, to that horizon that Du Bois announced as the heading of the problem of the Negro as a problem for thought—a global-level order of "the problem of the color-line" (Silva 2007; Young 1998; Young 1987; Chandler 2012).

Bibliography

Abrahams, R. D., and J. F. Szwed. 1975. Introduction. In *Discovering Afro-America*, ed. R. D. Abrahams and J. F. Szwed. International studies in sociology and social anthropology. Leiden, Germany: Brill.

————. 1983. *After Africa: Extracts from British travel accounts and journals of the seventeenth, eighteenth, and nineteenth centuries concerning the slaves, their manners, and customs in the British West Indies*. Ed. R. D. Abrahams. New Haven, CT: Yale University Press.

Allen, T. 1994. *The invention of the white race*. London and New York: Verso.

Althusser, L. 1970. *For Marx*. Trans. B. Brewster. New York: Random House, Vintage Books.

————. 1971. *Lenin and philosophy and other essays*. Trans. B. Brewster. New York: Monthly Review Press.

Andrews, W. L. 1986. *To tell a free story: The first century of Afro-American autobiography, 1760–1865*. Urbana: University of Illinois Press.

Appiah, K. A. 1986. The uncompleted argument: Du Bois and the illusion of race. In *"Race," writing, and difference*, ed. H. L. Gates, 21–37. Chicago: University of Chicago Press.

————. 1989. The conservation of "race." *Black American Literature Forum* 23 (1) (spring): 37–60.

————. 1992a. Illusions of race. In *In my father's house: Africa in the philosophy of culture*, by A. Appiah, 28–46. New York: Oxford University Press.

————. 1992b. *In my father's house: Africa in the philosophy of culture*. New York: Oxford University Press.

————. 2005. Ethics in a world of strangers: W. E. B. Du Bois and the spirit of cosmopolitanism. *The Berlin Journal: A Magazine for the American Academy in Berlin* 11 (fall): 23–26.

Aptheker, H. 1968. Editor's preface. In *The autobiography of W. E. B. Du Bois: A soliloquy on viewing my life from the last decade of its first century*, ed. H. Aptheker, by W. E. B. Du Bois, 5–6. New York: International Publishers.

————. 1975. Introduction. In *Black folk, then and now: An essay in the history and sociology of the Negro race*, ed. H. Aptheker, by W. E. B. Du Bois. Complete published writings of W. E. B. Du Bois, 1–18. Millwood, NY: Kraus-Thomson Organization.

————. 1989a. *The literary legacy of W. E. B. Du Bois*. White Plains, NY: Kraus International Publications.

————. 1989b. The negro. In *The literary legacy of W. E. B. Du Bois*, 123–41. White Plains, NY: Kraus International Publications.

Aptheker, H., ed. 1990. *A documentary history of the negro people in the United States*. Vol. 1, *From colonial times through the Civil War*. New York: Carol Publishing Group.

Aristotle. 1966. *Metaphysics*. Ed. and trans. H. G. Apostle. Grinnell, IA: Peripatetic Press.

Baker, H. A. 1984. *Blues, ideology, and Afro-American literature a vernacular theory*. Chicago: University of Chicago Press.

————. 1987. *Modernism and the Harlem renaissance*. Chicago: University of Chicago Press.

Baldwin, J. 1985. *The price of the ticket: Collected nonfiction, 1948–1985*. New York: St. Martin's/Marek.

————. 1998. On being 'white' and other lies. In *Black on white black writers on what it means to be white*, ed. D. R. Roediger, 177–80. New York: Schocken Books.

Baraka, I. A. 1963. *Blues people: Negro music in white America*. New York: W. Morrow.

Benhabib, S. 1984. Obligation, contract and exchange: On the significance of Hegel's abstract right. In *The state and civil society studies in Hegel's political philosophy*, ed. Z. A. Pelczynski, 159–77. Cambridge [Cambridgeshire] and New York: Cambridge University Press.

————. 1986. *Critique, norm, and utopia: A study of the foundations of critical theory*. New York: Columbia University Press.

Bennington, G., and J. Derrida. 1993. *Jacques Derrida*. Chicago: University of Chicago Press.

Bernasconi, R. 2001. Who invented the concept of race?: Kant's role in the enlightenment construction of race. In *Race*, ed. R. Bernasconi. Blackwell readings in continental philosophy. Malden, MA: Blackwell Publishers.

————, ed. 2001. *Race*. Blackwell readings in continental philosophy. Malden, MA: Blackwell Publishers.

Bhabha, H. K. 1992. Race and the humanities: The 'ends' of modernity? *Public Culture* 4 (2): 81–85.

Bible. 1966. *The Jerusalem Bible*. Ed. and trans. A. Jones, et al. Garden City, NY: Doubleday.

Bible. 2005. The gospel according to Matthew. In *Greek-English New Testament; Greek text Novum Testamentum Graece, in the tradition of Eberhard Nestle and Erwin Nestle.* 9th rev. ed. Tenth printing, ed. B. Aland and K. Aland, Universitaet Muenster, 1–87. Stuttgart, Germany: Deutsche Bibelgesellschaft.

Blackburn, R. 1997. New world slavery, primitive accumulation and British industrialization. In *The making of new world slavery: From the baroque to the modern, 1492–1800,* 509–80, esp. 554, and see epilogue, 581–93. London and New York: Verso.

Boas, F. 1911. *The mind of primitive man: A course of lectures delivered before the Lowell institute, Boston, Mass., and the National University of Mexico, 1910–1911.* New York: The Macmillan Company.

———. 1940. *Race, language and culture.* Chicago: University of Chicago Press.

———. 1989. *The shaping of American anthropology, 1883–1911: A Franz Boas reader.* Ed. G. W. Stocking. Chicago: University of Chicago Press.

Bontemps, A. 1969. *Great slave narratives.* Boston: Beacon Press.

Brundage, W. F. 1990. The Darien 'Insurrection' of 1899: Black protest during the nadir of race relations. *Georgia Historical Quarterly* 74: 234–53.

Chandler, N. D. 2006. The possible form of an interlocution: W. E. B. Du Bois and Max Weber in correspondence, 1904–1905, part I: The letters and the essay. *CR: The New Centennial Review* 6 (3) (winter): 193–239. Special issue: W. E. B. Du Bois and the question of another world, ed. N. D. Chandler.

———. 2007. The possible form of an interlocution: W. E. B. Du Bois and Max Weber in correspondence, 1904–1905, part II: The terms of discussion. *CR: The New Centennial Review* 7 (1) (spring): 213–72.

———. 2012. Introduction: On the virtues of seeing--at least, but never only--double. *CR: The New Centennial Review* 12 (1) (spring): 1–39. Special issue. Toward a new parallax: Or, Japan--in another traversal of the Trans-Pacific.

———. c. 1988. Writing absence: On some assumptions of Africanist discourse in the West. Unpublished master's seminar paper. University of Chicago.

———. Forthcoming. *The problem of pure being: Annotations on the early thought of W. E. B. Du Bois and the discourses of the Negro.* New York: Fordham University Press.

———. N.d. The Philadelphia negro project: W. E. B. Du Bois and the program for a study of the African American in the United States. Unpublished manuscript.

Cohn, B. S. 1987a. The census, social structure, and objectification in South Asia. In *An anthropologist among the historians and other essays,* by B. S. Cohn, 224–54. Delhi and New York: Oxford University Press.

———. 1987b. Lectures on colonial societies. October–December 1987. University of Chicago.

———. 1996. *Colonialism and its forms of knowledge: The British in India.* Princeton studies in culture/power/history. Princeton, NJ: Princeton University Press.

Craton, M. 1979. Changing patterns of slave families in the British West Indies. *Journal of Interdisciplinary History* 1: 1–35.

Craton, M., and G. Greenland. 1978. *Searching for the invisible man: Slaves and plantation life in Jamaica.* Cambridge, MA: Harvard University Press.

Craton, M., and J. Walvin. 1970. *A Jamaican plantation: The history of Worthy Park, 1670–1970.* [Toronto]: University of Toronto Press.

Cruse, H. 1967. *The crisis of the negro intellectual.* New York: William Morrow and Co.

Curran, A. S. 2011. *The anatomy of blackness: Science and slavery in an age of Enlightenment.* Baltimore, MD: Johns Hopkins University Press.

Davis, D. B. 1966. *The problem of slavery in western culture.* Ithaca, NY: Cornell University Press.

———. 1974. Slavery and the post-World War II historians. In *Slavery, colonialism, and racism,* ed. S. Mintz, 1–16. Cambridge, MA: American Academy of Arts and Sciences.

Deleuze, G. 1983. *Nietzsche and philosophy.* Trans. H. Tomlinson. Ithaca, NY: Columbia University Press.

Derrida, J. 1967a. *De la grammatologie.* Collection "Critique." Paris: Éditions de Minuit.

———. 1967b. Force et signification. In *L'Écriture et la différence.* Collection Tel quel., 9–49. Paris: Éditions du Seuil.

———. 1967c. *L'Écriture et la différence.* Collection Tel quel. Paris: Éditions du Seuil.

———. 1967d. *La Voix et le phénomène, introduction au problème du signe dans la phénoménologie de Husserl.* Paris: Presses universitaires de France.

———. 1972a. *La dissémination.* Paris: Éditions du Seuil.

———. 1972b. *Positions: Entretiens avec Henri Ronse, Julia Kristeva, Jean-Louis Houdebine, Guy Scarpetta.* Paris: Éditions de Minuit.

———. 1974. Introduction. In *L'origine de la géométrie: Traduction et introduction.* 2d ed., rev. ed., by E. Husserl, trans. and intro. by J. Derrida. Epiméthée, 3–171. Paris: Presses Universitaires de France.

———. 1976. *Of grammatology.* Trans. G. C. Spivak. Baltimore, MD: Johns Hopkins University Press.

———. 1978a. Force and signification. In *Writing and difference,* trans. A. Bass, 3–30. Chicago: University of Chicago Press.

———. 1978b. Introduction to "The origin of geometry." In *Edmund*

Husserl's The origin of geometry: *An introduction*, ed. David B. Allison, trans. J. P. Leavey, 25–153. Stony Brook, NY: Nicholas Hays Ltd.

———. 1978c. Violence and metaphysics: An essay on the thought of Emmanuel Levinas. In *Writing and difference*, trans. A. Bass, 79–153. Chicago: University of Chicago Press.

———. 1978d. *Writing and difference*. Trans. A. Bass. Chicago: University of Chicago Press.

———. 1981a. *Dissemination*. Trans. B. Johnson. Chicago: University of Chicago Press.

———. 1981b. The double session. In *Dissemination*, trans. B. Johnson, 173–286. Chicago: University of Chicago Press.

———. 1981c. *Positions*. Trans. A. Bass, interviewers H. Ronse, et al. Chicago: University of Chicago Press.

———. 1982a. Différance. In *Margins of philosophy*, trans. A. Bass, 1–27. Chicago: University of Chicago Press.

———. 1982b. *Margins of philosophy*. Trans. A. Bass. Chicago: University of Chicago Press.

———. 1982c. Ousia and grammē: A note to a footnote from Being and Time. In *Margins of philosophy*, trans. A. Bass, 29–67. Chicago: University of Chicago Press.

———. 1988. Afterword: Toward an ethics of discussion. In *Limited Inc.*, trans. S. Weber, 111–60. Evanston, IL: Northwestern University Press.

———. 1989. *Of spirit: Heidegger and the question*. Chicago: University of Chicago Press.

———. 1991. *Cinders*. Ed. and trans. N. Lukacher. Lincoln: University of Nebraska Press.

———. 1992a. *The other heading: Reflections on today's Europe*. Trans. P.-A. Brault and M. Naas. Studies in continental thought. Bloomington: Indiana University Press.

———. 1992b. "This Strange Institution Called Literature": An Interview with Jacques Derrida. In *Acts of literature*, ed. D. Attridge, trans. G. Bennington and R. Bowlby, 33–75. New York: Routledge.

———. 1994. "To do justice to Freud:" The history of madness in the age of psychoanalysis. *Critical Inquiry* 20 (2) (winter): 227–66.

———. 2002a. Declarations of independence. Trans. T. Keenan and T. Pepper. In *Negotiations: Interventions and interviews, 1971–2001*, ed. and trans. E. Rottenberg, 46–54. Stanford, CA: Stanford University Press.

———. 2002b. Force of law: The "mystical foundations of authority." In *Acts of religion*, ed. G. Anidjar, 230–98. New York: Routledge.

———. 2005. *Rogues: Two essays on reason*. Trans. P.-A. Brault and M. Naas. Meridian. Stanford, CA: Stanford University Press.

————. 2007. The laws of reflection: Nelson Mandela, in admiration. Trans. M. A. Caws and I. Lorenz. In *Psyche inventions of the other.* Vol. 2, ed. P. Kamuf and E. Rottenberg, 63–86. Stanford, CA: Stanford University Press.

————. 2011. *Voice and phenomenon: Introduction to the problem of the sign in Husserl's phenomenology.* Trans. L. Lawlor. Evanston, IL: Northwestern University Press.

Diawara, M. 1995. Cultural studies/black studies. In *Borders, boundaries, and frames: Essays in cultural criticism and cultural studies,* ed. M. Henderson. Essays from the English Institute, 202–11. New York: Routledge.

Dilthey, W. 1977. The understanding of other persons and their expressions of life. In *Descriptive psychology and historical understanding,* trans. R. M. Zaneer and K. L. Heiges, 123–43. The Hague: Nijhoff.

Douglass, F. 1982. What to the slave is the Fourth of July? In *The Frederick Douglass papers: Series one, speeches, debates and interviews.* Vol. 2, *1847–54.* 5 vols., ed. J. W. Blassingame. The Frederick Douglass papers, 359–88. New Haven, CT: Yale University Press.

Drake, S. C., and H. R. Cayton. 1945. *Black metropolis: A study of Negro life in a northern city.* Preface by R. Wright. New York: Harcourt, Brace and Company.

Du Bois, W. E. B. ca. 1894. Diary of My Steerage Trip Across the Atlantic. Manuscript. Series 3, Subseries C. MS 312. The papers of W. E. B. Du Bois. Special Collections and University Archives. Amherst, Massachusetts: W. E. B. Du Bois Memorial Library, University of Massachusetts Amherst.

————. ca. 1897. Beyond the veil in a Virginia town. Manuscript. Series 3, Subseries C. MS 312. The papers of W. E. B. Du Bois. Special Collections and University Archives. Amherst, Massachusetts: W. E. B. Du Bois Memorial Library, University of Massachusetts Amherst.

————. 1897a. The conservation of races. The American Negro Academy Occasional Papers, No. 2. Washington, DC: American Negro Academy.

————. 1897b. Strivings of the negro people. *The Atlantic Monthly: A Magazine of Literature, Science, Art, and Politics* 80 (478) (August): 194–98.

————. 1898a. The negroes of Farmville, Virginia: A social study. *Bulletin of the Department of Labor,* January.

————. 1898b. The study of the negro problems. *Annals of the American Academy of Political and Social Science* 11(1) (January): 1–23.

————. 1899. Final word. In *The Philadelphia negro: A social study, by W. E. B. Du Bois; together with a special report on domestic service by Isabel Eaton,* by W. E. B. Du Bois and I. Eaton. Publications of the University of Pennsylvania. Series in political economy and public law, 385–97. Philadelphia, PA: Published for the University; Boston, MA: Ginn [distributor].

————. 1900. The present outlook for the dark races of mankind. *A. M. E. Church Review* 17 (2) (Whole Number 66): 95–110.

————. 1901a. The freedmen's bureau. *The Atlantic Monthly: A Magazine of Literature, Science, Art, and Politics* 87 (519) (March): 354–65.

————. 1901b. The negro as he really is. *World's Work* (June): 848–66.

————. 1901c. The relation of the negroes to the whites in the South. *Annals of the American Academy of Political and Social Science* 18 (1) (July): 121–40.

————. 1903a. Of our spiritual strivings. In *The souls of black folk: Essays and sketches.* 1st ed., 1–12. Chicago: A. C. McClurg & Co.

————. 1903b. Of the black belt. In *The souls of black folk: Essays and sketches.* 1st ed., 110–34. Chicago: A. C. McClurg & Co.

————. 1903c. Of the dawn of freedom. In *The souls of black folk: Essays and sketches.* 1st ed., 13–40. Chicago: A. C. McClurg & Co.

————. 1903d. Of the sons of master and man. In *The souls of black folk: Essays and sketches.* 1st ed., 163–88. Chicago: A. C. McClurg & Co.

————. 1903e. *The souls of lack folk: Essays and sketches.* 2d ed. Documenting the American South: University Library, University of North Carolina at Chapel Hill, 2001. http://docsouth.unc.edu/church/duboissouls/dubois.html.

————. 1903f. *The souls of Black folk: Essays and sketches.* Chicago: A. C. McClurg & Co.

————. 1909. *John Brown.* American crisis biographies. Philadelphia, PA: G. W. Jacobs & Co.

————. 1910. The souls of white folk. *Independent* 69 (August 18): 339–42.

————. 1915a. The African roots of war. *Atlantic Monthly* 115 (5) (May): 707–14.

————. 1915b. *The Negro.* Home university library of modern knowledge, no. 91. New York: Henry Holt and Co.

————. 1917. Of the culture of white folk. *Journal of Race Development* 7 (April): 434–47.

————. 1920. *Darkwater: Voices from within the veil.* New York: Harcourt, Brace and Howe.

————. 1925. Worlds of color. *Foreign Affairs* 20: 423–44.

————. 1928. *Dark princess: A romance.* New York: Harcourt, Brace and Co.

————. 1935. *Black reconstruction: An essay toward a history of the part which black folk played in the attempt to reconstruct democracy in America, 1860–1880.* New York: Harcourt, Brace and Co.

————. 1937. Forum of fact and opinion. *Pittsburgh Courier,* May 1.

————. 1945. *Color and democracy: Colonies and peace.* New York: Harcourt, Brace and Co.

———. 1947. *The world and Africa: An inquiry into the part which Africa has played in world history.* New York: Viking Press.

———. 1962. *John Brown.* Centennial ed. New York: International Publishers.

———. 1968. *The autobiography of W. E. B. Du Bois: A soliloquy on viewing my life from the last decade of its first century.* Ed. H. Aptheker. New York: International Publishers.

———. 1973. *John Brown.* Ed. H. Aptheker. Complete published writings of W. E. B. Du Bois. Millwood, NY: Kraus-Thompson Organization.

———. 1975a. *Black folk then and now: An essay in the history and sociology of the Negro race.* Ed. H. Aptheker. Complete published writings of W.E.B. Du Bois. Millwood, NY: Kraus-Thomson Organization.

———. 1975b. *Darkwater: Voices from within the veil.* Ed. H. Aptheker. Complete published writings of W. E. B. Du Bois. Millwood, NY: Kraus-Thomson Organization.

———. 1975c. *Dusk of dawn: An essay toward an autobiography of a race concept.* Ed. H. Aptheker. Complete published writings of W. E. B. Du Bois. Millwood, NY: Kraus-Thomson Organization.

———. 1976. *Black reconstruction: An essay toward a history of the part which Black folk played in the attempt to reconstruct democracy in America, 1860–1880.* Ed. H. Aptheker. Complete published writings of W. E. B. Du Bois. Millwood, NY: Kraus-Thomson Organization Ltd.

———. 1977. The souls of Black folk. In *Book reviews,* comp. and ed. Herbert Aptheker. Complete published writings of W. E. B. Du Bois, 9. Millwood, NY: KTO Press.

———. 1980a. The Negro landholder of Georgia. In *Contributions by W. E. B. Du Bois in government publications and proceedings,* ed. H. Aptheker. Complete published writings of W.E.B. Du Bois, 95–228. Millwood, NY: Kraus-Thomson Organization.

———. 1980b. The Negroes of Farmville, Virginia: A social study. In *Contributions by W. E. B. Du Bois in government publications and proceedings,* ed. H. Aptheker. Complete published writings of W. E. B. Du Bois, 5–44. Millwood, NY: Kraus-Thomson Organization.

———. 1980c. Testimony before the United States Industrial Commission. In *Contributions by W. E. B. Du Bois in government publications and proceedings,* ed. H. Aptheker. Complete published writings of W. E. B. Du Bois, 65–94. Millwood, NY: Kraus-Thomson Organization.

———. 1982a. Credo. In *Writings by W. E. B. Du Bois in periodicals edited by others.* Vol. 1, *1891–1909,* comp. and ed. H. Aptheker. Complete Published Writings of W. E. B. Du Bois, 229–30. Millwood, NY: Kraus-Thomson Organization.

———. 1982b. My evolving program for Negro freedom. In *Writings by W. E.*

B. Du Bois in non-periodical literature edited by others, comp. and ed. H. Aptheker. Complete published writings of W. E. B. Du Bois, 216–41. Millwood, NY: Kraus-Thomson.

———. 1982c. The present outlook for the dark races of mankind. In *Writings by W. E. B. Du Bois in periodicals edited by others.* Vol. 1, *1891–1909,* comp. and ed. H. Aptheker. Complete published writings of W. E. B. Du Bois, 73–82. Millwood, NY: Kraus-Thomson Organization.

———. 1982d. The problem of housing the Negro. In *Writings by W. E. B. Du Bois in periodicals edited by others.* Vol. 1, *1891–1909,* comp. and ed. H. Aptheker. Complete Published Writings of W. E. B. Du Bois, 92–96, 100–104, 117–21, 122–25, 131–34, 135–38. Millwood, NY: Kraus-Thomson Organization.

———. 1982e. The souls of white folk. In *Writings by W. E. B. Du Bois in periodicals edited by others.* Vol. 2, *1910–1934,* comp. and ed. H. Aptheker. Complete published writings of W. E B. Du Bois, 25–29. Millwood, NY: Kraus-Thomson Organization.

———. 1982f. The study of the Negro problems. In *Writings by W. E. B. Du Bois in periodicals edited by others.* Vol. 1, *1891–1909,* comp. and ed. H. Aptheker. Complete published writings of W. E. B. Du Bois, 40–52. Millwood, NY: Kraus-Thomson Organization.

———. 1982g. The twelfth census and the Negro problems. In *Writings by W. E. B. Du Bois in periodicals edited by others,* comp. and ed. H. Aptheker. Complete published writings of W. E. B. Du Bois, 69–72. Millwood, NY: Kraus-Thomson Organization.

———. 1985. Beyond the veil in a Virginia town. In *Against racism: Unpublished essays, papers, addresses, 1887–1961,* ed. H. Aptheker, 49–50. Amherst: University of Massachusetts Press.

———. 1986a. The conservation of races. In *Pamphlets and leaflets,* comp. and ed. H. Aptheker. Complete Published Writings of W. E. B. Du Bois, 1–8. White Plains, NY: Kraus-Thomson Organization.

———. 1986b. Forum of fact and opinion [May 1, 1937, *Pittsburgh Courier*]. In *Newspaper columns.* Vol. 1, *1883–1944, Pittsburgh Courier.* 2 vols., comp. and ed. H. Aptheker. Complete published writings of W. E. B. Du Bois, 195–97. White Plains, NY: Kraus-Thomson Organization.

———. 1986c. A pageant in seven decades, 1878–1938. In *Pamphlets and leaflets,* comp. and ed. H. Aptheker. Complete published writings of W. E. B. Du Bois, 244–74. White Plains, NY: Kraus-Thomson Organization.

———. 1997. *John Brown: A biography.* American history through literature. Armonk, NY: M. E. Sharpe.

———. 2001. *John Brown.* Ed. D. R. Roediger. The Modern Library Classics. New York: Modern Library.

———. 2010. The Afro-American. *Journal of Transnational American Studies* 2 (1). http://escholarship.org/uc/item/2pm9g4q2.

———. Forthcoming (a). *The problem of the color line at the turn of the twentieth century: The essential early essays.* Comp. and ed. N. D. Chandler. New York: Fordham University Press.

———. Forthcoming (b). The relation of the Negroes to the Whites in the South. In *The essential early essays: Writings by W. E. B. Du Bois at the turn of the twentieth century,* comp. and ed. N. D. Chandler. New York: Fordham University Press.

———. Forthcoming (c). The study of the Negro problems. In *The essential early essays: Writings by W. E. B. Du Bois at the turn of the twentieth century,* comp. and ed. N. D. Chandler. New York: Fordham University Press.

Du Bois, W. E. B., and I. Eaton. 1899. *The Philadelphia Negro: A social study, by W.E.B. Du Bois; together with a special report on domestic service by Isabel Eaton.* Publications of the University of Pennsylvania. Series in political economy and public law. Philadelphia, PA: Published for the University; Boston, MA: Ginn [distributor].

Du Bois, W. E. B., and I. Eaton. 1973. *The Philadelphia Negro: A social study.* Ed. Herbert Aptheker. Complete Published Works of W. E. B. Du Bois. Millwood, NY: Kraus Thomson Organization Limited.

Durkheim, É. 1995. *The elementary forms of religious life.* Trans. K. E. Fields. New York: Free Press.

Ellison, R. 1989. *Invisible man.* New York: Vintage Books.

———. 1995a. *An American dilemma*: A review. In *The collected essays of Ralph Ellison,* ed. J. F. Callahan, 328–40. New York: Modern Library.

———. 1995b. Blues people. In *The collected essays of Ralph Ellison,* ed. J. F. Callahan, 278–87. New York: Modern Library.

———. 1995c. An extravagance of laughter. In *The collected essays of Ralph Ellison,* ed. J. F. Callahan, 613–58. New York: Modern Library.

———. 1995d. Indivisible man. In *The collected essays of Ralph Ellison,* ed. J. F. Callahan, 355–95. New York: Modern Library.

Equiano, O. 1969. The life of Olaudah Equiano, or Gustavus Vassa, the African, written by himself. In *Great slave narratives,* ed. and intro. by A. Bontemps, 4–192. Boston: Beacon Press.

———. 2003. *The interesting narrative and other writings.* Ed. V. Carretta. New York: Penguin Books.

Esch, D. 1993. Strategic exemplarity. *Alphabet City* 3: 24–26.

Eze, E. C., ed. 1997. *Race and the enlightenment: A reader.* Cambridge, MA: Blackwell.

Fanon, F. 1961. *Les damnés de la terre.* Paris: F. Maspero.

———. 1967. *Black skin, white masks.* New York: Grove Press.

————. 1975. *Peau noire, masques blancs*. Paris: Éditions du Seuil.

Faulkner, W. 1936. *Absalom, Absalom!* New York: Random House.

Feemster, R. 2003. The problem with public housing: Is Chicago solving it? *Ford Foundation Report*, spring. http://www.fordfound.org/publications/ ff_report/view_ff_report_detail.cfm?report_index=3.

Fernández Retamar, R. 1989. Caliban: Notes towards a discussion of culture in our America. In *Caliban and other essays*, by R. Fernández Retamar, trans. E. Baker, 7–72. Minneapolis: University of Minnesota Press.

Fields, K. 1996. Durkheim and the idea of soul. *Theory and Society* 25: 193–203.

————. 2002. Individuality and the intellectuals: An imaginary conversation between W. E. B. Du Bois and Émile Durkheim. *Theory and Society* 31 (4) (August): 435–62.

Fink, E. 1970. Husserl's philosophy and contemporary criticism. In *The phenomenology of Husserl*, ed. R. O. Elveton, 73–147. Chicago: Quadrangle Books.

Finkelman, P. 1996. *Slavery and the founders: Race and liberty in the age of Jefferson*. Armonk, NY: M. E. Sharpe.

Finley, M. I. 1960. The servile statuses of ancient Greece. *Revue Internationale Des Droits de l'Antiquité* 3rd series, 7.

————. 1973. *The ancient economy*. Berkeley: University of California Press.

Foner, E. 1982. Reconstruction revisited. *Reviews in American History* 10 (December): 82–100.

————. 1988. *Reconstruction: America's unfinished revolution, 1863–1877*. New American nation series. New York: Harper & Row.

Foner, P. S. 1975. *History of Black Americans*. Vol. 3, *From the bompromise of 1850 to the end of the Civil War*. Contributions in American history. No. 40. Westport, CT: Greenwood Press.

Foucault, M. 1969. *L'Archéologie du savoir*. Bibliothèque des sciences humaines. Paris: Gallimard.

————. 1972. *The archaeology of knowledge and the discourse on language*. Trans. A. M. S. Smith. New York: Harper & Row, Harper Colophon.

————. 1976a. Droit de mort et pouvoir sur la vie. In *Histoire de la sexualite: La volonté de savoir*, 177–211. Paris: Gallimard.

————. 1976b. *Histoire de la sexualite: La volonté de savoir*. Paris: Gallimard.

————. 1977. Nietzsche, genealogy, history. In *Language, counter-memory, practice: Selected essays and interviews*, ed. D. F. Bouchard, trans. S. Simon and D. F. Bouchard, 139–64. Ithaca, NY: Cornell University Press.

————. 1980a. *The history of sexuality*. Vol. 1, *An introduction*. Trans. R. Hurley. New York: Random House, Vintage.

————. 1980b. Right of death and power over life. In *The history of sexuality*. Vol. 1, *An introduction*, trans. R. Hurley, 135–59. New York: Random House, Vintage.

———. 1985. *The history of sexuality*. Vol. 2, *The use of pleasure*. Trans. R. Hurley. New York: Random House, Vintage.

———. 1997a. *"Il faut défendre la société" cours au Collège de France (1975–1976)*. Paris: Seuil/Gallimard.

———. 1997b. Preface to The history of sexuality, Vol. 2. Trans. William Smock. In *Essential works of Foucault, 1954–1984*. Vol. 1, *Ethics: Subjectivity and truth*, ed. P. Rabinow, 199–205. New York: New Press [distributed by W. W. Norton].

———. 2000. The subject and power. Trans. L. Sawyer. In *Essential works of Foucault, 1954–1984*. Vol. 3, *Power*, ed. J. D. Faubion, 326–48. New York: New Press.

———. 2003. *Society must be defended: Lectures at the Collège de France, 1975–76*. Ed. M. Bertani. Trans. D. Macey. New York: Picador.

Frankenberg, R. 1993. *White women, race matters: The social construction of whiteness*. Minneapolis: University of Minnesota Press.

Frazier, E. F. 2001. *The Negro family in the United States*. Intro. by A. M. Platt. Notre Dame, IN: University of Notre Dame Press.

Fredrickson, G. M. 1987. *The Black image in the white mind: The debate on Afro-American character and destiny, 1817–1914*. Middletown, CT, and Scranton, PA: Wesleyan University Press Distributed by Harper & Row.

Freud, S. 1965. *The interpretation of dreams*. Trans. J. Strachey. New York: Avon, Discus.

Fried, G., and R. Polt. 2000. Translators' introduction. In *Introduction to metaphysics*, by M. Heidegger, trans. G. Fried and R. Polt. Yale Nota bene, vii–xix. New Haven, CT: Yale University Press.

Gadamer, H. G. 1979. The problem of historical consciousness. In *Interpretive social science: A reader*, ed. P. Rabinow and W. M. Sullivan, 82–140. Berkeley: University of California Press.

Garnsey, P. 1996. *Ideas of slavery from Aristotle to Augustine*. The W. B. Stanford memorial lectures. Cambridge and New York: Cambridge University Press.

Gates, H. L. 1987. *Figures in Black: Words, signs, and the "racial" self*. New York: Oxford University Press.

———. 1991. *Bearing witness: Selections from African-American autobiography in the twentieth century*. Ed. H. L. Gates. New York: Pantheon Books.

Genovese, E. D. 1974. *Roll, Jordan, roll: The world the slaves made*. New York: Pantheon Books.

Gilroy, P. 1991. *"There ain't no black in the Union Jack": The cultural politics of race and nation*. Black literature and culture. Chicago, IL: University of Chicago Press.

———. 1993. "Cheer the weary traveller": W. E. B. Du Bois, Germany and the politics of (dis)placement. In *The black Atlantic modernity and double consciousness*, 111–45. Cambridge, MA: Harvard University Press.

Goldberg, D. T. 1993. *Racist culture: Philosophy and the politics of meaning.* Cambridge, MA: Blackwell.

Gordon, L. R. 2008. *An introduction to Africana philosophy.* New York: Cambridge University Press.

Gordon-Reed, A. 1997. *Thomas Jefferson and Sally Hemings: An American controversy.* Charlottesville: University Press of Virginia.

———. 2008. *The Hemingses of Monticello: An American family.* New York: W. W. Norton & Co.

Gramsci, A. 1971. *Selections from the prison notebooks.* Ed. and trans. Q. Hoare and G. N. Smith. London: Lawrence and Wishart.

Greene, J. P. 1970. Search for identity: An interpretation of the meaning of selected patterns of social response in eighteenth-century America. *Journal of Southern History* 3: 189–224.

———. 1988. *Pursuits of happiness: The social development of early modern British colonies and the formation of American culture.* Chapel Hill: University of North Carolina Press.

Guha, R. 1997a. Colonialism in South Asia: A dominance without hegemony and its historiography. In *Dominance without hegemony: History and power in colonial India*, 1–99. Cambridge, MA: Harvard University Press.

———. 1997b. *A subaltern studies reader, 1986–1995.* Minneapolis: University of Minnesota Press.

———. 2002. *History at the limit of world-history.* Italian Academy lectures. New York: Columbia University Press.

Guha, R., and G. C. Spivak, eds. 1988. *Selected subaltern studies.* New York: Oxford University Press.

Gutman, H. G. 1976. *The Black family in slavery and freedom, 1750–1925.* New York: Pantheon Books.

Hahn, S. 2003. *A nation under our feet: Black political struggles in the rural South, from slavery to the great migration.* Cambridge, MA: Belknap Press of Harvard University Press.

Hall, S. 1990. Cultural identity and diaspora. In *Identity community, culture, difference*, ed. J. Rutherford, 222–37. London: Lawrence & Wishart.

Hartman, S. V. 1997. *Scenes of subjection: Terror, slavery, and self-making in nineteenth-century America.* Race and American culture. New York: Oxford University Press.

Hegel, G. W. F. 1969. *Hegel's science of logic.* Trans. A. V. Miller, intro. by J. N. Findlay. The Muirhead Library of Philosophy. London: George Allen and Unwin.

———. 1975. *Lectures on the philosophy of world history: Introduction: Reason in history.* Trans. H. B. Nibet, intro. by D. Forbes. Cambridge studies in the history and theory of politics. Cambridge: Cambridge University Press.

————. 1977. *Phenomenology of spirit.* Trans. A. V. Miller, fore. by J. N. Findlay. Oxford: Oxford University Press.

————. 1991. *Elements of the philosophy of right.* Ed. A. W. Wood. Trans. H. B. Nisbet. Cambridge and New York: Cambridge University Press.

————. 1994. *Vorlesungen über die Philosophie der Weltgeschichte.* Vol. 1, *Die Vernunft in der Geschichte.* Ed. J. Hoffmeister. Philosophische Bibliothek, Band 171a. Hamburg: Felix Meiner Verlag.

————. 1996. *Vorlesungen über die Philosophie der Weltgeschichte: Berlin 1822/1823.* Ed. K.-H. Ilting, H. N. Seelmann, and K. Brehmer. Comp. K. G. J. v. Griesheim, H. G. Hotho, and F. C. H. V. v. Kehler. Hamburg: Felix Meiner Verlag.

————. 1998. *Phänomenologie des Geistes.* Ed. H.-F. Wessels and H. Clairmont. Intro. by W. Bonsiepen. Philosophische Bibliothek. Bd. 414. Hamburg: Felix Meiner Verlag GmbH.

————. 2011. *Lectures on the philosophy of world history.* Ed. R. F. Brown and P. C. Hodgson. Trans. R. F. Brown and P. C. Hodgson, assisted by W. G. Geuss. Oxford: Oxford University Press.

Heidegger, M. 2000. *Introduction to metaphysics.* Trans. G. Fried and R. Polt. Yale Nota bene. New Haven, CT: Yale University Press.

————. 1962. *Being and time.* Trans. J. Macquarrie and E. Robinson. New York: Harper and Row.

————. 1969. *Identity and difference.* New York: Harper and Row.

————. 1998. *Einführung in die Metaphysik.* 7th ed. Tübingen: Niemeyer.

Herskovits, M. J. 1990. *The myth of the Negro past.* Boston: Beacon Press.

Herskovits, M. J., and F. S. Herskovits. 1966. *The new world Negro: Selected papers in Afroamerican studies.* Ed. F. S. Herskovits. Bloomington: Indiana University Press.

Higman, B. W. 1984. *Slave populations of the British Caribbean, 1807–1834.* Baltimore, MD: Johns Hopkins University Press.

Holt, T. C. 1990a. Explaining abolition. *Journal of Social History* 24 (2) (winter): 371–78.

————. 1990b. The political uses of alienation: W. E. B. Du Bois on politics, race, and culture, 1905–1940. *American Quarterly* 42 (2): 301–23.

————. 1992. *The problem of freedom: Race, labor, and politics in Jamaica and Britain, 1832–1938.* Johns Hopkins studies in Atlantic history and culture. Baltimore, MD: Johns Hopkins University Press.

Huggins, N. I. 1990. Notes. In *The souls of Black folk*, by W. E. B. Du Bois. New York: Vintage Books/Library of America.

Hughes, H. S. 1977. *Consciousness and society: The reorientation of European social thought, 1890–1930.* New York: Vintage Books.

Hunt, D. B. 2009. *Blueprint for disaster: The unraveling of Chicago public housing.* Chicago: University of Chicago Press.

Hurston, Z. N. 1935. *Mules and men.* Preface by F. Boas, illus. M. Covarrubias. Philadelphia: J. B. Lippincott.

Husserl, E. 1954. Beilage III. Die Frage nach dem Ursprung der Geometrie als intentional-historisches Problem. In *Die Krisis der europäischen Wissenschaften und die transzendentale Phänomenologie,* ed. W. Biemel, by E. Husserl. Husserliana. Bd. 6, 365–86. The Hague: M. Nijhof.

———. 1960. *Cartesian meditations: An introduction to phenomenology.* Trans. D. Cairns. The Hague: Martinus Nijhoff.

———. 1970. *Logical investigations.* 2 Vols. Trans. J. N. Findlay. International library of philosophy and scientific method. London: Routledge and Kegan Paul.

———. 1978. The origin of geometry. Trans. D. Carr. In *Edmund Husserl's The origin of geometry: An introduction,* ed. David B. Allison, by E. Husserl and J. Derrida, trans. J. P. Leavey, 155–80.

———. 1980. *Ideas pertaining to a pure phenomenology and to a phenomenological philosophy.* The Hague and Boston: M. Nijhoff Distributors for the US and Canada, Kluwer Boston.

———. 1999. *The idea of phenomenology: A translation of Die Idee der Phänomenologie: Husserliana II.* Trans. L. Hardy. Dordrecht, Germany and Boston: Kluwer Academic.

Isaac, R. 1982. *The transformation of Virginia, 1740–1790.* Chapel Hill: Published for the Omohundro Institute of Early American History and Culture, Williamsburg, VA, by University of North Carolina Press.

Jefferson, T. 1972. *Notes on the State of Virginia.* Ed. W. H. Peden. New York: W. W. Norton.

———. 1984a. *Notes on the State of Virginia.* In *Writings,* ed. M. D. Peterson. Library of America, vol. 17, 123–325. New York: Literary Classics of the US. Distributed to the trade in the US and Canada by the Viking Press.

———. 1984b. *Writings.* Ed. M. D. Peterson. Library of America, Vol. 17. New York: Literary Classics of the US. Distributed to the trade in the US and Canada by the Viking Press.

———. 1999. *Thomas Jefferson, political writings.* Ed. J. O. Appleby and T. Ball. Cambridge texts in the history of political thought. New York: Cambridge University Press.

Jordan, W. D. 1977. *White over Black: American attitudes toward the Negro, 1550–1812.* New York: W. W. Norton.

Joyner, C. W. 1979. The creolization of slave folklife: All Saints Parish, South

Carolina, as a test case. *Historical Reflections/Reflections Historiques* 6:
435–53.

———. 1984. *Down by the riverside: A South Carolina slave community.*
Urbana: University of Illinois Press.

———. 1993. A single southern culture: Cultural interaction in the old
South. In *Black and White cultural interaction in the antebellum South*, ed.
T. Ownby, 3–22. Jackson: University Press of Mississippi.

———. 1999. *Shared traditions: Southern history and folk culture.* Urbana:
University of Illinois Press.

Judy, R. A. T. 1993. *(Dis)forming the American canon: African-Arabic slave
narratives and the vernacular.* Minneapolis: University of Minnesota
Press. .

———. 2000. Introduction: On W. E. B. Du Bois and hyperbolic thinking.
Boundary 2: An International Journal of Literature and Culture 27 (3) (fall):
1–35. A special issue, Sociology hesitant: Thinking with W. E. B. Du Bois,
ed. R. A. Judy.

Kamin, B. 1993a. Is that Cabrini-Green? Winning architects take a new perspective. *Chicago Tribune*, June 10, Section 2, 1–2.

———. 1993b. Results of the *Chicago Tribune* architecture competition for
public housing. Rebuilding the community: New ideas in public housing
are a return to the basics. *Chicago Tribune*, June 20, Special Section.

Kant, I. 1996a. Critique of practical reason (1788). In *Practical philosophy*, ed. M.
J. Gregor, trans. M. J. Gregor. Cambridge Edition of the Works of Immanuel Kant in Translation, 133–272. New York: Cambridge University Press.

———. 1996b. The metaphysics of morals (1797). In *Practical philosophy*, ed.
and trans. M. J. Gregor. Cambridge Edition of the Works of Immanuel
Kant in Translation, 353–604. New York: Cambridge University Press.

———. 1996c. Toward perpetual peace (1795). In *Practical philosophy*, ed. M.
J. Gregor, trans. M. J. Gregor. Cambridge Edition of the Works of Immanuel Kant in Translation, 311–52. New York: Cambridge University Press.

———. 1998. *Critique of pure reason.* Ed. and trans. P. Guyer and A. W.
Wood. New York: Cambridge University Press.

———. 2001. Über den gebrauch teleologischer prinzipien in der Philosophie. In *Schriften zur Ästhetik und Naturphilosophie: Texte und Kommen-
tar*, vol. 1, ed. M. Frank and V. Zanetti. Suhrkamp Tassenbüch Wissen-
schaft, 381–414. Frankfurt am Main: Suhrkamp.

———. 2007a. Observations on the feeling of the beautiful and sublime
(1764). Trans. P. Guyer. In *Anthropology, history, and education*, ed. and
trans. R. B. Louden and G. Zöller. Cambridge edition of the works of
Immanuel Kant in translation, 18–62. New York: Cambridge University
Press.

———. 2007b. On the use of teleological principles in philosophy (1788). Trans. G. Zöller. In *Anthropology, history, and education*, ed. and trans. R. B. Louden and G. Zöller. Cambridge edition of the works of Immanuel Kant in translation, 195–218. New York: Cambridge University Press.

Kelley, R. D. G. 1997. *Yo' mama's disfunktional!: Fighting the culture wars in urban America.* Boston: Beacon Press.

Kelly, K. 2005. Rising values. *The Chicago Reporter,* July/August. http://www.chicagoreporter.com/2005/7-2005/cha/chaprint.htm.

Kilson, M. 1976. Review [Roll, Jordan, Roll: The world the slaves made, by Eugene D. Genovese]. *The American Historical Review* 81 (1) (February): 209–10.

King, M. L., Jr. 1964. Letter from Birmingham jail. In *Why we can't wait*, 85–110. New York: Harper & Row.

———. 1991. I have a dream. In *A testament of hope: The essential writings of Martin Luther King, Jr.*, ed. J. M. Washington, 217–20. San Francisco: HarperSanFrancisco.

Kirk, G. S., and J. E. Raven. 1969. *The presocratic philosophers: A critical history with a selection of texts.* Cambridge: Cambridge University Press.

Lacoue-Labarthe, P. 1989. *Typography: Mimesis, philosophy, politics.* Ed. C. Fynsk. Cambridge, MA: Harvard University Press.

Lange, W. J. 1983. W. E. B. Du Bois and the first scientific study of Afro-America. *Phylon* 44 (3): 135–46.

Lewis, D. L. 1993. *W. E. B. Du Bois: Biography of a race, 1868–1919.* New York: Henry Holt.

———. 2000. *W. E. B. Du Bois--the fight for equality and the American century, 1919–1963.* New York: H. Holt.

Litwack, L. F. 1979. *Been in the storm so long: The aftermath of slavery.* New York: Alfred A. Knopf, distributed by Random House.

Locke, J. 1988a. The second treatise of government. An essay concerning the true original, extent, and end of civil government. In *Two treatises of government*, ed. P. Laslett. Cambridge texts in the history of political thought, 265–428. Cambridge and New York: Cambridge University Press.

———. 1988b. *Two treatises of government.* Ed. P. Laslett. Cambridge texts in the history of political thought. Cambridge and New York: Cambridge University Press.

Logan, R. W. 1997. *The betrayal of the Negro, from Rutherford B. Hayes to Woodrow Wilson.* New York: Da Capo Press.

Macpherson, C. B. 1962. *The political theory of possessive individualism: Hobbes to Locke.* London: Oxford University Press.

———. 1975. *Democratic theory: Essays in retrieval.* London: Oxford University Press, Clarendon.

Martí, J. 1891. Nuestra América. *La Revista Ilustrada de Nueva York*, January 10.

Marx, K. 1977. *Capital: A critique of political economy*. Vol. 1. Trans. B. Fowkes, intro. by E. Mandel. The Marx Library. New York: Random House, Vintage.

Mead, M., and J. Baldwin. 1971. *A rap on race*. Philadelphia, PA: Lippincott.

Meier, A., and E. M. Rudwick. 1986. *Black history and the historical profession, 1915–1980*. Blacks in the new world. Urbana: University of Illinois Press.

Mill, J. S. 2008. *On liberty and other essays*. Ed. and intro. by J. Gray. Oxford and New York: Oxford University Press.

Miller, J. C. 1977. *The wolf by the ears: Thomas Jefferson and slavery*. New York: Free Press.

Mintz, S. W., and R. Price. 1992. *The birth of African-American culture: An anthropological perspective*. Boston: Beacon Press.

Morgan, E. S. 1975. *American slavery, American freedom: The ordeal of colonial Virginia*. New York: W. W. Norton.

Morrison, T. 1992. *Playing in the dark: Whiteness and the literary imagination*. Cambridge, MA: Harvard University Press.

Moten, F. 2003. *In the break: The aesthetics of the Black radical tradition*. Minneapolis: University of Minnesota Press.

———. 2010. *B Jenkins*. Durham, NC: Duke University Press.

Naas, M. 1992. Introduction: For example. In *The other heading: Reflections on today's Europe*, by J. Derrida, trans. P.-A. Brault and M. Naas. Studies in continental thought, vii–lix. Bloomington: Indiana University Press.

Nelson, D. D. 1992. *The word in black and white: Reading "race" in American literature, 1638–1867*. New York: Oxford University Press.

Newton, A. Z. 1999. *Facing Black and Jew: Literature as public space in twentieth-century America*. Cultural margins. Cambridge and New York: Cambridge University Press.

Nietzsche, F. W. 1998. *On the genealogy of morality: A polemic*. Trans. M. Clark and A. J. Swenson, intro. by M. Clark. Indianapolis, IN: Hackett Pub.

Onuf, P. S. 2000. *Jefferson's empire: The language of American nationhood*. Jeffersonian America. Charlottesville: University Press of Virginia.

Orsi, R. 1992. The religious boundaries of an inbetween people: Street feste and the problem of the dark-skinned other in Italian Harlem, 1920–1990. *American Quarterly* 44 (3): 313–47.

Painter, N. I. 1996. *Sojourner Truth: A life, a symbol*. New York: W. W. Norton.

Partington, P. G. 1977. *W. E. B. Du Bois: A bibliography of his published writings*. Whittier, CA: Penn-Lithographics for Paul G. Partington.

Patterson, O. 1982. *Slavery and social death: A comparative study.* Cambridge, MA: Harvard University Press.

Patterson, T. R., and R. D. G. Kelley. 2000. Unfinished migrations: Reflections on the African Diaspora and the making of the modern world. *African Studies Review* 43 (1) (April): 11–45. Special issue on the diaspora.

Peden, W. H. 1972. Notes. In *Notes on the State of Virginia.*, ed. W. H. Peden, by T. Jefferson, 261–301. New York: W. W. Norton.

Plato. 1989. Theaetetus. Trans. F. M. Cornford. In *The collected dialogues of Plato, including the letters.* With intro. and prefatory notes, ed. E. Hamilton and H. Cairns. Bollingen series, 71, 845–919. Princeton, NJ: Princeton University Press.

Platt, A. M. 1991. *E. Franklin Frazier reconsidered.* New Brunswick, NJ: Rutgers University Press.

Pope, J. 2006. Ägypten und Aufhebung: G. W. F. Hegel, W. E. B. Du Bois, and the African Orient. *CR: The New Centennial Review* 6 (3) (winter): 149–92. Special issue: W. E. B. Du Bois and the question of another world, ed. N. D. Chandler.

Price, R. 1983. *First-time: The historical vision of an Afro-American people.* Johns Hopkins studies in Atlantic history and culture. Baltimore, MD: Johns Hopkins University Press.

———. 1990. *Alabi's world.* Johns Hopkins studies in Atlantic history and culture. Baltimore, MD: Johns Hopkins University Press.

———. 2005. On the miracle of creolization. In *Afro-Atlantic dialogues: Anthropology in the diaspora*, ed. K. A. Yelvington, 115–47. Santa Fe, NM: School of American Research Press.

———. 2006. *The convict and the colonel: A story of colonialism and resistance in the Caribbean.* Durham, NC: Duke University Press.

———. 2008. *Travels with Tooy: History, memory, and the African American imagination.* Chicago: University of Chicago Press.

Price, R., and S. Price. 1991. *Two evenings in Saramaka.* Chicago: University of Chicago Press.

———. 2003. *The root of roots, or, how Afro-American anthropology got its start.* Chicago: Prickly Paradigm.

Quarles, B. 2001. *Allies for freedom: Blacks and John Brown.* Cambridge, MA: Da Capo.

Reed, A. L. 1986. The "Black revolution" and the reconstitution of domination. In *Race, politics, and culture: Critical essays on the radicalism of the 1960s*, ed. A. Reed. Contributions in Afro-American and African studies. New York: Greenwood Press.

———. 1992. Du Bois's "double consciousness": Race and gender in progressive era American thought. *Studies in American Political Develop-ment* 6 (spring): 93–139. New Haven, CT: Yale University Press.

———. 1997. *W. E. B. Du Bois and American political thought: Fabianism and the color line.* New York: Oxford University Press.

Robinson, C. J. 2000. *Black Marxism: The making of the Black radical tradi-tion.* Fore. by R. D. G. Kelley. Chapel Hill, NC: University of North Caro-lina Press.

Roediger, D. R. 1991. *The wages of whiteness: Race and the making of the Amer-ican working class.* London and New York: Verso.

Rousseau, J.-J. 1994. On the social contract. In *Social contract; Discourse on the virtue most necessary for a hero; political fragments; and, Geneva man-uscript,* ed. R. D. Masters and C. Kelly, trans. J. R. Bush, C. Kelly, and R. D. Masters, 127–224. The Collected writings of Rousseau. Hanover, NH: Published by University Press of New England [for] Dartmouth College.

Said, E. W. 1983. *The world, the text, and the critic.* Cambridge, MA: Harvard University Press.

Saussure, F. d. 1986. *Cours de linguistique générale.* Ed. and comp. C. Bally, A. Sechehaye, A. Riedlinger, and T. De Mauro. Paris: Payot.

Saussy, H. 1993. *The problem of a Chinese aesthetic.* Stanford, CA: Stanford University Press.

Saxton, A. 1990. *The rise and fall of the white republic: Class politics and mass culture in nineteenth-century America.* London and New York: Verso.

Schneider, D. M. 1980. *American kinship: A cultural account.* Chicago: Uni-versity of Chicago Press.

———. 1984. *A critique of the study of kinship.* Ann Arbor: University of Michigan Press.

Shakespeare, W. 1982. *Hamlet.* Ed. H. Jenkins. Arden Edition. London and New York: Methuen.

Sharof, R. 2000. In Chicago, an attempt to upgrade a neighborhood. *New York Times,* September 10.

Shepperson, G. 1970. Introduction. In *The Negro,* by W. E. B. Du Bois, vii–xxv. New York: Oxford University Press.

Silva, D. F. d. 2007. *Toward a global idea of race.* Minneapolis: University of Minnesota Press.

Simmel, G. 1980. *Essays on interpretation in social science.* Ed. and trans. G. Oakes. Totowa, NJ: Rowman and Littlefield.

Smith, R. T. 1988. *Kinship and class in the West Indies: A genealogical study of Jamaica and Guyana.* Cambridge and New York: Cambridge Univer-sity Press.

Sobel, M. 1987. *The world they made together: Black and White values in eigh-teenth-century Virginia.* Princeton, NJ: Princeton University Press.

————. 1988. All Americans are part African: Slave influence on "white" values. In *Slavery and other forms of unfree labour*, ed. L. J. Archer, 176–87. London and New York: Routledge.

Spillers, H. J. 1991a. Introduction: Who cuts the border? Some readings on "America." In *Comparative American identities: Race, sex, and nationality in the modern text*, ed. H. J. Spillers. Essays from the English Institute, 1–25. New York: Routledge.

————. 1991b. Moving on down the line: Variation on the African-American sermon. In *The bounds of race perspectives on hegemony and resistance*, ed. D. LaCapra, 39–71. Ithaca, NY: Cornell University Press.

————. 2003a. *Black, white, and in color: Essays on American literature and culture*. Chicago: University of Chicago Press.

————. 2003b. The crisis of the Negro intellectual: A post-date. In *Black, white, and in color: Essays on American literature and culture*, 428–70. Chicago: University of Chicago Press.

————. 2003c. Mama's baby, papa's maybe: An American grammar book. In *Black, white, and in color: Essays on American literature and culture*, 203–29. Chicago: University of Chicago Press.

————. 2003d. Moving on down the line: Variations on the African-American sermon. In *Black, white, and in color: Essays on American literature and culture*, 251–76. Chicago: University of Chicago Press.

Spinoza, B. d. 1968. *Abrégé de grammaire hébraïque*. Trans. and ed. J. Askénazi and J. Askénazi-Gerson. Paris: J. Vrin.

Spivak, G. C. 1988a. Can the subaltern speak? In *Marxism and the interpretation of culture*, ed. C. Nelson and L. Grossberg, 271–316. Urbana: University of Illinois Press.

————. 1988b. Subaltern studies: Deconstructing historiography. In *Selected subaltern studies*, ed. R. Guha and G. C. Spivak, 3–32. New York: Oxford University Press.

————. 1989. In a word. *Differences* 1: 124–56.

————. 1990. *The post-colonial critic interviews, strategies, dialogues*. Ed. S. Harasym. New York: Routledge.

————. 1996a. More on power/knowledge. In *The Spivak reader: Selected works of Gayatri Chakravorty Spivak*, ed. D. Landry and G. M. MacLean, 141–74. New York: Routledge.

————. 1996b. *The Spivak reader: Selected works of Gayatri Chakravorty Spivak*. Ed. D. Landry and G. M. MacLean. New York: Routledge.

————. 1999. *A critique of postcolonial reason: Toward a history of the vanishing present*. Cambridge, MA: Harvard University Press.

Spivak, G., and W. Adamson. 1990. Interview with Gayatri Spivak, by Walter Adamson. In *Discourses: Conversations in postmodern art and culture*, ed.

R. Ferguson, W. Olander, M. Tucker, and K. Fiss. Documentary sources in contemporary art, vol. 3, 105–12. New York and Cambridge, MA: New Museum of Contemporary Art MIT Press.

Stepto, R. B. 1979. The quest of the weary traveler: W. E. B. Du Bois's The souls of black folk. In *From behind the veil a study of Afro-American narrative / Robert B. Stepto*. Urbana: University of Illinois Press.

Stocking, G. W. 1982. *Race, culture, and evolution: Essays in the history of anthropology*. Chicago: University of Chicago Press.

Stoler, A. L. 1995. *Race and the education of desire: Foucault's History of Sexuality and the colonial order of things*. Durham, NC: Duke University Press.

Stuckey, S. 1987. *Slave culture: Nationalist theory and the foundations of Black America*. New York: Oxford University Press.

Sundquist, E. J. 1993. *To wake the nations: Race in the making of American literature*. Cambridge, MA: Belknap Press of Harvard University Press.

Tagore, R. 1929. A message from Rabindranath Tagore. *The crisis: A record of the darker races* 36 (10) (Whole Number) (October): 333–34.

Tagore, R., and A. C. Chakravarty. 1997. Amiya C. Chakravarty for Rabidranath Tagore to W. E. B. Du Bois. Letter with enclosure, dated July 12, 1929, in *The correspondence of W. E. B. Du Bois*. Vol. 1, *Selections, 1877–1934*. Pbk. ed. with corrections, comp. and ed. H. Aptheker, 404–5. Amherst: University of Massachusetts Press.

Takaki, R. T. 1979. *Iron cages: Race and culture in nineteenth-century America*. New York: Alfred A. Knopf; distributed by Random House.

———. 1989. *Strangers from a different shore: A history of Asian Americans*. Boston: Little, Brown.

Taylor, C. 1959. *Looking ahead!* Album. LP S7562. E. Griffith, B. Neidlinger, and D. Charles. Los Angeles: Contemporary Records.

———. 1966a. Sound structure of subculture becoming major breath/ Naked fire gesture. Liner notes in *Unit structures*. Album. LP BST 84237. Blue Note Records.

———. 1966b. *Unit structures*. Album. LP BST 84237. E. G. Stevens Jr., et al. Blue Note Records.

———. 1973. *Solo*. Album. PA-7067. Tokyo: Trio Records.

———. 1974. *Spring of two blue-J's*. Album. LP 30551. J. Lyons, Sirone, and A. Cyrille. New York: Unit Core Records.

———. 1975. *Silent tongues: Live at Montreux '74*. Album. LP FLP 41005. London: Freedom Records.

———. 1977a. *Dark to themselves*. Album. IC 3001. R. Malik, J. Lyons, D. Ware, and M. Edwards.

———. 1977b. *Indent*. Album. AL 1038. New York: Arista Freedom.

———. 1978. *Air above mountains (buildings within)*. Album. IC-3021. Enja series. New York: Inner City Records.

———. 1982. *Garden*. Album. Double LP Hat ART 1993/94. Therwil, Switzerland: Hat Hut.

———. 1987. *For Olim*. Album. CD SN1150. Milan: Soul Note Records.

———. 1991. *In florescence*. Album. CD 5286. W. Parker and G. Bendian. Los Angeles: A&M Records.

Terry, D. 1992. Chicago housing project basks in a tense peace. *New York Times*, November 2, A-8.

Venkatesh, S., and I. Celimli. 2004. Tearing down the community. *NHI, Shelterforce Online* 138 (November/December). http://www.nhi.org/online/issues/138/chicago.html.

Walker, D. 1965. *One continual cry: David Walker's Appeal to the Colored citizens of the world, 1829–1830, its setting & its meaning, together with the full text of the third, and last, edition of the Appeal.* Ed. H. Aptheker. New York: Published for A.I.M.S. by Humanities Press.

———. 2000. *David Walker's appeal to the Coloured citizens of the world*. Ed. P. P. Hinks. University Park: Pennsylvania State University Press.

Wallerstein, I. 1974. *The modern-world system: Capitalist agriculture and the origins of the European world-economy in the sixteenth century.* Studies in Social Discontinuity. New York: Academic Press.

Ware, V. 1992. *Beyond the pale: White women, racism, and history.* London and New York: Verso.

Warren, K. 1993. Appeals for (mis)recognition: Theorizing the diaspora. In *Cultures of United States imperialism*, ed. A. Kaplan and D. E. Pease. New Americanists., 392–406. Durham, NC: Duke University Press.

Weber, M. 1964. *Max Weber, the theory of social and economic organization.* Ed. T. Parsons. Trans. A. M. Henderson. New York and London: Free Press Collier Macmillan.

West, C. 1982. *Prophesy deliverance: An Afro-American revolutionary Christianity.* Philadelphia, PA: Westminster Press.

———. 1987. Race and social theory: Towards a genealogical materialist analysis. In *The year left 2: an American socialist yearbook*, ed. M. Davis, et al., 74–90. London: Verso.

———. 1988. Marxism and the specificity of Afro-American oppression. In *Marxism and the interpretation of culture*, ed. C. Nelson and L. Grossberg, 17–33. Urbana: University of Illinois Press.

Wheatley, P. 1988. *The collected works of Phillis Wheatley.* Ed. J. Shields. The Schomburg library of Nineteenth-century Black women writers. New York: Oxford University Press.

Whitaker, D. 1992. Killing time: Rival gangs rap with a cop who walks a different beat. *Streetwise: A non-profit monthly newsletter empowering Chicago's homeless through employment* 1 (3): 6–8.

Wideman, J. E. 1990. Introduction. In *The souls of Black folk*, by W. E. B. Du Bois, i–xvi. New York: Vintage Books/Library of America.

Williams, P. J. 1991. *The alchemy of race and rights*. Cambridge, MA: Harvard University Press.

Wood, P. H. 1976. "I did the best I could for my day": The study of early Black history during the second reconstruction, 1960–1976. *William and Mary Quarterly* 35: 185–225. 3d Series.

Young, L. 1987. "Power and color: Japanese imperialism in a white world order." Unpublished master's thesis. New York: Columbia University.

———. 1998. *Japan's total empire: Manchuria and the culture of wartime imperialism*. Twentieth-century Japan. Berkeley: University of California Press.

Zamir, S. 1995. *Dark voices: W. E. B. Du Bois and American thought, 1888–1903.* Chicago: University of Chicago Press.

Zuckerman, M. 1977. The fabrication of identity in early America. *William and Mary Quarterly* 34 (2): 183–214. 3d series.

———. 1987. Identity in British America: Unease in Eden. In *Colonial identity in the Atlantic world, 1500–1800*, ed. N. P. Canny and A. Pagden, 115–57. Princeton, NJ: Princeton University Press.

Zumwalt, R. L., and W. S. Willis. 2008. *Franz Boas and W. E. B. Du Bois at Atlanta University, 1906*. Philadelphia, PA: American Philosophical Society.

Index

In this index books by W. E. B. Du Bois are listed as distinct entries, under their main individual titles only. See the end of the main entry "Du Bois, W. E. B." for a list of those main titles, for which the bibliography includes full citations. Articles and posthumously published material (except his *Autobiography*) written by Du Bois are listed under the main entry for his name.

common(s), as idea, 150
Cooper, Anna Julia, 12
Craton, Michael, 226n50
critical philosophy, 131. *See also* Kant,
    Immanuel
Crummell, Alexander, 12
Cruse, Harold, 172, 246n4; *Crisis of the
    Negro Intellectual*, 172
culture, as concept: and anthropology,
    in study of the Negro American, 210–
    11n61; as difference among humans, 88;
    and theory American culture, 129
Curry, Milton, xiii, xv

Daniels, Donna, xii
Dark Princess, 133. *See also* Du Bois, W. E. B.
Darkwater, 231–32n7. *See also* Du Bois, W. E. B.
David Graham Du Bois Memorial Trust, x
Davis, Dantrell, 182n7
Davis, David Brion, 203n43, 240n30,
death, as concept, 112, 127
Deleuze, Gilles, 244n48
Dent, Gina, 234n1
Derrida, Jacques, 64–66, 76, 109, 181n5,
    184n10, 185n1, 208n54, 212n67, 213n69,
    213n70, 244n48, 247n8; aconceptual
    concept, 12, 187n2; and the
    autobiographical, 218n22; on Baruch
    de Spinoza, 183n9; *différance*, 186n2,
    217n21; *Dissemination:* "Hors Livre...":
    a general strategy of deconstruction,
    186n2; "The Double Session," 183n9;
    and the idea of a double science,
    186n2; on Edmund Husserl, 82–83,
    209–10n58, 216n14, 218n23, 220n25;
    on Emmanuel Levinas, 188n5,
    209–10n58, 228n56; on *entre*, 183n9;
    on Europe, 230n66, 235–36n11; on the
    example, 235n10; on the foundation
    of authority, 205–6n51, 240–41n31;
    Of Grammatology, 204n46, 227n53,
    238n21; grammatology: idea of,
    64, 211–12n63; overturning, 187n2;
    Mallarmé, Stéphane, reading of, 7;
    paleonymy, 187n2; on philosophical
    opposition, 11, 222n34; *Positions*, 185n2;
    Rogues, 188n5; *Of Spirit*, 191n10; *sous
    rapture*, 187n2; on strategy, 65, 186n2,
    188n2; the trace, 201n38, 237n17; and
    ultratranscendental in, 215n6; the un-
    decideable, as idea, 184n10; *Writing
    and Difference:* and solicitation as
    idea in, 186n2. *See also* paleonymy

Descartes, René, 41
desedimentation. *See* Derrida, Jacques;
    Husserl, Edmund
Diamond, Sarah, 181n4
Diawara, Manthia, 189n50, 205n7
différence. See Derrida, Jacques
difference, 8, 16, 69, 86; as actual, 58;
    categorical difference, 29; and the
    human, 86; and law of identity, 37;
    mathesis: question of difference as
    excessive to, 86–87; in principle, 58; the
    problem of human difference, 88; in
    relation to identity, 85; and sameness, 71
différend, 50
Dilthey, Wilhelm, 35, 201, 203n36n45
dissimulation, 5, 9, 10. *See also* simulation
double, as theoretical term, 59, 112, 155–56.
    See also force of the double
double displacement. *See* African
    American problematic; African
    American subject; *Dusk of Dawn*; Du
    Bois, W. E. B.; *The Souls of Black Folk*
Douglass, Frederick, 12, 58, 122, 210,
    231n6n60; "What to the Slave is the
    Fourth of July," 233n10
Drake, St. Clair, 221n31
Du Bois, Alexander, 97–98, 102–4. *See also*
    Du Bois, W. E. B.; *Dusk of Dawn*
Du Bois, Alfred, 98–99. *See also* Du Bois,
    W. E. B.; *Dusk of Dawn*
Du Bois, Augusta, 98niii
Du Bois, Burghardt Gomer, 98–99. *See
    also* Du Bois, W. E. B.
Du Bois, Chrétien, 98, 100
Du Bois, Jacques, 98
Du Bois, James, (Dr.), 98, 100–101, 102;
    common-law wife of, 98, 101–2. *See also*
    Du Bois, W. E. B.; *Dusk of Dawn*
Du Bois, John, 98nii, 102
Du Bois, Louis, 98ni
Du Bois, Nina Gomer, 98–99. *See also* Du
    Bois, W. E. B.
Du Bois, Nina Yolande, 98–99. *See also* Du
    Bois, W. E. B.
Du Bois, W. E. B. (William Edward
    Burghardt), 2–8, 31–40, 62–64, 171–72;
    1442, his notation of, as mark for the
    inception of modern historicity, 176;
    as an Africanist subject of discourse:
    12; as an Africanist subject of
    discourse: exemplarity of, 19; "The
    Afro-American," 237n18; ambivalence,
    as concept: systemic and structural

AMERICAN PHILOSOPHY

Douglas R. Anderson and Jude Jones, series editors

Kenneth Laine Ketner, ed., *Peirce and Contemporary Thought: Philosophical Inquiries.*

Max H. Fisch, ed., *Classic American Philosophers: Peirce, James, Royce, Santayana, Dewey, Whitehead, second edition.* Introduction by Nathan Houser.

John E. Smith, *Experience and God, second edition.*

Vincent G. Potter, *Peirce's Philosophical Perspectives.* Edited by Vincent Colapietro.

Richard E. Hart and Douglas R. Anderson, eds., *Philosophy in Experience: American Philosophy in Transition.*

Vincent G. Potter, *Charles S. Peirce: On Norms and Ideals, second edition.* Introduction by Stanley M. Harrison.

Vincent M. Colapietro, ed., *Reason, Experience, and God: John E. Smith in Dialogue.* Introduction by Merold Westphal.

Robert J. O'Connell, S.J., *William James on the Courage to Believe, second edition.*

Elizabeth M. Kraus, *The Metaphysics of Experience: A Companion to Whitehead's "Process and Reality," second edition.* Introduction by Robert C. Neville.

Kenneth Westphal, ed., *Pragmatism, Reason, and Norms: A Realistic Assessment— Essays in Critical Appreciation of Frederick L. Will.*

Beth J. Singer, *Pragmatism, Rights, and Democracy.*

Eugene Fontinell, *Self, God, and Immorality: A Jamesian Investigation.*

Roger Ward, *Conversion in American Philosophy: Exploring the Practice of Transformation.*

Michael Epperson, *Quantum Mechanics and the Philosophy of Alfred North Whitehead.*

Kory Sorrell, *Representative Practices: Peirce, Pragmatism, and Feminist Epistemology.*

Naoko Saito, *The Gleam of Light: Moral Perfectionism and Education in Dewey and Emerson.*

Josiah Royce, *The Basic Writings of Josiah Royce.*

Douglas R. Anderson, *Philosophy Americana: Making Philosophy at Home in American Culture.*

James Campbell and Richard E. Hart, eds., *Experience as Philosophy: On the World of John J. McDermott.*

John J. McDermott, *The Drama of Possibility: Experience as Philosophy of Culture.* Edited by Douglas R. Anderson.

Larry A. Hickman, *Pragmatism as Post-Postmodernism: Lessons from John Dewey.*

Larry A. Hickman, Stefan Neubert, and Kersten Reich, eds., *John Dewey Between Pragmatism and Constructivism.*

Dwayne A. Tunstall, *Yes, But Not Quite: Encountering Josiah Royce's Ethico-Religious Insight.*

Josiah Royce, *Race Questions, Provincialism, and Other American Problems, expanded edition.* Edited by Scott L. Pratt and Shannon Sullivan.

Lara Trout, *The Politics of Survival: Peirce, Affectivity, and Social Criticism.*

John R. Shook and James A. Good, *John Dewey's Philosophy of Spirit, with the 1897 Lecture on Hegel.*

Douglas R. Anderson and Carl R. Hausman, *Conversations on Peirce: Reals and Ideals.*

Rick Anthony Furtak, Jonathan Ellsworth, and James D. Reid, eds., *Thoreau's Importance for Philosophy.*

James M. Albrecht, *Reconstructing Individualism: A Pragmatic Tradition from Emerson to Ellison.*

Mathew A. Foust, *Loyalty to Loyalty: Josiah Royce and the Genuine Moral Life.*

Cornelis de Waal and Krysztof Piotr Skowroński (eds.), *The Normative Thought of Charles S. Peirce.*

Dwayne A. Tunstall, *Doing Philosophy Personally: Thinking about Metaphysics, Theism, and Antiblack Racism.*

Erin McKenna, *Pets, People, and Pragmatism.*

Sami Pihlström, *Pragmatic Pluralism and the Problem of God.*

Thomas M. Alexander, *The Human Eros: Eco-ontology and the Aesthetics of Existence.*

John Kaag, *Thinking Through the Imagination: Aesthetics in Human Cognition.*

Kelly A. Parker and Jason Bell (eds.), *The Relevance of Royce.*

W. E. B. Du Bois, *The Problem of the Color Line at the Turn of the Twentieth Century: The Essential Early Essays.* Edited by Nahum Dimitri Chandler.

Nahum Dimitri Chandler, *X: The Problem of the Negro as a Problem for Thought.*